PARALYSES

∞

PARALYSES

Literature, Travel, and Ethnography
in French Modernity | John Culbert

UNIVERSITY OF NEBRASKA PRESS | LINCOLN AND LONDON

© 2010 by the
Board of Regents of the
University of Nebraska
All rights reserved
Manufactured in the
United States of America

This book has been published with the support of a grant from Scripps College.

Portions of the introduction and chapter 1, "The Muse of Paralysis," were originally published as "Border Crossings/Crossing Borders: Paralyses of Travel in Literature and Anthropology" in *Western Humanities Review* 60, no. 2 (Fall 2006): 117–27. Chapter 3, "Slow Progress: Jean Paulhan and Madagascar," was originally published in *October* 83 (Winter 1998): 71–95. Portions of chapter 6, "The Wake of Ulysses," were originally published as "Haunting the *Métropole*" in *Formules* 14 (Spring 2010).

Library of Congress
Cataloging-in-Publication Data

Culbert, John.
Paralyses: literature, travel, and ethnography in French modernity / John Culbert.
p. cm.
Includes bibliographical references and index.
ISBN 978-0-8032-2991-4 (cloth: alk. paper)
1. Travel in literature. 2. French literature—History and criticism. 3. Travelers' writings, French—History and criticism. 4. Travelers in literature. 5. Ethnology in literature. 6. Imperialism in literature. 7. Travel—Philosophy. I. Title.
PQ145.6.T7C86 2010
840.9'32—dc22 2010022013

Set in Galliard.

For my parents

Contents

Acknowledgments	ix
Introduction	1
1. The Muse of Paralysis	51
2. Horizon of Conquest *Eugène Fromentin's Algerian Narratives*	95
3. Slow Progress *Jean Paulhan and Madagascar*	155
4. Frustration *Michel Leiris*	199
5. Atopia *Roland Barthes*	255
6. The Wake of Ulysses	313
Notes	357
Bibliography	407
Index	433

Acknowledgments

A book is always the record of debts beyond reckoning, which makes penning one's acknowledgments a task both impossible and necessary. This book reflects discussions and conversations with friends, students, and colleagues who contributed immeasurably to its composition over the years. Thanks are due first of all to my mentors, Emily Apter, Judith Butler, Neil Hertz, William Ray, and Ann Smock, and to my colleagues in the Department of Comparative Literature at UC-Irvine, especially Eyal Amiran, Jonathan Hall, and Rei Terada. Much of the material here draws on courses I taught at UC-Irvine, and I am grateful to the students who indulged my interests and helped me puzzle through challenging texts. I have benefited from conversations with Homi Bhabha, James Clifford, Celeste Langan, Françoise Lionnet, Catherine Malabou, Achille Mbembe, Gayatri Spivak, and David Wills. Emily Apter, Denis Hollier, and Richard Sieburth were kind enough to read portions of the manuscript and offer their comments and suggestions. Aron Vinegar invited me to present my work at a conference at Ohio State University at a crucial juncture in my research and writing. Claire Paulhan, at the Institut Mémoires de l'Edition Contemporaine in Paris, was very gracious and generous with her time as I researched the Paulhan archives.

    A resident fellowship at the Camargo Foundation in Cassis, France, allowed me to begin work on the book project. With a grant from the Harry Ransom Center at the University of Texas at Austin I was able to consult the mud-spattered manuscript of Leiris's *L'Afrique fantôme*. Travel grants from the UC-Irvine Humanities Center provided support for research in Paris, and a Borchard Foundation fellowship at the Château de la Bretesche gave me much-needed time to complete the writing of the manuscript. A research associateship at the UC-Irvine Critical Theory Institute provided me with the facilities and resources to edit the completed text.

Gerald Prince and Edward Dimendberg gave invaluable editorial assistance and helped find the manuscript a home. At the University of Nebraska Press, Ann Baker, Ladette Randolph, and Kristen Rowley guided the book through the various stages with patience and care. Sue Breckenridge copyedited the manuscript with meticulous attention to detail. I would also like to thank the anonymous reviewers of the manuscript for their helpful comments and editorial suggestions. I am thankful to the editors and publishers of the journals *October*, *Formules*, and *Western Humanities Review* for their permission to reprint previously published texts here.

It is a particular pleasure to thank the close friends who over the years lent me their support and gave intellectual and creative sustenance to this project: Chris Andrews, Ali Dadgar, Michelle de Kretser, Gareth Gollrad, Daniel Katz, Eric Peterson, James Petterson, Kavita Philip, Stefan Mattessich, Targol Mesbah, Ward Smith, and Malina Stefanovska. My family provided constant support even when my work must have seemed incomprehensible. Most of all I thank my partner, Dina Al-Kassim, whose love, strength, patience, and unconditional support made this book possible.

Unless otherwise noted, all translations from French sources are my own.

Introduction

Chiasmus, from *chiazein*, to mark with a chi [X]: an inverted relationship between the syntactic elements of parallel phrases (as in . . . *to stop too fearful, and too faint to go*). — *Merriam-Webster*

The bind and the knot are necessary in order to take a step. — Derrida

Paralyses

At the beginning of his collected essays in political anthropology, Pierre Clastres recounts a journey into the territory of the Yanomami Indians. The author opens his text with a portrait of himself exhausted, crawling in the mud, a "Molloy in the Amazon," as he puts it.[1] On the trail of what he calls "the last free primitive society," the grail of the ambitious ethnographer, Clastres is reduced to a clownish figure he identifies with a character from Samuel Beckett.

This scene may serve as an emblem of my concerns in what follows. Clastres's "Molloy in the Amazon" shares with all the texts I examine here a critique of the figure of the modern traveler and doubts as to the viability of travel itself. The anthropologist's wry self-portrait, I would argue, is more than a passing scruple or a literary flourish; it indicates, rather, a crisis in the representation of the traveler, whose authority is in question and whose story may confound narrative. Clastres's critique of the traveler threatens to undermine the journey and its claims to knowledge and mastery, thereby setting the tone for his text. Even as he bears witness to the threatened life-world of the Yanomami, Clastres also testifies to his own inability to prevent the disappearance of their distinctive culture, or worse, as Western interloper, his unwitting implication in the changes he describes. Anthropology as a result gives way to what Lévi-Strauss in *Tristes Tropiques* called *entropology*, "the name of the discipline concerned with the study of the highest manifestations of this process of disintegration."[2] Traveler and travelogue are thus marked with the signs of futility and exhaustion.

Clastres's travelogue is characteristic of a strain of postcolonial anthropology for which travel, both as means of approach to its objects and as organizing principle of narrative, is marred by a history of political control, commercial exploitation, and ideological abuse.[3] The development of mass tourism and the more recent encroachments of "ecotourism" exacerbate these problems by putting the ethnographer at odds with travel circuits that are seen to contaminate local cultures. For Clastres and his contemporaries, travel cannot serve simply to authorize experience and justify knowledge, but confronts them with the political and technological limitations that underlie that experience and knowledge. Contemporary ethnographic travel no longer considers itself apart from the vectors of imperial power that made it possible as a field of study, and this contradiction between travel's conditions of possibility and its avowed aims has yielded far-reaching insights in recent years into the epistemology and political genealogy of anthropology.[4] The moral plaints of "entropology" have thus led to a reflexive questioning of the discipline of anthropology itself as unwitting agent of colonial and imperial forms of controlling knowledge. Clastres made a vital contribution to these debates by arguing that Europe confronted an "epistemological impossibility" in the New World, and that the legacy of that original failed encounter is still maintained in anthropology today by ingrained Western political notions of state, as well as our implication in its insatiable and "ethnocidal" outgrowths, empire and capital.[5] If empire haunts anthropology as a discipline, there are, however, more insidious forms of power whose contradictions, and indeed "impossibility," may not lend themselves so readily to political and epistemological analysis. My aim in what follows is to examine such contradictions and their paralyzing logic. An intractable contradiction of anthropology, one that implicates travel as its method of knowledge, pits the intention to study alien cultures against the intrusion required to conduct such study. This is, so to speak, the enabling contradiction of ethnography, one that is aggravated by the discipline's traditional investment in "primitive" and purportedly pure cultures. As a result, Clastres's lyrical and elegiac line "a mortal shadow is being cast on all sides" is awkwardly complicit, as a consequence, with the prosaic disaster he foretells for the Amazon: "oil derricks around the *chabunos*, diamond mines in the hillsides, police on the paths, boutiques on the riverbanks" (*Archeology of Violence*, 27). This attitude, including both its mournful rapture and its bitter complaint, resembles nothing so much as the refrain of the tourist, who fruitlessly negates the very means that render his mediated experience possible. In drawing such a comparison, my intent is not to conflate the righteous militancy of a Clastres combating ethnocide with the tourist's mercenary demand for more local color. And yet the tourist haunts Clastres's own travelogue, and his ironic deflation of his role as explorer is the symptom of a paralyzing contradiction he shares with the ordinary traveler.

Lévi-Strauss speaks of this contradiction of ethnographic travel in *Tristes Tropiques*. "I wished I had lived in the days of *real* journeys," he reflects, while recognizing that his own travels are the source of more advanced anthropological knowledge, due to their very belatedness (43). The anthropologist is, as a result, "paralyzed by this dilemma," and feels travel's contradictions as the negation of all mobile options. "I have only two possibilities: either I can be like some traveller of the olden days, who was faced with a stupendous spectacle, all, or almost all, of which eluded him, . . . or I can be a modern traveller, chasing after the vestiges of a vanished reality." As a good dialectician, however, Lévi-Strauss converts his contradiction into a synthetic vision, and paralysis instead contributes to an immobilized structural order in which "evanescent forms" and the passage of time "crystallize into a sort of edifice" (44). The conversion of the traveler's paralysis into the stability of structure is enabled by a backward look at his journeys that distances his fieldwork in time. But rather than resolve the dilemma that first paralyzed him, Lévi-Strauss's distancing strategy may only displace that dilemma. In *Time and the Other*, Johannes Fabian argues that such distancing strategies are inherent to the methodology of anthropology, whose "politics of time" denies a shared temporality with the cultures and peoples it studies. Lévi-Strauss's case is exemplary for Fabian, since his "denial of coevalness" takes the radical form of a rejection of history and temporality as such in favor of structuralism's synchronic taxonomies. This appeal to structure, Fabian shows, goes hand in hand with a negation of fieldwork, the spatiotemporal experience of travel and exchange that nonetheless grounds anthropological understanding. The mournful tone of *Tristes Tropiques* takes on the character of a more violent sacrifice in the light of Fabian's critique: "Living in the Time of the primitives, the ethnographer will be an ethnographer only if he outlives them, i.e., if he moves *through* the Time he may have shared with them onto a level on which he finds anthropology."[6] For Lévi-Strauss a synthesizing backward look resolves the traveler's contradictions, and his paralyzing impasse is overcome. But, Fabian asserts, structuralist anthropologists "do not escape the aporia arising from the conflicting demands of coeval research and allochronic discourse" (60). For Fabian this inescapable impasse is constitutive of Lévi-Strauss's work and, indeed, all anthropology.

This impasse is famously expressed in the first lines of *Tristes Tropiques*: "I hate travelling and explorers," Lévi-Strauss says, only to add, "Yet here I am proposing to tell the story of my expeditions" (17). Lévi-Strauss's defiant rejection of travel is more than an authorial anxiety of influence or literary avant-gardism; it breaks radically with travel and the travelogue, providing instead a vision of universal structuring codes of human society. *Tristes Tropiques*, a monument of modern travel writing, would aim at nothing less than a rejection of travel as such. This attitude, however, has a long genealogy. The critique of travel is endemic to French modernity and is linked to cultural transformations that in fundamental ways alter travel as form of experience and mode of representation. Among these transformations are doubts as to the notion of progress and its attendant metaphors; a critique of colonialism, along with the figures of discovery, adventure, and conquest that sustain its ideology; the rise of popular tourism, mass transit, and globalization; and technological changes that defy inherited representations of travel and transportation, prompting anxieties about spatiotemporal displacements within the lived present of the modern metropole itself. In 1859 Baudelaire vilified the very idea of progress in speaking of "a victory every minute lost, a progress forever denying itself," a critique that would be echoed by the entire symbolist generation and beyond.[7] These doubts are scathingly represented as well in *Sentimental Education*, where Flaubert describes a painting showing "the Republic, or Progress, or Civilization, in the form of Christ driving a locomotive through a virgin forest."[8] Conrad, inheritor of Flaubert's ironic vision, would later insist on the stillness of the journey related in *Heart of Darkness* as his steamship and its "pilgrims" doggedly "crawled on."[9] Clastres's invocation of Molloy is only a newer version of this ironic vision. In a more playful mode, Jean Echenoz's recent novel *Courir* delights in the absurd style of Zátopek, the fastest runner of his time: "Emil seems to dig deep, or dig in, like a man in a trance or a workman shoveling the roadway. Far from all academic canons or any concern for elegance, Emil's progress is heavy, jerky, tortured, all fits and starts."[10] The "impossible style" of the runner is like Echenoz's own, which seems to take up the baton from Beckett and his memorable descriptions of Molloy's stumblings and Watt's ridiculous gait.

Such paralyses may be found in all modern literature, but are particularly insistent motifs in French writing. Even the exceptions to this tendency confirm the rule; Le Clézio, perhaps the happiest traveler in today's more distinguished canon of writers, has been called "the most English of French writers."[11] A recent resurgence of travel literature in France, spearheaded by the manifesto *Pour une littérature voyageuse*, as well as the annual literary festival Etonnants Voyageurs, defines itself explicitly as a challenge to French literary tradition in advocating for "le 'travel writing' à la française."[12]

As Charles Forsdick points out, however, this movement is not without a touch of nostalgia and indeed "neo-exoticism."[13] It may even be seen to reprise an effort in the early twentieth century to reinvigorate French colonialist writing through the example of the adventurous Conrad. The opening salvo in *Tristes Tropiques* against travel reflects this cultural context, and like other ambivalent statements of its genre, fails to settle accounts with journeys to which it remains indebted. In what follows, then, I will sketch the salient features of a modern French resistance to travel in literature. In so doing, I will draw a distinction between the traveler's habitual frustrations, disavowals, and negations on the one hand, and their more paralyzing contradictions on the other. The negation of travel is, in other words, symptomatic of a crisis of travel. But as symptom, it masks contradictions its author cannot resolve: aporias that are not negated or overcome, but that remain paralyzing dilemmas in the travelogue.

"Every story is a travel story," Michel de Certeau has pointed out.[14] We might say that Lévi-Strauss's misgivings about telling his story struggle with the discursive fatality that narrative must plot itself out in space and time like a journey. More specifically, however, Lévi-Strauss's rejection of travel expresses a defining exclusion upon which his discipline is founded. As Fabian notes, "anthropology became an academic discipline when scientific discourse replaced narration—when, to put it simply, the monograph replaced the travelogue." Moreover, Fabian adds, this entailed "stationary fieldwork taking the place of travel." This replacement, Fabian insists, is no innocent evolution but rather the result of a more suspicious "disavowal,"[15] and his work undertakes a reevaluation of the discipline in light of its traveling precursors, the missionaries, explorers, and amateur ethnographers who laid the groundwork for modern anthropology. Fabian proposes a rehabilitation of these travelogues, while at the same time offering some of the most incisive demystifications of the ideology of travel by examining the complex and multiform practices of knowledge construction in the field. Fabian is thus able to avoid the symptomatic rejection of travel and offers instead a more nuanced view of its complexities in his study of explorers' accounts, *Out of Our Minds*. Interestingly for our purposes, this entails a reconsideration of travel and motion as they relate to immobility and stasis: "What is difficult to reconcile with the image of the intrepid traveler is that much, probably most, travel was stationary." This distinction allows Fabian to challenge anthropology's disavowal of travel and the travelogue. "Both travel and stay, motion and stillness . . . shaped these expeditions. This would be a truism, except for the realization that, while movement defined expeditions ideologically, in practice stops took up by far the larger portion of the total time spent." By displacing and reversing the opposition of travel and stasis, Fabian applies a deconstructive strategy to his reading of the genealogy of ethnography; the myth of exploration, he says, "calls for deconstructive literary analysis."[16] But the deconstructive strategy of reversal and displacement, a key method in destabilizing the terms of a founding opposition, is only a means to a further critical aim: that of undoing the opposition itself and its binary logic. To do so would be to articulate another relation of mobility and stasis, of travel and stillness, one that I am pursuing here and call *paralysis*.

Paralysis is a recurrent symptom of the modern crisis of travel. Index of travel's exhaustion as theme and mode of knowledge, paralysis is travel's ordeal, a trial suffered and undergone by the traveling subject, an experience less object of knowledge than symptom of the traveler's unwitting passion. Paralysis is what remains of travel, what holds back and stays the traveler beset by contradictions. In this sense, and despite its negative connotations, paralysis remains close to travel's etymology in the French word *travail*, for labor, toil, and torment. *Travail* itself derives from the Latin *trepalium*, an instrument of torture, from which French also draws the word *entraver*: to shackle, impede, and restrain. The travails of travel thus originate, as one etymologist ingenuously has it, in "the toil of travelling in olden times."[17] However, we might add, this toil is no less mythic than historical; in literature and mythology, travel's ordeals are sanctioned by theological and metaphysical motifs relating to sacred terrors, rites of passage, and mortal trespass. Within this metaphysical horizon, only difficulty, or indeed impossibility, would seem to consecrate a journey worth relating. Paralysis, then, would be travel's negative companion, but by a ruse common to our dialectical and metaphysical heritage, its negating power would serve a redemptive logic of useful toil, salutary travail, and mortal trespass. To read against the grain of this redemptive logic would be to consider paralysis otherwise than as negation or difficulty to overcome.

Derrida once ventured the term *paralyse* for the form of reading and interpretation called forth by such paths of thought.[18] In texts on Freud's death drive and Blanchot's fictions, Derrida discerns a logic of death and negativity that articulates a different figure of death as border, and thus of the metaphysical figures of motion organized there, including transgression, mortal trespass, survival, and passing on. *Paralyse*, or paralysis, dwells at this border that yields nondialectical figures of mobility and stasis: *pas*, *démarche*, and *dérive* are among the duplicitous terms that Derrida employs to name these problematic border crossings. To think, as to travel, would be "the experience of the aporia," neither stopping at the impasse nor passing beyond it, in the attempt to reckon with the paralyzing trace of the path.[19] What Derrida says of Blanchot in "Pas" might well be extended to a broader scope of texts: "If a science or a theory of reading these narratives were to constitute itself, coming round in the end, or resorting to its name, I would call it *paralysis* [la *paralyse*]."[20] *Paralyse* suggests itself here as a near-synonym for Derrida's own methodology, though Derrida qualifies his own statement with conditional verbs, and his "en venir à son nom" is rife with ambiguities. If Derrida subsequently took his distance from the term, this retraction is already anticipated here, and is not unlike his hesitation in committing to a master term for what came to be called deconstruction. *Paralyse*, in other words, goes "under erasure."[21] Other terms thus challenge the singularity of *paralyse*: *contre-allée*, for instance, combines, in aporetic form, the ideas of both traveling "with" and "against."[22] Adopting the orphan term *paralyse* for my own purposes here, *Paralyses* will demonstrate its broad resonance with the discourse and cultural politics of modern French travel.[23]

"Molloy in the Amazon." If I am stuck on this image it is due to the crisis of travel it captures, and because, linking ethnography and literature in one stroke, it emblematizes the textual analysis and politics of translation that have become hallmarks of contemporary critical anthropology. This image also stays with me because the name of Beckett is tied to the most difficult and challenging figurations of paralytic motion. Clastres may well have been thinking of Foucault when he penned his lines, since "The Discourse on Language," which was published shortly before Clastres's own text, also begins with a Beckettian reference: "I must go on; I can't go on; I must go on; I must say words as long as there are words, I must say them until they find me, until they say me—heavy burden, heavy sin; I must go on . . ."[24] At grips with discourse, obligation, and sin, Beckett's contradictions and perplexities serve to develop Foucault's argument on the will to truth, conceived as an ordering of discourse by means of strategic systems of exclusion. Foucault allows us to reconsider Lévi-Strauss's denial of travel as symptom of the will to truth and its denial of power and desire. "I hate travelling and explorers. Yet here I am proposing to tell the story of my expeditions." This contradiction, Fabian would argue, structures anthropological knowledge as a constitutive aporia. In Lévi-Strauss's autobiographical salvo we hear, in other words, the anonymous voice of anthropology echoing that of Beckett's character: "I must go on; I can't go on . . ."

It is ironic that Beckett's famous epigram should have become a password of sorts, translated by many commentators into all-too-meaningful statements about futility and the absurd. On the other hand, the emphasis is warranted, since Beckett remained doggedly attached to such statements, from his earliest works to *Worstward Ho*. The latter text's minimalist reiteration of *The Unnamable* strikingly renders its epigram as the alternating play, at once chiastic and aporetic, of the two mere words "no" and "on."[25] Only in recent years have critics taken Beckett's paralytic statements as more than negations or contradictions. Leslie Hill, for instance, observes that "all Beckett's protagonists set out on a journey which ends in an impasse," and adds that to read the journey's impasse thematically and teleologically would be to confer on Beckett's travels a progression and destination they deny at every step. As Hill points out, "Beckett's rewriting of the quest narrative is not an attempt just to toy with the forms of the past," but reflects instead "an aporetic crisis in the whole articulation of subjective space." What Hill calls "a system of self-cancelling alternatives" is characteristic of this aporetic crisis. "The space of journeying, like writing, becomes a space of indifference, . . . of movements made and then undone, advanced but annulled, of opposites set up and then abolished, of unity assumed and then divided."[26] Interestingly, as Hill's own commentary shows, it is seemingly impossible to convey these aporias without asserting a sequence of textual moves ("and then, and then"), so that the critic himself falls in with Beckett's double injunction "I can't" and "I must." This is what Leo Bersani calls "impeded reading," an effect of the Beckettian text's self-obstruction.[27] Bersani sees these impediments as enabling, through the near-ruin of representation, access to domains of affective experience repressed by narrative's ordering principles and spatiotemporal coordinates. Beckett's paralyses thus do not simply negate travel or motion but allow for other transports at the limits of representation.

Travel and narrative are intimately linked. To tamper with the narrative codes of travel, as Beckett does, is to challenge the basic storylines with which we order our lives. Accordingly, the aim of the following chapters is to show how paralyses undo the certainties of knowledge, presenting alternatives to the normative codings of travel, transports, and narrative. These alternatives, raised in moments of paralysis, may be political, sexual, or affective. At the limit—and paralysis always concerns a problematic limit—what presents itself may be more than a mere option and a decision; the alternative instead poses the challenge of the radically *other*. For this reason my focus has been on anthropological discourse, which traditionally concerns other worlds, other peoples, and other times. Anthropology thus has an implicitly ethical bent, oriented as it is toward the strange, the foreign, and the other. At the same time, however, one may argue that the ethical relationship is incomplete unless it calls language into question, unmastering the account one makes of the journey and the encounter. For this reason, as Fabian notes, language is a vital companion to the anthropological journey, not as a mere stylistic turn but as an exploration of the limits of language, narrative, and knowledge. Attuned to the "poetics" of its practice, anthropology today increasingly figures itself as a mode of cultural translation.[28] Translation, of course, implies transport: *trans* (across) and *latus* (borne) suggests a spatial transfer of meaning across languages. The figure and the practice always have an essentializing tendency, however, as what seems to be carried over is the "spirit" of the letter, not the material particularity of the source text. Translators have long been aware of this conundrum, of course, but only contemporary theory has been able to articulate the properly *paralyzing* implications of translation as a task both impossible and necessary. In recent years, and in response to the challenge of poststructuralist ethics, translation studies have complicated the classical model of translation as travel, suggesting that a certain *untranslatability* is the measure of fidelity and responsibility. "The translator's task is inevitably an ethical one," Sandra Bermann says, while recognizing that "language imposes internal barriers to appropriative understanding as well as to transparent communication." Translation, accordingly, is modeled less on metaphors of transport and delivery than on figures of interweaving and imbrication, in which the unmasterable otherness of the translator's language links with the unassimilable idiom of the other. "Linguistic ligatures," in Bermann's words,[29] being "tied up or trussed," and "entwined" in a "tangle," in Spivak's, speak to new models of translation as the paralyzing weave of a double bind.[30] Confronting such binds, the journey comes to a halt, *breaking down*, as Judith Butler has it, paralyzing travel and narrative alike in an encounter that remains, even in its ethical responsibility, unnarratable and paradoxically *unaccountable*.[31]

Roland Barthes poses this challenge to travel and narrative in *S/Z*, where he asks us to imagine the story of a journey without arrival or departure. Staying without arriving; traveling without departing; neither arriving or not: Barthes's paradoxical journey defies the normative codes of narrative and suggests the "self-cancelling alternatives" Hill ascribes to Beckett. "A scandal of readerliness," as Barthes puts it,[32] such a journey would thus no doubt provoke Bersani's "impeded reading" as well. Barthes's narrative mutations are more than a mere aesthetic concern. At stake in such questioning of travel and narrative is the invention of mobilities that defy travel's presumed spatiotemporal coordinates and their normative coding in narratives of desire, conquest, and exploration. Such paradoxical transports, moreover, provide the means to understand new mutations of travel that contemporary commentators may be ill equipped to conceptualize. Indeed, new technologies raise the stakes in this effort to reconceive modern travel. Take, for instance, the formulations of Paul Virilio, whose diagnoses of modern technology's paradoxical transports seemingly echo the words of Barthes: "Currently

... we are seeing the beginnings of a *'generalized arrival'* whereby everything arrives without having to leave, the nineteenth-century's elimination of the journey ... combining with the abolition of departure at the end of the twentieth, the journey thereby losing its successive components and being overtaken by *arrival* alone." Unlike Barthes, Virilio's willful paradoxes of transport ("static vehicle," "virtual velocity," etc.) ultimately appeal to outmoded theological and metaphysical grounding: the "soul" and the "here and now." Virilio's paralyses thus fall in with the mournful tone of Clastres and Lévi-Strauss in his nostalgia for what he calls "the essence of the path, the journey," and "the voyage of the navigator or the trek of the lone explorer."[33]

Modernity has long been equated with movement, change, and instability, whether in Marx's sobering diagnosis of the economic disequilibrium fostered by capital or the Futurists' rapturous embrace of speed.[34] And while this modern predicament has always provoked resistance and prompted reflection on the value of tradition and stability, such responses often tend to fall back on nostalgic tropes, even when, as in Virilio, they compulsively invoke figures of paradox. Virilio's paradoxes should, however, be answered not in the mode of nostalgia, but instead in a more critical—and playful—spirit. Ross Chambers's *Loiterature* contributes to such an effort, drawing on Beckett to advance what he calls a "poetics of digression." Digressiveness is not only wayward and wandering, Chambers says, but is marked by a tendency toward narrative slowness and stasis. "Loiterature," as Chambers names it, is a potential feature of any text, but is most characteristic of literary modernity, whose slowness and digressions constitute disorderly challenges to the order of proper narrative, and as such, express errant pleasures that contest the rules of discursive conduct and social rectitude. The subversive force and elusive charm of such texts lie in skirting the norm and testing limits, rather than in confronting the law. As Chambers says, "there is a type of practice, the digressive, that perhaps offers a model of how the law can be more effectively subverted, since in it something that does not manifest itself as subversive nevertheless has the power to put the law into question."[35] Digression, then, is an alternative to the frontal assault of transgression, and if it gives up the path of confrontation, it gains, however, in its room for play and seduction.

The subversiveness of Chambers's loiterature and the poetics of digression owe something to the poststructuralist turn in the analysis of power and dissidence, and in particular to Foucault, for whom power is not simply wielded, confronted, or endured, but distributed in more complex ways among disciplinary subjects. Foucault's "A Preface to Transgression" sets out the program for this study of power in an homage to Bataille. Chambers himself refers to Bataille in drawing a distinction between transgression and digression, stating that, unlike digression, "transgression and the law are intimately bound up with each other such that the law requires transgression as that which confirms its status as law" (*Loiterature*, 89). Chambers's account of Bataille posits a mutually defining relationship between law and transgression that, however, returns Bataille to the very dialectical system he aimed to undo. For Bataille, after all, transgression is not dialectical but aporetic; like Blanchot, Bataille insists on the impossibility of transgression that brings the dialectic to a standstill.[36] Consequently, Chambers's wandering digression, such as he defines it, is insufficiently distinguished from the transgression he would oppose. Moreover, digression merges with the dialectical transgression he attributes to Bataille, for if digression exploits "loopholes" in the law, Chambers says, "the loophole that it represents in the law is itself subject to a law: the law of loopholes. And the law of loopholes is that they are, in turn, constrained by the very order that they disturb" (*Loiterature*, 93–94). Paralysis, as feature of Beckettian digression, is thus cast as a dialectical confrontation of opposites, and, indeed, a "metaphysical paralysis," as Chambers says (100). Chambers thus speaks of a "paralysis—etymologically, a "coming loose" or "coming unstrung"—that simultaneously alludes to a desired inertia and signifies the impossibility of its attainment, for this paralysis is a state of suspension that derives from digression's oxymoronic pull toward a state of stasis, on the one hand, and a need to move or even a desire to progress, that is, to move on, on the other" (93). If, as Chambers correctly notes, Beckett's fiction is both paralyzed and "aporetic" (101), Chambers's account of its digressive stasis remains wedded to formulations of opposition and contradiction. Chambers's analysis of Beckett is thus another case of "impeded reading," provoked by the challenge of such paradoxical expressions as Beckett's "gress," "gression," and "moving pause." In reference to the latter, Chambers says, "such a busy pause is the opposite of stasis: it is a suspension" (101). This supposed opposition, unconvincing in itself, seems a symptom of a reading that insists on a play of contraries, even where Beckett defies them. Chambers's account of Beckett's narrative thus inadvertently mirrors the critic's own difficult critical choices in the face of textual undecidability. "Constantly making choices—whether to go in or to come out, whether to move or to stay put, whether to move in this direction or that—but making choices in a world in which there is no reason to prefer any particular option over its alternative, results in aporia."

Such impeded reading is the almost inevitable consequence of reading Beckett's strange transports. But were we to pursue Chambers's "law of loopholes" with Derrida, a way out of the stalemate of sheer contradiction might be found. Paralysis as a "coming unstrung" would likewise yield a different sense than that of loosening or unlacing; Derrida proposes instead a model of "stricture" and "destricturation" that is paralyzing, precisely, due to its undecidability, as seen in his essay on Heidegger's analysis of Van Gogh's boots. Derrida's essay is digressive in an exemplary way: stubbornly off-topic, it dwells at length on what seems trivial and virtually irrelevant, ignored by Heidegger, and insists on a slowness that is nearly immobile: "We're getting nowhere. We're not even sliding around, we're floundering [*Nous piétinons. Nous ne patinons même pas, nous pataugons*])."[37] The critic willingly trudges and flounders, the latter verb less evocative of Heidegger's privileged terms "way" and "soil," no doubt, than Beckett's mud. In the course of this slow, but never slow enough reading, what emerges, in a manner characteristic of Derrida, is the seemingly marginal detail in the painting that displaces and eclipses the whole: in this case, the shoelaces. The lace (*lacet*) is also a snare (*lacet*), one that sets a trap: "Another type of trap and of what in 'Pas' was named paralysis [*la paralyse*]."[38] The lacing of the boots, their passing in and out of eyelets in crisscross fashion, provides Derrida a model for thinking of a linking and differentiating that is beyond the logic of duality, opposition, and dialectic. The "pair" of boots is thus only the first pairing that calls for deconstruction, and which includes margin/center, inside/outside, representation/represented, part/whole. The interlacing is a nonoppositional and differential relation that, like the framing parergon, links inside to outside, only to confound the two, according to "the figure or trajectory of the *lace*: a stricture by alternate and reversible passage from inside to outside, from under to over" (*Truth in Painting*, 321). The shoelaces thus provide another model, crucial to Derrida, of a chiastic interlacing of asymmetrical terms.[39] Such is the paralyzing logic of the margin: delimiting the border of a given work, it simultaneously unworks that border and the distinctions it would support. "The picture is caught in the lace which it yet seems to include as its part" (*Truth in Painting*, 331). Nothing is more natural than to trip on these shoelaces which, both tight and loose, differentiate every pairing without opposing, contrasting, or negating: "the trap always works in the interlace, whether it misleads, lets go, or paralyzes."[40]

It is with such a paralyzing trap that Derrida opens his famous critique of Lévi-Strauss's Amazon journeys in *Of Grammatology*. *Tristes Tropiques* delivers a compelling version of anthropology's fatal contact narrative, cast by Lévi-Strauss as the violent intrusion of writing into the world of the Nambikwara. As Derrida argues, this representation of writing as contaminating agent is allied to one of metaphysics' most pervasive claims, the opposition between writing and speech, an opposition that articulates some of the fundamental distinctions of metaphysical thought. In Lévi-Strauss's account, the fatal contact with writing supports a portrait of the Nambikwara as innocent, autonomous, and natural. But writing, as constitutive exclusion of Western thought, troubles the vital distinctions it would claim to uphold, and vitiates, indeed, the very object of traditional anthropology: the "primitive," or "peoples without writing." For Derrida, these distinctions are troubled at the outset by the path that leads to the Nambikwara, opening their world to the outside; indeed, writing is inscribed in this very path. Quoting from Lévi-Strauss, Derrida stops him, so to speak, in his track: "a *picada* (a crude trail whose 'track' is 'not easily distinguished from the bush')." Derrida suggests that "one should meditate upon all of the following together: writing as the possibility of the road and of difference, the history of writing and the history of the road, of the rupture, of the *via rupta*, of the path that is broken, beaten, *fracta*, of the space of reversibility and of repetition traced by the opening, the divergence from, and the violent spacing, of nature." As a consequence, Derrida says, "it is difficult to imagine that access to the possibility of a road-map is not at the same time access to writing."[41] The logic of the *trace*, here, follows the meanings of "path" and "footprint" that have become obsolete, or nearly so, in English.[42] By anticipating writing in this way, the native path brings the anthropologist up short in his quest. Moreover, if the "territory of the Nambikwara is crossed by the line of an autochthonic picada," as Derrida says, the word "crossed" (*traversé*) suggests not only *crossing through* but *crossing out*: a line, that is, lying as much *across* the path as it does *along* it. The native path, in other words, confronts the traveler with an aporia: both line of demarcation and passageway, a line that both marks vital distinctions and passes through them. Neither writing nor speech, the native path is the trace of what Derrida calls "arche-writing" or "arche-violence," inscribing the inevitable loss of the proper that Lévi-Strauss's moral fables and Clastres's "archeology of violence" narrate in the mode of mourning. The native path as aporia, deconstructing the anthropologist's moral plaints, thus provides another means to understand what Renato Rosaldo has called "imperialist nostalgia." Rather than being mere hypocrisy or bad faith of the anthropologist, Rosaldo's "mourning for what one has destroyed"[43] should be traced back to the path as *entame* that both "breaches" and "broaches," as Spivak's translation has it, in one stroke. Instead of merely immobilizing the traveler, "the experience of the aporia," Derrida says in one of his texts on mourning, "gives or promises the thinking of the path."[44] Accordingly, *Of Grammatology* reclaims Rousseau from Lévi-Strauss, for whom the philosopher represents the founder of ethnology.[45] Derrida instead argues that the crucial contribution of Rousseau lies not in his theories of natural man or his mournful critique of cultural decline, but rather in the duplicitous figures, such as the *supplement*, that waylay his philosophy, narratives, and travels.[46]

Attention to such a paralyzing logic exposes a thread common to modern narratives of travel: a tendency toward stasis that belies the journey and its ostensible purpose. In touristic narratives, moments of stasis tend to express, in symptomatic form, the traveler's conventional frustrations: a bid for originality and authenticity always threatened by rivalry and mediation; an experience of otherness frustrated by mere spectacle and convention; and a desire to capture history from within a touristic consciousness blind to its own historical nature. In this way, frustrated travel is at grips with difficulties all too easily overcome—if only by compensatory illusions—or alternately, too readily taken as sheer obstacle. Paralysis, however, expresses more than contradiction; as we have seen, its aporias expose the stymied traveler to what is both necessary *and* impossible in transport and translation. These aporias lie in the very *track* of the traveler as they do the unaccountable *trace* of his narrative. If, as Ross Chambers has argued, literature is by nature dilatory and slow, paralyses could be considered, in their insouciance to difficulty, an expression of the loiterly and playful resources of literary writing. The tragic aspect of paralyses would be the counterpart to this tendency: not a loiterly playing with transgression, but a painful confrontation with absolute limitations. Aporia, however, expresses neither of these options. Only a reading that is slow enough, indeed paralyzed, can account for the transports of the paralyzed traveler. Paralysis, then, is not only the object of these studies but the name of their critical approach.

Hesitations

My argument so far has drawn on Western travels to show how the encounter with the other provokes a breakdown in the journey and its narrative. I have argued that such breakdowns stage an ethical encounter that, however, often remains incomplete and symptomatic. The task of a paralyzed reading is to dwell at such problematic moments in the text to bring out the text's implicit challenge to its own motives, drives, and transports. Postcolonial authors, for their part, have rewritten narratives of travel to contest and subvert accounts of Western discovery and conquest. Such postcolonial journeys are a critical counterpoint to Western travel, exploiting the contradictions and lapses of the colonial vision. And while contestation and subversion are valuable resources in this challenge to the norms of travel, some of the most far-reaching postcolonial critiques lie not only in political opposition but also in an exploration of shared complicities and knotted histories. For such writers, as in our examples so far, discovery and conquest may become the site of a paralyzing encounter as well.

James Clifford has shown how the contemporary Native American is constrained by a double bind whose logic demands that the aboriginal be utterly different—at the risk of isolation and death—yet make himself known in the language and culture of the colonizer—at the risk of losing his identity. To escape this double bind Clifford suggests that "along with the history of resistances we need a history of hesitations."[47] Such hesitations may not be the stuff of adventure and drama, but are the persistent and necessary strategies of survival that defy the either-or logic of resistance and submission, assimilation and isolation. Even a story of postcolonial revolution, such as C. L. R. James's *The Black Jacobins*, confirms Clifford's "history of hesitations"; James aptly speaks of Toussaint L'Ouverture as embodying "vacillation" at a key point in his struggle for Haitian independence from France.[48] What Clifford calls hesitation I have, for my part, been calling paralysis. Paralysis lies at the *crux* of the matter, a place of crossed identities and crossed destinies, where decisions are made in the absence of clear alternatives, where vital distinctions are needed yet lacking. This crux, moreover, has the crisscross form of a double bind. I would argue, then, that its paralyzing logic is not so easily dispatched, and indeed provides the means to articulate a way beyond the alternatives of aboriginal resistance and opposition.

Such a paralyzing crux is found in Jamaica Kincaid's "In History," an essay that revisits the journeys of discovery to the New World. Claiming that all modern history bears the trace of slavery and the slave trade, Kincaid says she would like to mark that trace with an asterisk. The asterisk would indicate where a footnote to the "official story" of Western travel is needed.[49] What Kincaid modestly calls her own "addition" to this official history does not, however, do justice to the transformations and displacements this footnote would entail, which her searching, wide-ranging, and allusive text amply proves. Such a footnote cannot simply be added, since it would threaten to undermine and overflow the official story. The asterisk thus indicates an impossible yet necessary addition. Moreover, the spot marked by this asterisk is not that of a place or a boundary; it is, like the crux, that of a limit both crossed *over* and crossed *out*.

INTRODUCTION

The crux, then, does not simply mark the spot; its crosswise suture marks instead an overlapping of sites, histories, and identities. To encounter the crux is to be paralyzed.

In her imaginary journey home to her native island of Antigua, Kincaid tries to imagine her people and her land as seen through the eyes of Columbus. At the same time, traveling with Columbus, she tries to counter that discovery with her own claiming of Antigua, to "speak of it as if no one has ever heard of it before" ("In History," 3). The journey thus mimes that of Columbus, yet aims instead at an undiscovered aboriginal Antigua. Is this other, older Antigua "in" history, or outside of it? Can Kincaid's asterisk displace what is already, as she says, a "footnote" to history in Columbus's own account, his passing mention of her island? And her footnote to this footnote, can it find a proper place in the text of history? Kincaid's journey home is a belated return, of course, and so finds itself on the side of colonial history, its language, and its texts. Her discovery can only be a rediscovery of Antigua, and a return not to her home but only to the moment of fatal contact, perhaps to the very line of demarcation between a historical before and after. But it would be too simple to assert that Kincaid's belatedness condemns her to this side of history, much as she insists that it is "the human imagination that I am familiar with, the only one that dominates the world in which I live." Kincaid's asterisk indicates, instead, a point of discrepant history, where the myths of travel and progress are shadowed by another temporality. Indeed, the asterisk does not allow for a clear demarcation of a historical before and after, of the time of a people without history and that of Western history. Kincaid's belatedness is, rather, that of a continuous present, the postcolonial moment of an "open wound" that sutures *and* divides past and future, "each breath I take in and expel healing and opening the wound again and again, over and over" (1). Kincaid's journey is thus neither simply opposed to that of Columbus, nor fated to follow in its wake. Rather, it finds its subversive potential in traveling "tout contre" (right next to/completely against), as Derrida says, in the strange complicity of a paralyzing "counterpath."

Due to her predicament of belatedness, Kincaid's pared down, disarmingly simple language is marked with duplicity and repetition even at the crucial moment in her imaginary journey when she arrives home. "What were the things growing on the land?" Kincaid asks. "I pause for this. What were the things growing on that land and why do I pause for this?" ("In History," 3). The "why" of Kincaid's pausing is as important here as the "what" she indicates. This pause, hesitation, or paralysis is more than an occasion to stop and take stock of a momentous occasion. It indicates, rather, what defies indication, and even the index of an asterisk. The minimal alteration of "the land" to "that land" is pregnant with this impossible referent: the home as seen by the other, where her people suddenly "make an appearance" in history, but also, simultaneously, the one unknown to history, to which Kincaid also claims to belong. This is surely a decisive moment, for the appearance of her people foretells the impending consequences of genocide, slavery, and, more recently, the neocolonial economy of tourism. A decisive moment Kincaid would surely choose to change. Why, then, her indecision and hesitation? What gives pause here is not simply that the past cannot be altered, that the fatal contact has already occurred, but that Kincaid's voice cannot extricate itself from the crux that binds her aboriginal land to its simultaneous appearance and disappearance in the text of history. This is, moreover, the same double bind that requires that she voice her story from within the story of her own eradication. Kincaid thus speaks from the place of the subaltern, where the voice of counterhistory expresses what is constitutively erased or foreclosed from history, and confronts that erasure as the enabling condition of her speech. In this postcolonial paradox, she attempts to reclaim, in the language of colonization, an identity destroyed by that language. In a sense, her reclaiming of her history and her home owes itself to the erasure of that history, and her journey with Columbus simply revisits the erasure of her home. This does not amount, of course, to a submission to that language and its history, but neither is it the dialectical overturning of that history. It is, instead, a voice that articulates itself with the trace of the other, a trace that cannot be authored or appropriated. This postcolonial predicament makes Kincaid herself, like her homeland, an ambiguous referent, "I, me," both subject and object, fixed in the gaze of the uncomprehending other, yet stubbornly claiming recognition: "the person you see before you" ("In History," 4); "the person standing in front of you" (3).

Kincaid's insistence on her present visual *appearance*, marked by her black and aboriginal heritage, is a claim to history in the name of "all who look like me" ("In History," 1). To make this claim the text thus narrows in on the very moment of discovery when, Kincaid says, "I and the people who look like me begin to make an appearance" (4). A repetitive and obsessive motif in Kincaid's text, this "making an appearance" is the ironic moment of a discovery that grants yet denies identity, that recognizes only through misrecognition: the postcolonial legacy of Columbus, "who started the narrative from which I trace my beginning." Kincaid does not, however, bow to the necessity of this beginning, since she insists as well on speaking from the standpoint of one who is "not yet in the picture" and, indeed, claims that "I have not yet made an appearance" (1). This is more than an attempt to turn back the clock of history or to defy the narrative of "discovery." It is, rather, to dwell at the crux of discovery, to "trace my beginning" to the moment of encounter, a moment that is also, moreover, that of her present appearance "standing in front of you." Kincaid's rebellious text thus *makes a scene*, talking back to history, but does not simply claim or reclaim a lost or neglected identity. Instead, she marks the *trace of her beginning*, a trace that neither appears or not: the trace, in other words, of a "pre-emergent" self, to use Gayatri Spivak's formulation, which testifies to an identity foreclosed by history.[50] This trace lies in the margins of Columbus's journey, and as "a reader of this account of the journey" ("In History," 2) Kincaid occupies the place of Columbus's foreclosed other, the Antiguan native. Kincaid's evocation of the Antiguan aboriginal would, then, be neither fiction nor history, but rather, in Spivak's terms, "the (im)possibility of a vicarious (un)reading, the perspective of the "native informant" (*Critique of Postcolonial Reason*, 35).

Kincaid's "In History" indeed provides a striking illustration of Spivak's theory of the "native informant." The native informant, as Spivak defines it, is neither the data-providing interlocutor of the ethnographer nor the postcolonial agent of an autonomous speech act. Rather, the native informant lies in the margins of the dominant discourse of Western history as a figure paradoxically necessary to the truth-claims of that discourse, yet occluded from the scene. This "foreclosure" is thus more than a denial or a disavowal of the other; it is, instead, the mark of a structuring absence upon which the dominant text depends. Like Kincaid reading Columbus, Spivak reads Kant for evidence of the aboriginal "raw man," and shows that "Rhetorically crucial at the most important moment in the argument, it is not part of the argument in any way" (*Critique of Postcolonial Reason*, 13). Strictly speaking, there is no "arguing" with this discrepancy in Kant; Spivak thus warns against the "opposition between master and native" (37) that can unwittingly produce a mere "legitimation-by-reversal" (39). The postcolonial critic's task is, instead, to move "from opposition to critique" and explore the "complicities" that bind the master discourse to its others (147). I have argued that Kincaid's *crux* is the index of such a complicity with history's official story. Similarly, Spivak's "complicity" is the place at which Kant's text relies on an aboriginal other—the Australian aboriginal and the South American Fuegan—that it nonetheless forecloses. These paralyzing contradictions in Kant's text are overcome all too easily in the "axiomatics of imperialism" (34) that consigns the other to a mere supplement. An important moment in Spivak's critique comes when she tries to take stock of the history and culture of the aboriginals Kant summarily dismisses. This entails a long footnote on colonialism and anthropology that runs to four pages: "the manuscript got stalled for years," Spivak says, admitting that "I cannot write that other book that bubbles up in the cauldron of Kant's contempt" (28). Like Kincaid's asterisk, this footnote indexes an infinite labor in the margins of official history: "a parenthesis, in a note, on the note on a note" (48).[51] This infinite supplementarity, both paralyzing and motivating, follows the trace of the other in the master discourse.

Kincaid's voice is thus a testimony to what Spivak calls the founding foreclosure of the aboriginal in colonial thought and Western reason. A challenge to Columbus's appropriating mission, the crux of Kincaid's text indexes what cannot be claimed or reclaimed, an aboriginal world more ancient than Antigua itself: the trace of the other that resists historical appropriation and persists as the infinite supplement to history and the postcolonial present. Kincaid's opposition is asymmetrical to colonial history in that it does not presume to reappropriate the aboriginal or claim redress or reparations. And yet, of course, the wounds of history can inform political action in favor of the aboriginal. This aboriginal is, however, not only the victim of violence, but also the testimony to an "arche-violence" more ancient even than Antigua.[52] To speak as an ab-original is to speak as one *deriving* from an origin that can be neither appropriated nor denied. To speak for the oppressed is thus to take sides where sides are lacking, where the crisscross suture "heal[s] and open[s] the wound again and again." Talking back to Empire and writing her way back home, Kincaid testifies to the impossibility of any simple return address. Indeed, her text seems finally to circle only around a handful of paralyzing questions: "and now how to go on," she asks in a Beckettian vein ("In History," 6); "What to call the thing that happened to me?"; "Should I call it history?" (1); "what is history?" (2). These paralyzing questions touch on what is perhaps the very origin of Kincaid's text. "It is almost as if what is told," Spivak says, "is the result of an obstinate misunderstanding of the rhetorical question that transforms the condition of the (im)possibility of answering—of telling the story—into the condition of its possibility. Every production of experience, thought, knowledge, all humanistic production, perhaps especially the representation of the subaltern in history or literature, has this double bind at its origin."[53] *Out of* this origin, always a supplement, Kincaid voices the necessary yet impossible claiming of her aboriginal home. Her faltering prose undermines both the journey and its telling to narrate not a return but a departure from the certainties of home, origin, and belonging.

And yet, *departure* too loses its conventional bearings as a result of this absent origin. The figures of transport provoked by this predicament are necessarily vexed, but still enable mobile tactics of identification and desire. For Glissant, such mobile tactics arise precisely from the lack of any possibility of a return, and in the promise of a Caribbean identity free of the illusion of an original self. In Glissant's terms, "reversion" to an origin is thus expressed in duplicitous "diversions," themselves oriented toward an "entanglement" akin to Kincaid's paralyzing crux. "Diversion," Glissant says, "is nourished by reversion: not a return to the longing for origins, to some immutable state of Being, but a return to the point of entanglement, from which we were forcefully turned away." Due to this insight, even the most violent cuts do not call for reunification, but rather for a closer attention to a visceral entanglement. "The machete, more twisted than knotted entrails."[54] Voicing a historical trauma, Kincaid invites us "to listen to departure," as Cathy Caruth puts it, calling on us to bear the responsibility for a traumatic event and a singular place that are always belated, always displaced, but which endure in the stubborn index of a historical asterisk.[55]

"Only the impossible can make me still," Kincaid says in *A Small Place*. Litotic and devastating by turns, Kincaid's searing monologue buttonholes the tourist and confronts his insouciant pleasures with the postcolonial realities of Antiguan life.[56] To be "still" is not so much a desire for calm and repose as it is the demand coming from an ignorant and tormenting other—the touristic "you" of Kincaid's insubordinate address—that she stop her ranting and retribution.[57] Here the polemical "you" is the site of another entanglement that Kincaid, for all her righteous hostility, cannot solve, since her own language embodies the hateful colonizing other from whom she wants to extricate herself. And yet within that entanglement surely the promise of another stillness is voiced, that of a hoped-for peace and resolution that could finally heal her wounds. In this sense, then, Kincaid asks for the impossible: a stillness that will not stop, and a "way" that can only be traveled in the travails of language, voiced in a rhetorical question that does not know whether it questions, affirms, or denies: "only the impossible can make me still: can a way be found to make what happened not have happened?" (32). There is no *solution* here, no *analysis* that that can assuage Kincaid's paralyses. The cherished name "Antigua"—translation, misnomer, and erasure of the proper—is the postcolonial allegory of this quest for selfhood, defying the claims of the explorer and tourist yet unclaimed by Kincaid herself, whose countervoyage is too aware of its fateful entanglement not to persist in demanding the impossible.

Transgressions

French literature forms the basis of this study of paralyzed travel, which spans a period from the early nineteenth century to the postcolonial present. As shown by our examples from Beckett and Kincaid, however, paralyses of travel are not limited to the French context. And yet it is in this context, and particularly in French modernity, that the critique of travel and paralytic transports becomes a culturally dominant motif. Moreover, French modernity provides both the most striking symptoms of paralysis and their most insightful critical theories. The French example serves here, then, both as a singular case and as an example with which to compare other cultural instances of travel's paralyses. This raises an interesting problem of cultural comparison and translation, however. If translation in its classical sense implies the transfer of meaning across cultural codes, such transfers and transports are called into question by travel's paralyses. As mode of cultural translation, paralysis dwells on the *untranslated*: that which does not cross borders, that which does not carry over. This is not to imply, however, that paralyses simply impede communication and reinforce cultural closure and singularity. Rather, paralyses prevent the facile transfer of meanings at the expense of language's figural thickets. It is, indeed, in the thickets of language that one reads the symptom as "a failure of translation," to borrow Freud's expression.[58] Extending Freud's notion of the symptom to a cultural level, one may speak of cultural "failures of translation" that bring travel to a halt. Far from remaining unmoved and static, however, the "to-be-translated," as Laplanche puts it, is the core of the desire to understand, communicate, and travel (259). The "to-be-translated" is, in this sense, the very source of the "drive to translate" (164), even if that source itself remains unmoved and untranslated.[59]

A diagnosis of the specifically French cultural motif of paralysis is provided by the Spanish critic José Ortega y Gasset in his 1925 *The Dehumanization of Art*, an early assessment and theorization of modernism. Ortega calls the novel "a sluggish genre" that, in his account, tends toward an increasing diminution of action, story, and adventure in favor of the exploration of literary form, character, and psychology.[60] Conrad might be cited as a key instance of this development; a hinge figure in literary modernism, Conrad exploits the resources of traditional adventure tales but tends to stall his journeys in reflexive psychological meditations.[61] For Ortega, Proust is the last great example, though an extreme one, of the modern novel's sluggishness. "So slowly does the action move," Ortega says of Proust, "that it seems more like a sequence of ecstatic stillnesses without progression" (*Dehumanization of Art*, 79). Indeed, in what he calls Proust's "paralytic novel" (87), "the permissible measure of slowness is overstepped" (80). Some amount of action is necessary to narrative, though Ortega approves its near-abolition in favor of hermetic formalism and psychological analysis. Ortega's modernist manifesto thus contrasts the French tradition, including the rigor of its classicism—as in the conversing "statues" of Racine's plays (73)—to the popular tradition of Spanish literature, still wedded in his time to models of chivalry, adventure, and the picaresque.

The rejection of adventure and the picaresque is a common thread in modern French literature, which voices an ironic doubt as to narratives of escape, adventure, and discovery. One may argue, further, that the breakdown of plot and narrative characteristic of modern literature corresponds to the demise of overarching spatiotemporal narrative structures modeled on travel, adventure, and conquest. This allows us to trace a longer genealogy to what Lyotard, in his celebrated formulation of 1979, calls postmodernism's "incredulity toward metanarratives." As Lyotard says, "the narrative function is losing its functors, its great hero, its great dangers, its great voyages, its great goal."[62] The political reasons for this rejection are lacking, however, in Ortega's analysis, though it betrays throughout a suspicion of mass culture and popular forms of literature. At the other end of the political spectrum, Michael Nerlich's *Ideology of Adventure* offers more pointed political reasons to critique the tradition of adventure. Nerlich argues that Western adventure narratives were born in a transitional historical stage between feudalism and early capitalism, Spain being a main context for this historic shift. Having lost his role within the feudal system, the knight's purpose was glorified in narratives that emphasized honor and romance. Interestingly, however, the rise of the tale of chivalry coincides with the obsolescence of the knight, serving as an ideological mask for his decreased social status in an increasingly mercantile and capitalist world. Taken up in turn by the rising merchant class, *adventure* similarly justified and masked the political role of the capitalist through the glorification of financial risk and adventure. And since profit negates the very risks undertaken in capitalist travel, it is only in promoting an ideology of risk that narratives of adventure, like the discourse of speculator, investor, and merchant, justify their profitable returns. Heroic adventure, in Nerlich's analysis, is thus the mere alibi of this closed economy, whose aim, in fact, is "to remove adventure as far as possible from any incalculable risk."[63] Nerlich's historical approach allows us to see how the decline of adventure in modern literature may be a symptom of the breakdown of bourgeois confidence in its historical mission. This doubt dominates in the literature of the nineteenth century, though the ideology of adventure persisted in popular media, just as it does today in the touristic discourse of so-called "adventure travel."[64]

Claude Simon's great war novel *The Flanders Road* provides a late instance of the demise of chivalry and adventure. Interestingly, in so doing the novel also contrasts the two cultural traditions of Spain and France. Horsemanship, horseracing, and the French cavalry are dominant themes in Simon's novel, whose story weaves back and forth between the history of an aristocratic officer, routed in the Napoleonic war with Spain, and the experience of the narrator, a soldier in the French cavalry in World War II. The retreat from Spain, remembered in the context of World War II, allows Simon to embroider a vast historical tapestry, from the origins of French literature in *La Chanson de Roland* up to the recent past. The narrative comprises a series of shifting and repeated tableaus that are strikingly static; the text insists on the immobility of all the soldiers' actions, as in the description of "the four riders and the five horses somnambulistic and not advancing but lifting and setting down their hooves almost motionless on the road."[65] The book's emblematic image is that of a dead horse lying in the mud, repeatedly invoked as frozen in motion or petrified like a fossil: "it seemed to have been there forever, like one of those fossilized animals or plants that had returned to the mineral kingdom, with its two front feet bent into a foetal posture of prayer" (26). This static and frozen figure connects the narrator's obsessive memories, though it cannot be located in a determinate time in the narrative. Indeed, the dead horse seems to fall outside of time in a kind of infinite acceleration, "as if the margin of time normally necessary for the passage from one kingdom to the other (from the animal to the mineral) had this time been crossed at once" (104). It remains for us to determine how and why such a paralyzed image coincides with a sudden *passage* and *crossing*.

The originality of Simon's novel lies in its insistence on a time that is not so much historical as geological. Indeed, all seems petrified or frozen in the novel, caught in the imperceptible movement of a glacier, "that Olympian and cold progression, that slow glacier moving since the beginning of time" (*Flanders Road*, 284). Time, conceived as a glacial substance containing all the novel's characters and events, suspends chronology and causality to offer instead a web of episodes linked not in a single temporal chain but rather as static elements in a contemporaneous frozen space. This bold narrative gambit of an impersonal glacial and geological time nonetheless betrays recognizably psychological obsessions and conventional narrative structures: "I the horseman the booted conqueror coming from the depths of time coming to seduce to carry off the lily-white princess" (272). This seduction, moreover, bears the traits of a Freudian family romance; the mother of Georges, the protagonist, hails from an aristocratic lineage, and Georges, in seducing the wife of his aristocratic officer, seems to flirt with incest and defy his father's peasant lineage. Georges's paralyses can then be ascribed to a neurotic fixation that sustains both his desire and its prohibition in images of frozen motion. This ambivalence also marks the novel's relationship to the adventurous narratives it aims to challenge and dismantle. In this respect, then, Georges—and Simon himself—would be similar to Georges's mother, who is "animated by contradictory sentiments, probably uncertain herself if in narrating these scandalous, or ridiculous, or ignominious, or Cornelian stories she wanted to deprecate that nobility, that title she had not inherited, or on the contrary give it more luster, so as to further gorge her pride with the consanguinity and the glamour reflected from it" (58). The reference to Corneille, appropriately enough, refers us to that classic tale of Spanish chivalry, *El Cid*. But in taking leave of such literary history, Simon's novel betrays an anxiety of influence that paralyzes his narrative. This ambivalent tension reaches a climax in the elaborate scenes of lovemaking at the end of the novel. The woman's body is identified with all that is earthly, mineral, and geological; a misogynist fantasy thus lays the blame for corruption and death in the fatal desire "to return to the moist and secret hiding place, the dark mouth" of his lover's sex (296). We have seen how the frozen image of the dead horse also invokes a sudden "passage" into another realm. Petrified and timeless, and yet suddenly crossing over a limit, the dead horse shares with Georges a similar paralyzed motion in the act of lovemaking, as he indulges in fantasies of guilty transgression. Women and the earth are insistently compared in such figures as "the matrix of pale ochre earth" (161), and the "ancient matrix" (221). Thus, Georges is described as "paralyzed with cramps, and as motionless as the dead nag, his face buried in the thick grass, the hairy earth, his whole body flattened as if he were trying to vanish between the lips of the ditch, to melt, to slip, to sink altogether through the narrow crevice to rejoin the original matter (matrix)" (249). Here, sex and desire seem to give way to Freud's death drive. I will return, in what follows, to this key notion in Freudian theory. Here let me briefly indicate that Simon's approach to the death drive resembles Freud's in its speculative delirium, as well as in its attempt to encompass a negativity that reaches beyond narrative and structure. But if the death drive opens onto sheer negativity and the loss of meaning, a compensatory move usually allays the costs; in Simon's novel, that move would be a grounding of meaning in a mythic feminizing of the work of destruction: "[B]ut what could you call that: not war not the classical destruction or extermination of one of the two armies but rather the disappearance the absorption by the primal nothingness or the primal All of what a week before were still regiments batteries squadrons of men, or better still: the disappearance of the very notion of a regiment a battery a squadron of men, or better still: the disappearance of any notion of any concept at all" (305).

What transports remain when the main thrust of narrative is seemingly abandoned, as we see here? What subjects replace the hero, adventurer, and conqueror? In Simon's case, the avant-gardism of his prose subtly perpetuates chivalry in the very dismantling of its literary codes; in this sense it is akin to all adventure tales that, as Nerlich argues, are inherently belated and anachronistic. I have argued, further, that a Freudian account of the text serves as a key to the narrator's paralyses. In what follows, I will further develop the stakes of a Freudian critique to show how modern literature's discourse of adventure is inflected away from the conventional domain of adventurous plot and action and toward psychic risk, rebellion, and transgression.

In an account of the demise of adventure in Western literature, Paul Zweig's *The Adventurer* argues for a rehabilitation of the adventurous hero, understood as an indispensable figure who dramatizes the defining boundaries of the social order through transgression and risk. Zweig's modern exemplar of such a hero is Nietszche, whose transgressive philosophy rejects the bad conscience of the criminal in favor of the overman. Zweig's celebration of adventure in literature fails to account, though, for what remains normative in such tales of masculine risk, discovery, and monstrosity. Interestingly, Zweig's first invocation of risk goes by way of *paralysis*: "Haven't all of us, now and then, experienced moments of abrupt intensity, when our lives seemed paralyzed by risk?"[66] This paralysis may well evoke the moment of suspense before action; it also points, however, to a breakdown of transport, a hesitation at the place of transgression. I would suggest that such paralyzed transgression can be approached through psychoanalysis, which offers some of the richest accounts of the paradoxes of transport. In contrast to Zweig's hero, the psychoanalytic subject would be that other criminal whose desire, in its byways and displacements, confronts the motivating and paralyzing force of prohibition. Neurotic travel reveals the structuring role of an internalized prohibition that the subject vainly attempts to circumvent. As the subject's alibi, travel, then, may be the scene of a failed reflexive turn; within the modern adventurer lies the ironic figure of a Rat Man, whose obsessions, fixations, and frenetic wanderings are so many frustrated attempts to bring to light his compromised desiring motives.[67] The reflexive turn away from adventure and toward the everyday is a hallmark of modernism and the Nouveau Roman; in Sarraute's early work, the emotional transports of her characters are reduced to minimal "tropisms" in a stifling atmosphere of anxiety and claustrophobia.[68] In its characteristic reflexivity, modern literature shares with psychoanalysis a suspicion of travel, or what Paul Morand calls the "délit de fuite" ("hit and run"; literally "crime of flight"), and the breakdown of heroic narrative confirms literature's quest for other transports, at the cost of paralysis.[69]

From conquistadors and chivalry to the modern cavalry, it is a small step to the *corrida*, belated holdover of an ideal of masculine heroism. Here again we find a paralyzed transgression, such as stands at the beginning of Michel Leiris's autobiographical project. Despite its promising title, Leiris's *Manhood* (*L'Age d'homme*) is no account of heroism, except in suggesting an impossible ideal: that of the matador to which the author aspires in his poetics of risk. As stated in the essay that opens the autobiography, Leiris aims at exposing himself to a "danger" analogous to that of the bull's horn by submitting himself to an absolutely truthful self-portrait.[70] Leiris notes that his writing is intended as an "act" of confession inspired by the experi-

INTRODUCTION 37

ence of a prior psychoanalytic treatment. This act, however, tends irresistibly toward paralysis, since the "sculptural" model to which Leiris aspires is that of a matador whose "feet remain motionless," controlling the passing bull with his cape (161). Further, Leiris says that he wants his autobiography to present him as a "solid block" in protection against death—adding that, paradoxically enough, this contradicts his own intention to "risk everything" (162). This crucial equivocation between self-constitution and absolute risk, unresolved by Leiris, points to a crisis of identity at the site of transgression, a crisis marked by castration anxiety, tellingly evoked by the threatening horn of the bull. Dedicated to his friend Georges Bataille, Leiris's *Manhood* bears the stamp of his friend's Nietzschian philosophy of transgression, and thus seems to confirm Zweig's argument; and yet, Leiris's examples of the *corrida* and sacred ritual fall more fully within the scope of a psychoanalytic predicament. Here, transgression conveys nothing so much as the compromised status of neurotic desire, both sustained and inhibited by a reigning prohibition. Thus, the matador, as embodiment of a ritualized transgression, is seen as submitting to a *rule* of conduct with respect to the dangerous bull. There is "an immediate connection between obedience to the rule and the danger incurred," Leiris notes (160). Indeed, the rule, "far from being a protection, contributes to his danger." The *rule*, then, submits to another imperative, that of the symbolic *law* conveyed by the phallic horn. Leiris's paralysis in the face of this threatening law is the price of his wayward, transgressive desire.

Another way of approaching the paralytic aspect of Leiris's work would be by means of the register of identification and desire that Jacques Lacan terms the *Imaginary*. As the primary mode of the subject's identification, the Imaginary initially serves to stabilize the infant as a specular ego in resistance to its bodily disorganization. Lacan emphasizes the inertia, fixation, and resistance that characterize the specular ego in its "formal stagnation," a stasis akin to the face of an actor in a film that has been stopped.[71] In the adult subject the persistence of the Imaginary represents above all a vain effort of self-constitution in resistance to the symbolic law of castration. Leiris's frustrated writings and travels would thus be structured and limited within the scope of an impossible and illusory effort of self-realization. It is worth recalling that Lacan defines egoical identity as an aspect of the subject that is intractable and permanent. While defined by a moment of development Lacan isolates as a "stage," the mirror stage is not one that is overcome, but is incorporated within the subject and in Lacan's discourse in an increasingly complex structuring network, overlapping and interfering with the Symbolic and the Real. At the same time, if this Imaginary regime that "fixates" the subject is irreducible, it contains within its own dynamic the seeds of its own dismantling. This is the topic of Lacan's essay "Aggressivity in Psychoanalysis," where he highlights the frustrating nature of the ego and the characteristic violence it fosters. Like Freud, Lacan considers aggression against others to be determined by an original aggressivity toward oneself. Lacan refines this point by tying its logic to "a primary identification that structures the subject as a rival with himself."[72] Accordingly, aggressivity, in Lacan's analysis, is fundamentally aggressivity turned against the specular ego; the ego, in its frustrations, is seen as undertaking the destruction of its own claims to integrity—such as Leiris's "single solid block"—and ultimately aiming beyond the Imaginary. In this account, then, Freud's primary narcissism is directed less at defense and self-constitution than toward the very overcoming of its illusions. Lacan thus parts company with Freudian ego psychology, which makes the ego the very core of the well-adjusted individual. In contrast, Lacan states that egoical frustration and aggression point the way to the emergence of the *subject* in the place of the ego. This self-realization is undertaken by means of the death drive, whose tireless work compels the subject to dismantle its cherished illusions. Leiris's "autocritique" can be usefully situated within this problematic, and the symptoms of

Leiris's masochism may be located at this primordial level, where the work of self-reflection and autobiography is directed at the demolition of the image of selfhood. Accordingly, a crucial feature of Leiris's travel accounts is their self-deflating presentation of his imaginary desires and motives. I examine Leiris's work and travels in chapter 1, where I compare him with two precursors, Nerval and Gautier, and more at length in chapter 4, where I examine his ethnographic travels.

Psychoanalysis thus provides a means to reconsider the topos of *imaginary travel*, usefully recast as a phantasmatic domain of vexed identification, rivalry, and frustrated transports. In his *Prospero and Caliban: The Psychology of Colonization*, Octave Mannoni addressed the imaginary motives for traveling to underdeveloped countries: "Baudelaire felt, as we all do, that savage countries and savage peoples were the nearest imitation he could find in the real world of that of his childhood—of paradise. We may go further and say, with but slight exaggeration, that there would be no ethnographers, explorers, or colonials 'among the savages' if it were not for this *vocation*." Mannoni links this vocation to a fundamental *ambivalence* that plays out in the colonial drama: "civilised man is painfully divided between the desire to 'correct' the 'errors' of the savages and the desire to identify himself with them in his search for some lost paradise."[73] What accounts for this ambivalence, and how does it serve to motivate the traveler? Mannoni's formulations here provide the elements of a Lacanian analysis. The traveler's picture of the native would be framed in the Imaginary, that register of desire in which the subject projects the illusory figments of an impossible plenitude by means of mirroring relationships with images of the self and others. This specular resolution is purchased at a great cost to the subject, however, as the ironic consequence of the subject's imaginary strivings for identity is to see itself only as an *other*. The ego is thus constituted as a relationship to a field of projections that the self cannot fully assume; for this reason, Lacan says, the ego is "frustration in its essence." All imaginary relations are as a result structured by an unresolvable dynamic of identification and rivalry as the subject struggles with the terms of his specular alienation. Mannoni points to such a dynamic when he asserts that the traveler is painfully divided by the desire to "identify" with the primitive and to impose himself on him. The alter ego is always prey to such violent alteration by the egoic subject due to the aggressivity inherent to his specular frustration.[74] With its focus on the case of French Madagascar, Mannoni's *Prospero and Caliban* provides me with some of the terms with which I approach the work of Jean Paulhan in chapter 3. In close readings of Paulhan's work, including his linguistic study of Malagasy proverbs, I underscore characteristic turns and reversals that bear persistently on a dynamic of mastery and submission. Paulhan's linguistic studies in Madagascar thus symptomatically enact a problematic of *subjection*, in which questions of agency and authority vie with intractable doubts and anxiety. These vexing figures of uncertain agency defy accountability, and as a result, Paulhan's cultural estrangement and dislocation yields no clear narrative but only paralyses and paradoxical transports.

Insofar as the traveler follows the vectors of an imaginary desire, his travels will be marked, then, by a defining frustration. Psychoanalysis thus provides useful terms for a political critique of imaginary travel. One might, for instance, recast Dean MacCannell's well-known sociological study of tourism in Lacanian terms. If, as MacCannell puts it, the tourist's journey is "a search for authenticity," his travel is, however, fundamentally nostalgic and illusory, sustained by figments of stereotyped elsewheres and others.[75] Frustration habitually accompanies the quest for authenticity, which misrecognizes its true purpose, Jonathan Culler points out, as "a quest for an experience of signs."[76] The habitual resentment by the tourist of other tourists could be attributed to specular rivalry, and the friction between the tourist's cherished illusions and the awkward mediation of his experience could be cast as a struggle between the

Imaginary and the Symbolic. Moreover, imaginary travel allows us to see how touristic travel can survive, and even sustain itself, in its very nostalgia and belatedness; the traveler's disenchantment—and even his failure—can console him in his illusions. We have seen how "imperialist nostalgia" stakes its claim to lost authenticity in a loss it perpetuates and dissimulates. Similarly, imaginary travel lays hold of images and stereotypes whose frustrating nature fosters an evermore imperious fixation. This is captured in Malek Alloula's catalogue of colonial Algerian postcards.[77] The postcards document the power of the stereotype in authorizing French claims for colonial domination, exposing in a striking way the role of the sexual phantasm in the discursive hegemony of colonial rule. A victory of the gaze, such postcards disavow their own frustrated access to women who remained in large part out of reach and sight of the French colonial.[78] In chapter 2, I explore this ambiguous colonial fascination in Fromentin's rapturous description of an Algerian harem, and argue that Fromentin's Algerian journeys demonstrate the belated traveler's jealous hold on colonial illusions.

Psychoanalysis also presents novel insights into one of the most time-honored examples of paralyzed travel: Zeno's arguments on the impossibility of movement. Several recent Lacanian essays have turned their attention to Zeno's paradoxes, the best known of which represents Achilles in pursuit of a tortoise. Zeno's argument purports to demonstrate that although Achilles is faster than the tortoise he will be forever unable to catch up to it. Since the tortoise has an advance on him, the argument goes, Achilles must make up first the distance between them, plus the advance. This advance, however short, becomes infinite in Zeno's argument, for once a given distance is covered, an advance always remains, which itself becomes a distance to cover, and so on. The prey thus infinitely recedes in smaller and smaller increments. Slavoj Žižek points out that psychoanalysis allows us to recognize in this seeming sophistry what is in fact the most common of experiences, namely the dream of running in place.⁷⁹ Zeno's paradox thus holds true at an unconscious level of experience. What the tortoise would represent, in this analysis, is the subject's *goal*: not any particular object but the object as such, whose promise of infinite satisfaction provokes its infinite regress. Zižek's argument concerning Zeno draws on the Lacanian notion of the *objet petit a*. In an important scene from Freud's *Beyond the Pleasure Principle*, the child conjures up an object that would cover over the absence provoked by the mother's departure. Lacan's reading of Freud asserts that the absence bears less on the mother herself than on the child's identity; out of the child's sense of lack he precipitates an object—the ego—with which his integrity can be assumed. This object Lacan terms the *objet petit a*, an object that the child attempts to recover but which, paradoxically, was not there to begin with. This object is inversely figured in the mirror stage, where the child anticipates an identity in the form of an image that his body cannot yet correspond to. The imaginary object thus exists within a temporality that cannot coincide with the subject: on the one hand, an impossible nostalgia posits retroactively what *must have been*; on the other, a dream of fulfillment to come conjures up a future perfect, what *will have been*. As cause of desire, the imaginary object propels the subject in a quest for what cannot be attained.

A second paradox of Zeno's posits that an arrow in flight is motionless. Since at any point in its trajectory it must occupy a certain space, it is claimed to be perpetually at rest. The logic of both paradoxes relies on the principle of cutting up motion into increments. Joan Copjec ties this logic to the rationale that leads Aristotle, in his theses on movement, to posit the Prime Mover, an immobile agent at the heart of any motion. What dictates that the identity of the arrow or the substance of a given being must interrupt its own motion? In Copjec's analysis, it is the primal cut between the Imaginary and the Symbolic that accompanies the subject's every move and threatens him with paralysis even as it causes his very flight. "The subject constructed by language finds itself detached from a part of itself. And it is this primary detachment that renders fruitless all the subject's efforts for a reunion with its complete being. The arc of its strivings appears to the subject as Zeno's arrow—an endlessly interrupted flight that can only asymptotically approach its goal."[80] Lacan adds to Zeno's paradox of Achilles and the tortoise the clarification that the subject (Achilles) may well be able to *overtake* the object (the tortoise), he simply cannot *attain* it. The most obscure moment of the paradox thus becomes that of the limit point where the subject crosses over or crosses out the place of the object: a point of coincidence without contact, a point of presence without present. "Clearly," Lacan says, "Achilles can only overtake the tortoise, he cannot catch up with her. He rejoins her only in infinity."[81] Copjec ties this question of infinite regression to the problematic of the signifier. In a linguistic order founded on difference, the infinite deferral of meaning, how, she asks, can the sign ever reach a point where meaning can coincide with the sign? Copjec suggests that the limit that suspends these alternatives is the subject's finitude, the incompletion that precipitates the subject's impossible object of desire. This finitude motivates the subject; the cause of his actions originates in an impasse whose overcoming is the impossible object. In Milner's words, Zeno shows that "the impossible is necessary."[82] The solution to the paradox lies with the limit: it is because the subject is finite or castrated that the limit is overcome, not once and for all but endlessly. Copjec says, "The psychoanalytical subject is not infinite, it is *finite*, and it is this limit that causes the infinity, or unsatisfiability, of its desire. One thing comes to be substituted for another in an endless chain only because the subject is cut off from that essential thing that would complete it."[83] A recognition of this unsatisfiability would be, then, the condition for an ethics of traveling desire. Ethical transports, renouncing the imperious image and its objects, would be modeled on the Freudian *drive*, a sheer impulse without object but its own tireless quest.

As Copjec's essay makes clear, her Lacanian analysis of the paradoxes of transport aims to rebut a deconstructive theory of linguistic difference. Derrida's critique of Lacan involves a challenge to the theory of the Symbolic as structuring linguistic order, with castration and transgression as its linchpins. Even among Lacan's dissenters, including many of his feminist critics, castration, transgression, and the law provide orienting terms for a questioning of symbolic norms and their social instantiations. Derrida's deconstruction of Freud and Lacan disorients these terms in a radical way. There is, as a result, a hint of anxiety in Copjec's invocation of an unstructured infinity, whose limiting cut, for all its painful consequences, offers a structuring reassurance. Indeed, her very argument with Derrida betrays a structuring reflex of opposition, one that, moreover, pits infinity against its contrary. However, Derrida's analysis of the limit does not itself posit the infinite Copjec would attribute to him. Neither finitude nor infinity, Derrida's limit poses the problem of an aporia more paralyzing than Lacanian theory, and more paradoxical even than Zeno.

Among Derrida's most searching inquiries into the figures of transport is his essay on Freud's death drive, where he suggests the name *paralyse* for the critique he undertakes.[84] Freud's metapsychological *Beyond the Pleasure Principle*, with its focus on death, finitude, and the "beyond," allows Derrida to question the role of the limit in Freudian thought. This limit is Freud's very topic—the limit of life—but as Derrida shows, it is also the limit of Freud's own discourse as it comes up against its unthought margins and boundaries. Derrida thus displaces the question as Freud poses it, to show how the text's unworking of its argument stages its own death-work at the limits of knowledge. Derrida emphasizes the erratic, stumbling, and wayward progress of Freud's argument, his *démarche*, underscoring how Freud's textual tarrying with the limit entails a fruitful paralysis. Metaphysical and spiritual figure par excellence, the notion of the "beyond" is significantly critiqued in Freud's own analysis, but it is only his inadvertent stumblings and paralyses that constitute a deconstruction of that notion. The value of Freud's inquiry lies, therefore, not so much in his theory of a purported biological death drive as in its enacting of a "destruction drive," the persistent undoing of the text's own argument.

Derrida thus finds Freud an ally in the deconstruction of death as theme or dialectical negation. Death as the radically other, Derrida argues, cannot be appropriated or set to work by the dialectic; its otherness is not opposed to life or the pleasure principle, nor is it sublated in a movement that transcends that opposition. Similarly, in an essay on Blanchot, Derrida reduces the movement at the limit to the mere step or "trace" of a "pas": a step beyond that is simultaneously the negation of that same step. The grand pathos of Bataille's theory of sacrifice and the grim negativity of Blanchot amount as a result to a mere pun. Derrida is careful to caution, however, that such a pun risks being mistaken as mere voluntary play or, as in Freud, a successful, if momentary, transgression of the censoring law.[85] The duplicity of the "pas" (step/not) aims instead to convey, in a pairing of nonopposed contraries, the differential stroke that inscribes otherness within any given sign. Likewise, Derrida's witty and punning intervention into Freud's *Beyond the Pleasure Principle* aims not to make light of the death drive, but to bring out, in Freud's own inquiry, what resists death's appropriation as theme or *telos*. Death is not dialectical otherness and negation; it is, instead, a paralyzing confrontation with a minimal limit that, always already crossed, binds the sign to its duplicitous other. Derrida's "pas" conveys this play of otherness and iteration that confounds any account of presence, paralyzing both writer and reader in their encounter with its paradoxical trace.

In *Reading for the Plot*, Peter Brooks has named the theory of the death drive as "Freud's masterplot."[86] It is noteworthy that in using Freud's text for his narratological purposes, Brooks's focus is on nineteenth-century literature, and not on more-modern fictions—

such as Claude Simon's, for instance—that dismantle and problematize the arc of conventional narrative. Moreover, Freud's *Beyond the Pleasure Principle* is not so much a *plot* as a tangle of fits and starts, of retractions and reversals. Reading for the *plod*, so to speak, we bring out paralyses in Freud more akin to the texts surveyed here: the trudging fictions of Beckett, the wayward self-scrutiny of Leiris, the drifting of Barthes. To catch the drift of Barthes's texts is to read desire in its paradoxical transports, in tropisms and paralyses that belie narrative order. As I show in chapter 5, Barthes's early *Mythologies* took to task the political, ideological, and colonial economies of travel and tourism as expressed in the popular media of the France of the 1950s. Subsequently, Barthes theorizes other transports that go by the names of *dérive* and *atopie*. Such transports reflect a turn in Barthes's work, begun with *S/Z*, toward the theorization of sexuality, pleasure, and desire. *S/Z* also marks Barthes's departure from the structuralist paradigm, and his espousal of paradoxical transports carries him away from structural models of sexual identity, plot, and narrative. This proves a significant means of challenging gender norms as embedded in traditional narrative and plot, and as perpetuated in narrative theory.[87] One of Barthes's tactics in the face of such normative sexual roles is to redistribute them along the lines of gender. Thus, pointing to the convention that "Woman is sedentary, Man hunts, journeys," Barthes claims the privilege of the former: "sedentary, motionless, at hand, in expectation, nailed to the spot, *in suspense* [*en souffrance*]."[88] This paralysis defines the principal role of the lover in *A Lover's Discourse* as one who suffers the absence of the other: "in any man who utters the other's absence *something feminine* is declared: this man who waits and who suffers from his waiting is miraculously feminized. A man is not feminized because he is inverted but because he is in love" (14). Barthes's appropriation of a conventional topos of amorous narrative thus yields a queer alternative to its sexual essentialism and elaborates an ethics of desire that refuses the spoils of romantic adventure and chivalrous conquest.

Barthes's suspicion of travel in *A Lover's Discourse* entails a rejection of narrative, to the extent that the latter is wed to motives that would deny or attenuate the force of a desire aiming beyond ends, needs, and morals. Paralysis and fragmentation, as opposed to the language of mastery and adventure, nonetheless allow for other forms of transport. The language of absence provides for a space of play, a rhythm of attachment and separation. A frequent model of such transports for Barthes is the *fort-da* game from *Beyond the Pleasure Principle*, by which the child mimes the comings and goings of his mother. Barthes is close to Lacan in taking this scene as exemplifying the force of the drive in its impossible relation to a forever absent object. Indeed, Barthes specifically adopts the term *dérive* (drift) from Lacan to name the paradoxical transports of desire. Unlike Lacan, however, Barthes holds to *dérive* and its relation to the maternal object in resistance to the Symbolic as such. Barthes thus departs from the psychoanalytic critics we have surveyed so far, and attempts to reclaim the Imaginary as an alternative to the normative constraints of social and sexual identification. This alternative ultimately entails a rehabilitation of imaginary travel as an ethical relation in which the subject makes room for his *atopic* desire as the space of his necessary illusions and queer transports.

Barthes launches the challenge of such atopic transports in *S/Z*: "What would be the narrative of a journey," Barthes asks, "in which it was said that one stays somewhere without having arrived, that one travels without having departed—in which it was never said that, having departed, one arrives or fails to arrive?"[89] Barthes's impossible journey and its paradoxical transports resonate with all those explored in this book. As we will see in the next chapter, such an impossible journey is highly evocative of the spatiotemporal complexities of the immigrant experience. It also speaks to the nightmare of marginality and discrimination as described by

Boudjedra, the focus of my final chapter. Barthes's analysis thus not only can inform atopic pleasures and drifts but also contribute to a political critique of the exclusion of *sans-papiers* and migrants from the dominant narratives of travel. Such insights are enabled in part by cultural and political criticism, as seen in *Mythologies*, but also, more significantly, by the paralyzed reading in *S/Z*, a patient, exhaustive, *"slow motion"* and *"step-by-step"* approach (12). Neither arriving nor failing to arrive, as Barthes has it, the transports of such reading are a pleasurable *dérive*. At stake in this drift, once again, is the figure of an aporetic boundary, a *rive*—"shore" or "bank"—that defies access. Barthes's paradoxical drift thus accords with Derrida's in "Pas": "What arrives would always arrive *at the border*. Affecting the border. But by remaining there: by not arriving."[90] Neither movement nor stasis, the "non-arrivé" is an impossible arrival at each and every step.[91] At the same time, however, the "non-arrival" is promising, as it suggests not only paralysis but also transports, translations, and destinations still to come. For the *rive* or border is also a *crossroads*; here at this crossroads we will meet the *arrivant*, the twin and reversible figure of the colonist and immigrant, each paralyzed by the legacy of modern French travel.

At the end of *Sentimental Education*, Flaubert gives a summary indictment of bourgeois travel: "He travelled. . . . He returned."[92] One hundred years later, Barthes's *S/Z* offers a similarly telegraphic synopsis: *"To depart/to travel/to arrive/to stay*: the journey is saturated" (105). Between the two and stretching beyond into a wider nineteenth- and twentieth-century modernity, French literary culture expresses a pervasive mistrust of travel. One might call this a dominant literary *discourse* against travel, akin to the modern French denigration of vision studied by Martin Jay in *Downcast Eyes*. Unlike Jay's, however, my own approach aims not at a comprehensive cultural history, and does not claim to fully represent even a literary history of the period. In this respect, I share Jay's own qualifications regarding the limitations of "discourse" as an organizing principle of cultural historiography. Jay quotes from James Clifford on this point: "Discourse analysis is always in a sense, unfair to authors. It is interested not in what *they* have to say or feel as subjects, but is concerned merely with statements as related to other statements in a field."[93] A similar problem arises when treating travel as unitary theme or motif; Clifford's work, eminently sensitive to travel's complexities, has pursued the seemingly contradictory, but more precisely oxymoronic and paralyzing implications of "traveling cultures" and "dwelling-in-travel."[94] Likewise, to avoid the risk of overgeneralizing claims and illusory themes, in what follows I pursue close readings of the work of a select number of authors; a sustained focus on their texts brings out the particular lineaments of their paralyses within a discursive context they evoke, contest, and alter. It is, in fact, only from a synoptic perspective—such as that of Flaubert and Barthes above—or by means of selective quotes and broad themes, that one could make the claim for a simple, consistent, or uniform modern French negation of travel. A closer, slower approach reveals that paralyses are always challenges not to travel as such but to the norms and constraints of travel and translation. In this sense, the critique of travel is a "counter-discourse," as Richard Terdiman defines it; not simply the discourse of antagonism and resistance, but a more imbricated contestation within the dominant order.[95] Paralyses, as distinct from critique, would occupy the very site of this imbrication: between discourse and counterdiscourse; between the colonizer's vision and the recognition of the other; between touristic mentality and the experience of alterity. Given the omnipresence of figures of transport in language, the vexations of paralyzed speech threaten all the terms by which we represent our motions, emotions, motives, and meanings. As a result, language too becomes the site of contestation, its powerfully freighted metaphors paralyzed by poetic insight into more problematic turns of speech. Even at their most stymied, however, paralyzed travels always speak to new mobilities, and it is to a more detailed study of such paradoxical transports that we will turn next.

Having opened this introduction with a discussion of Beckett's paralyzed travels, I will index in closing a late manuscript of his titled "The Way." Beckett accompanied his drafts of this brief, unfinished, and unpublished text with the image of a figure eight, alternately drawn upright and horizontal. Each image figures a "winding one-way way," the path of a perpetual circuit. "The one way back was on and on was always back."[96] The cover of this book is indebted to Beckett's simple and evocative image that conveys a journey both infinite and infinitely stymied. Beckett's "Way" may serve as a map to the chapters that follow.

1. The Muse of Paralysis

I know why the volcano stirs again . . .
Your light foot, passing, touched it yesterday,
And suddenly ash blanketed the sky. — Nerval

Discrepant Journeys

In 1955, the year Lévi-Strauss proclaimed "an end to journeying" in *Tristes Tropiques*, Michel Leiris published *Scraps* (*Fourbis*), the second volume of his autobiography, *Rules of the Game* (*La Règle du jeu*). Like Lévi-Strauss's book, Leiris's *Scraps* offers a picture of disenchanted travel at midcentury. The parallels between these two texts are instructive, as they present differing perspectives on literature, anthropology, and the politics of travel. Lévi-Strauss's travelogue opens with a memorable evocation of colonial Martinique, first stop on his narrative journey; Leiris's first chapter, "*Mors*," written after his return from the Antilles, invokes Martinique as well. These similarities, however, mask striking differences between the two texts. The negation of travel in Lévi-Strauss finds its rejoinder in Leiris's more complex and ambiguous paralyses. Far from echoing him, Leiris's paralyses constitute a challenge to Lévi-Strauss's anthropological journeys, their politics, and their narrative ordering. Leiris's text thus may serve as a corrective to Lévi-Strauss's portrait of the midcentury predicaments of autobiography, travel, and anthropology. Even as it dwells on mourning, loss, and nostalgia, Leiris's essay defeats its own claims to repair or represent its losses, and thus it avoids the pitfalls of moralizing conscience and compensatory disenchantment, the stock-in-trade of post-exotic travel narratives.

The year our pair of texts appeared was also the year of the Bandung Conference, which paved the way for decolonization around the globe. In 1955 representatives from twenty-nine states, many of them newly independent, gathered at the Asian–African conference in Indonesia to oppose colonialism and the threats of postwar neocolonialism. The year 1955 was thus the turning point in a global political mobilization against colonialism that was already underway; in the coming years the process of decolonization would accelerate, particularly in Africa. The year before Bandung, the Algerian war of independence began, while the defeat of French forces at Dien Bien Phu led to the recognition of Vietnam's independence. Tunisia and Morocco would gain their independence in 1956. Martinique, for its part, had ended its colonial rule but opted for the status of Département d'Outre-Mer. In this context, the declaration of "an end to journeying" on the part of the anthropologist may seem politically dubious. While overtly an indictment of amateur travel, mass tourism, adventure, and missionary evangelism, Lévi-Strauss's nostalgia also hearkens back to an era in which the anthropologist's journeys were less politically fraught. Barthes's scathing indictment, in his 1957 *Mythologies*, of the exoticist film *The Lost Continent* might well be applied to this nostalgic impulse in *Tristes Tropiques*: "the 'beautiful pictures' of *The Lost Continent*," Barthes says, "cannot be innocent: it cannot be innocent to *lose* the continent which found itself again at Bandoeng."[1] Similarly, Lévi-Strauss's "end to journeying" is contested by those who traveled to Bandung, whose transits between colony and metropole forged postcolonial identities, and whose diasporic networks of travel and affiliation gave rise to the consciousness of a new map of the globe, including the Third World, *négritude*, and the "black Atlantic."[2]

Aimé Césaire's *Notebook of a Return to the Native Land* exemplifies these new networks of postcolonial travel. First published in 1939, Césaire's poem follows the arc of a journey home to colonial Martinique, one that merges with the tortured journeys of his ancestors in the hold of slave ships. Césaire's journey of self-discovery and self-renewal descends into the depths of abjection in order to transform history's black passengers into postcolonial travelers. This journey is a negation of the white traveler, his conquering and exploration, and an affirmation of "those who have known voyages only through uprootings."[3]

> Pity for our omniscient and naïve conquerors!
>
> Eia for those who never invented anything
> for those who never explored anything
> for those who never conquered anything (36)

If Césaire's indictment of the colonizer's world entails a rejection of the journey of discovery, conquest, and exploration, what transports remain for his own return home? In a passage that portrays the mutiny of a slave aboard a ship, Césaire emphasizes less the reclaiming of the privilege of travel than a stubborn resistance within the motion of the journey.

> And the nigger scum is on its feet
>
> the seated nigger scum
> unexpectantly standing
> standing in the hold
> standing in the cabins
> standing on the deck
> standing in the wind
> standing under the sun
> standing in the blood
> standing
> and
> free (48)

The insistent "standing" of the mutinous slave seems to defy not only his masters but the journey itself. *Négritude*, coined here in Césaire's poem, is likewise defined as an "upright patience" (*Notebook of a Return*, 35) whose ardent passions and emotions resist, throughout the journey home, the tainted transports of white travel. The "motionless veerition" (51) with which the *Notebook* closes conveys, in its oxymoronic combination of stasis and motion, as well as in its strange and inventive neologism, the need to express an experience of travel for which words are lacking, and whose passionate transports occupy the space of a colonial contradiction. Christopher Miller opines that it is "too bad" Césaire's "motionless veerition" offers no clear possibility of escape.[4] However, what stirs us in the *Notebook* are transports that do not simply narrate the hope and promise of emancipation but dwell instead within the bind of subjection as fraught and conflicted agency. In this light, one might compare Césaire's journey to the colony with Genet's invocation of Guyana in *The Thief's Journal*. In a willfully perverse turn of fantasy, Genet bemoans the abolition of the penal colony, to which former convicts were ferried in a "procession on the sea . . . performed with bowed head."[5] Like Césaire, Genet discovers lyrical resources in a rehabilitation of the abject, and for all its vagabondage, his picaresque narrative tends invariably toward arrest and incarceration in order to savor in a passionate struggle with the law the transports of queer desire. Genet's work, exemplarily committed to the cause of the colonized, figures desire as a force that dwells in transgression, its transports not so much a dialectical passing beyond the limit as tending always downward, deeper, in what Foucault termed a "spiral" of transgression.[6] Frantz Fanon's 1952 *Black Skin, White Masks* cites amply from Césaire's *Notebook* to argue that the contradictions of black colonial experience do not square with the progressivism of dialectical history. In "The Fact of Blackness" Fanon thus resists Sartre's claim that "negritude appears as a minor term of a dialectical progression," a "transition," and a "means." The "fact of blackness" is not only an index of the white man's "intractable" racism, but is also the resistant core of what, in spite of the author's torment and impatience, leaves Fanon "waiting" and "paralyzed" at the end of the essay.[7] If Hegel's dialectic of master and slave narrates a "journey of desire," as Judith Butler argues,[8] queer and postcolonial writers would tangle with the legacy of that journey's tacit exclusions and discover vital though conflicted transports within what its idealist progressivism sacrifices and purports to leave behind.

Such fraught stories of travel are characteristic of colonial and postcolonial narratives of immigration, emigration, and diaspora, which struggle with the need to relate an experience of journeys that fall outside the codes of the master discourse. Postcolonial immigrant narratives are often fragmentary and episodic, rather than progressive and end-driven, a narrative tendency that reflects their characters' position in a social order that frustrates expectations of progress, development, ends, and goals. In an interesting account of the experience of illegal immigration from North Africa to Europe, Fawzi Mellah underscores how the journey of immigrants defies the genre of the travel narrative. The dangers risked, the courage of the travelers, their discoveries and explorations, all invite comparison, Mellah says, with "mythic adventurers" and such historic predecessors as the Spanish explorers of the New World.[9] And yet, as Mellah points out, "A clandestine immigrant spends more than half his time (his life?) simply waiting" (50). This stasis reflects the restriction of the time and space of the immigrant to solving immediate needs and problems, a condition that seemingly puts any real future out of reach. The difficulty of describing and narrating the space-time of immigrant travel is dramatically illustrated when the clandestine boat surreptitiously crosses the path of a passenger liner. As he tries to imagine the world of the passengers on board that ship, Mellah says, "I no longer had the feeling that I lived the same temporality as the honest, regular passengers of the liner: they were traveling resolutely and on a straight line toward a known destination that had been chosen ahead of time; as for us, we were creeping shiftily toward a port we hadn't chosen and about which we didn't know much" (33). This confusion of the space-time of the immigrant traveler, Mellah says, is more than a factor of illegality, but of "a new temporality. A novel way of sensing duration. A completely different rhythm than ordinary humans. No longer belonging to the same time, the passengers of the liner and us, lowly cargo of our sorry boat, we no longer lived in the same space either." The encounter with the passenger liner resumes the "jolting rhythm" of the immigrant traveler's experience as a whole: "Out of sync with others, he moves around in a temporality made up of forced stopovers and unpredictable fits and starts" (34).

When, as he relates at the beginning of *Tristes Tropiques*, Lévi-Strauss's passenger liner arrived in Martinique in 1941, he was one of a handful of passengers who, despite his refugee status, benefited from a separate cabin, an anomalous and belated holdover from the privilege he had enjoyed in earlier transatlantic passages. Lévi-Strauss was accompanied on board by an unusual conglomeration of some 350 passengers fleeing Nazi-occupied France, crammed like livestock, Lévi-Strauss says, in the cargo hold. Among those passengers was none other than André Breton, with whom Lévi-Strauss had struck up a friendship during the crossing. Breton's arrival in Fort-de-France is the occasion of a remarkable encounter in the annals of literary history: wandering the streets of the town, Breton comes across the work of Césaire in a shop window and, captivated by his writing, arranges a meeting.[10] The friendship between Césaire and Breton would lead to literary and political collaboration over the following years, and Breton would be instrumental in broadening the reach of Césaire's work and renown. Lévi-Strauss would not be part of this encounter, and his visit to Martinique as a whole constitutes something of a missed appointment. Nothing could contrast more with Lévi-Strauss's bitter and misanthropic picture of Fort-de-France than Breton's rapturous discovery of a new world in the making. Breton is not of course blind to the poverty, racism and political backwardness of Martinique, doubly colonized, in a sense, by Vichy France. However, Breton, unlike Lévi-Strauss, recognizes the colonial nature of the social ills on the island, and sees the literary work of Césaire as a promise for the future. Indeed, as schoolteacher, poet, mayor of Fort-de-France, and finally deputy to the French Assemblée Nationale, Césaire would leave a long and lasting influence on postcolonial Martinique and beyond. Césaire was teacher and inspiration to Fanon, the most influential of postcolonial theorists and activists; with Léopold Sédar Senghor, he fathered the pan-Atlantic movement of literary *négritude*; and as a politician, he would steer Martinique out of the doldrums of colonial rule.

Former surrealist and fellow communist Leiris followed Breton in meeting with Césaire in the course of an ethnographic mission to the French Antilles in 1948. Leiris's encounter with Césaire would radicalize his perspective on the collusion of anthropological knowledge with colonial power, as seen in his groundbreaking essay of 1950 on ethnography and colonialism. From the perspective of its colonialist history, Leiris sees ethnography's exclusive focus on primitive cultures as perpetuating a "myth" of objectivity blind to the relationship of authority and domination it maintains with respect to such cultures.[11] Coming from within the field of anthropology itself, Leiris's critique of its colonial politics was the first of its kind and anticipates issues that have shaped anthropological debates in recent years. A history of anthropology today departs from the recognition that its work was made possible by colonial appropriation and the technical and economic expansion that accompanied it.[12] The conscience of anthropology in the face of this predicament is most famously voiced in *Tristes Tropiques*, both elegy to the primitive world and despairing portrait of a modern world Lévi-Strauss sees as turning increasingly monocultural. In contrast to Lévi-Strauss's moralizing nostalgia, however, Leiris takes the position of political commitment to anticolonialism and espouses an ethics of hybridity and difference. Leiris's critique of anthropology and his friendship with Césaire thus place him at the center of the key political and cultural realignments of French and Francophone culture at midcentury. In James Clifford's *The Predicament of Culture*, Leiris's ethnography is a key witness to the complex cross-cultural exchanges of the twentieth century, not least because his ethnography's very authority is contested by the shifting cultural boundaries that it inhabits.[13]

Following such work as that of Clifford's, my reading of Leiris locates his work within a political and historical context that gives rise to an epistemological mutation in the traveler's rapport with other cultures. Further, my analysis attempts to account for the traveler's desire insofar as it motivates his approach to cultural others. Such an approach is essential to a portrait of the traveler that would ground his political and ethical responsibility not in abstract principle but in his affective transports. As regards Leiris in particular, this approach necessarily answers to the dual nature of his writing, both ethnographic and autobiographical. The autobiographical element of Leiris's work, significantly informed by psychoanalysis, places desire at the heart of the project of writing, and this unruly desire is a feature that fruitfully contaminates the account of his first ethnographic mission recounted in *L'Afrique fantôme*. It is thus at the level of Leiris's affective transports and sexual phantasms that I locate, in chapter 4, the key stakes of such texts as his ethnographic monograph on ritual possession in Ethiopia. Leiris's reflexive engagement with his sexuality allows for an unsettling of his own self-interested impulse for travel, resulting in a broader critique of ethnography's unspoken motives, including its exoticism and identification with narratives of heroism, conquest, and adventure. A suspicion as to his own affective transports thus leads Leiris toward a critique of travel's dominating thrust.

Anthropologists have recently turned their attention to the sexual politics of fieldwork, confirming the motivating and compromising role of desire in ethnography as exposed by Leiris. One author has suggestively linked ethnography's hermeneutic thrust with a masculine prerogative; narrative itself, to the extent that it is organized in terms of penetration and appropriation would thus be aligned with the main vector of sexual domination.[14] Similarly, Clifford observes that Leiris's writings "betray an unease with narratives of escape and return, of initiation and conquest."[15] Such a suspicion of narrative, as we saw in my introduction, resonates with a significant feature of modern French literature. Leiris provides a striking instance of this dismantling of narrative's conventional transports. Unlike Lévi-Strauss's summary rejection of travel, Leiris dwells on the frustrations and lures of the exotic, indulging and critiquing his traveling motives, and persistently slowing his journeys to the point of paralysis. In what follows, I will pursue this logic of paralysis in an autobiographical text of Leiris. A close reading of the paradoxical transports of this text will illuminate the politics and ethics of Leiris's affective journeys.

Johannes Fabian argues that "autobiography is a *condition* of ethnographic objectivity,"[16] and no writer answers better to Fabian's call, perhaps, than Leiris, who spent a lifetime in the dual practice of autobiography and anthropology. At a time when French anthropology was constituting itself as a modern discipline, Leiris joined the first major ethnographic expedition across Africa, during which he wrote and subsequently published an autobiographical account that laid bare his personal foibles and the colonialist failings of the expedition. This book, *L'Afrique fantôme* (1934), would be followed by *Manhood* and a four-volume autobiography, *Rules of the Game*; the latter texts are striking innovations in the genre of autobiography, foregoing chronology and narrative in favor of associative chains of reflexive meditation. Leiris's autobiography is more than a subjective addition to his work as anthropologist, and does not serve simply as remedy to the claims of scientific objectivity. To adopt Clifford's expression, it exposes the "partial truths" of anthropology, the inherent limitations of its discourse as "mediated by the claims of rhetoric and power."[17] A scholar working, as he says, "in the borderlands of anthropology,"[18] Clifford has had a special interest in Leiris, whose work exposes in an exemplary way the political, discursive, and disciplinary boundaries of anthropology, its problematic edges and policed borders.[19] Another boundary and border, however, is traced by the work of Leiris: that which marks a paralyzing limit located neither inside nor outside his work, and affecting all of his writing. If Leiris's autobiography is a "condition" of anthropological objectivity, as Fabian has it, we might best understand this in deconstructive terms, as condition of possibility *and* impossibility, as an enabling impasse or aporia. The experience of such an impasse is at the heart of Leiris's work, and is the key to the ethics and politics of his travels.

Leiris's 1955 *Scraps* opens with a chapter titled *"Mors,"* and embroiders on the meaning of death in Leiris's life and travels. *"Mors"* begins, like Lévi-Strauss's *Tristes Tropiques*, with a traveler's disavowal, but to different ends. Speaking of his recent trip to the Antilles, the author says,

> In many respects this trip certainly delighted me: sites at the end of the world and the beginning of time, palm trees, breadfruit trees, bamboos, tree-ferns, in short, all the enumerable features of a tropical setting that—without racking my brains any longer, and ceasing to stick at each idea and each word—I would perhaps not hesitate to describe as "enchanting" if, that is, this were really the sort of memory I wanted to talk about.[20]

Needless to say, the picturesque exotic is not Leiris's interest, but he incorporates this needless saying the better to retract it. This rhythm is characteristic of Leiris's halting and digressive prose; the text and traveler thus advance and retreat, "stick[ing] at each idea and each word" and impeding their progress. Thus, in the midst of a writing block, Leiris complains, "I can't get started; my confidence being at its lowest, I mark time for months and months. Passing beyond that crisis of confidence, shouldn't I go on despite everything . . . ?" (*Scraps*, 3). Such frustrations and the contradictions they express are hardly surmounted, even as Leiris continues to write. "No other way out, then—ceasing to slave over minute corrections . . . redoubled at each stroke of the pen—no other way out than to push my reflection further" (48). Continuing to write, however, Leiris comes to feel that his autobiography, lagging behind his life, is replacing that life that inexorably advances: "isn't the mad race I'm running (a dream gallop that is galloped without moving) a 'race to the death'?" (9). Moreover, through writing Leiris feels he is already surviving himself, or, as he says, "no longer existing except through writing" (64). Surviving through writing converts failure into success and success into failure (3), thus spurring on endless reiterations of frustrated motion. The untimeliness of Leiris's writing seemingly makes his autobiography posthumous in advance of the death he fears, and the end of life, like the ends, or purposes of writing, are inscribed by a limit that is always already crossed and yet always in advance.

Leiris's difficulties with writing and the paradoxes of motion they entail converge in the question of death as trespass, as figure of a limit and border. In his writing block Leiris attempts to grasp this "limit . . . drawn as the strict separation of two worlds" (*Scraps*, 37) and obsessively makes what he calls "imaginary voyages to the border between life and death" (39). Death as limit evokes an absolute boundary, a barrier to thought and figuration, and this brute reality confronts Leiris at every step: "the decisive break that is the fact of dying remains so inconceivable that the imagination furnishes only the poorest symbols of it" (17). And yet, if death defies representation, there is also an "art of dying" (40); indeed, Leiris says, "death . . . is assuredly the most theatrical of events" (41). That death should inhabit theater makes its borderline problematic, passing as it does through art, and not, so to speak, on its far side. The shifting boundary of death thus contaminates the vital distinctions Leiris explores in the course of his essay, including reality and artifice or memory and invention. Survival, as complication of the distinction life versus death, reveals the unaccountable debt Leiris's self-portrait owes to the thanatography of the trace. The autobiographical dream of "wholly possessing ourselves" (16) is explicitly tied by Leiris to the need to *personally* and *properly* grasp the figure of death, yet at the cost of a writing process that dispossesses its author and unworks the text. It is the measure of Leiris's accomplishment that this dogged effort exposes his text to ruin, and thus to the work of death. "This principle of ruin," Derrida says in *Aporias*, "is nothing other than death: not the dying-properly but, and it is quite different, the end of the properly-dying."[21] This aporetic principle yields less a *work* than an *event* defined by a rigorous engagement with its constitutive borders.[22]

Let us, then, follow this aporetic logic in Leiris's travels. Leiris's object in *"Mors"* is not so much, as he dryly puts it, "to speculate on the great theme of death" (*Scraps*, 60) as it is to have death *countersign* his work, thus exposing it to Derrida's "principle of ruin." To be sure, Leiris's essay does not escape a thematics of death, and the author is not immune to the ruses by which any autobiographer reckons with finitude so as to feign profit from absolute loss. The search for a "rule" of conduct, the erection of a monument to posterity, or proposing as elements of a "mythology" his scraps of recollections are some facets of this inevitably failed reckoning. We have seen, however, how the figure of a border may resist both thematics and figuration itself; at its most searching, Leiris's text neither appropriates nor domesticates the radical alterity of death. But if death is not appropriated in these pages, neither is it consigned to the utterly unknown. Rather, as the author's countersignatory, death is the text's internal other, authenticating and legitimating the text, both with and against its author. Death as the unrepresentable thus serves as Leiris's richest means to explore the impossibility of his own autobiography.

If there is a center or a destination to this wandering text of "forked paths" (*Scraps*, 50) and "indirect routes" (53) it would be the passages in which Leiris attempts to recapture in memory the first occasion of his "sudden awareness of death" (17). Leiris's quest is thus for an origin, a journey whose failure is prefigured by the *mise en abyme* (a favored figure of Leiris) according to which the remembered scene is a trip itself: an ostensibly ordinary walk in the country with his family during which the young Leiris hears a disturbing and fearsome sound. We are anticipating only slightly when we say that this quest for an origin, by a logic common to such narratives, will defeat the claims for that origin. Origins are among the most highly invested of mythological and metaphysical figures, and it is appropriate, then, that Leiris speaks of *pilgrimage* with respect to his textual undertaking in *"Mors"* (14). An atheist's pilgrimage—a paralyzing contradiction in itself—Leiris's journey unfolds in the contradictory space of a quest for an ever-lacking object, a lack compensated only by what he calls "wayside shrines on a sort of initiatory journey" (14). In the course of this journey, Leiris admits, "I have done nothing else, . . . though without discovering anything positive, than try, one after another, various paths and passageways. Lacking experiences capable of enlightening me, might I not have some resting places that—whether bastions or oases— might function as wayside altars for my anguish?" (70). What might be taken as a metaphor of pilgrimage here would better be read as *allegory*, and the penitent's shrines as consequences of the author's allegorical impulse. In this light *"Mors"* nicely confirms Joel Fineman's observation that "self-conscious texts eventually realize their responsibility for the loss upon which their literariness depends, and . . . when this happens, this responsibility is itself thematized as sin."[23] Appropriately enough, Fineman's formulation is developed out of a reading of a pilgrimage text, *The Canterbury Tales*; but if such textual effects have a long history, it is only the resources of poststructuralist theory that have fully enabled a deconstruction of their characteristic "piety and nostalgia for the lost origin" (44). If allegory is the trope of sustained correspondence to a prior and superior order of meaning, it is, however, and unlike the more stable metaphor, a perpetual displacement from that order. Allegory as figure thus provides the means to uncover the hidden lack of structure upon which a given structural order authorizes itself. What results from such an analysis is a paralyzing contradiction of allegorical desire and the journeys they occasion: the quest is paradoxically bent on repairing a lack that is itself the enabling condition of the journey. Thus, without discounting Leiris's individual penchants and character traits—masochism, castration anxiety, neurosis—such allegorical desire speaks to a more scriptural economy, a death-work that dictates and countersigns another logic of failure and suffering. As Fineman says, "the text holds out the promise of a meaning that it will also perpetually defer, an image of hermeneutic totality martyred and sacralized by and as the poetical" (44–45). In the final analysis, the text aims for a *signifier* that might arrest its errant ways, but which instead provokes continual desire.

It is in such an allegorical mode that Leiris's text converges on a minimal sound, a sign that, if not from the world beyond, is pregnant with the meaning of the other. Tied to a single time and place, this elusive sound constitutes the crucial *event* Leiris strives to recapture. "The paramount event that I have always been incapable of recapturing (for the simple reason that it must never have occurred, either because there isn't even the possibility of such a discovery . . . or because it acts only by degrees and in a surreptitious way as the end approaches) is in fact that which would have been constituted, for me, by my sudden awareness of death (*Scraps*, 17). That Leiris attempts a recollection of such an event in spite of these misgivings—in the face, indeed, of the impossibility of his task—is less a sign of an overriding faith, confidence, or belief on the part of his anamnesis than it is a dogged will to capture the event in its duplicity, as marked by its originary fracture—the very point at which it escaped him. On the country road at dusk, Leiris remembers hearing "a high-pitched, apparently distant noise" that frightens him. "The noise that makes such a deep impression on me is a sort of rapid and continuous rattling, surely an insect's buzzing (but at that time I am incapable of such an identification)" (18). It is worth noting that this initial sound is received as an "impression," which thus instantly converts the phonic into the scriptural, a first impression already secondary to the phonic source. An impression of travel accompanying "the noise of our footsteps on the road" (21), this singular event is drawn along the sequence of a journey just as it falls into a metonymic slide of textual associations, an allegory of lost origins. This fatal secondariness of the scriptural to the phonic is one of the most stubborn claims of metaphysical thought in its bid to ground meaning in full, unmediated presence. Even if Leiris falls prey to this allegorical desire, he also, however, expresses another scriptural economy according to which "many experiences . . . have marked me forever even though as events they left no trace in me" (15). This *mark leaving no trace* suggests the arche-writing constitutively effaced by Lévi-Strauss's writing lesson, and confirms the deconstructive insight that any given structure begins with a retroactive erasure of its starting point. It is thus fitting that following the critique of Lévi-Strauss in *Of Grammatology*, Derrida's *Margins of Philosophy* should open with a lengthy citation from Leiris's "Persephone," whose meditation on the aural and scriptural accompanies and countersigns Derrida's deconstruction of that metaphysical opposition.[24] Notably, Leiris's evocation in "Persephone" of the ear's "tympanum, a fragile membrane threatened with perforations" (cited in Derrida, *Margins of Philosophy*, xvi) and "subject to a fear of being injured" (xix) leads him to formulate the object of his search in terms of "a margin, a fringe surrounding the object, isolating it at the same time as it underlines its presence, masking it even as it qualifies it" (xxiv). "*Mors*" picks up where "Persephone" left off, the piercing and intrusive sound of the insect providing another means to dwell on such delicate and marginal distinctions as the eardrum played in the earlier text. "*Mors*," moreover, revisits and corrects aspects of that earlier text, filling in a missing memory that Leiris recognizes, after the fact, to have been at the source of important passages of "Persephone." This process of correction and reiteration is one of the most distinctive aspects of Leiris's textual self-exploration; it is also, however, a means by which the text unworks itself in perpetual allegorical digression. If Leiris's work fails as a result to deliver a singular masterwork such as *Tristes Tropiques*, it also avoids the false assurances of that work's claims for structural order. Thus, the missing link to "Persephone" serves not as a conclusive discovery but instead as the link to the meditation that follows.

Leiris's long reflection on the haunting sound in *"Mors"* finally yields an insight that we can only call remarkable.

> [W]hat, then, did this noise—an insect's rasping or the thin rattle of a carriage whose axles and spokes might be no more than frail dry limbs—what did this noise, in its uniqueness, come murmuring to me?
>
> After careful consideration, I think the noise said one single thing and the unique thing that it said was that it was *unique*. (*Scraps*, 22)

Here, at the point of origin, the unique sign affirms itself in a tautology whose very insistence carries it away in repetition. A uniqueness that bears repeating, the sound, moreover, calls for more than one formula from Leiris's pen: *"solitary from a strange world* (or *peculiar isolate*) *in nocturnal intrusion"* (*Scraps*, 23) (*"solitaire d'un monde étrange* [ou *isolé insolite*] *en nocturne intrusion"* in original [*Fourbis*, 28]). The haunting sound thus corresponds to what Derrida, in a text on Barthes, calls "the unique disappearance of the unique," according to which the claim for a *point* of origin (Barthes's singular *punctum*) is undone by the metonymy of *punctuation*. I devote a longer analysis to Barthes in chapter 5 of this work; here I will note only that, like Leiris's haunting sound, the singular *punctum* has the force of a traumatizing message. As Derrida says of Barthes's *punctum*, "It pierces, strikes me, bruises me, and, first of all, seems to concern only me. Its very definition is that it addresses itself to me."[25] Likewise, the traumatizing nature of Leiris's sound is indexed by its penetrating *intrusiveness* ("the intrusion of the isolated, unexpected voice") (*Scraps*, 22) as well as its absolutely enigmatic address ("a fragile sound that will not have carried any message") (23). Indeed, we might say that the sound is traumatic to the extent that it seems to carry no message, while being addressed, nonetheless, to Leiris.

This address implies an additional division of the unique, between the message *sent* and *received*, a division already inherent in that between the sound and its impression. This discrepancy is more than a matter of interpretation, however, according to which accuracy and fidelity to the original might be supposed or divined. Rather, we are in the vicinity of what Jean Laplanche calls the *enigmatic signifier* and the traumatic origins of sexuality. For Laplanche, sexuality and fantasy derive from messages received at infancy from an adult caregiver, messages that, because unconscious on the sender's part, are opaque both to the adult and to the child. The messages have a sexual content and, implanted in the child, give rise to the question, "What does the other want from me?" Born of trauma and secrecy, the child's sexuality is formed in an unconscious fantasy that supplies a possible, but only approximate, answer to that nagging question. The isolation, uniqueness, and stubborn tautology of Leiris's haunting sound, as well as its traumatic nature, correlate substantially with Laplanche's formulations. The original event at stake for Leiris would be, in Laplanchian terms, primal repression and the constitution of the first *source-objects* of the drive. Tellingly, the initial implantation, or indeed "intrusion" of the enigmatic signifier gives it a liminal status "both internal-external" as Laplanche puts it.[26] Further, Laplanche says of enigmatic signifiers that "isolated by the sender, they are addressed to the subject"; once implanted they leave a repressed remainder that "loses its status as representation (as signifier) in order to become a thing which no longer represents (signifies) anything other than itself."[27] Leiris's account of the intrusive *isolé insolite* would then, in Laplanchian terms, relate the implantation of traumatic signifiers that, following a process of repression, leave a stubborn remainder: "thing-like presentations [*représentation-choses*], which take on an isolated status, outside of communication and signification."[28] This becoming-object of the repressed element is strikingly suggested by Leiris's description of himself as becoming "'*tout chose*'" (upset) at the moment of hearing the sound.

Laplanche's enigmatic signifier also provides the means to interpret why the sound Leiris hears is only a noise, and not yet an address, until it is drawn into a parental scene in which questions posed yield only fear, suspicion, and doubt. To Leiris's question concerning the noise and its source, his father responds that it is only a distant carriage, an answer that Leiris finds suspicious, "as though I had detected its falseness and thought it was only a white lie meant to *hide* from me something that I might have feared for good reason" (*Scraps*, 19). Consequently, a major cause of Leiris's fear is the father, since "it seems to me that if my fear increased, it was in fact because of that explanatory phrase and its inadequacy." Several fantasies are sketched out here, the mysterious sound now rich with the fantasy life of a susceptible child in bed and "unconscious while the grownups are still busy with their occupations." Leiris thus provides the basic givens of Laplanche's primal seduction in the child's "openness to an adult world saturated with unconscious sexual significations."[29] When Leiris wonders of his father, "what motive could have impelled him" to deceive the boy, Leiris shifts the blame for the haunting sound to the father. It is the duplicity of the father that now stands in for the duplicitous sound, a compensatory move placing a cruel, castrating father against his Oedipal son. Such scenarios of castration are familiar to readers of Leiris; we should hardly be surprised, also, that the quest for a missing origin should find its remedy once again in a more readily narrative framework of rivalry, guilt, and sin.

This Oedipal scenario that structures and organizes difference has its correlative in Leiris's fantastical account of the abjection of women as consequence of the duality of the sexes: "woman . . . represents, more than her partner, a sinister element, as though it were clear that . . . one recognized implicitly in her the one term out of the duality that existed *in addition* to the first and had consequently—since it was radically *other*, occurring as an intrusion—to be held responsible for the pernicious dichotomy" (*Scraps*, 60). It is noteworthy, here, that the other imposes itself again as an *intrusion*. Moments such as these often relate to a quest for a point of origin, which in this case is nothing less than an "attempt to repair the original lesion" causing both death and sexual difference (59). Leiris's text, in its quest for origins, frequently reaches back to moments of minimal difference and primal separation, as, for instance, when he evokes "that phase of mental life in which we are still so close to the state of a baby who scarcely emerges from his sleep except to suck on his mother's breast" (30). Neil Hertz names such textual moments as occurring "at the end of the line," an end point that characteristically divides figures of minimal distinction. As such insight into minimal difference is difficult to articulate or sustain, Hertz says, resolution is characteristically asserted through an Oedipal scenario of "conflict and structure" or misogynistic scapegoating.[30] Leiris's example of the child at the breast thus serves him to imagine death taking form at this time as "the childish fear we have of being eaten" (*Scraps*, 30). A Kleinian psychoanalyst might see what Leiris calls "the most rudimentary form of aggression" as the projection of the child's aggressivity onto the mother, according to Klein's dynamic of the "good" and "bad" breast. Laplanche, faulting such a view for the primary agency it would ascribe to the child, asserts here as elsewhere the "primacy of the other" in the subject's formation;[31] in this light, Leiris's fear of being eaten would derive instead from a breast whose sexual messages precipitate the formation in the child of a paradoxical "internal foreign body."[32] Laplanche's theory of the origins of sexuality thus leads us, like Hertz, to "the end of the line," where self and other are minimally differentiated, and the desire of the other may be absorbed as an internal alien.

Having traced Leiris's account of the haunting sound to an enigmatic signifier, have we not reasserted the claim to a unitary *source* deconstructed by a Derridean reading? Laplanche insists, however, that the origin of fantasy always goes hand in hand with a fantasy of origins; recollection and reconstruction are invariably caught up in the double movement whereby the enigmatic signifier is both cause and effect of the subject's desire.[33] Laplanche, the most deconstructive of psychoanalysts, thus comes closest to positing a psychic theory of the wounding *punctum* or the arche-violence of the trace. The work of memory in such a psychoanalysis will be allegorical to the extent that its rules of order are founded on an origin that is constitutively ruled out. In innovating Proust's project by means of psychoanalysis, Leiris's *Rules of the Game* makes not "involuntary memory" but a more *intrusive memory* the hallmark of his autobiography, at the cost of a past that cannot be recaptured. At the end of the line, the enigmatic signifier yields itself up neither to a causal account of personal history nor to the work of interpretation; it would lie, rather, as Leiris aptly puts it, "between recollection and invention" (*Scraps*, 28). Interpretation, and even such self-interpretation as that of Leiris, is oriented toward the meaning of the other, and gravitates toward sounds heard and things felt in scenes of primal seduction. This institutes at the basis of writing and interpretation a model not simply of communication and exchange but of properly enigmatic transmissions.

It is on such a basis, and by means of a dual work in deconstruction and psychoanalysis, that Neil Hertz has placed the messages of art and culture under the heading of *paralysis*: "the "'paralyzing' powers of art," Hertz says, are evidenced in "moments of shared 'unconsciousness,' when important transmissions are taking place."[34] Recalling that Freud's earliest work included studies of motor paralyses in hysterical patients, Hertz underscores how Freud at key moments in his own reflections is prey to experiences of standstill, immobilization, and what he himself names "paralysis." The "spell" of paralysis shows itself in Hertz's reading to be a productive source of knowledge and experience since, as he says, "the spell is crucial to one's experience of the work, as constitutive of it as the analytic effort that succeeds and dispels this 'paralysis'" (xvii). Hertz's essay thus contributes toward releasing paralysis from its normative coding as pathological symptom in such cases as female hysteria and male castration anxiety, the latter memorably invoked in Freud's essay on the Medusa, to which Hertz devoted an earlier study.[35] Likewise, we have seen how in Leiris, an author dramatically beset by castration, the moment of becoming *tout chose* indicates something other than an Oedipal crisis, and constitutes a paralysis worth dwelling on. It remains for us to elaborate the consequences of such paralyses in a few narratives of travel, and in so doing, we will trace the literary lineage of a paralyzing message that echoes in the pages of "*Mors*."

Impressions of Travel

A final example from Leiris provides the link we will pursue in the following readings. Leiris's "*Mors*" weaves numerous elements from a recent trip to the Antilles into his meditations, among which one stands out—a literary *motif*, one would say, were it not so immobile and paralyzing. This is the statue of a woman in Saint-Pierre de la Martinique, depicting the rebirth of the city after the eruption of Mont Pelée in 1902. "It represents a woman of African type lying flat on her front and leaning on her two arms, her face lifted toward the sky and her naked body half upright" (*Scraps*, 43). Leiris's personal impression of the statue is marked above all by its eroticism and ambiguity. For him it represents "the very equivocal nature of the expression of carnal pleasure and, more generally, ecstasy—

which also partakes of death." This equivocal quality of manifesting death in life is shared by other things and creatures Leiris describes as coming "*from a border region*," a border marked out "between pleasure and pain" (49). Leiris's list of similarly ambiguous entities—somnambulists, automata, and mannequins—seems to locate his thoughts in the neighborhood of what Freud calls the *uncanny*. In drawing such a comparison, however, we risk passing over what, in Freud's own text, and in spite of its ostensible claims, does not reduce itself simply to a catalogue of themes. For "The Uncanny" is matched only by *Beyond the Pleasure Principle* in its vexed attempt to settle accounts with sheer otherness,[36] or, as Derrida puts it, "alterity—to which Freud gives the metaphysical name of the unconscious."[37] Like Freud's text on the death drive, which Derrida submits to a critique he names "paralysis," Leiris's meditation in "*Mors*" frames its topic not merely as theme but as the very border at which the text undoes itself.

The statue in Martinique ultimately fascinates Leiris for the unofficial legend attached to it: according to this story, the woman depicted would have plunged into the water to escape the volcano's burning ash only to boil herself in that water's scalding heat. The woman thus "died twice," as Leiris puts it (*Scraps*, 43), a double death certainly suggestive of the sexual *petite mort*, but also another death that, unaccountably, occupies Leiris in the act of writing. This "second death" (50) yields a paralyzing logic Leiris compares to *torpor*. "Free of all true passion, all vice, and even all ambition, I am, while still alive, subject to a torpor similar to that of the museum figures who once intruded into my sleep, and the acts that I perform are scarcely more than the gestures of an automaton or the mechanical works of a zombie" (58). What Leiris seems to recognize in the statue is a figure of himself who, in the act of writing, lives an anticipatory posterity. Obsessed as anyone else might be by the question of death, but characteristically held "in check," "inhibited" and "reticent," Leiris is, more specifically, *paralyzed* by the evidence of his other death, that which is traced "at each instant" by his literary survival: "no longer existing except through writing and, at each instant, attempting to formulate sententious phrases with the distant tone of last words, as though my fingers were already squeezed by the stone gauntlet of death" (64). Death "at each instant" would be another figure for "the unique disappearance of the unique," or the punctuated *punctum*—the paralyzing trace of the other in the same. Here as elsewhere Leiris homes in on a figure of minimal distinction, sharpening the blade that marks a division and a problematic limit, as when he evokes "The statue, of an iron gray color rather like the gray of a stone for sharpening scythes" (44). Leiris's description here evokes a cutting tool that need not be that of castration; similarly, his dubious speculation that "a sin with fateful repercussions" (58) accounts for the eruption of Mont Pelée would be merely the structuring reflex attendant on finer and more originary divisions. Leiris's survival, his unaccountable living on, marks him as being, like his statues, "from a border region," living on the border, paralyzed at the aporetic limit of life and death.

Underlying Leiris's Antillean "nymph of the volcano" (*Scraps*, 49) is a lineage of literary texts of which Leiris was certainly aware, as indexed by the thinly veiled reference to "the daughter of fire and water" (44) and a passing allusion to Pompeii (69). The most famous of these texts is *Gradiva*, by Wilhelm Jensen, to which Freud devoted a significant and lengthy essay, "Delusions and Dreams in Jensen's *Gradiva*." Jensen's story provides a signature case study of fixation and paralyzed travel. The story tells of Norbert Hanold, a young lecturer in archaeology, who becomes fascinated with an antique bas-relief depicting a girl in midstride, raising her skirt to reveal her sandaled feet. Hanold's obsession with this sculpture leads to fantasies and dreams that flesh out a delusional hypothesis about its origin: Gradiva—the name he gives to the girl in the sculpture—must have died in Pompeii on the day of the eruption of Mount Vesuvius. In a dream Hanold is transported to Pompeii on that fateful day and witnesses Gradiva's death and burial in the volcanic ash. Hanold soon finds himself journeying to Rome, then onward to Naples and Pompeii, all unaware, however, of the motive of his trip and its underlying erotic impulse. In Pompeii, Jensen's tale takes a turn toward the fantastic; Hanold, aimlessly wandering among the archaeological ruins, happens upon an apparition: Gradiva herself. Several meetings with Gradiva take place over the following days, during which Hanold struggles with the question of her physical nature, all the while deaf and blind to the evidence that might dispel his delusion. In the end, Gradiva's identity is revealed to be that of his neighbor and childhood sweetheart, Zoë, accompanying her father on a trip to Italy. Hanold comes to understand that his obsession with the figure of Gradiva derived in fact from this long-forsaken girl, replaced in his thoughts by the dry science of archaeology.

One of the features that most appeals to Freud in the story is the series of conversations Zoë has with Hanold in his state of delusion. Acting the part of Gradiva, Zoë carefully enters into Hanold's delusion in order to gauge the workings of his mind. As Freud observes, Zoë behaves as an analyst, using the dynamics of transference to help Hanold express his fantasy and its latent meaning. Hanold's delusion thereby reveals its purpose as a compromise-formation that hides a repressed memory of love within the lifeless cast of an archaeological relic. The conclusion of the story has Hanold making plans to wed his rediscovered childhood sweetheart. This happy ending makes *Gradiva* a satisfying case study for Freud; not only do the workings of Hanold's dreams and other symptoms confirm the psychoanalyst's theories, but the delusional protagonist ultimately undergoes a successful cure.

"Delusions and Dreams" is Freud's first substantial effort in literary interpretation, and persuasive as it may be, his analysis of the story is somewhat didactic. This may be due in part to the normative and conventional qualities of Jensen's charming tale, which, notwithstanding its supernatural features, remains far from the perverse and disturbing character of fantastic fiction's more devious works. When, twelve years later, Freud devotes a study to Hoffmann's fantastic tale "The Sandman," the result is the significantly more subtle and speculative essay "The Uncanny." And yet, as Sarah Kofman demonstrates in *Freud and Fiction*, both of Freud's essays display marked tendencies on Freud's part to limit the literary text's "undecidability" and "plurality of textual codes" in favor of a somewhat reductively diagnostic methodology.[38] Even at this level of analysis, moreover, Freud skirts some of *Gradiva*'s more perverse leanings, including castration, foot fetishism, and masochism. Indeed, at the conclusion of the story, a latent atmosphere of *Venus in Furs* imbues the final therapeutic scene with the distinctive qualities of "suspense" and "frozen progression" that Deleuze attributes to the fiction of Sacher-Masoch.[39] In that scene, Zoë, seated in a position above Hanold, is transformed into an impatient and ill-humored "school-mistress" before whom the young man felt he was "running the risk of slipping into the role of a big school-boy scolded and slapped in the face."[40] Similarly, and reading against the grain of the therapeutic model, Barthes sees the kindly and sensible Gradiva as masking "an evil Gradiva," one who "drives me insane" and never stops "bringing me back to my impasse." It is not merely *love* but a more passionate *delirium* that is sustained by such an evil Gradiva, who, Barthes says, "puts me in contradiction with myself (with the result of paralyzing my speech)."[41]

Such a "paralyzing" Gradiva may challenge not only the therapeutic model but also the theory of repression on which it is based. For Freud, the Pompeian themes of *Gradiva* metaphorically render the force of repression as both a calamitous burial and an enduring conservation of the past. Freud thus notes "a perfect similarity between the burial of Pompeii—the disappearance of the past combined with its preservation—and repression."[42] Freud was fond of archaeological metaphors and would return to a similar image of memory in his famous evocation of ancient Rome in *Civilization and Its Discontents*. The conflicting forces of burial and preservation are condensed in the bas-relief of Gradiva, whose static and lifeless nature takes on, in Hanold's eyes, spellbinding signs of life and mobility. Hanold's admiration for the bas-relief's apparent liveliness, indexing the return of the repressed, is, however, symptomatically marked by disavowal and negation: "the young woman was fascinating, not at all because of plastic beauty of form, but because she possessed something rare in antique sculpture, a realistic, simple, maidenly grace which gave the impression of imparting life to the relief" (*Gradiva*, 4) Hanold's fascination narrows in on a detail of the right foot that "touched the ground only lightly with the tips of the toes, while the sole and heel were raised almost vertically." Here, what Hanold had called the "impression" of life becomes a singularly "double impression": "This movement produced a double impression of exceptional agility and of confident composure, and the flight-like poise, combined with a firm step, lent her the peculiar grace" (4–5). Hanold's double impression conforms to the logic of the symptom, or the conflict that combines "satisfaction" and "annoyance" (10–11) at every turn, "transform[ing] the desirable thing into quite the opposite" (84). This conflict in itself holds the key to its resolution; as Freud points out, archaeology, the very means by which Hanold negates his erotic life, is the medium of the return of the repressed.

Gradiva thus presents, in Freud's reading, a cautionary tale concerning repression and its possibly delusional consequences. Hanold's long archaeological detour was hardly necessary, after all, to discover the true object of his quest, who, "without his having any suspicion of it, was his contemporary" (*Gradiva*, 12). Baudelaire offers a similar warning to archaeologists such as Hanold: "Woe be to him who, in antiquity, studies anything besides pure art, logic and general method! By plunging into the past he may well lose the memory of the present [*la mémoire du présent*]"⁴³ Baudelaire's deceptively simple injunction puts us on the trail of a "double impression" that does not yield itself up readily to therapeutic recollection. Commenting on this line of Baudelaire's, Derrida brings out the problematic division of the present it implies. "What if," Derrida asks, "there were a *memory of the present* and that far from fitting the present to itself, it divided the instant? What if it inscribed or revealed difference in the very presence of the present, and thus, by the same token, the possibility of being repeated in representation?" (60). Similarly, Baudelaire's phrase *the representation of the present*, as de Man points out, "combines a repetitive with an instantaneous pattern without apparent awareness of the incompatibility" (cited in Derrida, *Mémoires*, 60). Hanold's "impressions" are marked by the same incompatible appeal to the present; when he first spies Gradiva in a dream, she "walked across the flagstones of the Forum to the Temple of Apollo . . . and because of a feeling that the living reality would quickly disappear from him again, he tried to impress it accurately on his mind" (*Gradiva*, 12). Hanold's immediate appeal to the mediating impression, one that grasps the present only as memory, may already prefigure the paralyzed form of a statue—a fatality confirmed in Baudelaire's great poem about another elusive woman in the street, "To a Woman Passing By": "A woman passed me, with a splendid hand / Lifting and swinging her festoon and hem; / Nimble and stately, statuesque of leg."⁴⁴

The textual evidence of such impossible and paralyzing presence has guided many of Derrida's readings of Freud. In *Archive Fever: A Freudian Impression*, Derrida makes a brief foray into *Gradiva* in order to bring out, he says, "a point which is never taken into account, neither in Jensen's reading nor in Freud's."⁴⁵ Derrida quotes from *Gradiva*:

> Something "came into his consciousness for the first time [*zum ersten mal*]: without being aware himself of

the impulse within him, he had come to Italy and had traveled on to Pompeii, without stopping in Rome or Naples, in order to see whether he could find any traces of her. And 'traces' in the literal sense [*im wörtlichen Sinne*]; for with her peculiar gait she must have left behind an imprint [*Abdruck*] of her toes in the ashes distinct from all the rest." (99)

This idea of Hanold's—to find the "literal" trace of Gradiva's footstep—seems to outdo his other dreams and fantasies in its extravagant delusion. And yet such is the habitual target of the narrative quest, and it lies at the basis of any claim to memory or presence, whether that of an archaeologist or his psychoanalytic reader.[46] The quest for such first impressions Derrida names *archive fever*. Archive fever, Derrida says, "is to have a compulsive, repetitive, and nostalgic desire for the archive, an irrepressible desire to return to the origin, a homesickness, a nostalgia for the most archaic place of absolute commencement" (*Archive Fever*, 91). Gradiva's imprint in the ash, the motivating cause of Hanold's journey, does not, then, fall under the categories of truth or delusion, and is not pathological in a Freudian sense. It is instead both impossible and necessary, and expresses what Derrida calls, aporetically, a "truth of delusion." How, after all, without positing an originary trace, can one imagine the source of an impression? But is that unique impression not also the imprint of an original division? Thus, if Derrida's archive fever spurs on a journey, it is one that is paralyzed at each step, yet motivated by the "traces of a past that has never been present."[47]

At the risk ourselves of archive fever, we will develop this literary genealogy of paralysis by turning to a text that served as inspiration to *Gradiva*, Théophile Gautier's fantastic tale "Arria Marcella." Situated as well in Pompeii, the tale concerns a young man's erotic fixation on a sculptural fragment of a woman's body, which leads to a fantastical journey back in time to reanimate the woman from whom it comes. In Gautier's story, the sculptural object of fixation is the actual cast of a woman's breast, preserved in the hardened ash of Vesuvius's eruption. The outcome of Gautier's story suggests nothing like a therapeutic cure, and presents a more challenging case study for psychoanalytic interpretation. An admirer of Hoffmann, Gautier provides less a neurotic romance than an uncanny tale whose fantasies are not so easily dispatched. Moreover, the fantasy of the breast preserved in stone leads us into temporal disturbances not fully accounted for in Freud's notion of deferred action. To explore these complications and their paralyzing consequences I will turn again to Jean Laplanche and to his reformulation of *Nachträglichkeit* in the light of his theory of primal seduction.

At the beginning of Gautier's story the protagonist Octavian is transfixed by an object on display in the archaeological museum of Naples:

> What he was studying so carefully was a piece of coagulated black ash with a hollow imprint [*une empreinte creuse*]: one would have taken it for a fragment of a statue's mold, broken in the process of making a cast; an artist's eye would have readily recognized the form of an admirable breast and a flank as pure in style as that of a Greek statue. . . . That lava, cooling about the body of a woman, had kept its charming contours. Due to the caprice of the eruption that destroyed four towns, that noble form, fallen to dust nearly two thousand years ago, has reached us; the curve of a breast has crossed centuries while so many fallen empires have left not a trace![48]

The motif of burial and preservation in Gautier's text anticipates, as in Jensen, an erotic resuscitation of the past. Gautier's "splendid bosom, triumphant over the ages, which destruction itself sought to preserve" ("Arria Marcella," 355) thus seems to conform to Freud's theory of repression as conserving destruction. And yet Gautier's tale links themes of life and death without clearly resolving their tension. All of Gautier's work testifies to an equivocal desire to capture an ideal in durable form, succinctly rendered as supreme aesthetic credo in the poem "l'Art," which states, "Le buste / Survit à la cité [The bust / Outlives the city]."[49] Just as "destruction itself sought to preserve" the breast, so Gautier the poet, siding with that negating force, expresses a passion for a supremely ambiguous object: a permanent lifelike form haunted by deathly stillness.[50] Moreover, Gautier's *object* as first described is no more than an *imprint*, and is thereby suggestive of Jensen's "literal trace" of Gradiva. This "hollow imprint," once become flesh, ultimately belongs to a woman of monstrous qualities.

The breast as occasion for a journey back in time, driven by what Gautier calls a "retrospective love" ("Arria Marcella," 328) and "a retrospective ideal" (335) nicely frames the stakes of deferred action or *Nachträglichkeit* in Freudian theory. To illustrate this temporal concept, Freud recounts the following story: "A young man who was a great admirer of feminine beauty was talking once . . . of the good-looking wet-nurse who had suckled him as a baby: 'I'm sorry', he remarked, 'that I didn't make a better use of my opportunity.'" The humor in the story Freud recounts lies in the temporal anachronism that transports the adult in his erotic fantasy back to a time before his sexual maturity, and simultaneously projects the infant prematurely forward into sexual adulthood. I have taken this anecdote of the "admirer of feminine beauty" from an essay of Laplanche, in which he cites also the line from Freud: "Love and hunger . . . meet at a woman's breast."[51] For Laplanche, this last statement is rife with problems, glossing over as it does the primal relation between need and desire and their problematic distinction. One of the things at stake for Laplanche in the supposed "meeting" of love and hunger is the "propping" effect whereby sexuality per se emerges in the perversion of biological appetites and functions. Further, Freud's anecdote betrays contradictions inherent in the notion of *Nachträglichkeit*, for which Laplanche offers the English neologism "afterwardsness." Reading the anecdote in the light of his own general theory of seduction, Laplanche points out that Freud omits the nurse herself from the scene, and in so doing casts the scene as involving an infant and a mere object. This omission of the role of the other person, Laplanche argues, causes Freud to overlook as well the formative role for the infant of the unconscious of the other, source of enigmatic and seductive messages. To place the other in this primal scene is to decenter the psychoanalytic subject and to assert the primacy of the other in the formation of sexuality and the unconscious. This primacy of the other leads Laplanche to question Freud's temporal notion of *Nachträglichkeit*, arguing that the past to be reinterpreted contains a message from the other that defies both progressive and retrogressive models of development, and likewise challenges both deterministic theories and hermeneutics.

In this reconception of the development of the infant, with its emphasis on an external and thus in a sense doubly unknowable unconscious, what becomes the proper *object* of psychoanalysis? Laplanche's answer involves a surprising recourse to the model of archaeology. Of this Freudian archaeology, Laplanche says, "It is an archaeology which is not subordinated to history, as modern science would have it, but which subordinates history solely to the revivifying of the object."[52] The object of psychoanalysis is thus modeled on the singular artifact on exhibit, completely shorn of its pedagogical and historical supports: "the wonderful object of the exhibition." Laplanche says, "This unique object, isolated (and in this sense genuinely *archaeological*), displayed in a casket of light and preferably, in a separate sanctuary draped in black velvet, this object made of an indestructible material . . . this timeless object, having journeyed through centuries and millennia to address itself directly to us . . . what does it want from me?" (*Essays on Otherness*, 146–47). Laplanche's psychoanalytic archaeology aptly captures the affective state of Octavian in the Naples museum, who, in his private contemplation of the ancient breast, contrasts with the "tourists busy turning over their guide-books," and who is startled at the approach of his companion "like a man whose secret has been surprised" (Gautier, "Arria Marcella," 315). For Laplanche, the psychoanalytic object is an object of desire, provided we understand that desire as bound up with an enigmatic question addressed to the subject. Implanted by the other in the subject's infancy, enigmatic signifiers leave as a residue such thing-like mental archaisms that pose the question of the subject's desire.

One readily imagines Gautier's Octavian standing before the museum case as being erotically drawn to the petrified breast, attracted to its form and stimulated by its beauty. Octavian is, however, motionless and transfixed, like a man in a trance; this passivity contrasts with the active verbs conveying the eruption that created the object and that describe its forward journey in time. Laplanche's theory of primal seduction helps us to see Octavian less as an agent than as being subject to the force of these verbs and submitting to a question he can answer only in the temporal riddle of desire's "afterwardsness." The question "what does it want from me?" places the "it" of the object-source of desire, residue of the other's unconscious, in the position of subject. Laplanche thus speaks suggestively of "a fixed mover of temporalization" with respect to "the other thing in the other person."[53] The imprint of the breast would be such a paradoxical "fixed mover" that sets Octavian on his fantastic journey into the past.

Like Freud's comic anecdote of the admirer of feminine beauty, Gautier's "Arria Marcella" makes this journey into something of a joke as well. Having left the Naples museum, Octavian and his friends press on to Pompeii: "The three friends alighted at the Pompeii Station, amused by the mixture of antiquity and modern times naturally suggested to the mind by the title 'Pompeii Station'; a Greco-Roman city, and a railway terminus!" (318). This anachronism becomes deadly serious, however, when Octavian is shown the spot in Pompeii at which the remains of the woman whose breast he admired were found, in the cellar of the house of Arrius Diomedes—the very site of Hanold's conclusive meeting with Gradiva: "His breast heaved, his eyes were moist; the catastrophe effaced by twenty centuries of forgetfulness impressed him like a quite recent misfortune; the death of his mistress or of a friend would not have moved him more, and a tear, two thousand years late, fell . . . upon the spot where had perished, stifled by the hot ashes of the volcano, the woman for whom he felt himself filled with a retrospective love" (328).

Octavian's obsession drives him to return to the ruins after dark, and to his surprise ancient Pompeii is fully resurrected in this nocturnal setting. In a particularly effective use of the ruins as oneiric space of unconscious desire, Gautier says that "Octavian observed that he was traversing portions of Pompeii that had not yet been excavated, and which consequently were wholly unknown to him" ("Arria Marcella," 355). When Octavian meets up with Arria Marcella, time is abolished, and Gautier conveys this timelessness in lofty terms borrowed from Goethe:

> For, in truth, nothing dies; everything goes on existing. No power can annihilate whatever has once been created. Every act, every word, every shape, every thought which has fallen into the universal ocean of things makes circles which go on broadening to the far confines of eternity. . . . Octavian had just lived one day in the reign of Titus, and had made himself beloved of Arria Marcella, who was lying at this moment by him on an antique bed, in a city that for every one else was destroyed. (358–59)

It is in no less lofty terms that Freud, in what he calls "a flight of fancy" evokes the ruins of Rome, the Eternal City, to illustrate the timelessness of the unconscious in *Civilization and Its Discon-*

tents. On the basis of this analogy Freud asserts, like Gautier, that "in mental life nothing which has once been formed can perish."[54] Laplanche's model of primal seduction offers another means to account for this apparently timeless permanence. Insisting that the breast that feeds an infant is always a sexual breast—primarily on the mother's part—Laplanche asserts that this breast is the source of exciting and disturbing implantations from the unconscious of the adult to the child. The question "what does it want from me?" gravitates around an internalized enigma that has the character of a fixed, unmetabolized, and immutable object. We have seen in a similar primal scene from Leiris how the image of a suckling child provokes a fear of aggression. Laplanche would account for this fear as deriving from the attack from within the child of the other's enigmatic message, and this attack of the "bad" breast—an anachronistic sexual breast—is nothing other than "the attack of the death drive."[55] This persecutory breast would account for the reversal, at the conclusion of "Arria Marcella," of the desired woman into a virtual vampire. "Arria did not eat," Gautier says, "but she often bore to her lips an opalescent Myrrhine cup filled with dark purple wine, like coagulated blood" (358). In this final scene, which teems with clues as to the woman's secret monstrosity, Arria is not so much nourishing Octavian as feeding on him. This reversal, however, is implicit in the initial fascination of Octavian for the ancient breast; the protagonist's erotic journey back in time is motivated—and paralyzed—by the originary question of the desire of the other.

Laplanche's theory of primal seduction, as we have explicated it here, is coded by a quasi-universal scenario of mother-child exchange, and this would account for the commonalities we have established between Gautier's text and Laplanche's model. Laplanche is at pains, however, to explain that the other's unconscious is in each case a *particular* other. Despite the similarity of vocabulary, then, Laplanche's "desire of the other" is not reducible to that of Lacan, in which the capitalized Other stands in for the structural symbolic order.

Likewise, the "thing" in the unconscious for Laplanche is otherwise paralyzing than Lacan's Thing, barred from the subject by castration and the Symbolic. In this light, the origin of Octavian's fantasy and the nature of his object is complicated by the fact that "Arria Marcella"—and, plausibly, *Gradiva* as well—derives from another author, Gautier's friend Gérard de Nerval, and specifically from the latter's Pompeian tale "Octavia." Laplanche himself, of course, does not discount the role played by cultural objects in enigmatic transmissions. But is this a matter of the archive of biography—or of literature? And if fiction, are we dealing with traces or, as Jensen oddly has it, "'traces' in the literal sense" (*Gradiva,* 99)? Jensen's formula may well intend an indexical claim to sheer presence, but his "imprint ... distinct from the rest" (99) is already the imprint, as we have seen, of its own difference from itself. This, the very object of Hanold's quest, is not an enigmatic but a "fractured" signifier, as Fineman puts it.[56]

At the further risk of archive fever, then, let us take an additional step backward to Nerval's "Octavia." Gautier adopts the name Octavian from Nerval's "Octavia," the name of the girl who is the object of the poet's obsessive fascination in his own Pompeian tale.[57] Ross Chambers emphasizes the motif of slowness that opens the story and its journey.[58] On the passage to Naples, the girl is portrayed with a strange and arresting detail. Nerval says that Octavia, "impatient with the ship's slow progress, was imprinting her ivory teeth in the rind of a lemon."[59] The image of the girl's teeth imprinted in a lemon is a cryptic one. How might this impression motivate Nerval's impressions of travel? Is this impression the precursor to the hollow mold of Gautier's breast? Might it also be at the source of Jensen's obsessive trace? It is indeed noteworthy that in *Gradiva* at the first moment of physical proximity with Zoë, Hanold dwells not on her feet but her "dainty and perfect teeth," which, "in biting the crust caused also a crunching sound so that they *gave the impression* of being not unreal phantoms, but of actual, substantial reality."[60] The impression given by Zoë's teeth would seem to confirm Derrida's insight that what is at stake in *Gradiva* is not so much connected to the overt themes of the foot as it is to a paralyzing impression and its impossible archive.

Any reader of Nerval will recognize in Octavia's teeth an image from Nerval's sonnet "Delfica." Several images from the sonnet are borrowed from the song of Mignon in Goethe's *Wilhelm Meister*, including the lemon, but the impression of the teeth are the invention of Nerval.[61] The significant lines are:

> Do you recognize the TEMPLE with its immense peristyle,
> And the bitter lemons that have the imprint of your teeth?
> And the grotto, fatal to its careless guests,
> Where the vanquished dragon's ancient seed lies asleep?[62]

The poem condenses a theme that is dear to Nerval, and which the Pompeian tale "Octavia" reprises: the promise of a return of classical paganism to the disenchanted Christian world. In "Delfica" as in "Antéros," the image of the dragon invokes the sowing of the dragon's teeth by Cadmus to give birth to the armed Spartoi, founders of Thebes. In "Antéros" Nerval thus speaks of "the old dragon's teeth," while in "Delfica," however, the teeth belong to Dafné, the addressee of the sonnet—or perhaps even to Nerval's lover, Jenny Colon, to whom he dedicated his first version of the poem. The "ancient seed," which substitutes for the dragon's teeth in "Delfica," is thus also in a surprising position of substitution with Dafné's teeth, and this gender reversal is carried into Nerval's Pompeian story. For all her youthful and innocent charms, Octavia is a femme fatale, brandishing a switch with which she playfully threatens Gérard on the ship deck at the beginning of the story. She is also, ominously, accompanied by her invalid father, and by the end of the story has married another man who, "shortly after their wedding, had been stricken with total paralysis; he lay there on a couch, his features entirely dead except for his two large dark eyes"

(*Selected Writings*, 203). This apparent suffering masks a deeper desire of paralysis on Nerval's part. For Gérard's obsession with Octavia takes him further back into Antiquity to resurrect the Egyptian pair Isis and Osiris, and with Octavia he plays out the parts of these two in the ruins of Pompeii. The goddess Isis, Nerval points out in his other Pompeian text "Isis," is the archetype of Mary, whose love of her child only reenacts an earlier story of a tragic couple: "A deified woman, mother, wife or lover, bathes with her tears this bloody and disfigured body."[63] Nerval's syncretism would seem to confirm Freud's observation in *The Future of an Illusion* that childhood helplessness lies at the heart of the compensatory raptures of religious experience. One might also read in the image of Octavia's teeth the latent threat of castrating dentata, which would anticipate the paralyzing charms of Jensen's Medusa-like sculpture. The ambiguous charms of the femme fatale lie in the symptomatic reflexes of an embattled masculinity that oscillates between the poles of misogyny and mystified devotion, and whose raptures, as Deleuze points out, are marked by a paralyzing *suspense*. Fascination with the femme fatale always risks settling on her banishment or "textual eradication," as Mary Ann Doane says, though her subversive force is best gauged not in such outcomes, but rather in the paralyses she provokes.[64] Moreover, before her "textual eradication," her lover is paralyzed by a *trace* he can never master, and whose prior erasure will always already escape the bid to rub her out.

"Octavia," in its complex turns of memory and travel as well as in its haunted affections, anticipates in many ways Nerval's great novella *Sylvie*. Proust's high regard for *Sylvie* and its influence on his own work are well known. In his excellent annotated selection of Nerval's writings, Richard Sieburth points out that "Proust discerned in the condensed compass of Nerval's novella the germ of his own *magnum opus* to come."[65] What if "Octavia," more condensed even than *Sylvie*, contained the "germ" of the later novella, and thus of Proust's *Remembrance*? Might the *impression* we have been tracing here be at the source of Nerval's influence, not only on Gautier and Jensen, but also Proust, as well as the surrealists, Leiris and Robbe-Grillet?[66] Others might be added to this lineage as well, notably Yves Bonnefoy, late surrealist and faithful inheritor of Nerval's poetry and travels.[67] Nerval's impression, as we have seen, is linked to a promise of the future: the "ancient seed" of Nerval's dragon, a seed itself linked to Dafné and to the oracular sibyl. The germ of modernity? We have no doubt fallen prey to archive fever. For Proust's, Sieburth's, and our archive fever would thereby overlook what is *disseminated* in the singular germ of Nerval's texts: teeth whose impressions are sown between two poems and the Pompeian story, scattered even as they gather in one cryptic image of a source. This fertile dissemination defies the claim to a unique origin even as it holds out its promise. Neither masculine nor feminine, its trace is felt in the queer transports that resist the symbolic law, from Nerval to Proust and beyond. Neither one nor the other, this paralyzing trace suspends all oppositions; it is *neutral*. "Il-la paralyse," Derrida ventures to name this neutral trace, duplicitous source of difference that marks each step of the journey with a paralyzing *pas*.[68]

This trace often seems to simply defeat the journey. "Perhaps," Nerval says in "Isis," "one should fear that readings done ahead of traveling will spoil the first impression of famous sites."[69] But what would such a first impression be? Nerval, stopping over in Pompeii, has just returned from his celebrated journey to the Orient, and his statement ironically undercuts the mountains of archival material with which he authorized and partly fabricated his Orientalist vision, laying claim instead to an authentic and unmediated vision. In his passionate backward journey to the source of his desire, and back beyond Latin and Greek antiquity to the original mother goddess, Nerval cannot help, however, admitting the loss of this first impression. "Perhaps I owed to the dazzling memory of Alexandria, Thebes, and the pyramids the nearly religious impression made on me by a second viewing of the temple of Isis of Pompeii."[70] If on the one hand Nerval's first impression seems the most authentic and desirable, on the other hand, the secondariness of his return trip yields an "almost religious impression" due to the charms of memory and comparison. In an abyssal structure of memory and repetition characteristic of Nerval, these two options are shadowed, moreover, by another: that indexed by the *second viewing* of the temple itself. For Nerval's trip to Pompeii comes not only after his journey to the Orient, but is subsequent to an earlier journey, several years earlier, and unaccounted for in the text. If there were a first impression, it would belong to this earlier trip, itself virtually under erasure, and posited only retroactively. Nerval's decadent imagination would seem here to conform to a common touristic struggle between mediation and authenticity. In Ali Behdad's expression, Nerval would be a "belated traveler," following in the footsteps of literary precursors and arriving only to take stock of what he has missed.[71] But Nerval's belatedness is not a mere factor of chronology and historical lateness; rather, its temporality is that of an "afterwardsness" in quest of a primal origin. In other words, the *mediation* of the traveler's experience is troubled by a more disturbing *supplementariness* of the origin. Nerval's slim Pompeian texts, bookends to his massive *Voyage en Orient*, contain impressions of travel that defy the space and time of the travelogue, but in so doing reveal the paralyzing motives of the textual journey as archive fever. There is no first impression, Nerval shows us, that is not doubled by its other. Jensen too, attests to this in his description of Gradiva, in the passage that comes as close as possible to capturing his motivating fixation: "The left foot had advanced, and the right, about to follow, touched the ground only lightly with the tips of the toes, while the sole and heel were raised almost vertically. This movement," Jensen says, "produced a double impression" (*Gradiva*, 4).

In the introduction to his 1835 *Mademoiselle de Maupin*, Gautier invoked the image of Montmartre as a volcano threatening to bury Paris. In so doing, Gautier contrasted the classical legacy of Pompeii with the poor relics that Gautier felt a buried Paris would leave to future excavators. This gesture owes a great deal to the vision of cultural decline in Hugo's Romantic *Notre-Dame de Paris*. And as in Hugo, this critique cannot help but provoke a recuperative gesture; Hugo's Gothic revival—inspiration for a broad movement for French historic preservation—would become in Gautier a cult of form, modeled on classical beauty.[72] Each author expresses a contradiction bequeathed by the French Revolution to the nineteenth century: founding a new secular state and a modern culture on the vestiges of a religious past.[73] Further, the Romantic turn away from a perceived vulgarity of contemporary French culture is compensated by ideals sought elsewhere: not only in the past, but in an Orient seen as the living presence of the past, yet fast disappearing. That present past is claimed by Nerval in Egypt and by Gautier in Algeria, an oxymoron sustained by what Dina Al-Kassim calls "a touristic delectation in loss, disguised by a ressentimental hatred of the West." As Al-Kassim makes clear, such disavowals and displacements are the habitual privilege of masculine travelers and their "paternalistic orientalism."[74] Nerval's and Gautier's journeys outward and away from French vulgarity thus ironically confirm the colonial enterprise. This reflects a persistent contradiction of French leftist politics that combined oppositional critique of the state with advocacy for colonial expansion.[75] Nerval's Isis expresses this contradiction to the highest degree. His critique of modernity and quest for ancient ideals leads him to venerate a god resurrected by Napoleon's conquest of Egypt. And Isis is none other than the figure Napoleon chose as the emblem of a new Paris, rebuilt on the ruins of an apocryphal Parisis. This imperial archive fever has far-flung consequences, as the bid to ground national identity accompanies a politics of colonial appropriation. On the first page of his *Orientalism*, Nerval's is the first name Said invokes. Ironically enough, it is linked to an evocation of the recent destruction of Beirut.

Gautier's Parisian volcano, then, is highly problematic. It serves as a challenge to the Paris of the July Monarchy, opposing its modern decadence with a vision of an uncorrupted *art pour l'art*. But the vision of past grandeur is maintained in his glowing portrait of France's imperial reach into Africa, where modernity and the mirage of antiquity can merge under the banner of colonialism. In the next chapter we will see how Fromentin's Algerian journeys convey a similar conquering melancholy. And yet, as we have seen, both Nerval's and Gautier's Pompeian tales leave a legacy that defies the economy of loss and redemption, of disenchantment and exoticist delights. In the texts of each author a paralyzing archive interrupts the journey and its illusions. This archive is the trace of the other; not a pathological fixation, but the "fixed mover" of the texts, whose narratives of sin, transgression, and desire constitute its compromised aftereffects, carried forward into each story and beyond. Inheritor of this archive, Leiris would make it the paralyzing source of his postcolonial travels.

Gradiva's Archive

In 1927 Leiris embarked on his first of many journeys. Inspired in part by Nerval, he traveled to Egypt, where he began writing the first of his significant works of prose, *Aurora*. Like Nerval's final work, *Aurélia*, whose title it echoes, Leiris's narrative is a mystical exploration of dreams and fantasies that have as their obsessive focus a haunting and mysterious woman. Since his days among the surrealists, for whom Nerval was a beacon in the unconscious, Leiris developed what would be a lifelong passion for Nerval's writing. Nerval is Leiris's "secret sharer," as Richard Sieburth puts it, and his cryptic traces may be seen in all of Leiris's subsequent work in the exploration of dreams, autobiography, and ethnographic travels.[76] When, at the end of his life, Leiris founded a journal devoted to the study of the history of French anthropology, he titled it *Gradhiva*.[77]

The archives of French anthropology, including Leiris's own work, would be watched over by Jensen's muse.

Gradiva as guardian of the archive: a fitting emblem of archive fever. More than a literary flourish, Leiris's choice reflects his desire to bind ethnography to a work of self-scrutiny, a work that passes through the difficult medium of literary composition. Muse of the surrealists, Gradiva, as name of the journal, hearkens back to the "surrealist ethnography" at the origins of Leiris's interest in primitive societies,[78] and suggests not only the force of unconscious memory and the necessity of anamnesis but the delusions that haunt the traveler's quest. Leiris never masked the delusions and dreams that accompanied his professional tasks, and which infect the scientific study of others with the otherness of the ethnographer's own desire. The "nymph of the volcano" that Leiris discovered in Martinique is emblematic of this scrupulous self-critique.[79] If the statue evokes a postcolonial rebirth of the Antilles to which Leiris was committed, it also exposes the complex web of exoticism, obsessive fascination, and self-analysis that problematize Leiris's journeys and, indeed, paralyze them. In chapter 4 I return to Leiris to explore the politics of ethnography as they relate to Leiris's autobiography and travels. If Leiris holds an important place in these studies, it is because he exemplifies a paralyzing logic of travel whose lineage we have traced from Nerval to Gautier and Jensen, and which, passing through Freud, has inspired critical reflection on the paradoxes of traveling desire. What we have examined as the traces of a paralyzing impression of travel among Leiris's precursors become in Leiris, however, a more sustained exploration of the motivating paralyses at the heart of the autobiographical and ethnographic quest. The aporias of literary self-understanding lead Leiris to dismantle the myths and figures of transport, and this ethical work of self-critique informs a critique of travel that undoes the colonial discourse of mastery and appropriation, pointing the way to a postcolonial ethnography.

2. Horizon of Conquest
Eugène Fromentin's Algerian Narratives

Was there still an obstacle that he could not get past to reach the immense uncertain space, or did this obscure and devastated space (serial desert) constitute the only impediment, the last obstacle? — Blanchot

Stop here! The great desert unfurls. — Gide

The Colonial Arrivant

In a provocative essay titled "On the Superiority of Anglo-American Literature," Gilles Deleuze and his cowriter Claire Parnet take French literature to task for its apparent failure to travel. In contrast to this inability to "cross the horizon" and follow "lines of flight," the authors say that "American literature operates according to geographical lines: the flight toward the West, the discovery that the true East is in the West, the sense of the frontiers as something to cross, to push back, to go beyond.... There is no equivalent in France."[1] Deleuze and Parnet's comparative analysis of French and Anglo-American travel writing yields striking insights into the subversive and emancipatory force of mobile desire and travel writing. In invoking the figure of the frontier, however, the authors show a striking insensitivity to the mythopolitical—and imperial—dimension of this motif in the American cultural imaginary. Unwitting exoticists, the authors resurrect the dubious "Frontier Thesis" of the late nineteenth-century American historian Frederick Jackson Turner. As a result, literature and travel risk becoming allies of a romance of national identity, manifest destiny, and the ideology of expansion.

Deleuze and Parnet would not deny, of course, that for all its transformative potential, the frontier can always be "reterritorialized" by claims to identity, structure, and order. Their task as critics, however, would be to affirm the "deterritorializing" potential that challenges such calls to order: the "becoming-other" of the traveler, the "event" of encounter, the very "disappearance" of the writer in the midst of circumstances that exceed his authorship, authority, and identity. The frontier, then, is at best a site of conflict between these rival forces. If this is so, then the absence of the frontier in

French literature, we might say, is an absence not only of its potential force of liberation, but also, and more importantly, of the seductive power of ideological identification with the lines of force of imperial expansion. Moreover, the authors' polemic against French writing fails to account for the subversive force of the French resistance to travel. Far from being mere symptom of cultural boundedness, allergy to change, or denial of discovery, modern French travel writing provides a rich critique of travel's illusions and ideology. When, for instance, Paul Nizan says in his Arabian travelogue, "I reject navigation and itineraries,"[2] he voices a denial of travel that is neither complacent nor comfortable, but stubborn and militant in its indictment of exoticism, mercantilism, and colonial ideology. In contrast to Deleuze and Parnet, one might point out that an important cause of French resistance to travel writing can be traced back to doubts and suspicions concerning the colonial project. These doubts may account for the striking fact that French Algeria, France's counterpart to manifest destiny and the American frontier, yielded almost no literature of consequence in the nineteenth century. Literary writing on Algeria consisted mainly of short stories rather than novels, and travelogues of a documentary nature; French Algeria thus contributed no examples of the major genres of French literary production of the day. The literary resistance to travel writing is linked to a liberal sensibility that, if not anticolonialist, could not, however, invest in mythologizing settler mentality, military conquest, and colonial frontiers.

One might perhaps regret this lack of literary investment in French Algeria. Literature provides some of the most synthetic and complex representations of cultural production, and thereby provides as well a reflexive dismantling of culture's authorizing fictions. Daudet's critique of French Algeria in *Tartarin de Tarascon* does not perform such a work of cultural reflection; the novel flounders in mere pastiche and farce. Flaubert chose classical Carthage over contemporary Algeria as the topic of his great North African novel.

Deleuze and Parnet, then, are partly correct in their assessment of French writing. There is no Melville of nineteenth-century French literature, no Conrad of its colonial imagination. If French Algeria did not benefit from French literary attention, however, one need not, like Deleuze, take this lack as a mere failing. As we will see, the breakdown of colonial travel may itself constitute an act of political resistance, and the very paralysis of the travel account yields transports that challenge the ideology of colonial travel.

A telling indication of this literary attitude toward Algeria is provided by the 1885 novel by Guy de Maupassant, *Bel-Ami*. At the beginning of the novel, the protagonist, nicknamed Bel-Ami, has just been released from military duty in Algeria and reflects on his colonial adventures as he strolls aimlessly in Paris: "he remembered his two years in Africa, how he used to prey on the Arabs in the little outposts in the South. . . . In Paris, it was another matter entirely. You couldn't set off on a nice little looting expedition, with your sabre at your side and your revolver in your hand, safe from the arm of the law."[3] Bel-Ami embodies the greed, hypocrisy, and self-interest of the Paris of the Third Republic, and Maupassant clearly links his dizzying rise to success during the course of the novel to attitudes forged in the experience of colonial predation. Bel-Ami, in other words, is the quintessential *arriviste*, and his entry into high society is enabled, significantly, by a colonial travel account. Happening upon an old military acquaintance now become a newspaper editor, he is invited to contribute a piece to the paper. Maupassant's Flaubertian irony embroiders on Bel-Ami's difficulty in capitalizing on his colonial experience as he sets out to write his "Recollections of an African Cavalryman":

> On his sheet of paper he wrote: "The town of Algiers is completely white . . ." but was unable to say anything more.
>
> In his mind's eye, he could see the lovely bright city, its low, flat-roofed houses cascading down the mountain

into the sea; but he could no longer find a single word to express what he had seen, what he had felt. After a great struggle, he added: "It is partly inhabited by Arabs . . ." Then he flung his pen down on the table. (30)

Ambitious but lazy, Bel-Ami seeks out his friend the editor for help with writing the piece, and falls instead upon the latter's wife, who lends him her assistance. In the face of Bel-Ami's utter lack of ideas, however, the editor's wife takes up the pen herself and launches into a fictional concoction of colonial clichés and colorful details, going so far as to include various exotic romances in her text. This episode of the fabricated travelogue anticipates the larger social questions of Maupassant's novel, including the manipulation of opinion through the popular media, and Parisian political and financial intrigue with Tunisia as colonial backdrop. The symbolic capital of Bel-Ami's colonial experience, however ineptly managed on his part, enables his entry into this world of corruption. Maupassant's novel demystifies colonial travel writing as an ideological construct in the service of empire. And yet, by having the travel account be written by a woman, Maupassant slyly makes the other sex accountable for this deflation of heroic travel, as if the prattle of colonial discourse were the work of women. In this way, colonial travel would be less negated than *disavowed* in the novel; Maupassant's social critique runs up against its ideological limits and falls back on the dubious consolations of irony and disillusionment.[4]

Among the literary elisions, evasions, inanities, and symptomatic negations of French Algeria, the work of Eugène Fromentin holds a place apart. Orientalist painter, art critic, and novelist, Fromentin was the author of two major Algerian travel narratives, *A Summer in the Sahara* (*Un Eté dans le Sahara*) and *Between Sea and Sahara* (*Une Année dans le Sahel*). Fromentin's travels between 1846 and 1853 coincide with the early period of the French conquest and colonization of Algeria, and his texts portray in an original way the French phantasms and identifications that structure relations of power, desire, and knowledge in the apprehension of the culture and territory of the Algerians. Fromentin's encounter with Algeria subtly undoes the discourse of colonial mastery, and this subversion of colonial authority makes Fromentin's work a valuable counterpoint to both popular imperial discourse and his literary contemporaries. Fromentin's subversion of the colonial travelogue involves a characteristically French negation of travel, one that, however, serves a different purpose than in the texts and authors mentioned above. If a travel relation conventionally aspires to an exercise of knowledge and authority, Fromentin's texts suggest a different rapport to his subject. Resistant to the forms of the travel narrative as such, Fromentin flirts with the impossible: a journey without a traveler, a narrative without narration.

> I'm not a traveler.... I am at most a wanderer. If I were to undertake an expedition, my contribution wouldn't even be to rouse the curiosity of others to follow in my footsteps. In vain I would travel all the roads of the world and geography, history or science wouldn't benefit from a fresh piece of information. What I remember about things is often not worth the telling, for even if quite accurate, it never carries the solidity of a document acceptable to all.[5]

In spite of these disclaimers, Fromentin's travelogues are exceptional testimonies in the storehouse of exoticist clichés, political propaganda, and outright fabrications of nineteenth-century French writing on Algeria. Though his writings fall short of a critique of French colonialism, they avoid many of the pitfalls of contemporary exoticist discourse. This is due in part to the defiance of certain codes of the travelogue; it is also due, I argue, to a motive force that goes against the grain of travel itself. The encounter with the other takes place for Fromentin in an experience of self-dissolution that interrupts the drive to knowledge. Against the models of military and sexual conquest narratives, Fromentin's writing proposes other transports and other drives, and tends toward a point where the alternative to travel becomes a nonvoyage and paralysis.

Fromentin's first book, *A Summer in the Sahara*, recounts the artist's passionate discovery of the desert when, on a quest for pictorial subject matter, he accompanied a military convoy into the Algerian south. Whereas he was expected to paint military subjects in return for the trip, he focused exclusively on landscapes and portraits of Algerians, and his narrative turns a critical eye on the French. The popular and critical success of this book led to his second, *Between Sea and Sahara*, inspired by a year he spent in the vicinity of Algiers. Though minor classics, Fromentin's travel texts, along with his lone novel *Dominique* (1863), are commonly seen to fall somewhat short of a literary oeuvre, and his work is usually overlooked in studies of colonial and Orientalist literature. Fromentin's name does not, for instance, figure in Said's *Orientalism* or *Culture and Imperialism*, which cite Chateaubriand, Nerval, Loti, and Gide; nor do his writings figure significantly in the large body of critical work that has developed in response to Said's work. Such an omission is striking given that Fromentin's works were hailed by important contemporaries, and his painting was seen to stand, with Delacroix's, at the head of the French Orientalist school. If, as Said defines it, Orientalist discourse may be seen as a closed system of mutually corroborating representations, Fromentin's citational prose certainly merits a place of distinction. Indeed, as a practitioner of two media, Fromentin was ideally placed to authorize one of the most fantastic confirmations of an Orientalist stereotype: the entry into the harem where, writing with a painter's eye, he sanctions every detail of Delacroix's *Women of Algiers*. At the same time, Fromentin comes closer to the life of the Arabs than any other writer or painter of his time, attempting to capture what he calls the "nobility" of their existence in a land whose beauty impresses him above all for its radical difference. The Algerian landscape confronts Fromentin with a palette and a subject matter that compel him to challenge the dominant conventions of Orientalist painting. His experience of discovery results in a persistent tension with the norms of representation and an awkward allegiance to his French identity, since Fromentin laments the French presence in Algeria to the extent that it corrupts the native customs he admires.

This tension, of course, is not in itself either progressive or anticolonial. Indeed, it reflects the characteristic predicament of modern tourism, as outlined in my introduction; caught between a wish for contact and frustration at his mediated experience, the tourist habitually feels his alienation in the mode of belatedness and nostalgia. Further, as Renato Rosaldo has pointed out, such nostalgia can support the insidious bad faith of imperialist desire, slyly converting the dispossession of the other into one's own narrative of loss.[6] "[T]he myth making of travel has vanished," Fromentin says at the outset of his second travelogue. "Speed has eliminated daring adventure; everything is simpler, more direct, not at all mythic, less beguiling."[7] Such nostalgia is a familiar trope of touristic consciousness, but Fromentin offers a vision that substantially complicates the narrative of belatedness and disillusionment. This may elucidate Fromentin's status as a traveler who denies the role of traveler, and who is seemingly confined within Orientalist knowledge and yet pushing beyond it. At stake, I will argue, is a conflict between motion and stasis, whose point of articulation is that of the boundary or limit that Fromentin is unsure of crossing. A conflict between limits crossed and respected accompanies Fromentin in the course of his journeys, throwing a barrier across his lines of flight. "To penetrate further than is permitted into Arab life seems to me a mistake of curiosity," Fromentin says.[8] This aesthetic credo concerning the artist's proper distance extends to a respect for holy sites, such as the mausoleum next door to Fromentin's home in Algiers: "If it weren't for my great respect for these grounds," he says, "I could in one leap easily get myself on to its terrace."[9] And yet, despite these scruples the artist exults in playing a part in the larger territorial penetration of the French: "No French painter that I know of has penetrated further than us into our southern possessions."[10] This contradiction and its paralyzing tensions are nowhere more apparent than in Fromentin's journey into the Sahara, a landscape that defies his painting and leads him to take up the pen in an attempt to capture a sublime and intractable alterity. Unlike his Romantic predecessors, Fromentin did not follow the prescribed itinerary of Orientalist travel; instead of revisiting the familiar Orientalist *topoi*, he undertakes, as his editor remarks, "an itinerary that had no sites."[11] This evacuation of the traveler's sites is conveyed most strikingly in *A Summer in the Sahara*, with its painterly evocations of desert light, spatial expanse and infinite distance. Fromentin's experience of the desert, seen through disenchanted romantic eyes, is rendered in prose of an occasionally startling modernity. Above all, to the platitudes of Orientalist literature Fromentin answers with the "flat line of the horizon," ceaselessly invoked from start to finish of *A Summer in the Sahara*. With no site for destination, the travel account tends toward a perpetual horizon that sustains and defies the purpose of Fromentin's Algerian journey. What kind of encounter occurs in the contact zone of an unapproachable horizon? Does this horizon represent a political and ideological frontier or a Deleuzian line of flight? How might Fromentin's "mysterious line of the desert"[12] reconfigure the critical terrain of colonial contact?

In one sense, Fromentin's horizon suggests itself as a symbol of the artist's avant-gardism; indeed, the military metaphor regains its primary sense in Fromentin's painterly urge to capture images from the furthest outposts of French Algeria. In spite of his scruples, the artist's ambition allies him with the penetrating force of conquest; Algeria defined Fromentin's career as Orientalist painter and launched a second career as writer upon his return to France. Fromentin's early texts and letters from Algeria are filled with the excitement of discovery and the sense of ambition confirmed. Writing to his mother Fromentin says, "[T]his country . . . has made me what I am."[13] Like Bel-Ami, then, Fromentin can be seen as an *arriviste* climbing in French society by means of his colonial experience. His Algerian texts and paintings belong to the spoils of war. These spoils and their cost are most apparent in Laghouat, the Saharan town Fromentin visited six months after the terrible massacre that brought it under French control. In Laghouat Fromentin describes finding the bodies of three Arab women, victims of the French conquest, come unburied from the desert sands. He picks up the detached hand of one woman and continues on his way, until, overcome with horror, he drops it in the cemetery. Assia Djebar lingers on this scene of Fromentin's in *Fantasia*, her great postcolonial fresco of Algerian history. Djebar imagines placing a pen in the hand dropped by Fromentin in order to write her people's story of resistance and liberation. Djebar's invocation of Fromentin reveals an appreciation of the French traveler's experience that transcends the violence of war and the quest for profit, and speaks to an encounter shared between cultures in spite of the ravages of conquest and colonization. Djebar says, "I . . . greet the painter who has accompanied me throughout my wanderings like a second father figure. Eugène Fromentin offers me an unexpected hand—the hand of an unknown woman he was never able to draw."[14] In an uncanny repetition of the scene from *Bel-Ami*, Djebar, like the editor's wife, ghostwrites the Algerian travelogue of a Frenchman. Djebar's gesture is an ambiguous one, however, aiming both to correct the failings of the Frenchman's account and to pay homage to his unique testimony. In its strategic duplicity, Djebar's gesture resembles the bitter thanks she offers to the French general who slaughtered an entire Algerian village—but who left to the historical archive a precious firsthand account of the awful event and its victims: "their rigid carcasses, their paralysed embraces, their final paroxysms" (78). Haunted and belated though it is, Djebar's is a postcolonial gesture of hospitality to the colonial traveler.

That Fromentin provokes such a response calls on us to consider his colonial journeys as a fertile act of cultural translation. This is not, of course, to dispense with the texts' colonialist opportunism, but to attend to the trace of an encounter within the limits, transgressions, and horizons of Fromentin's texts. Rather than *arriviste*, then, Fromentin provides a figure for the *arrivant*, as Derrida defines it. Derrida's notion of the *arrivant* names not only the person who arrives, the "newcomer," but also whatever arrives or happens, the unexpected event, be it belated or untoward—such as the hand Djebar calls "unexpected." "The new *arrivant*," Derrida says, "this word can . . . mean the neutrality of *that which* arrives, but also the singularity of *who* arrives, he or she who comes, coming to be where s/he was not expected, where one was awaiting him or her without waiting for him or her, without expecting *it* [*s'y attendre*], without knowing what or whom to expect . . .—and such is hospitality itself, hospitality toward the event." If hospitality is by definition hospitality toward the other, for Derrida such receptivity must extend to otherness without determination; it must become sheer exposure to the unforeseen: "The absolute *arrivant* does not yet have a name or an identity. It is not an invader or an occupier, nor is it a colonizer, even if it can also become one. This is why I simply call it the *arrivant*, and not someone or something that arrives, a subject, a person, an individual, or a living thing."[15]

The notion of the *arrivant* reflects Derrida's broader deconstructive project, which pits the structure of a given system against that which exceeds it, in order to demonstrate how logic, order, and structure take shape only by virtue of marginal elements that are habitually repressed or excluded. The *arrivant* poses a challenge to such exclusions, and reorients our thought toward an ethical practice of radical hospitality. But in so doing, the *arrivant*, in its sheer otherness, exposes us to what resists comprehension, what cannot be taken in, and thus lies outside hospitality. The possibility of hospitality lies in this apparent impossibility. For my purposes here, the notion of the *arrivant* resonates with questions of transport, providing the means to figure the traveler's space of encounter as an openness to the other. At the same time, following Derrida, such a space always poses the problem of an *aporia*—a limit, obstacle, or threshold that defies passage. In this sense, to arrive is to arrive above all *at the limit*, and thereby to call the boundary into question, as well as all the distinctions it serves to demarcate. Indeed, the *event* of arrival is nothing other than this tampering with the limit. "Paradoxically," Derrida says, "the absence of horizon conditions the future itself. The emergence of the event ought to puncture every horizon of expectation."[16] Fromentin's desert horizon, I will argue, suggests such a troublesome limit. The frontier and horizon, as well as the artist's avant-gardist ambitions, give way, unexpectedly, to an event of encounter that paralyses the colonial journey.

Precursors of the Travelogue

As a writer Fromentin was not given to drama; his denial of travel ("I'm not a traveler") accords, then, with a resistance to the primary narrative codes of crisis, intrigue, and adventure. This is a noticeable stylistic trait in *Dominique*, whose love story unfolds within the static tableaus of a country setting imbued with the narrator's nostalgic sensibility. Similarly, *Between Sea and Sahara* is more a patchwork of scenes and episodes than a travelogue. *A Summer in the Sahara* is the exception in Fromentin's work; the spatiotemporal order of the Saharan journey contrasts markedly with the introspective and cyclical structures of all Fromentin's later works.[17] In what follows, then, I will pay particular attention to *A Summer in the Sahara*, Fromentin's most mobile and dramatic narrative. As we will see, however, the germ of Fromentin's later paralyses lies within the very forward drive of his Saharan travelogue.

A Summer in the Sahara delivers a dramatic and compelling account whose narrative thrust is that of a march southward into the desert. Written in the form of a journal addressed to his friend Armand Du Mesnil, the narrative of *A Summer* stays close to the movement and the events that make up the march, and the descriptions convey the thrill of discovery and the confirmation of Fromentin's artistic ambition. The Saharan journey and its narrative find their forward force in the story of French conquest. This story subtending Fromentin's experience is referenced obliquely, in passing and seemingly without judgment, and yet it conveys the story as much as the military convoy transports the artist. The identification of the artist's ambition with colonial drive is expressed in the Orientalist avant-gardism of Fromentin's personal letters, which speak for the first time of a projected written account of his journey, as if the journey's imaginary fulfillment were dictating the trip before the fact. This anticipation of a story to tell is also the hope for a future profit: "It is absolutely necessary that this journey be profitable to us because of the effort, trouble and money it will have cost us."[18] Fromentin's colonial ambition goes so far as to imagine a dedication to the duc d'Aumale, in order to place the name of the governor-general of Algeria at the head of the text. "This could be very profitable to us," he says.

Such collusions of empire and narrative are endemic to the travel literature of the period. The desire to turn a profit also inscribes Fromentin's journey within the economy of return, of travel as mercantile adventure.[19] Fromentin's editor notes that in *A Summer in the Sahara* there is no account of the return trip; the narrative concludes at its Saharan terminus on the eve of departure.[20] And yet the circular colonial economy already anticipates this domestic return, as do the letters themselves. Indeed, as we shall see, such a complication goes to the heart of Fromentin's journey, yielding a profoundly conflicted narrative. To the extent that Fromentin recognizes his implication in the colonial economy of conquest and appropriation, he betrays doubts about his journey. The journey's narrative thereby emerges less as adventure than as a composite of fixity and motion, advance and stasis.

Fromentin's identification with the penetrating thrust of empire yields a contradiction that is pointedly addressed in his private letters. While the French presence in the Sahara makes possible Fromentin's aesthetic exploration, he is acutely aware that it disfigures the people and the landscape he would capture. Venturing into the outlying areas of French control, Fromentin hopes to see "the real African country, with its caravans of camels, its palm forests, and its population more or less intact." This last qualification, the price paid for the right of inspection, is repeated later, where Fromentin evokes a landscape "more or less intact, since we haven't had the time to disfigure it."[21] A telling disavowal, however, follows: "I have told you and I repeat, that we are the only French painters who will have gone so far. This country will be virgin territory." That Fromentin's dramatic *A Summer in the Sahara* stands out in his work is due partly to its identification with the forward push of colonial mastery, the "sheer historical momentum" Said speaks of with respect to Conrad's compelling *Heart of Darkness*.[22] And like Conrad's story, but a blazing, nearly infernal version of that ambivalent text, *A Summer* conveys the doubts and anxieties that accompany the vision of the European mission in the heart of Africa. As we have seen, this is due to the contradiction that makes Fromentin's paintings of the Algerians party to French domination. Fromentin neither accommodates nor denies this contradiction; it becomes, rather, a symptomatic anxiety accompanying the voyage, rendered in figures of transgression and paralysis. Indeed, the voyage as narrative drama is a feature at odds with the text itself. One might say that Fromentin's exceptional narrative *borrows* this larger narrative of empire and conquest that underwrites his text. The borrowed narrative of *A Summer* is not fully claimed by the narrator, and the drama of the march southward—into the Sahara, toward France's future African possessions—is the invention of others.

Who speaks in the colonial travelogue? Whose drama is recounted in the tale of adventure? How to identify the voice of Fromentin in the citational patchwork of his borrowed Orientalism? These questions of narrative and enunciation may illuminate both the authorship and the authority of Fromentin's colonial discourse as well as the vexed figures of motion and stasis in his narratives. Author of a Saharan travelogue, Fromentin is at the same time *authorized* by colonial discourse and the forces that carry him into the desert. Roland Barthes's famous question, "Who speaks?" sheds light on this eclipsing of the author, indeed his death, within a discourse that both overdetermines and disseminates the semantic codings of the text.[23] Applied to Fromentin's case, Barthes's "death of the author" can help undo the postures of mastery and judgment that support the traveler's narrative perspective. Further, and to lend a sharper political edge to Barthes's insight, one can bring it to bear on Albert Memmi's analysis of the psychology of colonization. Despite Fromentin's will to impartiality, to the purported innocence of what Albert Memmi calls the *colonial*, Fromentin voices the attitudes of a host of other characters diagnosed by Memmi: the colonizer, the colonialist, the colonial who accepts, and the colonial who refuses. Indeed, as Memmi asserts, these more politically charged positions lie hidden behind the mask of all purported impartiality in the colony: "the colonial," Memmi says, "does not exist."[24] Fromentin's journey of near self-immolation could be seen as betraying the symptomatic proof of Memmi's dictum, abolishing the "innocent" *colonial* in the adventurous narrative of the *colonizer*. In this way, Memmi's negation of the colonial would confirm Barthes's insight into the death of the author; each is a mirage, a false claim to coherence in a field of complex loyalties and dubious authority. But in its strict Manichaeism, Memmi's anticolonial militancy is not able to account for the more complex narrative enunciation described by Barthes. At the same time, however, one should not allow undue alibis to the colonial travelogue, as if the polyvocal text were redeemed simply by its more inclusive complexity. The death of the author should not serve merely as his textual alibi; it imposes, rather, the responsibility for his lack of authority. For Memmi, that responsibility ultimately lies in recognizing the "factual position" (17) of undue privilege the French subject invariably occupies in the political reality of the colonial context.

While sympathetic to Memmi's point here, I think his bid to ground politics in factual reality would sacrifice too much of the *scene* of enunciation in Fromentin's case. Jean Laplanche and Jean-Bertrand Pontalis provide another means to approach this scene and its multiple voices, provided, however, we take it as a colonial scene of *fantasy*. "In fantasy," the authors say, "the subject does not pursue the object or its sign: he appears caught up himself in the sequence of images."[25] As a result, "the subject, although always present in the fantasy, may be so in a desubjectivized form, that is to say, in the very syntax of the sequence in question." In such a scene, they say, the subject "cannot be assigned any fixed place." The complex desire articulated in this scene can illuminate violent defenses that are as much personal as political: disavowal, projection, turning against oneself, and reversal into the contrary. These are indeed visible features of Fromentin's texts, and they yield insights into the politics of his colonial desire. Such colonial desire cannot be dispelled as mere bad faith or hypocrisy; colonial ideology must contend not only with reality, as Memmi argues, but with the phantasmatic scenes that lend its illusions their psychic power.

Such a scene of colonial power, politics, and phantasmatic polyphony is dramatized in Fromentin's descriptions of his mistress Hawa and her apartment. The entire narrative development of this conventionally exotic love story, from illicit contact to the tragic death of Hawa at the end, is largely due to the invention of Fromentin's friend Armand Du Mesnil.[26] Fromentin's text is virtually ventriloquized by the voice and desire of his friend, and it is due to this borrowed intrigue that Fromentin's text achieves a level of narrative drama missing in his habitually static texts. Fromentin made many changes in adapting Du Mesnil's story; as Fromentin's editor, Guy Sagnes, notes, Du Mesnil was somewhat more of a "novelist" in his approach to the subject matter. Indeed, the difference between their perspectives, as Sagnes points out, is best gauged by the interiors in particular, which Fromentin renders in an impressionistic, "Baudelairean" manner.[27] The descriptions of Hawa are not, therefore, merely imitative of his friend but also contest the codes of masculine penetration and conquest. In adopting his friend's story, Fromentin as protagonist finds himself within a scene of conflict and rivalry, particularly with the Orientalist painter against whom he hopes to measure up, Delacroix, and his masterpiece, *Women of Algiers*. "I'll be going to see whether Hawa's apartment resembles Delacroix's admirable painting," he writes his friend.[28] And on returning, he reports, "Yes, my friend, just like it. It also has charm. But is not more beautiful. . . . When we got to the entrance of her mistress's room the black servant turned her head slightly toward me making exactly the same gesture as she parted the muslin curtain that you can see in the Delacroix painting. As I entered I saw Hawa, who had been waiting for me." Fromentin's discretion in placing himself in this scene is noteworthy: "I sat down, not beside her but at her feet and not too near so that I could get a good look at her" (96). Confirming Delacroix's picture requires that Fromentin retain a viewing distance from his subject such that she remains a superficial image. "The pull she exerts is strange as well: it's very strong yet superficial, not going I would imagine deeper than the heart's outer layer. . . . You listen to her, contemplate and admire her, and are captivated by something that's charming without being drawn to it" (109–10). As a mere image, "bizarre," "useless" and "delightful," in Fromentin's words (110), Hawa sustains denials and equivocations that are characteristic of Fromentin's both evocative and evasive prose. Barthes's essay on the death of the author departs from a similar instance of discourse in Balzac: "'This was woman herself, with her sudden fears, her irrational whims, her instinctive worries, her impetuous boldness, her fussings, and her delicious sensibility.' Who," Barthes asks, "is speaking thus?"[29]

The penetration of the harem is one of the most highly invested masculine Orientalist tropes. Fromentin, however, provides a version in which mastery and appropriation are significantly skirted. Indeed, entering the phantasmatic scenario of his superior rival Delacroix, one might say that he performs a tribute less to the Oriental mistress than to the virile desire of that rival. The scene, moreover, concludes with Fromentin leaving Hawa's house as a child outside spits on the ground in "a sign of sovereign loathing" (*Between Sea*, 98). In a letter to a friend Fromentin conveys the ambivalence of a penetrating gaze that would nonetheless resist exploitation: "I have seen *Aïcha* again. I have spoken of this to Armand, as well as others.—I don't know what to say about it; I want to penetrate deeply into the intimate lives of this people. I am so far from any sensual ideas that I will confront without danger these places in which others would debauch themselves."[30] The multiple addressees of Fromentin's account indexes a homosocial convention of the sexual conquest exchanged between men, subsequently banalized in the Algerian colonial postcard.[31] And yet Fromentin's trespassing gaze denies itself the conquest of others; his approach, "not too near," as he says, seems to suspend the transgression that it nonetheless savors.

Fromentin makes this castrated spectatorship into aesthetic credo in *A Summer in the Sahara*. "To penetrate further than is permitted into Arab life seems to me a mistake of curiosity. One must observe these people from the distance that it suits them to show themselves: men up close, women from afar; the bedroom and the mosque, never. To describe a woman's quarters or to paint the ceremonies of Arab religion is in my opinion more serious than fraud: it is to commit, as far as art is concerned, an error of perspective." The landscape painter would thus limit himself to exterior views. By a double debt to Delacroix and his friend Du Mesnil, then, Fromentin delivers an Orientalist spectacle that he would avoid painting, and which he would render in writing as a virtual anti-narrative. "I'm really hard put to tell you," Fromentin says, "what we do in her company or how we pass the time."[32] This impossibility of narrative plays, of course, with literary conventions of modesty and suggestiveness; in a more Laplanchian vein, however, it indicates desire's inarticulateness in the scenario of sexual conquest. These scenes with Hawa include the narrator's friend, the adventurer and explorer Vandell, who serves here and throughout the travelogue as a virile contrast to the sensitive and more passive painter. By means of this opposition, or splitting of roles, both of Fromentin's Algerian narratives exploit a distinction between a conventional masculinity of conquest and a marginal masculinity that would resist such a version of travel. The triangular structure of the interactions with Hawa suggests an Oedipal pattern of desire, rivalry, and interdiction, no doubt, but rather than portraying instances of mimetic desire, these scenes are pregnant with the shifting positions of Laplanche's subject of fantasy. Further, Fromentin's immobility finds an insistent theme throughout his text in the pleasures of the home as nest and place of passive observation and repose—aspects of a queer *séjour* akin to Loti's Orientalized transvestism, which link Fromentin to Hawa not so much as object of desire as of identification.[33] Narrative's impossibility in Hawa's interior speaks to what remains inarticulate in the Laplanchian "syntax" of the fantasy's enunciation.

Such a predicament lends a static and paralyzing nature to Fromentin's descriptions and to his journeys themselves. It is precisely upon leaving Hawa's chambers that Fromentin delivers the lines quoted above in which he summarily disavows his Algerian journey: "I'm not a traveler" (*Between Sea*, 114). Placed in this specific context, the statement suggests a resistance to the demand for narrative imposed by Orientalist conventions and by the romance invented by Fromentin's friend. It also serves as an explicit counterpoint to Vandell, embodiment of the intrepid colonial traveler. Fromentin's negation of travel, moreover, falls under the sign of interdiction, as he speaks of himself in contrast to Vandell as "not daring to dream of expeditions that are forbidden to me."[34] A characteristic network of motifs thus links a forbidden woman and passive contemplation with an interdiction that prohibits travel. This neurotic condition compromises the mobility of Fromentin's journey, making its every move a repetition of the lure of trespass and the paralysis of interdiction. Fromentin's parents, his father in particular, objected to Fromentin's first Algerian journey, which he took nevertheless without their consent and without informing them. Fromentin's father, himself an amateur painter, may then lie behind both Vandell and Delacroix as figures of rivalry, and Fromentin's troubled transgressions would enact the symptoms of this unfinished contestation and failed revolt against the paternal law.

Other voices also contribute to the scene of Fromentin's colonial desire; here again, stasis and inarticulateness are compensated by the structuring narrative Fromentin borrows from a masculine voice. A major precursor to Fromentin's Saharan journey is General Eugène Daumas, whose popular books *Le Grand désert* and *Le Sahara algérien* provided some of the period's most detailed accounts of the cultural and religious life of the Algerians. *A Summer in the Sahara* refers frequently to Daumas's *Le Grand désert*, which Fromentin admiringly calls the "Odyssey" of the Sahara.[35] Daumas's career in the Algerian Bureaux Arabes led to the position of Director of Arab Affairs and ultimately Director of Algerian Affairs at the Ministry of War. Like his fellow officers in the Bureaux Arabes, Daumas occupied the compromised stance of a benevolent paternalism that defended the indigenous population from the demands of the French settler population. An admirer of the Algerian Arabs, Daumas's proto-ethnological writings display in a striking manner the function of social-scientific study as instrument of discipline and control. Analysis "from a reconnaissance point of view," in Patricia Lorcin's words, characterizes the military scholarship of Daumas and his colleagues, which became the raw material for much subsequent ethnography and anthropology.[36] By the mid-nineteenth century no European had yet crossed the Sahara; Daumas's narrative is placed in the mouth of an Algerian native informant who makes a caravan crossing to traffic in goods and slaves. As the author notes in his preface, his previous book, *Le Sahara algérien,* had successfully served a French trader as a "guide" for his travels.[37] To such ends *Le Grand désert* includes a "Vocabulaire d'histoire naturelle," a "Code de l'esclavage chez les musulmans," and a large color map by the cartographer Oscar MacCarthy—who served as model for Fromentin's fictional Vandell. The text, then, is both a reference source and an advertisement for French interests and territories beyond the Sahara. As Daumas says, "Interests of the highest gravity are bound up, for us, with the knowledge of central Africa, which, in a more or less distant future, may be opened up to the commerce of our colony" (v). One of the dubious claims made by the author is an argument for French management of the slave trade, so as to import "servants" into the colonies who, thereby "initiated into a moral education" would be later repatriated as "missionaries of civilization" (ix). Daumas's vision of French interests beyond the Saharan desert prefigures a colonial dream that would be frustrated until the turn of the century.[38]

Textual references to Daumas serve to authenticate Fromentin's descriptions in *A Summer in the Sahara* and, indeed, *Le Grand désert* may have been a chief inspiration for his journey. As Jean-Pierre Lafouge remarks, "the reading of Daumas's works allowed him to make . . . a sort of first voyage in his imagination."[39] When Fromentin pushed as far as Laghouat on his 1853 journey, he had reached the southernmost point of French control in Algeria. The emir Abd-el-Kader's revolt had been suppressed, but the town of Laghouat had been taken by the French only months earlier, and the area immediately beyond remained independent. The last leg of Fromentin's journey is a trip to the holy town of Aïn Mahdy. What Fromentin calls a "travel dream" realized at Aïn Mahdy is a destination beyond French jurisdiction.[40] In a letter to his mother Fromentin writes, "Aïn Mahdy is not ours, and it is a boon for its appearance is that we have never had a garrison there."[41] The text of *A Summer*, however, is more circumspect about judging the contaminating presence of the French. This circumspection, or "discretion" with respect to colonialism, as Lafouge would have it (*Etude sur l'orientalisme*, 129), seems dictated by the narrative structure of the story. How, without betraying his hosts or exacerbating a contradiction, might Fromentin object to the expedition that makes his journey possible? The achievement of Fromentin's *A Summer in the Sahara* is that it captures a historical moment from within its ideological confines, yet conveys an anxiety and doubt that calls into question the voyage itself. Transported by a journeying convoy, scripted into an ideological narrative, Fromentin dwells on the static figure of an inaccessible horizon. Progress itself is called into doubt in Fromentin's narrative. The journey as conquest, adventure, or civilizing mission is suspended by the perpetual presence of Fromentin's enigmatic line. Fromentin's paralyses thus provide an alternative to the story of French conquest, but at the cost of narrative itself.

"Beau fixe"

Barthes's essay on the death of the author has helped us register the complex voice speaking in Fromentin's colonial narratives. In one of his essays on critical mythology, Barthes asks another question we might apply to Fromentin's travelogue and its obsessive figure, the horizon: "how can you visit a line?"[42] Barthes's question resonates with the many analyses of travel and tourism that make up his *Mythologies*; indeed, as instances of the "impotence to imagine the Other," travel and tourism are privileged objects of Barthes's project of demystification.⁴³ Barthes's "impossible line," calling for the "transgression of laws," also anticipates the transgressive semioclasm of Barthes's later hedonist works, where the text of pleasure is sought in figures of other transports. A guiding thread in these works is the infraction of the gender boundary, and the pleasures of this line transgressed yield the queer transports of an "atopic," "drifting" subject, refractory to the narratives that would order him. Such works focus on a hedonistic *romanesque* alternative to the Oedipal *roman*, seeking affective transports that give the lie to the paternal symbolic. Travel narratives are contested by the queer "sojourns" of Loti, while adventurous narratives of conquest are replaced by Barthes's autobiographical "incidents" of loiterly cruising.⁴⁴

Barthes offers such a queering of Fromentin in an essay he devotes to *Dominique*. With a nod to Gide, who counted *Dominique* among his favorite books, Barthes invites us to place Fromentin in a queer literary lineage. "Dominique is a double name: masculine and feminine," Barthes notes, and this ambiguity illuminates a division according to which the story of a self-denying melancholy hero— "sensible," "conformist," and indeed "reactionary,"—is doubled by another.⁴⁵ Dominique's *masochism*, Barthes says, provides the key to the love story as to its social drama: desire and its frustration give shape to the narrator's tormented attachments and his unfulfilled class potential. The novel stages a moral drama within this masochistic logic, according to which youthful passion and ambition are thwarted and eventually compensated by the extinction of desire in the hero's virtuous self-abnegation. We have seen the traces of this neurotic predicament in Fromentin's travelogues as well. If this is the narrative arc of *Dominique*, its "dramatic system," as Barthes terms it, there is, however, a second level of passion and frustration that contests that system and its moral thrust. Barthes thus opposes a "ludic system" to the "dramatic system" at work in *Dominique*. The dramatic system, necessarily suspenseful, puts into play a conventional structure of crisis and struggle that the plot must resolve. "Yet," Barthes says, "the dramatic structure is suspended at a certain moment and permits itself to be penetrated by a ludic structure: this is my name for any *motionless* structure articulated on the binary oscillation of repetition—as we find it described in the *vort/da* game of the Freudian child: once passion is established and blocked, it oscillates between desire and frustration, happiness and misery, purification and aggression, the love scene and the scene of jealousy, in a literally *interminable* manner" ("Fromentin: *Dominique*," 101–2). Barthes's queer reading thus escapes the narrative logic of Fromentin's tale and its moral confines. Modeled on Freud's *death drive* and *repetition compulsion*, the play of desire and frustration no longer responds to a pathology of masochism but rather to a primordial splitting of the subject. This play escapes narrative in that it provides the fundamental coordinates of a repetitive drive whose conflict is never resolved for the desiring subject. To the extent that one gives play to this drive—as Barthes claims Fromentin does—one espouses a desire without object and a salutary egoic destitution Barthes names "dérive," or "drift." However, since this drift escapes the "dramatic system," its passions are not so much mobile, as its name suggests, as they are *suspended* and *motionless*. Further, such suspensions defy the binary logic of crisis that "paralyzes and exalts" Dominique (98). Following Barthes, then, we must see a *different* paralysis at work in Dominique's queer drifts.

In his essay on Loti's Orientalist tale *Aziyadé*, Barthes takes the image of a drifting boat as the emblem of this queer desire as drift. To this purpose, Barthes might have cited from the scene of the drifting boat in *Dominique*, where Fromentin's narrative seemingly holds its breath in a languorous atmosphere of enchantment. As the protagonist Dominique says, "the boat drifted on [*le bateau s'en allait à la dérive*]," while he and his companions were lulled into a state of forgetfulness by "the rocking motion of the calm water."[46] The rocking of the boat and the loss of self-awareness suggestively renders an infantile regression. Fromentin however lends this peaceful rocking all the violence of a self-rending split: "Nothing could have been more innocent all round, and yet I look back on these hours of languor and apparent repose as perhaps the happiest and the most dangerous of my life [*les plus dangereuses peut-être que j'aie traversées dans ma vie*]." Tellingly, the scene insists on a near total immobility in drift: "the boat, gently swayed by imperceptible currents, stopped almost still [*le bateau ne marchait presque plus*]." This frozen suspense is accentuated by the evocation of a ship on the horizon, that privileged referent of Fromentin: "a single ship, so far out that it was cut in half [*déjà coupé à demi*] by the line of the horizon, waiting under full sail for the return of the land breeze" (149; 484). Just as this boat is divided by the horizon line, caught at a moment of unfulfilled aspiration, so is Dominique divided by contrary passions. Absorbed by the spectacle of his desired Madeleine sleeping in the boat, he asks himself, "Was it rapture? Was it torment? [*Etais-je ravi? Etais-je torturé?*]" (149; 485). Dominique's desire is not to resolve this question but rather to prolong it. "I wouldn't for the world have made the slightest movement which might break the spell [*qui pût en suspendre le charme*]" (149; 485).

As the last line confirms, Fromentin's scene is unmistakably indebted to Lamartine's elegy "Le lac," and its morbid sense of temporality and dedication to an ideal of impossible love echoes a host of Romantic predecessors. In his study of Fromentin, Jean-Pierre Richard takes this scene from *Dominique* as emblematic of what he calls Fromentin's "poésie du sillage," or poetry of the wake, a nostalgic sensibility emblematized in the narrator's contemplation of the boat's trail in the water.[47] Only memory can answer to what Richard calls Fromentin's "need for permanence" (244), a need tragically fulfilled only in belatedness and aesthetic mediation. In Richard's analysis, Fromentin's academic tendency in painting, his doctrine of *habit*, his affective moroseness all devolve from a betrayal of the sensory life of impressions and experience. "No one had more than he the love of fixity," Richard says of Fromentin (232). As exception to Fromentin's "frozen ardor" (261), the critic singles out *A Summer in the Sahara*, whose striking vivacity, Richard says, is subsequently betrayed by later writings. Fromentin's vigorous exploration thereby gives way to a career of more measured "promenade" (260); only his early writing retains the "freshness of his impressions" (238) and avoids the morality and conservatism of the return home.

What Richard calls Fromentin's "doctrine" of failure confirms the masochistic self-thwarting Barthes ascribes to the novel's protagonist. And yet, Richard's assessment of Fromentin's career as the unfortunate story of a downward arc and return home reflects only one facet of his narratives: the "dramatic structure" by which Barthes says one may read the story of *Dominique*. And whereas Richard laments Fromentin's "love of fixity," Barthes valorizes the "*motionless* structure" that speaks to other transports and desires. Barthes's *dérive*, desire without object, traumatic repetition of frustration and desire, thus challenges the terms by which the phenomenologist would assert sensory immediacy. Indeed, for Barthes the story of failure is compensated not by Richard's vital "life of the impression" (236) but instead by the death drive and the destitution of the subject. Moreover, like most of Fromentin's critics, the phenomenologist overlooks the colonial dimension of Fromentin's Saharan tale. The aspects of *A Summer in the Sahara* that Richard values—Fromentin's ambition, discovery and "exploration,"—are layered onto a story of colonial conquest, and this conquest is a crucial aspect of *A Summer*'s narrative thrust. Richard's valorization of adventure and exploration is made at the cost of this colonial elision. And, moreover, while Richard opposes Fromentin's Saharan tale to his later writings, the figure of the horizon puts into play a paralysis that text shares with his more overtly static texts. Barthes's queer transports speak more aptly of this paradoxical immobility, and provide the means to analyze the text's subversion of its own dramatic structure, of the time, space, and narrative of the colonial travel account.

It is ironic, in this light, that Fromentin's work should be anthologized in that mythological text par excellence, the *Michelin Blue Guide*, Barthes's emblem of the French bourgeoisie's "cultural alibi." In spite of his double disclaimer of travel and traveling posterity, Fromentin would be a pathbreaker for many followers. Fromentin's descriptions would indeed provide the template of all subsequent Algerian travel accounts, as Martine Loutfi points out: "The models of the points of view, of the paintings, of the moments described in *A Summer in the Sahara* ... that is what travel writers seek in North Africa. So much so that a given scene is not noticed unless it matches the literary memory."[48] That Fromentin is echoed by so many followers no doubt indicates the complicity of his representations with French colonial ideology, and the figure of the horizon is complicit with that ideology in a particularly subtle way. "Horizon," Michel Foucault reminds us, "is a pictorial, but also a strategic notion."[49] Similarly, Derrida warns that the furthest limits of knowledge always tend to be reclaimed by the mind's assimilating grasp: "a horizon is always a horizon of the same."[50] Fromentin's literary and pictorial horizon is defined by the forward march of the military caravan he accompanies into newly conquered desert lands, and this second dimension to the pictorial image seems to haunt the text as its unavowed political meaning in the ideology of conquest and the advancing frontier. The mystique of the horizon, in its very intangibility and natural allure, merges the fascinated traveler with the forces of politics and ideology that carry him forward into foreign territory. The horizon thus functions as a duplicitous "prospect," to use Mary Louise Pratt's term: a joining together of an aestheticizing colonial view with an aim to claim and exploit it.[51]

This joining of the strategic and pictorial in a seemingly innocent image lends a compelling force to Fromentin's narrative. Haunted by its other horizon, the pictorial frontier masks the traveler's political desire and colonial identity, even as it calls them forth. Fromentin is thus prey to the summons of a seemingly imperious force: "I do not know where I am going; something as vague as an instinct, but as violent as the strongest passion, pushes me into a furrow whose end I cannot see, and I do not know where it leads me."[52] Interestingly, passion, instinct, and desire call up the image of a "sillon," or furrow, as if the novelty of Fromentin's trajectory is already marked by the rut of a well-worn path. Thus, while Richard sees Fromentin's attachment to the *wake* or "sillage" congealing in *Dominique*'s nostalgic moroseness into a "poésie du sillon," the very path of the colonial journey is already compromised in its earliest impulse. Fromentin's desire conveys in its very inarticulateness the urgency of artistic ambition awakening in the face of an overwhelming otherness. Just as important, however, is the way in which Fromentin's own ambition is haunted by colonial authority and desire. This results in a tension in which Fromentin submits to Orientalist codes that he also resists, and the colonial horizon stages a similar play of desire, complicity, and resistance in a landscape reduced to the line of an impossible transgression.

"What did I come looking for here . . . ? What did I hope to find?" Fromentin asks himself in Laghouat. His troubled questions concern an aesthetic vantage point with respect to the desert Arabs, alternately viewed as historical abstractions of humanity and specific types suitable to genre painting. The aesthetic question, however, hides a broader question about the justification of Fromentin's presence in Laghouat and the purpose of his quest within the French project of colonial conquest. Most readers of Fromentin have noted the originality and symbolic resonance of his painterly landscapes; few, however, have noticed how the landscape, and particularly its evacuation, supports the equivocations and evasions of Fromentin's political conscience. Viewed within the colonial economy of return, one might ask why Fromentin's text is so elusive as to its means, motives, and ends. Indeed, the fundamental question as to why Fromentin undertakes his journey is pointedly elided; desire is rendered in the text less as ambition than as a virtually abstract force.

Likewise, the object of his desire is defined in terms of sheer absence and lack, as seen in the opening section of *A Summer in the Sahara*: "I believe I have a clear objective. Should I ever attain it, it will speak for itself; if not, why speak of it here? Allow me simply to say that I passionately love the color blue, and that there are two things I am burning to see again: the cloudless sky, above a desert without shadow" (*Un Été*, 18–19). The furthest point of his projected journey is a great blank space on the map bearing the name *Land of Thirst*. "Others would retreat before the nakedness of such an itinerary; I admit it is precisely that nakedness that spurs me on" (18). Once revealed, this nudity undergoes a further subtraction, as if the sexual suggestion were too strong: "nakedness brings out the Sahara's true physiognomy," Fromentin says, adding, "what I like most about the place where we are camped is its sterile appearance" (56). This inhospitable land of thirst and privation appeals to Fromentin for its negation of all objects of attachment: "I always experience the same calming of the spirit in feeling myself so utterly deprived of everything." (83). This ascetic deprivation, however, only heightens the force of desire, sustained in the absence of its object.

The colonial journey claims its ultimate justification in abstracting away all objects for the benefit of an overweening and imperious desire. René Caillié's famous African travelogue opens by evoking "a strong desire to become a traveller," one deriving from his "earliest infancy." Like Fromentin's, Caillié's ultimate aim imposes itself on the explorer like a singular compulsion: "Timbuktoo became the continual object of all my thoughts, the aim of all my efforts, and I formed a resolution to reach it or perish."[53] Here lies also the vulnerability of desire's colonial alibis, its seemingly mystical raptures and abstract joys; in a playful and elegant turn of creative citation, Abdourahman Waberi quotes from Caillié and inverts the explorer's raptures in arriving in Timbuktu to make his words evoke instead those of a clandestine French refugee desperate to find asylum in a fictional "United States of Africa."[54] Waberi's satire latches effectively onto the compulsive desire of the explorer the better to undermine it. "At length," Caillié says, "we arrived safely at Timbuktoo, just as the sun was touching the horizon. I now saw this capital of the Soudan, to reach which had so long been the object of my wishes. On entering this mysterious city, which is an object of curiosity and research to the civilised nations of Europe, I experienced an indescribable satisfaction."[55] Tellingly, the aim of the journey is rendered here as both "the object of my wishes" and that of larger forces of European science and commerce. This duplicity is betrayed in a passage where Caillié speaks bluntly of opening up interior routes to enable future African "tribute" to France, followed by the faithful acknowledgment of his own personal "tribute" to his native country (2:vii, viii). Clearly, as Waberi suggests, both immigrant and explorer are economic migrants, though with markedly different privileges. But perhaps most revealing here is how the explorer's desire is itself colonized, serving empire in its most intimate drives and childhood fantasies. When the traveler chooses to reclaim a personal desire in the colonial scenario, that desire will be haunted by political negations, elisions, and circumlocutions.

Thus, deep in the desert, Fromentin says, "My mind calls up, with incredible spasms, a giant cup filled to brimming with that icy and limpid mountain water. It is an *idée fixe* I cannot dispel [*que je ne puis chasser*]. Everything in me is transformed into sensual appetite; everything gives way to this sole concern: to slake my thirst" (*Un Eté*, 183). This passage, remarkable for its sensuality, speaks to a desire stripped bare, reaching a fever pitch in deprivation, though it maintains the driving force of his journey as a cipher of desire. It is this desire sustained in lack, rather than its satisfaction, that is targeted. Such prose has a strikingly modern quality, anticipating Gide in particular, and like Gide's early Algerian narratives, Fromentin stages colonial alibis of desire, in which travel is sustained in and as the suspension of means, ends, and desire. A burning desire, an objective expressed in intimations and retractions: in more than one way, Fromentin anticipates the circumlocutions of Gide's *L'Immoraliste*, whose hero Michel, crossing Fromentin's path in Algeria, conveys an anguish of desire torn between self-discovery and self-abnegation. Fromentin's march into the rising summer heat of the desert suggests a similar tension between burning passion and self-immolation. Such conflicted desire, heightened by the abuses and contradictions of colonial presence, makes Fromentin's landscapes the ambiguous theater of colonial desire. Less generously, one might say that Fromentin's "sole concern" for survival evacuates all other concerns and issues, notably the aggressive French politics of "pacification" in the Sahara. In this sense, his ordeal is akin to the desert death-march Saint-Exupéry narrates in *Terre des hommes*, where the adventurer's pat humanism finds its ultimate alibi in his own *sole concern*: the pathos of a single life in extreme peril.[56] And indeed, *A Summer in the Sahara* performs a number of political elisions to pare down the journey to its bare essentials.

In accompanying a French convoy to Laghouat, Fromentin was expected to provide paintings on military topics, including the siege itself, which he never did.[57] He does, however, give a textual account of the siege, doing so reluctantly, he says, "to be over and done with a story that is foreign to my own idea of travel."[58] The text of *A Summer in the Sahara* contrasts dramatically with the manuscript, where one reads a more critical account whose emphasis is on the Algerian death toll: "Such a fierce battle, such boldness in the attack, an exceptional heroism on the part of the defense, so many brave people struck dead, so many poor people exterminated on their own walls, getting killed rather than giving up, so many victims, . . . one third of the population destroyed, and by what right, for what offense or threat, and for what dubious result?" Fromentin attenuates these bitter remarks with a retraction: "I have no right to relate or judge a victory of this sort." Other variants show the extent to which Fromentin was moved by the plight of the inhabitants of Laghouat, and how at the same time he attempts to maintain his distance: "Moreover, don't ask me for decisive opinions on all that I see. I observe without judging [*Je regarde et ne juge point*]."[59] Other variants include "Je regarde et ne critique point," and "Je transcris," none of which survive in the final text.

The plight of Laghouat nonetheless continues to haunt *A Summer in the Sahara*. If for practical reasons Fromentin avoided political commentary and judgment, his account of Laghouat in *A Summer* does not spare the graphic details of the massacre and its aftermath. Laghouat presents Fromentin with a crisis of conscience whose solution is not censorship so much as a subtle self-implication in the crimes committed. On a tour of the town, Fromentin says in a telling phrase, "We followed more or less the path of our soldiers' bullets and bayonets" (*Un Été*, 92). Fromentin also repeatedly signals the similarity of the Arab words for *painter* and *thief*, so as to foreground the transgression that haunts his innocent spectatorship. "I am visiting this country as one examines one's prey," Fromentin writes to Du Mesnil. "I've never felt such detachment from a place, in spite of the keen desire to make the most of it." Unlike the text of *A Summer*, Fromentin's letters reveal a bitterness combined with the fascination of discovery and a passionate need to create: "No landscape has charmed me less and moved me more."[60] Like the attenuation of his political criticism, this contradiction is muffled in the text of *A Summer*. And yet, in Fromentin's textual landscapes of the desert one enters a vision that pairs extreme emotion with desolation, death with passion, desire with frustration. The horizon focuses these contradictions as a figure that symptomatically conveys the political impossibility of his journey.

The negation of travel is echoed in Fromentin's paintings, which are characteristically static and portray figures at rest. A few titles speak to this tendency: *The Halt*; *Halt in the Desert*; *The Arab Camp*; *A Halt on the Banks of the Nile*; *Resting*; *Halt of Travelers at the Entrance to the Sahara Desert*. Moreover, it has been noted by critics that Fromentin seemed unable to render figures in movement. His best paintings excel instead in capturing remarkable tones of atmosphere, with finely rendered figures and horses set off against an immense landscape and distant horizons. Distance and stasis reflect fundamental features of the artist's viewing pleasure. "I love to look," Fromentin says, "but not to go and look."[61] Less often, Fromentin painted horses in motion, with results that compare unfavorably with his Orientalist contemporaries. Toward the end of his career, Fromentin made a few attempts at dramatic paintings, inspired by episodes from his desert journeys. The most ambitious of these is *The Land of Thirst*, a painting that is, however, clearly derivative of Géricault's great *Raft of the Medusa*. Comparing the two, James Thompson and Barbara Wright point out that in Fromentin's painting "the drama is more passive than active" (242). Fromentin's waving figure gestures toward no distant caravan but only empty space. In a subsequent version, this figure is removed along with the central rock that rises above the horizon. The result is an image even more static, whose figures are crushed under an oppressive horizon and a sky filled with threatening birds. Might the paintings be an oblique testament to the deaths that preceded Fromentin's visit to the conquered Algerian south? Both take as their title the final words of Fromentin's Saharan travelogue. A "passive drama," in the words of our critics, they translate the ambivalence of those closing lines of *A Summer in the Sahara*: "I will salute with deep regret that menacing horizon, so desolate and so rightly named the *land of thirst*."[62]

It is perhaps not surprising that, as a landscape artist, Fromentin's aesthetic interests lie in the motionless, the static, and immutable. Fromentin's static tableaus, however, speak not only to their pictorial nature but also to the artist's affective paralysis. The immutable clear weather of the desert landscape reflects this fixity of Fromentin's spirit: "the weather invariably determines my outlook. Both for the past month, if I can put it that way, have been steady fair [*au beau fixe*]."[63] Fromentin's *beau fixe* might stand as an emblem of his life and work, provided we see in the perfect weather an unnatural stillness that casts a pall on the world. Indeed, Fromentin's *beau fixe*, as denial of time's passage, of changeable nature, virtually freezes the sun in place; this haunting dark side of the immutable may be seen in the striking description he gives of the desert transformed by the midday sun into "a dark plain."[64] Fixity, much as it should preserve and console, nonetheless turns sunshine into a deathly pall. Thus Fromentin speaks of "a radiant immobility, the somewhat gloomy fixedness of fair weather" (123). That sunlight does not confer joy is confirmed in one of the most important passages of *Between Sea and Sahara*, where Fromentin says, "Gaiety isn't what pleases me in light. What delights me is the precision it lends to contours. Of all the attributes that go with grandeur the most beautiful as far as I'm concerned is immobility. To put it another way, I have a genuine fondness for things that last; I can only consider with some passion things that are stationary" (67).

This penchant for immobility is expressed as early as Fromentin's youthful correspondence: "I have no great liking for what runs, flows, or flies; every motionless thing, every stagnant water, every perched or gliding bird, causes in me an indefinable emotion."[65] Fromentin speaks here of his ambition to render this "feeling of repose," while fearing at the same time that it speaks to a "sterile inertia." Fixity, as symptom of paralyzed desire, will always be haunted by the ultimate stasis of death. We have seen how the Sahara answers this anxiety about sterility, though the journey allows Fromentin to exorcise its internal threat as a spectacle of nature. The alien desert, sterile and immutable, thus shows itself to be strangely familiar—uncanny—as answer to Fromentin's quest for the *beau fixe*. In this quest, Fromentin's torment would be any flux and motion, such as the stormy sea: "A floating surface and an undecided perspective of unmanageable forms [*formes insaisissables*] . . . not one feature that doesn't vanish as soon as it materializes."[66] The horizon, by contrast, promises a straight and unwavering line that orients his view and stabilizes the scene. And yet, interestingly enough, the horizon line is itself cast as *ungraspable*, as in the quote above, defined as it is as "la ligne insaisissable d'un horizon plat."[67] The line of the horizon, minimal figure of form and definition, can thus be located neither on the side of Fromentin's desired fixity and permanence, nor simply on the side of the motion and instability he rejects. This tension, as we will see, governs the development of his entire desert travelogue. Figure of a *colonial sublime*, the horizon provides the key to Fromentin's paralyzed journey.

The Paralyzing Horizon

There is "nothing in the world," Fromentin says, "so beautiful to look upon than the undefined emptiness of a flat horizon."[68] This horizon, as Fromentin's editor points out, gives "the structure which serves as the line of force of *A Summer in the Sahara*, an avid march toward the desert."[69] But the leitmotif of the horizon in *A Summer* functions as a cipher in the narrative of Fromentin's journey. In the context of colonial war, it suggestively renders both the advancing frontier of French conquest and an unattainable destination. Perpetually deferred, the horizon would seem to function as an alibi of colonial desire that sustains the contradictions of French ambitions in the Sahara. Fromentin's horizon presents itself as deeply ambiguous, and his images of perpetual striving and frustration are features that remain seductive to contemporary readers. I would argue, however, that the horizon graphically figures what Homi Bhabha has called "an aporia in the inscription of empire." Fromentin's desert horizon is a dramatically paralyzing instance of such "imperial aporia," flirting with the mirages, phantasms and sheer inarticulateness of the "senseless signifiers" and "colonial non-sense" that Bhabha analyzes.[70] In so doing, however, it also exposes the space of ambivalence and contradiction as a fertile terrain to challenge the colonial order of discourse and the representation of the other.

A Summer in the Sahara begins with an atmosphere of urgency. But this urgency is less one of desire than *flight*, as the author is pushed and driven forth into the desert. The traveler's flight, moreover, tends not toward speed but immobility. "It is thanks to the rain that I discovered, for the first time . . . the land of perpetual summer; it is in fleeing it headlong that finally I encountered the cloudless sun."[71] To express his flight in the rain, Fromentin evokes a Rembrandt engraving that portrays "two travelers hurrying along, fleeing, the wind at their backs. It shows," Fromentin says, "all the agonies of the traveling life [*les transes de la vie de voyage*]." *Transes*, Fromentin's choice of noun here, denotes a peculiar transport that can only be approximated by the term *agonies*; derived from the verb *transir*, to die or go beyond, it also names a certain paralysis. This sense of being paralyzed or transfixed in motion is reinforced in the narrative that follows, in which it is a question of reaching another boundary: "I arrived at *El-Kantara*, at the boundary of the Tell of Constantine, exhausted, agonizing [*transi*], pierced through the heart, but determined not to stop until facing the unmistakable southern sun" (15). In the course of his journey, Fromentin often marks significant moments with a narrative pause; arrivals in particular call for slow motion: "let yourself be led step by step to the entry of the desert. . . . Something would be missing from my arrival in this amazing country if I left out the slowness . . . of the final miles" (74). Step by step, Fromentin's perpetual entry into the desert is a kind of constant arrival at the limit.

The opening of *A Summer in the Sahara* puts into play a set of contrasts: sun and rain, past and present, darkness and light. These oppositions lead the reader to the dividing line that separates winter from summer and the mountainous Tell from the Sahara: the "marvelous bridge" of El-Kantara. "Remember this name," Fromentin writes in a letter to Du Mesnil, "it will be the *rendez-vous* of all my memories."[72] Once over the bridge, Fromentin says, "You are in the Sahara." This sudden arrival in the Sahara, the revelation and release represented by the magnificent site of El-Kantara are developed at length in *A Summer* and Fromentin's letters. One is tempted to see in the *rendez-vous* of Fromentin's memory a lingering on the bridge that suspends the passage across in order to dwell on the frontier, *transi* at the boundary. This suspension at the bridge is in part a factor of memory, the future appointment already anticipated in the present. *Fixer une image, fixer un rendez-vous*: in Fromentin's art of travel, an anticipation of retrospection already freezes the present moment. "The memories will become extraordinary," Fromentin declares in his letters, "and if ever I write them they will take a literary form."[73] This temporal predicament, according to which the present is already grasped as past image, gives a second sense to the title of *Un Eté dans le Sahara*. "And what did you see there?" a friend asks Fromentin on his return from the desert. "Summer," he simply answers ("L'été").[74]

This temporal dislocation illuminates the beginning of *A Summer in the Sahara*, which, despite its format of a daily journal, does not in fact coincide with the actual trip underway. Indeed, the entire episode of El-Kantara constitutes a false start in the narrative, referring as it does to a previous but shorter trip, Fromentin's first into the Algerian south. No doubt the impact of Fromentin's initial discovery plays a role in his rememoration. And yet the reason for overriding the travel narrative with a backward loop seems to lie rather in a retrospective impulse that cedes the present to the past. The scene of writing is thus framed, in the opening lines of the text, as a preliminary paralysis, suspending travel and promoting a belated narrative. "My friend, I had not expected to write you until the first stopover; but my forced inaction makes me open, without waiting, my travel journal" (*Un Eté*, 13). Bad weather is the ostensible cause of this "inaction forcée," but the writing of the journey seems to dictate that the present journey fall under the sign of the *été*. And while the bridge of El-Kantara interrupts the present journey and promotes a paralyzing halt at the limit, it remains, however, a clear marker of passage and transition: the "golden door" of the site reveals a "lifting of the curtain" on the Orient. By contrast, Fromentin says, "there is no El-Kantara on the uniform and well-planned route I will be following" (18). The bridge, site of passage and fixation, is replaced in this journey by the more complex and elusive figure of the horizon.

Guy Barthèlemy has devoted an extensive analysis to the figure of the horizon in Fromentin's work. Writing in a Deleuzian vein of the "deterritorializing" quality of Fromentin's text, the critic speaks of a "paroxystic alterity" represented by the desert horizon.[75] Oddly enough, this book-length study grants a mere footnote to colonization and the brutal taking of the Saharan town Laghouat just before Fromentin's arrival there. To indicate this lapse is not only to invoke the importance of the historical context of Fromentin's journey; it is to attend to the imbrication of literary and colonial representation, as well as to the author's complex and conflicted politics of desire. Barthèlemy's reading of Fromentin avoids such questions and, despite its claims for "a poetics of alterity," in fact reinscribes an aesthetics of the ineffable by means of the figure of the horizon. "The encounter with the Orient is thus that of a limit: Fromentin, betrayed by his art, seeks to push back that limit by means of writing" (55). What ensues, as Barthèlemy shows, is a play of perpetual deferral in which Fromentin holds out a promise that is never delivered. Unfortunately, the critic conflates this textual deferral with the desert itself, which consequently takes on a conventional mystique couched in postmodern jargon: "the paroxystic alterity of the improbable desert spatiality." If, finally, in this analysis what is presumably at stake are the limits of representation, the critic, by a certain subreption, focuses instead on the representation of limits: the "symbolism of the threshold" (73), as he puts it.

A purported "symbolism of the threshold" in fact skirts what is the main challenge of Fromentin's horizon as the text's organizing motif. Fromentin did, indeed, sense the inadequacy of painting to capture the views that confronted him in the desert, and his textual descriptions are marvelous evocations of the subtle hues of color and light, the formless expanse, and above all, the ineffable line that framed the terrain. If, however, he thus recognized the limits of his painterly art, his text does not so much "push back that limit" as *supplement* it in writing. Anxious, melancholy, and self-doubting, Fromentin was acutely aware of his artistic limitations, and Delacroix's Romantic grandeur was one model against which the artist measured himself. Fromentin's limitations yield more, however, than failure and self-critique; attuned to his own limits, he also questions the limits of painting and representation. Fromentin's journey into the Sahara would thus test his limits in more than one way. His letters home confirm that this project is born out of the failure of painterly representation. "It is violently beautiful," he writes home to his wife from the desert. Speaking to her of the variations of desert light during the day, he says, "The most striking for me is noon, but it defies all expression." To a friend he writes, "None of this can make it into my painting," and confides the plan for the written work that would become *A Summer in the Sahara*. This text would seem, then, to promise a remedy for the deficiencies of his vision, rendering by means of narrative temporal aspects and dimensions of sensory experience lacking in visual representation. But more importantly, I would argue, the literary text supplements and displaces that lack. Thus, rather than provide a more inclusive and totalizing vision, the text exacerbates the tensions that gave rise to its composition; the horizon, as key to this tension, becomes both image of a limit and the limit of the image.

To be fair, however, Barthèlemy's error with respect to such limits is perhaps an inevitable consequence of reading. The *limits of representation* is a terribly ambiguous phrase, combining as it does the objective and subjective genitive "of," and thereby conveying two distinct and not necessarily compatible meanings: the limits *of representation* and the representation *of limits*. If the horizon is an instance of such limits, we may approach it, on the one hand, by means of the techniques, codes, and conventions that render it as a figure of the limit, in the field of painting, for instance. On the other hand, the *limits of representation* suggests the limitations of the medium, the bounds of its competence or authority, the edge of its domain. It is not the same limit in both cases. One falls "within" the domain of representation, while the other, even if constitutive and defining, cannot be contained "inside" that domain. The double genitive speaks, moreover, to a chiastic folding together of these two limits, such that each may be at stake in the same case. Indeed, in any representation worthy of the name of "art," where the representation of the limit is concerned, both are imperatively involved. But what limit can represent the boundary between these two, which are simultaneously opposed, reversible, and indifferent? Such questions lead into the question of the sublime as unlimited limit, as experience of ambiguous rapture, and of the very definition of the beautiful in art.

Early in his Saharan journey, at what he calls an "abominable" campsite, Fromentin expresses an ambiguous rapture in the face of the desert.[76] "Was it fatigue? Was it an effect of the locale? . . . [I]t was a great formless thing, almost colorless, nothingness, like the forgetfulness of God; receding lines, uncertain undulations."[77] Here Fromentin attempts to render something at the limits of representation, and beyond the bounds of his painterly craft: an experience of the sublime. We recognize in Fromentin's descriptions the attraction and repulsion Kant identifies as characteristic of sublime feeling. As Kant defines it, the experience of the sublime confronts the subject with a limitless spectacle beyond all measure and form, and this provokes both wonderment and anxiety. The very failure of the sensuous imagination to represent this experience becomes the means by which reason asserts, over and against the body, its ability to apprehend the unlimited. This claim of reason, however, may be seen as a claim to represent the unrepresentable, and one can pursue this problematic bid of Kant's in the figuration of the sublime as limitless limit. To do so is to question the metaphysical limitations of Kant's framework and the authority it borrows to surpass its own limits in positing a transcendental beyond. This metaphysical dimension is apparent in Fromentin's text, though it makes few references to articles of faith. In Fromentin's desert travelogue, the Kantian ambivalence of a "stupefying and stimulating" experience, as one critic puts it,[78] harmonizes with what are of course the dominant Christian conventions of the desert as site of mortifying ordeal, religious revelation, and mystical rapture. True to the sublime, Fromentin's horizon suggests a limit whose metaphysical infinitude vies with finitude. At the limit, the travelogue stages a drama at the frontier of death. The voyage as journey of death is established, as we have seen, at the outset of the text, lending a paradoxical motion-in-stasis whose figure is that of transgression or trespass. Fromentin's journey thus expresses more than mere ambivalence of desire; its fevered passion tends, rather, beyond the pleasure principle.

To make this claim is to displace the sublime as Kant frames it into a psychoanalytic context. We know from Kant that sublime feeling entails a combination of pain and pleasure, and one can bring Kant's sublime and its play of repulsion and attraction into relation with what Freud calls the "vacillating rhythm" of the death drive. "One group of instincts rushes forward," Freud says, "the other group jerks back to a certain point to make a fresh start and so prolong the journey."[79] Kant's formula is strikingly similar: "This agitation . . . can be compared with a vibration, i.e. with a rapid alternation of repulsion from, and attraction to, one and the same object."[80] Reading Kant psychoanalytically, the struggle between sensory imagination and the claims of reason may be translated into a question of the boundary between the psychical and the somatic explored by Freud in his essay on the death drive. Following Lacan, Slavoj Žižek, among others, has indicated points of contact between these two works. In this optic, Kant's claims for reason in the face of the formless would be the assertion of the illusory autonomy of the ego over its constitutive unboundedness. Lacanian psychoanalysis translates this struggle as occurring between the registers of the Imaginary and the Real; the Symbolic, figured as bar of interdiction, would set the absolute limit of the ego in its illusory strivings; the Real is intimated in formless objects that the Symbolic aims to reclaim from their all-too-threatening otherness. Zižek helpfully indicates how ideological captation is enabled by "sublime objects" that may stand in the place of the desiring subject's determinate lack.[81] Along these lines, one may posit that in spite of its threatening unboundedness, Fromentin's desert horizon functions as a sublime object of colonial ideology. This indeed may be what captivates such readers of Fromentin as Barthèlemy, and which may seduce even such an astute critic as Richard. However, I would argue that Fromentin's horizon does not constitute an object but a limit. This limit, as we will see, may challenge Lacan's model of the sublime as encounter with the paternal function and its bar of interdiction. As such, it offers another way to define what Žižek and his dialectical approach posit as line of transgression and determinate lack.

To bring Kant and Freud together on the sublime is not, moreover, to relate common themes or common emotions, or even to pursue in Kant a supposed "philosophical neurosis," as Lyotard puts it.[82] "The Analytic of the Sublime" and *Beyond the Pleasure Principle* hold similar positions with respect to each author's works. The "Analytic," ostensibly an "appendix" to the *Critique of Judgment*, has had a posthumous influence analogous to Freud's rebarbative text, functioning as an indispensable supplement, as part that eclipses the whole. This supplementarity results from the manner in which each stakes their respective claims at the limits of representation. The challenge posed by Freud's problematic limit is recognized by his best readers.[83] Such accounts of Freud's work, however, often leave in suspense the definition of the unaccountable limit they themselves invoke. To account for this strange limit and its supplementarity is to pursue a logic that does and undoes the text at its limits, bringing forth its constitutive impasses or aporias. The "lack" that Kant himself acknowledges in his work, Derrida points out, may in fact be its *frame*: the unrepresentable limit at which the text is both bounded and unbounded, defining at once its limits and its limitations.[84] As Derrida says, "The work exceeds itself, it surpasses the limits of the concept of itself that it claims to have . . . while presenting itself. But if the event of the work thus exceeds its own borders . . . then it would do so precisely at this locus where it *experiences the aporia*."[85]

Working between psychoanalysis and deconstruction, Neil Hertz takes up this aporetic logic in his examination of the sublime as an experience of "blockage." The key treatises on the sublime and their Romantic inheritors display a striking array of pathological and symptomatic responses to the sublime limit, and its effects on the overmastered subject tend to betray the force of a fearsome superego. Hertz's analysis, however, challenges psychoanalytic models that would see the sublime as the subject's passionate encounter with the symbolic fatality of the law of the father as interdiction. As Hertz shows, a different logic may be discerned in the subject's relation to this extreme limit, for the experience of "blockage," he argues, may be secondary to a more paralyzing "difficulty" with the very figure of the boundary. What Hertz calls "the sublime of conflict and structure" would then be the compensatory reflex by which a problematic boundary is sublimated into a more stable and normative limit, that of an Oedipalized site of conflicted transgression.[86] (In this light, and to invoke Barthes's "dramatic system" again, narrative as the coding of "conflict and structure" might itself be cast as a compensatory order.) At this limit, Hertz says, the subject undergoes "an identification with the blocking agent that is the guarantor of the self's own integrity as an agent." Thus, despite his trouble and suffering, the subject's blockage is a reassuring one, for it replaces a more archaic and difficult limit, opening onto an experience of chaos, with a structuring boundary. As Hertz says, "although the moment of blockage might have been rendered as one of utter self-loss, it was, even before its recuperation as sublime exaltation, a confirmation of the unitary status of the self." For our purpose here of reading the complex enunciation of colonial travelogues, Hertz speaks aptly of the "flux and dispersion of the subject" (58) that precedes the drama of sublime blockage. Hertz uncovers the trace of this earlier state of flux and dispersion in the insistent figuration, in key places of highly reflexive texts and images, of a line of minimal differentiation that marks out "a difference without a distinction" (211). Hertz's analysis thus helps us to see in Fromentin's problematic horizon neither a theme nor symbol "but an engagement with the act and with the medium of painting or writing condensed almost to the point of nonreflective opacity" (219). To read "at the end of the line," in Hertz's phrase, is to examine this characteristic staging in literature and art of an "attenuated subject and divided object" (223). Developing on this model, Hertz emphasizes the politics of rivalry and abjection latent in every bid for identity when the subject encounters such a problematic limit and attempts to pass beyond it.[87]

The politics of this encounter with the limit is dramatically staged by Fromentin when his narrative journey reaches the end of the line. The high point of *A Summer in the Sahara* narrates Fromentin's raptures as he observes the great expanse of the desert from a lofty vantage point on a tower above Laghouat. The scene and its descriptions revolve around the fixed center of Fromentin's static position held during the entire length of a day, like a sentinel dominating the conquered city. Immobile as it is, this fixed position and its tableaus are, however, oriented toward the horizon and beyond, toward the lands further south. The phenomenologist Richard devotes his attention to the admittedly rich descriptions of the changing aspects of the desert light in this scene. I would emphasize instead how the static scene is mobilized and driven forth by an imperious colonial project. Fromentin's descriptions thus evoke a colonial sublime, oscillating between otherness and identification, movement and stasis, dispossessive rapture and appropriative gaze. This colonial sublime is not so much contradictory as oxymoronic, given that the sublime, opening the subject onto sheer otherness, tends to fold itself back into what Levinas has called phenomenology's "imperialism of the same."[88] Fromentin's sublime raptures allow us to take Levinas's formula at its word, and to see how the horizon, as figure of the infinite, may be politically invested by a totalizing grasp of the journeying imagination. J. M. Coetzee nicely articulates this duplicitous quality of the politics of the sublime in colonial literature. "[W]hile it by no means follows that the sublime must be sympathetic to the politics of expansion, conquest, and grandeur, it is certainly true that the politics of expansion has uses for the rhetoric of the sublime."[89]

From his lofty vantage point Fromentin says, "One asks oneself . . . what might be this silent land, cloaked in a dubious tone that seems the color of the void; where no one comes, where no one goes, and that ends in a line so straight and clear against the sky" (*Un Eté*, 126–27). In the "stupor" of midday, with his sketch pad curling in the sun, his paint box crackling like burning wood (125), and his paints mixing with sand and reduced nearly to mortar (129), Fromentin reaches the extreme of his painterly craft; he indeed goes temporarily blind as a result of sunstroke. This ordeal of representation is indexed by the "dubious" color of the "void" and the terminal limit of the horizon in his description. Here as elsewhere the horizon line is described as a clear and distinct graphic line, and as such, it would seem to belong more to the domain of visual representation than to the verbal art of narrative. As visual line, moreover, it fixes and stabilizes a boundless, amorphous, and shifting scene; similarly, in a passage from *Between Sea and Sahara*

Fromentin, troubled by the sight of the sea's sublime confusion of churning waves, says "I'm working and console myself with clear colors, rigid forms, and well-defined lines" (67). The ambiguity of the sublime thus converges in this limit, which is figured at the limit of painterly representation, and yet within the totalizing scope of the imagination. Writing allows Fromentin to raise the stakes of this bid to grasp the sublime limit. Only in writing can Fromentin evoke a line that is not one, and only writing, in its compulsive drive, can render in its very repetitions the singularity of what, Fromentin says, "must be rendered in a single stroke" (43). Thus Fromentin's line escapes writing as well, and only appears there as an obsessive and archaic trace. Fromentin's desert ordeal is an instance, then, of what Derrida calls *archive fever*, which strikingly captures the passion of Fromentin's quest. Of such a fever of representation, Derrida says, "It is to burn with a passion. It is never to rest, interminably, from searching for the archive right where it slips away. It is to run after the archive, even if there's too much of it, right where something in it anarchives itself. It is to have a compulsive, repetitive, and nostalgic desire for the archive, an irrepressible desire to return to the origin, a homesickness, a nostalgia for the return to the most archaic place of absolute commencement."[90]

In this way, the horizon motivates and orients Fromentin's journey and testimony, but its graphic line uncovers a differential trace that cannot be represented. To seek this archaic trace is to try to suture an original division that is itself the origin of the quest. This nostalgia within the very journey of exploration is seen, moreover, when Fromentin compares a lakeside desert scene with a landscape of Normandy; as Anne-Marie Christin points out, the metaphoric impulse of Fromentin's "Normandie Saharienne" lies as much in conveying identity as it does duality.[91] Throughout his descriptions the desert's flatness seems an uncanny version of Fromentin's childhood home in the utterly horizontal countryside of coastal La Rochelle.[92] *Dominique*'s insistence on flatness and the horizon confirms this nostalgic vocation in the desert journey, the home as secret archive of the Saharan travelogue.[93]

This secret affinity of the desert with the flat coastal home lends a different sense to Fromentin's invocation of the conventional metaphor of the desert as a sea, as in his phrases "a limitless ocean" (*Un Été*, 76) and "the immobility of this solid sea" (126). Likewise, this economy of metaphor, the homeward turn of the trope of comparison, illuminates how, in what follows, the adventurous crossing of the horizon entails an appropriative grasp. The passage in question follows on the description of the "straight and clear" line of the horizon as *end* of the field of vision: "Were one not to know it, one senses that it does not end there and that it is, so to speak, but the beginning of the high seas" (127). There ensues an evocation of what lies beyond that horizon, due south. Fromentin invokes the "prestige" of Saharan names known from maps, from the Tuareg to Timbuktu, and his reverie continues southward to conjure up territories far into black Africa and across the equator. Fromentin's imagination thus rehearses the itinerary of Daumas's *Le Grand désert* and its trans-Saharan ambitions, linking up with the territories discovered by Caillié; the limit, once sensed, is transgressed with the borrowed authority of the colonial imagination. And yet Fromentin persists in his desire to overtake the colonizer, to outdistance his conquest, and this desire leads him back at the end of his reverie into the unknown: "And then what? Nothing clear, unknown distances, an uncertainty, an enigma. I have before me the beginning of this enigma." Fromentin's adventure, to borrow Emily Apter's phrase, thus ends up as an "impotent epic."[94] This powerlessness is always prey, as we have seen, to the lure of power and appropriation. A different powerlessness, however, may be seen in Fromentin's dealings with the trace and its figures of boundary, limit, and horizon. To cross such a limit would entail a passive transgression that yields other figures of trespass and hospitality, as we will see.

Thresholds

On approaching the town of Aïn Mahdy, terminus of his Saharan journey, Fromentin says, "I fulfilled in that moment [*en ce moment*] one of my oldest dreams of travel."[95] This dream fulfills the virtually impossible wish to reach an inviolate town, unknown to the French. Aïn Mahdy is evoked as "pious, grave, and haughty," a town whose "ramparts" recall a recent battle fought and won against an aggressor (164). Fromentin's divided loyalties are contradictorily maintained in these proud ramparts, since the town's resistance was not, after all, directed against the French but Abd-el-Kader, whose year-long siege in 1838–39 failed to win the town over to his side in the war against the French. In this way, the dreamlike Aïn Mahdy suspends the contradictions of Fromentin's political reality, yielding an intact and resistant space that may yet be visited in all innocence. The narrative, however, is centered on figures of threshold and horizon, transitions and divisions that mark the embattled distinctions of Fromentin's self-division and troubled conscience. The manuscript elaborates at length on the walls of the town, as well as on the city gate, where a particular detail captures Fromentin's attention. Within the doorway are two vestibules, "as if the stranger had to stop there to wait for permission to enter, and as if hospitality in this town were given only at the threshold" ("Notes et variantes," 1347). The threshold offers a space to stay, if not inhabit; within the very walls of the fortified city, this interstice suspends the alternatives of passing or not passing the threshold. This transitional space, neither inside nor out, responds to Fromentin's ambivalent status as traveler, providing a figure by which to read the affective domain of his journeying conscience. As a space to stay, the vestibule stays all oppositions, and figures the possibility of a space within the dividing line. How might this remarkable space call on us to reconceive the topology of the boundary, and thereby of the intruder, the guest, and the host? Can this space within the line reconfigure the space of transport, of passage and trespass?

Hospitality "at the threshold," as Fromentin so strikingly puts it, seemingly translates the author's difficult status as colonial guest. It is also an impossible figure, an aporia that interrupts the very terms it mobilizes. It figures the boundary as a problem, a space of delimitation *and* indistinction; what happens here, we might say, happens above all *to* the threshold. In spite of himself, Fromentin stumbles on a figure that renders hospitality, or the ethical relation, as a kind of interruption. At the gates of the holy town, that is, Fromentin figures himself as the *arrivant*. As Derrida says, speaking of the *arrivant*, "One does not expect the event of whatever, of whoever comes, arrives and crosses the threshold—the immigrant, the emigrant, or the guest, or the stranger. But if the new *arrivant* who arrives is new, one must expect—without waiting for him or her, without expecting it—that he does not simply cross a given threshold. Such an *arrivant* affects the very experience of the threshold."[96] What Derrida calls the "experience of the threshold" conjoins the notion of experience as passage with the boundary as impasse. What is at stake then is, at the limit, an impossible experience, an experience of the aporia, which is not of the order of a personal encounter, phenomenal intuition, or sensation.[97] The experience of the impasse, Derrida points out, "is neither stopping at it nor overcoming it." It would be, instead, the trace of the event or of the encounter, altering the event "itself" such that it can only occur as other than itself, as iteration. This alteration is what "comes to pass," so to speak, in the event, never presenting itself as such. Fromentin's boundaries are so many inscriptions of this impossible experience, this traveler's paralysis.

Once inside the town of Aïn Mahdy, the visitors are greeted by the Kaïd, whose reception falls noticeably short of hospitality. Moreover, the meal that is delivered to the guests is of the poorest quality and borders on insult. The reason for this cold reception is soon made apparent: whereas the travelers had left Laghouat the previous evening at the end of Ramadan, in Aïn Mahdy the crescent moon had not yet been spotted. The travelers had thus inadvertently imposed themselves on their hosts, intruding in the holy town and transgressing the fast. While explanations are made, the sun, meanwhile, is setting. "At that moment [*à ce moment*]," Fromentin says, "the kaïd stretched his arm toward the horizon; and we saw . . . appear in the pale twilight the long thin circle of the new moon. It stood out as clearly as a silver thread against the perfectly clear sky" (*Un Eté*, 171). Here, Fromentin is witness to a highly charged sacred and symbolic occasion, one that he frames, however, in terms of trespass and intrusion, and which homes in on a minimal moment and the finest of lines, the horizon itself and the "silver thread" of the moon. The message conveyed by this episode is enigmatic: does it serve as a critique of the French contamination of Algerian sacred space? or is it, rather, an instance of Orientalist voyeurism that transforms the foreign culture into an exotic spectacle? This ambiguity is sustained by the travelogue's splitting of Ramadan's end into two places and times; the narrative of transgression thereby claims its alibi, and a conflict of cultures becomes a mere instance of local disagreement. The narrative thus treads a fine line between violence and misunderstanding, a line, moreover, that Fromentin would lend to the sacred moment itself: "The daily fast begins and ends at that very fictive minute when, supposedly, one '*cannot distinguish a black thread from a white thread*'" (145). The critical moments of Fromentin's text are figured by lines and boundaries such as this; like the vestibule of the city ramparts, they draw lines only to call them into question.

One might read Fromentin's equivocations here as rhetorical instances of what Johannes Fabian has called "the politics of time."[98] As spectacle, ritual and phenomenon subject to debate, the end of Ramadan would stand opposed to the rational temporality of the Christian traveler; Fromentin's description of the event thus shares in anthropology's epistemological separation of the time of the Western observer from the time of the Other, or what Fabian names a "denial of coevalness." Beyond the objective distinction between Christian calendar and Muslim hegira, Fromentin's temporal drama conveys the time of the Other as a picturesque atavism, reinforcing claims to colonial superiority in the most abstract of terms, as temporal and developmental advance. His travelogue makes clear throughout, moreover, that Fromentin indulges in the Orientalist notion of the Algerian as a living remnant of the biblical past. The stakes of a politics of time during Fromentin's stay are dramatic, particularly in Laghouat and Aïn Mahdy: by a popular Saharan belief, the messiah or mahdy was expected to come and deliver the Algerians from the French in the year 1854, one year after Fromentin's visit.[99] Perhaps this politics of time is what haunted Fromentin years later when, after having abandoned poetry for more than thirty years, he penned "La Fin du Ramadan," a poem that reflects the scene of Aïn Mahdy, but in which the crescent moon notably fails to appear.[100]

Though Fromentin confirms an Orientalist denial of coevalness in this episode at Aïn Mahdy, his text amply expresses a concern about intrusion and sacrilege. A second alibi, however, functions with respect to the traveler's sacrilege. The great religious leader of Aïn Mahdy, Tedjini, had died only four months earlier, and the prestige of the town in Fromentin's eyes is tied to the "heroism," "grandeur," and "saintliness" of this man (*Un Eté*, 169). In contrast, the kaïd, Fromentin says, "suitably represents civil authority in this municipality now become bourgeois and pious" (170). Thus, Fromentin suggests that Ramadan has been already desacralized before his own arrival in the town. Such a displacement and projection of blame is symptomatic of the traveler's disavowed contamination of the sites he visits. In his colonial nostalgia, Fromentin thus reinforces the familiar temporal predicament of the Orientalist traveler as examined, for instance, by Ali Behdad, whose journey makes "the melancholic discovery of its impossibility."[101] However, belatedness in Fromentin's case is not simply, as Behdad flatly puts it, "an anxiety of coming after what had come before" (13), but displays a more vexing problem with time. As Coetzee says in *Waiting for the Barbarians*, "We have crossed the limits of the Empire. It is not a moment to take lightly."[102] Likewise, it is the moment "itself" that obsesses Fromentin; a moment that marks the limit of both empire and the assimilating grasp.

As a privileged "moment" in Fromentin's narrative, the sighting of the new moon echoes the moment of arrival, the dream fulfilled. One might indeed read the "en ce moment" of arrival and the "à ce moment" of the sacred ritual as parallel but asymmetrical versions of the passing moment and the means to inhabit them. To take these prepositional phrases at their word is to bring out the anxious figures that mark the space and time of encounter, of entry and residence for Fromentin. Here, "in" and "at" convey a different temporal impossibility than that of Behdad: an impossible present, jealously laid claim to but escaping that same claim. Fromentin, as we have seen, often marks significant moments with a narrative pause, as he had done in first arriving in Laghouat: "This time, I arrived," he says, "as I had hoped, at the hour without shadow; it was just past noon." (*Un Eté*, 76). The *arrival* at this sublime destination, taking place once and for all, is marked by a characteristic slowness: "waiting" and "stopping" are emphasized in the static tableau that Fromentin views to "seize hold of it forever." Even Fromentin's claim to exact duplication bears the trace of the problematic line and limit that confounds his journey: "Here, straightforwardly and copied line for line, is what I saw." But the moment of arrival cannot fail to escape Fromentin. "This time" ("Cette fois") is already a moment in a series of initial arrivals, and the "un peu plus de midi" indicates a slight fall from the zenith of noon: the "shadow" of time, once denied, reasserts itself in this minimal difference.

Fromentin's power of memory is legendary.[103] This power is what enabled him to paint from memory and to narrate such scenes as this, not, as his story would have it, the very evening after, but upon his return to France. "To seize hold of" the scene ("m'en emparer de") expresses this power's colonizing grasp of the conquered town of Laghouat which, Fromentin later says, "truly smells of death" (*Un Eté*, 181). His return from Aïn Mahdy provokes this regretful admission, and it is here that Assia Djebar greets the colonial *arrivant*. But as we have seen, the first moment of arrival already bared the traces of an inherent belatedness; Fromentin's rapture is a grasping powerless to capture the moment of presence. The "anti-conquest," to borrow Mary Louise Pratt's expression, is in Fromentin's case not so much a false claim to innocence as an undoing of the author's power of expression in the articulation of its claim to power.[104] Fromentin thus testifies, but in the margins of his narrative, to what Djebar calls "the conquest of the Unconquerable," joining ranks with a host of invaders whose own language betrays their colonizing claims: "invaders who imagine they are taking the Impregnable City, but who wander in the undergrowth of their own disquiet."[105]

Fromentin's powerlessness to fix the present scene, "line for line," as he says, is expressed in the very insistence on its faithfulness: "I reproduce, without changing anything, what has imprinted itself as a picture within my mind" (*Un Eté*, 76). The power of memory is thus delegated to what prints *itself*. Such a claim to presence is the characteristic bid of archive fever: the selfsame is posited at once as a singular *impression* and as the latent trace of its repeated iterations. In this way, Fromentin's pictorial imagination seems blind to the contradiction that binds duplication to singularity. Moreover, this contradiction is more precisely aporetic, and thus paralyzing, given that it binds identity to alterity in a single stroke, that of the differential trace. Fromentin's insistence on what prints *itself* in his mind answers Derrida's speculation on this trace of memory: "What if there were a *memory of the present* and that far from fitting the present to itself, it divided the instant? What if it inscribed or revealed difference in the very presence of the present, and thus, by the same token, the possibility of being repeated in representation?"[106] The memory of such an elusive present can only be narrated, and thereby attenuated, in tales of nostalgia, quests for origins, or sins of illegitimate conquest. But such "dramatic structures," in Barthes's expression ("Fromentin: *Dominique*," 101), pass too quickly over what resists the march of narrative and the experience of the journey: the trace of an impossible present that both gives and takes the traveler's every impression.

We must see, then, in Fromentin's slow arrival the latent *precipitation* of the instant, the *movement* within the *moment*. "This acceleration," Derrida says, "is incommensurable, and thus infinite and null at the same time; it touches the sublime" (*Mémoires*, 62). What Derrida calls "the discontinuity of this rhythm" sheds light on the "vibration" of Kant's sublime and the "vacillating rhythm" of Freud's death drive addressed above. Each converges in the sublime as limit, touched but not surpassed. Jean-Luc Nancy's "syncopation" of sublime experience echoes Derrida's formulation of the sublime as a touching of the limit. Glossing Kant, Nancy says, "This is, in fact, the sense of the word *sublimitas*: what stays just below the limit, what touches the limit. . . . Sublime imagination touches the limit, and this touch lets it feel 'its own powerlessness.'"[107] In the experience of the sublime as in Kant's own text, such a feeling of powerlessness is all too readily recuperated in a compensatory recoil of the subject from its limit or in a metaphysical appeal to an absolute beyond the extreme limit. Thus, in Nancy as in Derrida there is an emphasis on touching the limit without surpassing it, and on sensing without comprehending what defies knowledge. To touch the limit would require, then, a questioning of the very representation of the limit to the extent that the limit is itself confined to knowable form. Likewise, as Nancy points out, the motion that would claim to attain or surpass this limit calls for deconstruction: "The sublime will always invoke . . . an aesthetics of movement as opposed to an aesthetics of the static or the state. But this movement is neither an animation nor an agitation, as opposed to immobility.

... It is perhaps not a movement in any of the available senses of this word" (36). I have, for my part, been calling this paradoxical movement and the critical reading it requires *paralysis*.

If, finally, Fromentin's travel narrative is a nonvoyage, it is because the landscape itself, the vast space of the Sahara, becomes the nonsite of an imperceptible limit. "There is no agreement on the etymology of the words Tell and Sahara," Fromentin says. "General Daumas . . . suggests an etymology that I like because of its Arab origin, and which is good enough for me. . . . Sahara would derive from *Sehaur*, a difficult moment to grasp, that precedes the break of day and during which one can still, in the time of fasting, eat, drink, and smoke" (*Un Eté*, 34). The Sahara is thus compressed into a "difficult moment to grasp," that corresponds in temporal terms to what Fromentin calls the horizon's "ligne insaisissable" (65). In its intangibility, this line may seem to fall short of Nancy's sublime touch. But here as elsewhere, Fromentin strives and necessarily fails to render what touched him at the limit of his colonial journey. This *striving*, as Nancy indicates, is not so much that of a subject and his exertions as it is of the limit itself; its *tendency* is not toward any project, program, or object. "What tends, and what tends here toward or in the extreme, is the limit," Nancy says ("Sublime Offering," 45). Fromentin himself renders the horizon's limit both in terms of a *tending toward* a limit and a limit itself in *tension*. Found at the very opening and in the concluding lines of the text, these passages and their tension thus span the entire Saharan journey: "my eyes scanned the horizon. Whatever imperceptible threads that held my heart grew for a moment tighter [*se tendirent un moment plus fort*] than I would have thought" (*Un Eté*, 21). Near the last page of the journey, Fromentin evokes a similar moment of tension: "the moment we crossed back over the pass . . . was revealed stretched out before us [*tendue devant nous*] the mysterious line of the desert" (181). Both temporal and spatial figure, this line would be the key to Fromentin's narrative, the minimal symbol of his journey in space and time. But it is, more importantly, a figure that tends toward the unfigurable, conflating in sheer contradiction the merest trace of a line with absolute space: "a final ashen line," Fromentin says, "but so fine that it must be rendered in a single stroke, determines the real depth of the landscape, and sometimes measures enormous distances" (42–43).

Haunting Returns

Despite his indictment of the Algerian travelogue in *Bel-Ami*, Maupassant made his own journey to colonial Algeria. Both *Au soleil* and *La Vie errante* convey the contradictory posture of their author in his portrayal of the politics of colonization. While he is scathing in his critique of what he calls the French "expropriation" of the native, Maupassant's portrait of the native Algerian is frankly racist: "Arab means thief, without exception [*Qui dit Arabe dit voleur, sans exception*]."[108] Bent on escape from the routines of life and what he saw as the vulgarity of contemporary Paris, Maupassant finds Algeria itself transfigured by French rule and petty colonial culture; at the same time, however, he cannot fully recognize the value of the culture that is being displaced. In its frustration and self-thwarting, Maupassant's journey is an instance of what Marc Augé calls the "impossible journey" of the tourist.[109] Colonization makes this touristic predicament a more pointedly political impossibility, one that inhibits the traveler in his innermost drives and ambitions, linked as they are to exploitative fictions and imperial dreams. In a revealing phrase, Maupassant thus speaks of feeling himself "drawn to Africa by an imperious need [*un impérieux besoin*]" (*Au soleil*, 5). Once in Algeria, his desire follows the colonial drive southward into the desert and beyond, a drive Maupassant casts not as invasive but as invading him. "Once you have set foot on this African land," he says, "a singular need overcomes you [*vous envahit*] to go still further, southwards" (22). Is it Fromentin's ambiguous raptures that speak through Maupassant? "The South! The desert, the nomads, unexplored lands and then the Negroes, a whole new world, like the beginning of a universe! The South! How powerful that becomes on the frontier of the Sahara" (63).

Maupassant had no doubt read his Fromentin, though he does not mention him in his travelogues. An uncanny influence seems to have laid hold of Maupassant, however. In "The Horla," his great supernatural story of paranoia and haunting, Maupassant seems to have patterned his protagonist's decent into sickness and terror on an Algerian episode of Fromentin. When writing his disturbing tale, Maupassant was beginning his personal decline into sickness and dementia; within a few years he would attempt suicide and later die. At the beginning of his story, Maupassant's character, feeling unwell, takes a stroll that only confirms his worsening state: "Where do they come from, these mysterious influences which turn our happiness into gloom and our self-assurance into distress? It is as if the air, the invisible air, were full of unfathomable powers, whose mysterious proximity affects us."[110] These lines echo those of Fromentin: "Are you aware, my friend, of the incalculable effects that result when the barometer goes up or down? Have you ever noticed to what extent this little instrument rules us?"[111] Fromentin, like Maupassant's character, is taking a stroll, "as if a recuperating patient," Fromentin says (68), and both scenes share a springtime setting by the water; each text also has the format of a diary. Fromentin's text takes a curious turn toward the supernatural: "Perhaps all of us while alive live dependent on certain occult forces whose actions we are subjected to without our either acknowledging them or being able to pin them down. Perhaps buried in the destiny of us all are miserable little secrets that we don't talk about out of fear of confessing our enslavement, thereby humiliating in the presence of mere matter a human soul pretending to be free" (69). These occult themes of subjection, "imprisonment" at home and being "face-to-face with my shadow," as Fromentin says, take the form, in Maupassant, of the onset of a delirium of possession by an alien being: "Everything about us, everything we see without looking at it, everything we brush past without knowing it, everything we touch without feeling it, everything we meet without noticing it, has swift, surprising and inexplicable effects on us, on our senses, and through them on our ideas, on our very hearts" ("The Horla," 314). As Maupassant's story develops, the narrator becomes convinced of the occult presence of the Horla, an invisible being that heralds the total subjection of man. The tale of supernatural possession thus translates Fromentin's colonial scene as one of alien invasion, and in an uncanny reversal, the colonial guest is transposed into the host of that threatening alien. The risk—and opportunity—of such a substitutability of guest and host, as Mireille Rosello argues, is the haunting colonial legacy of the politics of contemporary hospitality, which "constantly tests the host's and the guest's thresholds of fear, and their willingness to live with that fear, and with their malaise."[112]

Despite its outlandish themes, then, Maupassant's tale of possession, domination, and uncanny hospitality is an apt inheritor of Fromentin's influence. In its delusions, phantasms, and illusory bids for power, French colonial discourse, betrayed even in Fromentin's best readers, would be prey to the seductions and uncanny influence of Fromentin's subtle portrayal of colonial power: masochism and defeat compensated for by an unavowed mastery; a sublime and disorienting experience that falls back into the merely picturesque; and a misrecognized Other who would, in the end, prove an underestimated challenge to French rule in Algeria. And yet, as I have shown, a different thread runs through Fromentin's travelogues. "The Horla" was written shortly before Maupassant succumbed to syphilitic paresis, or general paralysis.[113] It may be this impending fate that drew Maupassant to Fromentin's text and to the particular episode he seems to have borrowed, for it is preceded by Fromentin's aesthetic credo: "Of all the attributes that go with grandeur the most beautiful as far as I'm concerned is immobility" (*Between Sea*, 67). In falling under his influence, Maupassant would seem to have recognized, but only as threat and horror, the lure of Fromentin's paralysis.

Speaking of Delacroix's *Women of Algiers*, Assia Djebar states that "what floats between these Algerian women and ourselves . . . is the forbidden."[114] Such taboos are, of course, the stock-in-trade of Orientalist exoticism. More even than Delacroix, Fromentin conveys the force of this forbidding dividing line in his Orientalist vision. But in making the transition from painting to prose, Fromentin turns his vision over to what cannot present itself as image and ultimately escapes figuration. Literature provides Fromentin the means to explore this breakdown in representation and to unsettle the basic coordinates of the traveler's experience. A newcomer to literature, Fromentin discovers a world that is both made and unmade in prose, contesting his visions and bringing the Oriental journey to a halt.

3. Slow Progress
Jean Paulhan and Madagascar

Master of the word you will speak,
Slave of the word you have spoken. —Paulhan

The Colonial Récit

Jean Paulhan was a casualty of the turbulent year of 1968. When Maurice Blanchot, in a eulogy to the longtime director of the *Nouvelle Revue Française*, said that in May '68 "Paulhan was beginning to leave us," he linked his passing to the end of an era.[1] If, in one sense, Blanchot's statement seemed to imply that Paulhan had been superseded by the generation of '68, in another, however, he bequeathed Paulhan's ghost to the intellectual afterlife of revolution. During the intervening years, Paulhan's work has suffered neglect only to experience a certain revival of late, reappearing in connection with various areas of renewed critical interest, including the Collège de Sociologie, early ethnography, and the politics of collaboration.[2] The ongoing publication of Paulhan's enormous correspondence and the recent appearance of previously unpublished autobiographical texts and early writings shed new light on this figure whose name is invariably associated with mystery. Paulhan's famed obscurity is matched only by the extraordinary influence he exerted over the literary scene of his day as director of the NRF.[3] His highly public post and often spectacular polemics never diminished his discretion and personal reserve. Indeed, by means of public exposure Paulhan deployed a characteristic self-effacement, guile, and ambiguity, often under cover of a pseudonym. As Denis Hollier has pointed out, Paulhan was seen to possess an "enigmatic authority," an authority, one might add, that was enigmatic above all to Paulhan himself.[4] The crux of Paulhan's work lies in this authority that escapes him, and his writings encode the ambiguous and reversible terms of his defining *subjection*. What follows is an exploration into this vexed authority in the light of Paulhan's colonial initiation.

In 1921 Paulhan published an unsettling short story, the account of a French military convoy in colonial Madagascar escorting a large group of Senegalese women across the country.[5] These women are to join up with a regiment of soldiers, themselves displaced from colonial French Senegal and enlisted in the pacification of Madagascar. The tale is complicated by internal and external strife: the three officers are uneasy with each other, while their subjects are unruly and the natives in revolt. A sense of malaise permeates the story as its two unreliable narrators grapple with a mysterious event they cannot fully account for. At the center of the text is the official log of the sergeant Aytré, an innocuous journal that betrays a glaring omission in its report. As Aytré, prey to some unnamed disturbance, "falls out of the habit" of his duties, he begins to venture impertinent remarks in the journal, going so far as to question colonial authority and the grounds of his knowledge of the natives. The log is framed by the narrative of Aytré's superior officer, who upon reading it comes to recognize his own implication in Aytré's guilt.

Paulhan's story was inspired by his stay of nearly three years in Madagascar, where, recruited by the governor-general Augagneur, he took the post of professor in 1908 at the newly established Collège européen in Tananarive. This turn of affairs indicates what colonial opportunity could represent at the time for a young man in Paulhan's position. Having recently failed his *agrégation*, Paulhan found his career ambitions in France limited. Madagascar also offered a chance for escape from his future wife, for whom his affections were undecided: "I would have fled to the ends of the earth," Paulhan says of his motives at this time.[6] Once installed in Tananarive, Paulhan promptly took up with a native mistress. Like the protagonist of his short story, Paulhan himself appears to have fallen out of the habit of his duties, devoting less time to his teaching responsibilities in order to pursue research into Malagasy proverbs, or *hain-teny*. This research, inspired by his studies in Paris with Emile Durkheim and Lucien Lévy-Bruhl, would leave its mark on all of his subsequent writings on language and rhetoric from his post at the *Nouvelle Revue Française*.

Madagascar holds a defining place, then, in the work of Paulhan, and it was an initiation into errors and misunderstandings that find early expression in his colonial tale. The will to knowledge of Paulhan's ethnographic studies in Madagascar is ironically echoed by the voice of Aytré's adjutant: "There are days when I would like to be a scholar: and I already know things about Malagasy customs, and their language, that no-one would imagine. It's just these revolts that I can't explain."[7] The adjutant realizes that Aytré mirrors his own presumption of knowledge: "He too wanted to be a scholar" (94). Knowledge on the part of each is vitiated by native resistance and by the officers' mission, which cannot help but evoke the forced transport of African slaves. In a particularly striking way, the text recalls Christopher Miller's definition of Africanist discourse, in which *theory* evokes a different *théorie*: a procession or convoy—as of slaves—or, as the *Petit Robert* puts it, "théories de femmes."[8] "We have women of three different races: Yoloffs, Bambaras, and Toucouleurs," Aytré notes. "They argue frequently . . . The threat of a few blows with the rope is enough to make them get back in line" ("Aytré," 88). Bending to the codes of colonial authority, Aytré's representations are inseparable from the subjugation of others. Aytré's log suggestively ends, however, with a reversal of the ethnographic gaze: "What idea do they have of us?" (93).

If "Aytré" resembles a detective story, it belongs to that modern variant whose detective, unseated from his privileged position, discovers himself implicated in the crime he seeks to solve. We will see later to what extent Paulhan's quest for what he calls the "secret" of proverbs is similarly marked by self-incrimination and the signs of culpability. Indeed, Paulhan's investigation into the duplicity and "failings" of language as emblematized by the *hain-teny* seems nothing so much as an attempt to corner the source of his own personal failings. This is the aim of the adjutant in "Aytré," who is troubled by the elusive signs of his guilt. On the brink of sleep, he attempts to pin down such an elusive sign. "This mark [*tache*] or this trace, although I've never really understood it, preoccupies me because of how carefully I am avoiding it" (77). Emerging from his dreams, he takes stock of his obsessive thoughts: "Escaping oneself is a singular thing. Yes, that's the idea that I was just now trying to avoid [*que je tâchais d'éviter*], and yet which was tempting me" (78). In this dizzying scenario, avoidance exerts an attraction, while attraction only draws the subject away from himself. This game of displacement points to a guilty symptom, plainly manifest when the adjutant points out a red stain ("une tache rouge") on the rice at dinner (30). Here, as in the previous scene, the word *tache* is followed by its homonym, *tâche* (effort); a stain, we might say, accompanies every effort, and every effort a stain. The incriminating efforts of the adjutant thus recall the euphemism given by General Galliéni to the technique of military pacification employed in Madagascar—*la tache d'huile*—although Paulhan's tale belies this peaceful conquest.

Blanchot is one of the few critics to have broached Paulhan's anomalous tale, curiously inquiring of "Aytré," "Where does literature begin?"[9] Blanchot's question is provoked by the obscurity of Paulhan's story, whose two voices testify to a breakdown of comprehension and a failure to communicate. By foregrounding such failures, "Aytré" points Blanchot to literature's emergence from the ruin of everyday discourse and its unquestioned habits. Literature, Blanchot says, begins by wandering away from "the security of ordinary language" to express a primary absence at the source of expression (70). The mystery at hand calls for no detective, it answers to a different law; closer to Mallarmé's "Mystery in Letters" it remains unavowable. Blanchot thus locates the source of the text in an originary *silence*.

Blanchot's reading of "Aytré" is apt, in turn, to provoke in the reader a certain suspicion or malaise. It is not for lack of intrigue that Blanchot elides the story told, a story whose mysterious crux centers on a violent crime. For in the midst of the story's troubled circumstances there occurs the murder of a colonial French woman hastily passed over by the account. Blanchot passes over it just as quickly. "From this little story," Blanchot says, "it does not follow that literature must necessarily begin with crime" ("Paradox of Aytré," 69). Blanchot's reading thus moves from the specifics of Paulhan's tale to a more general law of literature. As a result, the silence Blanchot invokes in his reading seems oddly complicit with that of the characters, as if confirming their alibis and discounting the story's incriminating context.[10] "The writer does not always begin with the horror of a crime that makes him feel his precariousness in the world, but he can hardly think of beginning other than by a certain inability to speak and write, by a loss of words, by the very absence of the means of which he has an over-abundance. Thus it is indispensable for him to feel at first that he has *nothing* to say" (68).

Silence, in Blanchot's account, precedes any incrimination, any culpability, testifying instead to an absolute negativity that threatens the undoing of the speaking subject. The death at the center of "Aytré," for Blanchot, is thus not of the order of an identifiable event, and is not to be found in the story as theme, drama or experience. Rather, this death is the work of a "fundamental dispossession" to which characters, plot, and action are subordinated ("Paradox of Aytré," 70). With the story's undoing, its events lose their place; another space opens up, harboring the mysterious origin of the work. "Aytré," in other words, belongs to that category of writing Blanchot calls *récits*: stories that step back from their ostensible events to recount only the event of the story's emergence. The idea of the *récit* in the work of Blanchot bears in part on the reflexive questioning of narrative self-assurance prevalent in Paulhan and endemic to modern literature. And yet, reflexivity in the *récit* turns on a fundamental paradox; rather than pointing to itself in a gesture of self-reflection, the *récit* turns back on an inscrutable origin.[11] All literature, Blanchot claims, bears testimony to the movement of the *récit*, which, foreign to the space and time of narrative, approaches the negation and absence from which the tale derives. The *récit*, even as it opens up the space of literature, is consequently the yawning of an insuperable void.

In his reading of "Aytré," Blanchot is drawn to those moments, characteristic of Paulhan, in which narrative breaks down to dwell on linguistic uncertainty and troubled memory. Accordingly, adventure and drama retreat from the scene in "Aytré," upstaged by affairs of communication, by obscure dreams and secret desires. And yet nothing would seem to prepare the reader for the dismissal of the crime Blanchot performs in his essay. This dismissal is the more intriguing given that the story of "Aytré," as Blanchot of course knew, draws substantially on Paulhan's personal experience in Madagascar. Blanchot would therefore remove an entire realm of lived experience from the story, disqualifying its biographical pretexts. Similarly, in another essay on Paulhan Blanchot evokes Lacan's reading of Poe's detective story "The Purloined Letter" to make a cautionary note: the notorious secrecy and obscurity that Paulhan cultivated throughout his career should not lead one to search for a missing object, Blanchot suggests, in the mistaken attempt to correct a fundamental absence or blind spot. At stake in the secret workings of language and of the *récit* is an *impersonal* agency, more originary and more defining than the biographical subject. To personify this agency would be to lend the text "a false appearance of being documents *à clé*," and to misrecognize that what speaks through any given subject is the neutral voice of language itself.[12] The mystery of the text, for Blanchot, would lie in this impersonal origin and not in any identifiable voice. While the text's origin is central and fundamentally determining, it is, however, only a fascinating lure that resists approach. Reading, for Blanchot, thus responds to the imperious demand of the text to solve an unsolvable mystery. In a well-known passage from *The Space of Literature*,

Blanchot defines the task of the reader as a paradoxical quest for what ultimately eludes contact: "The central point of the work is the work as origin, the point which cannot be reached, yet the only one which is worth reaching."[13]

Paul de Man observed that the criticism of Blanchot differs essentially from interpretation and exegesis, and that his readings, far from elucidating the mysteries they invoke, aim to "suspend the very act of comprehension."[14] Criticism for Blanchot is thus tied to a questioning that outlasts every answer; indeed, it is the simplest of questions to which Blanchot's work obsessively returns.[15] In this, Blanchot's question regarding literature's beginnings derives from Heidegger, for whom the origin and the question provide thought's fundamental coordinates. But it is equally the work of Paulhan that serves to inspire Blanchot's simple questions. In one of his stories, Paulhan's narrator says, "I would find out about the things that people think are complicated, but I know it's the simplest things which I miss, I don't want to cheat. Truly the simplest . . ."[16] Blanchot cites this passage in "The Ease of Dying" to assert that Paulhan's work as a whole testifies to a quest for *unity* and *simplicity*, provided, however, that those terms convey not a consoling metaphysics of presence, identity, and self-evidence but instead the "irreducible duplicity of the One" (135). Blanchot, then, recognizes in Paulhan a deconstructive effort to think identity and unity outside an oppositional and dialectical framework; at stake in the duplicitous One is "a supplementary mark of unity," a difference that, never present as such, betrays the One as "always already divided" (137). If the *récit* is a quest for the secret of this original difference, the very movement of the quest is beset by what Blanchot calls "the possibility of an impossible movement": toward an origin that is not *one*, and the passage across a division that cannot be fully grasped (127).

How, we might ask, can reading be possible for Blanchot, given that attempts at interpretation are ultimately vain, and that the simplest questions, for him as for Paulhan, remain unanswered?

The possibility of reading is tied to the question Blanchot raises in one of his first literary essays, entitled "Comment la littérature est-elle possible?"[17] In this essay, Blanchot follows the argument of Paulhan's *The Flowers of Tarbes* (*Les Fleurs de Tarbes*), which characterizes literary tradition as divided by two mutually defeating programs: one bent on the exclusion of rhetoric, the other committed to its defense.[18] Paulhan shows how literary claims for rhetoric, far from espousing form and artifice, are motivated instead by a desire for unmediated communication, while the desire for such direct communication in the other camp leads ultimately to rhetoric. In a relentless and dizzying series of chiastic reversals, Paulhan exposes the mutual misunderstanding that mars the dialogue of "Terrorist" and "Rhetorician," one that every speaking subject, himself embodying both roles, seems condemned to repeat. At the heart of this paradoxical debate is a struggle that inheres in the very notion of the sign, whose singular yet duplicitous nature reconciles radically opposed elements: form and content, sign and meaning, signifier and signified. Literary practice and criticism devolve from an inevitably failed attempt to account for the mysterious agency by which the sign's duality is overcome. This fundamental or original articulation, while necessary and simple, remains unaccountable and inconceivable to the subject of language. Following Paulhan, Blanchot thus sees language as "haunted by its own impossibility."[19] Given this paradox, the question of the possibility of literature remains an open one, tied as it is to an ineradicable impossibility.[20] One telling result of this predicament, which Paulhan never tires of demonstrating, is that readers and writers invariably misread one another.

Blanchot's work shows an abiding fascination with Paulhan's formulations of what we might call the constitutive impasses of expression. Beneath Blanchot's question concerning literature's possibility is an incredulity that resists any answer. For if, following Paulhan, any sign is not only prone to misunderstanding but also governed by a systematic failing, how can one avoid falling out of the habit of language, like Aytré? How can one not be drawn up short and paralyzed by the obstacles set in one's path by language? Blanchot's response to Paulhan's deadlock of Terrorist and Rhetorician is not a surmounting of the opposition but a radicalizing of that distinction to the point of "indifference." At stake, then, in the "mystery" of the "passage" from sign to sense is a more originary indistinction that, Blanchot says, escapes the view of Paulhan himself. Challenging Paulhan's analysis, Blanchot thus asks "if, instead of object, it were a matter of components that one isolates momentarily for the purposes of analytic exposition, but that do not exist outside of this analysis and that are thus justified in making themselves distinct only within the confines of analysis? Might the scandal actually not come from analysis itself?"[21] Blanchot's insistence on "analysis" and "analytic exposition" shows that he is taking to task a method that would *analyze*—in the literal sense of "undoing" or "loosening"— what is bound together and indistinct. This early essay thus already bears the marks of Blanchot's later writings on the originary and unlocatable "trace." The alternative to Paulhan's *analysis*, such as Blanchot critiques it here, is certainly not the dialectical *synthesis* of contraries; it is, instead, a more stubborn and confounding obstacle to thought, calling forth another mode of approach, which Derrida, speaking of Blanchot, later terms "paralysis."[22] Paralysis, in this sense, is not only a "loosening" but a binding together, according to the stricture of a double bind that connects, as Blanchot says, "two irreconcilable and inseparable halves" (*Work of Fire*, 50). To be fair, and despite Blanchot's critique, Paulhan offers his own versions of this paralyzing double bind, and it is this implicit message that Blanchot draws out of his texts. As Paulhan says, *"An author's thoughts are a reader's words, and an author's words are a reader's thoughts* [Pensée d'auteur, mots de lecteur; mots d'auteur, pensée de lecteur]."[23] Tellingly, the formula is chiastic: not a confrontation of opposites but their problematic interweaving and reversal. The "passage" that stumps Paulhan here as elsewhere may entail a blind act of faith, but it traces the chiastic truth of an unaccountable interweaving: in a characteristic moment of reflexive perplexity, Paulhan thus speaks of "pretending that the passage I spoke of doesn't exist at all, but that everything follows and is woven together into one."[24]

It is worth noting in this light that all of Paulhan's stories stage on a larger scale a certain narrative paralysis: from "Aytré," whose narrator lies in bed through the course of the story, to the invalid of "The Severe Recovery" ("La Guérison sévère"), to the soldiers of "The Diligent Warrior," ("Le Guerrier appliqué"), frozen in place on the front lines in World War I, "on the threshold of war."[25] Each story thus lays claim to the slow progress recounted in "Progress in Love on the Slow Side," whose narrator's stalled driving lessons are emblematic: "I had the impression . . . that I never managed to get past the point that I reached in the first place. I would have been only too happy if I had been able to stay there" (30). "What's more," the narrator says, "I'm not quick and I need adventures to happen to me more slowly than they do to others" (33). This stubbornness and slow progress is a feature not only of Paulhan's characters but the author as well: "You've hardly begun and you're already balking," Paulhan complains of himself in his journal.[26] Paulhan's translator has similarly noted that on a stylistic level "the language of the *récit* never seems to get going or to flow."[27] This aspect of Paulhan's work is crucial to Blanchot, who, in an essay that returns once again to the problems raised by *The Flowers of Tarbes*, acknowledges "the impossibility . . . of going beyond them."[28] And yet, those very obstacles that seem apparently intractable are effortlessly overcome in speaking any given word. Paradoxically, what is most paralyzing in such transports is the very *facility* of the passage that defies all account. As Ann Smock puts it, all Paulhan's *récits* "bring about an unlikely passage, a quasi-magical transition or transport."[29] Smock's formula is cautiously understated, and rightly so; the "unlikely passage" is not only surprising but improbable, indeed impossible. Both Paulhan and Blanchot seem as if transfixed by this linguistic factor that seemingly goes without saying. For Paulhan, the name of this agency is the "commonplace," that blind tribute paid in language to ensure the hardy passage from sign to sense and from self to other. Blanchot, reading Paulhan in the light of Kojève and Heidegger, sees the impersonality of the commonplace as the cipher of death, a negativity assumed by the subject at the cost of his dispossession. Blanchot thus casts the question of the obstacle in terms of an impossible transgression, effortlessly undergone: the *saving grace* of death that is the basis of Blanchot's reading of Paulhan in "The Ease of Dying," and which is developed more at length in *The Step Not Beyond*.[30]

Paulhan thus raises some of the fundamental questions of Blanchot's writing. Indeed, Blanchot's question regarding literature's beginnings could be seen as indicative of the originary and defining place Paulhan's oeuvre holds in his own work. In addition to the four essays mentioned above, it is noteworthy that Paulhan appears alongside the name of Hegel in one of Blanchot's most significant essays, "Literature and the Right to Death."[31] One is tempted, moreover, to see in Blanchot an identification with the person of Paulhan, an identification overdetermined by their overlapping biographies and troubled politics. To examine this shared biography is to resist the impersonality Blanchot imposes on his work, which he would extend to that of Paulhan. Writing on the question of impersonality in Blanchot, Paul de Man offers the same biographical caution as Blanchot: "One is never so far removed from the center as when one assumes to have recaptured the origin of the self in an empirical experience that is taken to be the cause."[32] In recent years, both Blanchot and de Man have come under scrutiny for the suspicion that such gestures toward impersonal agency are allied to a disavowal of their personal histories, specifically, in both cases, relating to reactionary and anti-Semitic positions taken in the pre–World War II period.[33] In the wake of this controversy, Blanchot recently published a text narrating his personal brush with death during the war. *The Instant of My Death* (*L'Instant de ma mort*) is unique in Blanchot's work for speaking of an apparently "empirical experience" that retrospectively informs the entirety of his writing, particularly those *récits* and essays addressing the question of death.[34] And yet, the subject of Blanchot's text is rendered in the third person; between the narrator and the person he remembers opens up the impersonal space of the *récit*. "It is not a question of a personal experience," Blanchot remarks elsewhere of the experience of death in Paulhan.[35] Such would be the claim Blanchot maintains as he zeroes in on this central experience of his life. It is striking that the very brief text of *The Instant of My Death*, which mentions Hegel once again, closes with the name of Paulhan. The presence of Paulhan at the conclusion of Blanchot's testament is both revealing and obscure. Paulhan's name is connected in this story to a failed search for a text lost in the course of the war, and is a seeming emblem for a failure to remember in the throes of historical drama. This gesture thus recalls Blanchot's characterization of Paulhan in "The Ease of Dying" as a writer who was given to publish in wartime, thereby leaving his works "anonymous" and "in the margins of time" (123). The experience of war and death, far from inspiring history and autobiography, only serve to occlude the writer and his tale. In this way, I would argue, the *récit*'s narrative failure points to nothing so much as the repercussions of *trauma*.

The convergence of trauma and the *récit* is suggestively voiced in Paulhan's "Progress in Love on the Slow Side" as the narrator struggles to find words to express untold pleasures: "As happens to the man who is wounded, and repeats to himself at first, to give himself courage: 'You don't feel anything, it is nothing.' Thus he lies in order to make himself go on."[36] *Going on*, here, is the product of a "lie," a denial, perhaps a repression, while the *récit* aims backward at the paralyzing source of the narrator's wounds and perplexities. Michael Syrotinski speaks aptly, in this light, of the "limping rhythms" of Paulhan's narrative style.[37] Freud's theory of traumautic neurosis offers a similar example as Paulhan's: "It may happen that someone gets away, apparently unharmed, from the spot where he has suffered a shocking accident. . . . In the course of the following weeks, however, he develops a series of grave psychical and motor symptoms, which can be ascribed only to his shock or whatever else happened at the time of the accident."[38] In this late essay of Freud's, the psychoanalyst's reference to "psychical and motor symptoms" hearkens back to insights developed in the course of his early studies of organic motor paralyses in hysterical patients.[39] Indeed, it is worth recalling that paralyses provided Freud a crucial link between the psychic and the somatic as his nascent psychoanalytic method emerged from his training in neurology. Freud's theory of trauma would undergo various alterations in the course of his career, but the scene of the accident above shares with his early studies a basic and common framework: the "fixation to traumas," as Freud puts it, involves a traumatic event, a forgetting of the trauma, and its return in a pathological form.[40] The graphic and literal cases of bodily paralyses studied early on by Freud would, then, be extended to a more encompassing model of psychic fixation. And while fixation is all too often invoked in common parlance and vulgar psychology within a developmental, and indeed normative framework, Jean Laplanche has insisted, rather, that fixation constitutes the very motor of the drive and the desiring subject.[41] It is this more paralyzing fixation that seems to lie at the heart of Paulhan's troubled *récits*.

Freud's theory of fixation and trauma aims of course at unknotting the subject's paralyses. And yet, at the limit, trauma poses a more stubborn knot that resists any undoing through analysis. Recent critics have turned to the theory of trauma to show how traumatic events often escape recollection and narration; indeed, the subject of the trauma is eclipsed at the moment of the event, which, paradoxically, only occurs to him belatedly, at another time and place.[42] Certain formulations of Blanchot are highly resonant with the theory of trauma, particularly as defined by Lacan as a "missed encounter."[43] In "The Sirens' Song," for instance, Blanchot says that the *récit* recounts "the encounter itself, always distanced from the place and the time in which it occurs."[44] What Blanchot in his identification with Paulhan may have recognized without naming, then, is a traumatic force at the heart of his *récits*, originary yet inaccessible. And yet, Blanchot's ontological approach tends to void the context from which Paulhan's narratives derive. While the *event* of trauma may always prove elusive, this need not warrant a general claim to "impersonality."

Significantly, in this light, Paulhan's most important rhetorical study, *The Flowers of Tarbes*, opens with an evocation of trauma, in the person of a soldier struck mute upon his return from battle in World War I. Two references are inescapable in this context: that of Freud, who derived the notion of the death drive from the repetition compulsion as manifested by the traumatic neuroses of soldiers, and that of Walter Benjamin who, in "The Storyteller," relates the modern demise of storytelling to the shock of World War I. "Was it not noticeable at the end of the war," Benjamin asks, "that men returned from the battlefield grown silent—not richer, but poorer in communicable experience?"[45] Paulhan's anecdote of "the silence of the soldier on leave" suggests that what he calls "a chronic illness of expression" would derive from the shock of war trauma;[46] indeed, the title of the book may be seen as an allusion to the severe case of pneumonia that near the war's end would almost kill Paulhan in Tarbes in 1918. Further, the birth of the *récit* in Paulhan may be traced to his first published story, "Le Guerrier appliqué," that recounts his own experience at the front. Blanchot himself points out the wartime backdrop of many of Paulhan's *récits*, but the insistence on trauma in Paulhan's work lends another inflection to Blanchot's observation that Paulhan is a wartime writer whose works are "anonymous" and lie "in the margins of time."

In 1992 Blanchot was confronted with an essay he had written in 1942, and in which the name of the fascist Charles Maurras is mentioned. In response, Blanchot claimed to have forgotten the essay, but conceded that his reference to Maurras in the context of the Occupation was "inexcusable." Most interesting, perhaps, is how Blanchot's brief response echoes the words above that he had applied to Paulhan: "What more to say? This text, not simple and indeed tangled, has the merit of remaining outside time."[47] Like Steven Ungar, who comments on this episode, my aim is certainly not to discredit Blanchot's postwar thought on this basis. And yet it points to a moment of difficult transition in which Blanchot was distancing himself from his reactionary prewar positions, a period, precisely, when Blanchot began writing on Paulhan. Interestingly, Ungar speculates that Blanchot's reading of *The Flowers of Tarbes* in 1941 provided one means of transition from politics to literature by "displacing the violence and radicality of political revolution onto the concept of literature itself" (120).[48] What Ungar calls a postwar pattern of "partial and oblique" disclosures on Blanchot's part to his political past can be traced, then, as far back as "La Terreur dans les lettres" and "Comment la littérature est-elle possible?" of 1941. The legacy of this past, in Blanchot's work and in its critical reception, is that of "aftereffect," a term Ungar borrows from psychoanalysis and the theory of trauma: aftereffect, Ungar says, is "the reference back to the initial shock at a temporal remove and . . . an extension of that past shock into the present" (131). In this light, Blanchot's choice of Paulhan as topic of study seems strangely apt. The silences, gaps, and temporal disjunctions of Paulhan's essays and *récits* provided Blanchot with the means to articulate his troubled transition from politics to literature, and thereby carry forward the legacy of his past as aftereffect. But in so doing, Blanchot inherited the trauma of another, one deriving from an earlier war, as well as from Paulhan's colonial experience in Madagascar. Such "contagion," as Cathy Caruth points out, is one modality of trauma's legacy, though it may carry less a *message* than a mute and opaque testimony to past pain.⁴⁹

Blanchot, as Paulhan's most distinguished reader, is no doubt correct in emphasizing the role of language and the paradoxes of the *récit* in his work. And yet linguistic expression operates within discursive fields of power relations and modes of exchange that Paulhan himself never took for granted. If it is true, as Blanchot says, that "Paulhan wrote nothing but *récits*" this is due in large part to the autobiographical element that is never absent from his writings.⁵⁰ Even Paulhan's rhetorical work draws substantially on personal anecdotes, and his studies of proverbs in particular show a development toward the increasingly anecdotal and subjective. That this autobiographical element is often a point of obscurity does not void its motive force. Indeed, ambiguous agency, impersonality, and alter egos—hallmarks of Paulhan's style—may indicate nothing so much as a crisis of the subject as it engages such difficult and traumatic terrain as politics and sexuality. Impersonality in Paulhan, then, points less to ontology than to a problematic of *subjection*, in which the quest for the self engages its discursive conditions, conditions that Paulhan tellingly casts as an ambiguous play of mastery and submission. To read with an eye to biography is, then, not to return the text to its singular cause, but to examine the constitution of the subject in the field of discourse. In this light, certain postformalist rejections of biography may be seen as equally reifying of the author as naïve biography. The recent furor over deconstruction's political genealogy is a symptom of this unresolved conflict. In the place of each, one may posit a *subject of discourse*, both object and agent of its textual context. Accordingly, the true dimension of the Paulhanian *récit* includes a wider context of ritual, ceremony, and duty; politics, morality, and more than one order of laws. If the *récit*, for Paulhan, is the privileged mode of tackling these issues, it is not because literature transposes them into an abstract order of language, giving them their unique—if elusive—source, but because it dramatizes social pacts and modes of address while dislocating them from their habitual world. Such is the context dramatized by "Aytré qui perd l'habitude" and found in all of Paulhan's texts deriving from the period of his stay in Madagascar.

What, then, of the literary origin postulated by Blanchot in his essay on "Aytré"? If we wish to look closer at this point of departure, it is not in order to reassert a naïve empiricism in the quest for a unitary origin, but to look into the specificity of a context. Madagascar was a beginning in many respects for Paulhan, and the context from which he drew a lifetime of work and reflections. His firsthand encounter with colonial politics led to a political positioning in which we may already recognize the older Paulhan of the *Nouvelle Revue Française*, and the ambivalences and contradictions of his political conscience. A "colonial misunderstanding," to use Octave Mannoni's phrase, lies at the origin of Paulhan's vexed dealings with language.[51] The secrecy and mystery surrounding Paulhan's persona and his stories is significantly illuminated by this troubled context. A noteworthy stain in Paulhan's biography comes at the end of his stay on the island. Paulhan is alleged to have murdered a local resident under circumstances that remain obscure.[52] Collusion with the French administration and the sympathy of the locals for Paulhan's side conspired to precipitate Paulhan's departure from Madagascar. Paulhan would never go back, but his writings would constantly return to the scene.

Of Trauma and Terror

In his introduction to Paulhan's *Traité du ravissement*, Yvon Belaval points out that ever since Madagascar Paulhan seemed to keep repeating himself, employing the same examples and returning to the same ideas. His observation inflects differently Blanchot's question of Paulhan's beginnings: "some commentators have cast doubt on his progress: everything is already there from the start."[53] While there is no questioning the formative nature of Paulhan's experience in Madagascar, doubt would seem to bear on his progress beyond the sticking points that would perplex him in his dealings with Malagasy, causing him to return continuously to the "défauts" (flaws) and "secrets" of language, and seeing all discourse, not only that of proverbs, as marked by miscommunication and ambiguity. In his obsessive quest for the "secret" of proverbs, Paulhan would extend to all language a tragic duplicity, belied only by the seeming nonchalance with which he demonstrates its fatal flaws.

Shortly after his return from Madagascar, Paulhan wrote a brief text that, coming close on the heels of "Aytré" and its incriminating background, can only give its reader pause. In the offhand manner characteristic of Paulhan's essays, "L'Innocence utile" ("Useful Innocence") throws into question the difference between guilt and innocence.[54] In this text, Paulhan questions the view that an innocent person, due to his naïveté, may defend himself less well than one who is guilty. Given his ability to spin ruses and anticipate his accusers, a guilty person may be considered, Paulhan says, to have a certain advantage. But are not guilt and innocence roles that each party plays, anticipating the audience? In this way, the innocent person plays at simplicity in the same way the guilty one elaborates a complex alibi. However, recognizing these roles, their auditor is thereby able to distinguish one from the other. Consequently, the very skill of the guilty person becomes his failing, and the simplicity of the other his protection. This "useful innocence" of the innocent party thus returns us to the commonplace view that innocence defends itself best. Paulhan's essay thus overturns a received idea only to set it back upright. But having infected innocence with its performance and implicated it in its audience, Paulhan destabilizes the very opposition he has demonstrated. Innocence would be the shared illusion that innocence is simplicity, when it is in fact doubly duplicitous, as unwitting performance and as tacitly recognized spectacle. Useful innocence is the means by which the innocent party's role-playing is taken as natural. Having thus restored faith in the force of the innocent, Paulhan, however, undermines the very notion of his innocence and the means to recognize it.

"How is it," the narrator of "Aytré" asks himself, "that I have stopped . . . granting myself the benefit of the doubt?" (*Aytré qui perd l'habitude,* 75). "Aytré" shares with the argument of "L'Innocence utile" a disorienting movement of role reversals, misperception, and mutual implication. Guilt in both of these texts spreads, extending even to the party that holds itself to be innocent. In his dealings with proverbs, Paulhan would similarly find himself unable to overcome his doubts about himself and language. In these rhetorical studies, we find Paulhan struggling with haunting questions that bear dramatically on his biography. One need only recall the subtitle of *The Flowers of Tarbes* to note that, as in "L'Innocence utile," it is the gravest and most compromising questions that Paulhan engages in his studies of language, questions that bear persistently on guilt.[55] It is in such terms that Paulhan provocatively takes stock of his experience with Malagasy proverbs: "Before I applied myself to acquire knowledge of proverbial language, I felt its existence in a very vivid manner because of the discomfort and, if I may say so, the harm it caused me."[56] Proverbs, for Paulhan, would be primarily a lesson in error. One such error is the exoticist illusion by which a traveler's misunderstandings are projected onto the other as linguistic singularity or cultural anomaly. This illusion, Paulhan says, "consists in taking as particularly representative of a language that aspect which, in our acquisition of the language, surprises and troubles us the most, and, if you will, develops in us the keenest awareness [*la plus vive conscience*]."[57] In this second formulation, which strikingly echoes the previous quote, "conscience" replaces "wrong," suggesting that the mistakes at issue in Paulhan's treatment of language bear not merely on knowledge or "awareness" but more dramatically on self-doubt. Would linguistic error, for Paulhan, be a wandering quest for an elusive conscience? "It's remorse, rather, that I lack, and which I would like to find, instead of all this distress,"

Paulhan says elsewhere, words that might well have been spoken by the protagonist of "Aytré."[58] This missing conscience, or failed reflexive turn, seems suggested by Paulhan's frequent evocations of the necessity—and impossibility—of self-reflection. An Orphic conscience may lie at the heart of Paulhan's question: "Who truly knows what he is thinking?"[59] But if one is blind to one's own thoughts, Paulhan says, it may be that we are not looking in the right place: rhetoric, proverbs, and clichés themselves display the "original thought" (63) or "secret text" each holds within him (68). It is with this in mind that we propose to read the biographical import of Paulhan's linguistic and rhetorical studies.

Originally intended as a university thesis under the direction of Lucien Lévy-Bruhl, Paulhan's "Sémantique du proverbe" would never see completion in this form. From 1910 until 1936 he worked intermittently on the thesis before the project was definitively abandoned. During this period, however, Paulhan's research on the *hain-teny* gave fruit to various other studies, the major works being his translations, each accompanied by an introduction, the first edition dated 1913, the second 1939.[60] In an essay on these separate editions, Silvio Yeshua traces the evolution that would lead Paulhan from an objective study of the proverbs, leaning on sociology and linguistics, to the later study in which the opacity and singularity of the phenomenon of the *hain-teny* would come to the fore.[61] From the beginning, Paulhan would be perplexed by the "authority" and "influence" of the *hain-teny*, a traditional form of poetry employed in arguments and discussions among older Malagasy and still found in use in the country at the time of Paulhan's stay in Madagascar. Paulhan determined that each *hain-teny* contained a proverb, often obscure and resistant to interpretation. Through his classification of themes and analyses of their usage, Paulhan attempted to unveil their messages and determine the means by which a given proverb would settle differences. His hypothesis that success in a debate was merely a factor of the sheer *number* of proverbs exchanged hardly clarified the question of their value, which Paulhan himself recognized in the *Hain-teny* of 1913 (*Hain-teny merina*, 57). Many semantic aspects of the *hain-teny* would remain opaque to the researcher. The later edition of Paulhan's study does not shy from such difficulties, aiming instead to relate the errors and confusions that beset him in his research, thus lending the text the markedly autobiographical quality already in evidence in "L'Expérience du proverbe" and "Sacred Language." *Les Hain-tenys* of 1939, Blanchot would say, becomes a *récit*. Yeshua ties the abandonment of the earlier format of the text and of his doctoral ambitions to the need on Paulhan's part to put himself into play, to become himself the object of inquiry. In so doing, Paulhan's work diverges from its claims to objectivity, opening up questions of subjectivity and method that are today on the agenda for reflexive anthropology.

One measure of the evolution from Paulhan's earliest to his final studies of the *hain-teny* is thus his distance from the object of study. The *hain-teny* decline in exoticism over the years, becoming ever more familiar even as they remain obscure. This shift is indexed by the change in the title of his thesis from "Sémantique du proverbe malgache" to the more general "Sémantique du proverbe." In his first thesis, Paulhan claims confidently, "this is the first study attempted on a phenomenon that counts among the most complex, and most foreign to any European logic, of Malagasy folklore."[62] Paulhan's formula bears the mark of Lévy-Bruhl, whose work of the period aimed to distinguish "primitive" thought—characterized as "mystical" and "prelogical"—from that of advanced societies.[63] By the time of "Sacred Language," however, Paulhan would be less sanguine about his ethnographic pretensions. The questions raised by proverbial language, Paulhan now realizes, apply to every aspect of speech, not merely to its more esoteric or "sacred" forms. "There is no need to go to Madagascar to experience the proverb."[64] And yet, we might add, only the estrangement undergone in the field would have allowed Paulhan to take stock of the strangeness of his own language. The "experience" at issue, Paulhan comes to realize, is the mysterious conversion by which word becomes idea, and idea word. To this movement is tied the fortune and influence of all signs, which, seen as mere words invariably fall flat, while taken as ideas exert their wanted influence. Proverbs dramatize this double nature by being at once strictly formalized expressions and vehicles of time-honored truths. Derived from common wisdom, their messages seemingly *go without saying*, and yet they are bound to a strict protocol without which they risk failure. Paulhan narrates many occasions on which failure ensues from deviation from form. But failure also comes from following form too closely; a certain ease and confidence, which Paulhan struggles to attain, is essential to their delivery. Indeed, what truly *goes without saying* is the means of transformation of each into the other. This unspoken cipher of language is the target of all Paulhan's rhetorical analyses, which see communication as riven by a difference as radical as it is insignificant. Neither form nor content, this ambiguous entity is properly unspeakable: "Neither thought nor word, but utterly suited to be the densest word or the subtlest thought" (320). Rather than theorize this linguistic entity, Paulhan would instead show how its duplicity is played out in endless disputes, misunderstandings, and polemics.

Paulhan's progress in proverbs is thus a development from exoticism to self-estrangement, in which what he first held to be "foreign to any European logic" comes to inhabit his own language as well. This would allow Paulhan in 1925 to take issue with Lévy-Bruhl's theory of primitive mentality, which holds that languages of "inferior" cultures are lacking in abstraction.[65] The "explorer's illusion," Paulhan says, is the ethnocentric bias by which failings common to all languages are projected onto others. According to the polemic Paulhan would subsequently argue in *The Flowers of Tarbes*, it is always the *other* who speaks in words, while oneself speaks in ideas. In a Lacanian intervention on "L'Expérience du proverbe," Roland

Chemama argues that Paulhan's experience is directed away from any *others*—along the axis of projection, dispute, or misrecognition—to engage instead with the symbolic *Other*.[66] In its impersonality, the proverb would allow access to the unconscious—Paulhan's "secret text"—which escapes the proper agency of the speaking subject. Chemama's reading thus reframes the question of the poetic duel, indicating that it is instead a dual subject at grips with the Other that takes center stage in Paulhan's text. Paulhan himself suggestively indicates at several points that the difference at issue in a debate is less a question of individual interests than of the symbolic as such. Arguments, then, would be the means of establishing that language itself may continue: "Language itself was put at stake [*s'y voyait mis en jeu*]: it was suddenly less a question of knowing whether this or that was the truth than of establishing whether language could go on—to help it go on."[67] Discussants find common cause in this effort, each, however, confronting the alterity of his own language become object. Chemama's reading of Paulhan takes its cue from Lacan, who makes a glowing reference to "L'Expérience du proverbe" in a seminar session dedicated to Roman Jakobson. In distinction to the work of Jakobson, Lacan says of himself, "It seems to me that it is difficult not to speak stupidly [*bêtement*] about language."[68] Lacan seems to identify with Paulhan, whose instructive stumbling in Malagasy exposes failures and misunderstandings essential to the psychoanalyst's approach to language. As Chemama points out, Paulhan's essay does not "systematize" what is more significantly "the description of an itinerary" ("L'Expérience du proverbe," 46). But what kind of itinerary would this be? At a certain point in his text, Paulhan says that he overcomes his difficulties to eventually master the language of proverbs; a turn of events that, however, remains unaccountable to Paulhan. The very notion of progress is elided by what Chemama calls a "blank" and an "interval" in the narrative. We are not far from Blanchot's *récit*: "Where one might expect to find the account of an apprenticeship," Chemama says, "nothing is mentioned that might refer to any progress." Unaccountably, the signifier "takes hold" of Paulhan: "Le signifiant, *ça prend, ça ne s'apprend pas*" ("L'Expérience du proverbe," 49). If Paulhan seems to master the proverbs, it is a mastery that escapes him; or better, a reversal of mastery into submission that corresponds to the "backward progress [*progrès retourné*]" described at the conclusion of *Les Hain-tenys* (96).

The paradoxical transports described in Paulhan's essays on proverbs bear on the idea of progress in general as concerns Paulhan. "What to do, in life, with a failing [*un défaut*]?" the narrator asks in "Progress in Love." "One has to wait for it to become a quality. Patiently, if possible."[69] For the shy, introspective narrator of "Progress," sexual initiation occurs unwittingly to him as his passivity and awkwardness eventually win him recognition as a lover. Crucial to this transformation is the role played by stock phrases and jokes, the language of love that plays in "Progress" a role analogous to that of proverbs. "Why does she talk like a book?" the narrator wonders of Simone's protestations of love, while he struggles to match his male friends' ease with words (37). At stake in proverbs and in the language of love is a certain authority that Paulhan cannot seem to muster, except blindly: "progress was made unwittingly and in an obscure way."[70] Any progress is thrown into doubt as Paulhan looks back uncomprehendingly on the linguistic impasses overcome and his passivity conquered. "There is nothing in the world more humiliating than to be able to do perfectly something one is incapable of understanding."[71] Indeed, as Paulhan fails to grasp the cause of his self-assurance, success itself invariably bears the mark of shame: "I gladly withdraw behind these successful words, I take my leave [*je me retire*], I almost ask to be forgiven for being so right."[72]

Perhaps the most memorable instance of paradoxical progress in Paulhan is his story of a motorcycle race in Madagascar. After a brilliant start, Paulhan leads the pack, only to be gradually overtaken by his competitors, finding himself eventually dead last. At this point, Paulhan says, he quits the race to lie down in a field, comfortably chewing the sugarcane. "Je me retire," in the above quote, here takes the blunt sense of "dropping out." As Paulhan returns to Tananarive, he is greeted by progressively more numerous and enthusiastic spectators: the other racers not having returned yet, Paulhan is taken as the winner, and he crosses the finish line "in triumph."[73] Somewhat wryly, Paulhan says that his unfair triumph was the greatest glory of his life. In this fable Paulhan seems to play the role of both tortoise and hare, alternately. Slowness yields always for Paulhan unexpected progress, while progress reverses into stasis. In Paulhan's characteristically light and nearly offhand way, his narrative invokes a moral tale while overturning its moral, implicating himself in the process, yet eliding the fraught context of his colonial victory. Paulhan's tale, then, does not amount to an illustration of Aesop's moral of "perseverance;" it is closer, instead, to Zeno's famous arguments on the impossibility of motion.[74] Likewise, Paulhan's Lacanian "stupidity" with proverbs suggests an obstinate encounter with the stumbling block of the "impossible real."

Paulhan's *récits* and tales of initiation dramatize torments less evident in his more self-composed works, notably *The Flowers of Tarbes*, in which a personal dynamic of subjection is replaced by a broadly generalized reign of error. But read in the light of his more personal writings, Paulhan's rhetorical essays can be seen to play out their own drama: that of a compensatory skepticism that enjoys putting the burden of contradiction on others. Judith Butler provides an account of the skeptic's motivations in her reading of the Unhappy Consciousness in Hegel: "The skeptic overrides his own contradictoriness in order to take pleasure in forcing others to witness their contradictions."[75] The "stubbornness" of the Unhappy Consciousness eventually gives way to an "ethical reflexivity" in which his outward scorn reverts on himself. Accordingly, a sadistic attitude, particularly apparent in Paulhan's political essays, thus complements the anxiety and self-doubt of the *récits*. To what extent, then, does Paulhan reflect the dialectical overturning of Hegel's skeptic and his "stubbornness"? The *récit*, following Blanchot, is a challenge precisely to the dialectical movement of Hegel's thought; for Blanchot ethics is to be sought not in the developmental and self-reflexive movement of becoming, but rather in the *paralyzing* logic of the "step not beyond." Such a paralyzing logic is indeed to be found in Paulhan's *récits*, and it lends its moments of ethical insight. But by challenging the impersonal claims of Blanchot's *récit*, and by folding Paulhan's biography into them, I have brought out the violence that mars his moments of textual ambiguity and reflexive opacity. Paralysis thus vies with mere stubbornness as the *récit* stakes its claims in the fraught contexts of colonial rule and sexual politics. This double aspect of Paulhan's work lends every question of agency liable to reversals in which the imposture of mastery is interrupted by doubt.

In his introduction to the English translation of Paulhan's stories, Michael Syrotinski points out a characteristic movement by which the narrator is periodically eclipsed. "Paulhan's texts always gravitate toward a point in their narrative where the entire analysis is turned on its head . . . and the resulting inability to fully account for this 'turn' becomes the subject of the text, which thereby enacts or performs the very reversal it is attempting to describe" (x). The "turn" or "reversal," as we have seen, is usually centered on a point of opacity Paulhan terms a *défaut*, in which the agency of the speaker and his words may be confused. As Syrotinski points out, an "uncertain participation" in the events narrated devolves from this predicament (xi). Language in such cases comes to the fore, superseding the will or intent of the speaker. Paulhan thus brings out an impersonal quality of language in order to dramatize a performative disjunction between sayer and said. What remains unanswered is why such "turns" in Paulhan are marked by guilt, or in the case of his stories, violent reversals of fortune. If the proverb entails a wrong and a transgression, it is due in large part to its particular agency, an agency that operates without regard for the subject. Impersonal, less spoken than cited, and following rules that escape the will of the subject, the proverb occupies the place of what Lacan calls "the place of the 'inter-said' [*l'inter-dit*], which is the 'intra-said' [*l'intra-dit*] of a between-two-subjects."[76] The proverb highlights a discontinuity between intention and meaning in the speaker, or what Lacan, drawing on Jakobson, identifies as the division between the subject of the enunciation (*l'énonciation*) and the subject of the statement (*l'énoncé*). Given this split and division, constantly traversed in discourse, speaking would always be a matter of transgression, or the *interdit*, lending the proverb the "sacred" nature Paulhan attributed to it. Unable to grasp the cut by which his thought is "amputated," as Paulhan is given to say, he finds himself placed on one side or the other, unable to account for the reversal itself.[77] Characteristically for Paulhan, this predicament entails a humiliating passivity as the subject is transformed by chiastic reversal from *speaker* into *spoken*.

The question of this passivity lies at the heart of Paulhan's introduction to a course in the Malagasy language, taught at the Ecole des Langues Orientales upon his return from Madagascar. In his first class session, Paulhan presents the foreignness of Malagasy thought as a property of grammatical structure, bound to alter the students' very patterns of thinking as they assimilate the language. "With Malagasy you will not only have to learn new words but also to become familiar with and adopt new reflections, new ways of thinking."[78] The students' initiation is one in which they give themselves over to the language to be transformed by it. Only in ceding the initiative to words will the student, like Paulhan, be able to gauge their true influence. The first lesson in language, then, is passivity, and it is the passive that Paulhan singles out for his students, the verb structure that dominates in Malagasy, as distinct from French. "Where a French speaker says: 'I see the house. I write a letter,' the Malagasy will say, 'seen by me the house, written by me the letter'—in other words man, the acting person, doesn't have in Malagasy the essential role he has in our languages." Through a dispossession of the speaker, Paulhan's experience of Malagasy points us in the direction of Lacan's "subversion of the subject" under the law of castration. And yet, Paulhan's speaking subject does not fall under the law that would legislate his place in the symbolic order. The troubling of agency in proverbs and in the Malagasy language leads Paulhan instead to question the disposition of gendered roles, altering gender distinctions in the same way that he alters self and other and "inferior" and "superior" cultures.

It is significant in this light that the *hain-teny* stage a sexual crisis, for whatever the topic they may be called on to arbitrate, the poems are couched in the vocabulary of love. It is precisely in its foregrounding of argumentation, negotiation, and disagreement that Paulhan sees the unique value of the Malagasy definition of love. "It is not the sensual and contemplative love of Arab poetry; nor the refined love of the troubadours; nor a simple whim or romantic passion. Rather, it is an intellectual and argumentative love that discusses and seeks less to move than to convince."[79] Love in the *hain-teny*, Paulhan says provocatively, is "better yet than love, an amorous quarrel." As Silvio Yeshua points out, "The quarrel (or discussion) between lovers appears then in these poems as a general metaphor for all debates, for every opposition of views or interests, for any confrontation; and love—as the universal metaphor of all binarisms" ("Jean Paulhan et les hain-teny," 342). According to the model set by this "poésie de dispute," all of Paulhan's work, marked by dualisms, controversy, and polemic, can thus be located within the conflict put into play by sexual contest. If, however, the *hain-teny* articulate sexually distinct roles, they also undo these roles in transposing them into a field of discursive performance. For whatever the sex of the parties in an argument, each ties his fortune to a role of his choice, male or female, in making his case. This possible reversal of roles is authorized by the *hain-teny* in their indifference to gender.

As Paulhan points out, "There is usually little difference between the *hain-teny* of the man and those of the woman." This reversible binarism can, moreover, be collapsed in the person of a single party, who thereby may argue "by himself the roles of the two rivals."[80] The embodiment of sexual difference within a single subject thus lends a particular urgency to Paulhan's linguistic *défaut*, providing a key to the troubling reversals of his *récits*. Far from theme or topic, and calling the subject himself into question, sexuality is no doubt the privileged locus of the Paulhanian *défaut*. Paulhan points us toward this mysterious crux when he suggests that we place at the beginning of his love stories a particular *défaut*, "a failing in love, to be precise."[81]

A chapter of "Progress in Love" entitled "Simone and the Quarrel" dramatizes this *défaut* in ways that elucidate the central crime of "Aytré." Sizing himself up against a more assertive friend, Paulhan's insecure narrator gains the ability to assert himself only by means of a quarrel in which he is unjustly accused of a theft. Thanks to this accusation, he discovers a "confidence," an "inner strength" and even a "joy" usually lacking in him; the accusation, we might say, thus repairs any self-accusation and self-doubt, restoring his sexual sense of self. It is telling that the narrator's self-possession in "Progress" is due to a crime against a woman, as in "Aytré." The narrator finds himself envying his companion, who, in the midst of the ensuing quarrel, insults the woman as a "catin," or "hussy," which he quickly regrets. "He was feeling sorry for himself with a violence, and a kind of joy that he no doubt got from having said the word, and from the energy he had gained thanks to this injustice" (27). It is striking that the reactions of the narrator and his friend mirror each other; but while the reaction of the one derives from his innocence, the other follows on a fault. This mirroring thus destabilizes the opposition from which each derives, echoing the conflation of guilt and innocence in "L'Innocence utile." The quarrel in "Progress" is emblematic of the "turn" characteristic to all Paulhan's *récits*, a point of narrative opacity that defies any account, and that swerves insistently toward *unaccountability*. What remains unaccountable to the narrator, as we have seen, is the means by which he overcomes his passivity and "indifference." Paulhan's affections are unjustifiable precisely due to the reversals that characterize his self-image. In a particularly lucid passage, the narrator says, "It is strange that I should desire a woman, not so much in proportion to how much she pleases me, but on the contrary, and in order that I might look down on her a little bit" (3–4). And yet, this sadistic position is unstable and elsewhere seeks confirmation of its guilt. Thus, under cover of the third person Paulhan says of his first wife, "she pleased him for giving him the exact picture of his own distrust with regard to himself."[82] Indifference is less a lack of affect than the position from which Paulhan, blind to his motives, gives play to his self-division in matters of love. It is only in later years, as we will see, that Paulhan takes on the questions of sadism and masochism implicit in his stories and journals.

Polemics

One of the dominant traits of Paulhan's work is the refusal to settle differences. His work repeatedly argues against the "illusion of totality" that sets aside exceptions and *défauts*, so many stumbling blocks in his slow progress in knowledge. As director of the left-leaning but centrist *Nouvelle Revue Française* he practiced a studied indifference in politics that is not, however, reducible to a position of complacency. As in his affections, indifference is the means by which Paulhan would embody rivalries in his own person, taking on the singular ambivalence of the *hain-teny*. In "La Mentalité primitive et l'illusion des explorateurs," we saw how Paulhan took issue with the exoticist projection of otherness, positing instead a duplicity and ambivalence inherent to the self and his "proper" language. It is worth recalling this text as it anticipates the terms with which he engages in his future polemics:

> This kind of interior debate and difficulty one may have with his language, a certain way of mistrusting it . . . all this goes away and disappears as soon as one faces a foreign language that is taken as strange and hostile— disappears like the internal struggles that had formerly divided a nation that goes to war, the scruples that had worried the orator as he prepared his speech, and for the lover who makes his declaration, all uncertainty on the meaning of *love*. (152)

Paulhan's formula indicates to what extent the subject's relation to language is implicated in sexuality and politics. Political "divisions," personal "scruples," and sexual "uncertainty" are falsely overcome by a complacent projection of otherness, an otherness that inhabits one's own language. The experience of Malagasy, for Paulhan, is an experience of estrangement that defuses all opposition, only to render them interior: "my advances with regard to proverbial language seemed to consist less in resolving than in prolonging, within me, the very differences and oppositions that had puzzled me from the start."[83] Paulhan does not allow himself the benefit of the doubt that would see fault in the other. By a reflexive turn of conscience, he looks instead to his own language, the embodiment of his enigmatic duplicity. In his sexual adventures Paulhan will not settle his ambivalence, just as in times of war he will not allow aggression to steal the scene from social division. On the model of Malagasy "poetry of dispute" Paulhan sees literary history as an intractable argument between Rhetoricians and Terrorists, an agonistic misunderstanding that Paulhan extends to his very definition of the social. *The Flowers of Tarbes*, in turn, sets the stage for Paulhan's notorious polemics of the postwar years, when the question of terror takes on a more urgent form: that of the violent purges carried out by the Resistance following the liberation of France. In a series of essays collected as *Of Chaff and Wheat* ("De la paille et du grain") and culminating in his notorious *Letter to the Directors of the Resistance* (*Lettre aux Directeurs de la Résistance*) Paulhan took exception to the purges and scapegoating undertaken against former collaborators with Vichy France and the Nazi occupation. Paulhan's reproach against righteous patriots echoes his formulation of 1925: "while a patriot is dangerously vulnerable to national wars, it would be wrong to ignore the fact that he has the good fortune to avoid civil wars."[84] The hypocrisy of war is that it overcomes internal differends at the expense of external others.[85] The error of the Resistance, Paulhan argues, is that it applies the same scapegoating mentality to its traitors, dangerously oblivious to more intractable social divisions and ambivalences: an otherness at the heart of the social.

The legacy of the war has amply demonstrated the persistence of a trauma that de Gaulle and a resurgent French nationalism would have settled. Paulhan raised his voice against the high cost of this jubilation. It is with this in mind that Frédéric Badré's recent biography characterizes Paulhan as "just": a clear and equitable conscience negotiating the hypocrisy and contradictions of a divided France.[86] Badré's formula, however, ascribes to Paulhan a moralizing position that Paulhan himself was at pains to refuse. Moreover, it fails to address Paulhan's motives, which, despite the issues with which they engage, remain remote from the restricted sphere of national politics. More importantly, such a reading does not account for the role of error that troubles the very definition of justice in Paulhan. Justice for Paulhan is always guilty, as exemplified by the words of the murderous Aytré: "I want perfect justice in everything" ("Aytré Who Gets Out of the Habit," 90). Implicated in errors that cannot be remedied, justice, for Paulhan, cannot be set in opposition to guilt. Justice, we might say, is justified by error, which, by overstepping the bounds thereby delimits the law. This transgressive aspect of Paulhan's thought, which Blanchot recognized, binds his work to that of Bataille, and finds its most succinct formula in *Of Chaff and Wheat*. Condemning the blacklist of collaborationist writers drawn up by the Comité National des Ecrivains, Paulhan defended such authors in the name of a "right to error"—*un droit à l'erreur*.[87] Paulhan's formula is as simple as it is paradoxical. Error would seem to call on a certain right, one that, however, is compromised by its own infringement. As regards many of the writers under accusation, the error in question, moreover, involves nothing less than treason. Paulhan's intervention as a "grammarian" into this political debate not surprisingly places its emphasis on language and rhetoric. Paulhan argues that the key term of the debate—the proverbial "nation"—is one that lends itself to inevitable misunderstanding. Like any word, Paulhan says, the nation is an entity at once material and ideal. The "mystery" and inevitable error involves taking the one for the other (*Of Chaff and Wheat*, 44). On the basis of this opposition, Paulhan points out that Vichy protected the physical nation that the Resistance could only defend in the abstract. Beyond these "partisan" positions Paulhan appeals to a "patriot" that may combine the two (45). The "nation," as a word among others, accommodates rival elements in a unity of "indifferent difference."[88]

In a somewhat malicious essay that traces a "speculative genealogy" from Paulhan's postwar writings to deconstruction, Jeffrey Mehlman has claimed that Paulhan's appeal for amnesty to collaborators finds its inheritors in poststructuralist thought devoted to forgetting the past.[89] Mehlman reads Paulhan's tropes of reversibility and indistinction as implicitly collaborationist, and claims that these tainted figures, under the dubious guise of Derrida's *différance*, for instance, fatally compromise the politics of deconstruction. My own account of Blanchot's reading of Paulhan has attempted to offer a more nuanced view of Paulhan's inheritance. Rather than reprise the controversy provoked by Mehlman's essay,[90] I would like to single out one aspect of his claims that is drawn from *Of Chaff and Wheat*. Paulhan, as we have seen, insistently invokes chiastic figures in his studies of language and rhetoric, and one such figure, seemingly innocuous, appears at the outset of the text. Paulhan mentions the French word *choucroute*, which strikes the ear as a near-homophone of the German *Sauerkraut*. However, as Paulhan points out, the French translation has transposed each part of the German word in crisscross fashion: "in *choucroute*, 'chou' (almost) means *croute*, and 'croute' means *chou*" (4). The example is rich in implications, as it exemplifies cultural and linguistic exchange across an intensely fraught border. Paulhan cites the word as an instance of language's general hospitality to foreign influence. I would go further and venture that it offers a figure of *chiastic translation*: a transfer of sense across a cultural divide, but by means of a cross-stitch that defies that very passage. And indeed, as Paulhan pursues examples of linguistic borrowing, he concludes not with a simple moral of hospitality, tolerance, and assimilation but a more vexed problematic of linguistic influence, allergy, and mutation. Mehlman, for his part, sees the word as an instance of Paulhan's supposed blurring of distinctions—such as between resistants and collaborators—which Paulhan casts, at one point of his argument, as "the difference between 'the following day' and 'the day following' [*c'est blanc bonnet et bonnet blanc*]" (44). From these examples Mehlman derives the conclusion that deconstruction's chiastic tropes perpetuate a negation of political distinctions and a denial of history: "Let the chiasmus survive, but let its painful political crux be voided" (7).

As chiasmus is a key figure of what I have been calling paralysis, I would propose instead a different "survival" of the term in contemporary critical discourse. At stake in Paulhan's *Of Chaff and Wheat* is the crucial distinction between resistance to power and submission to power, a distinction hardened by hindsight on the Occupation, and which Melhman accuses Paulhan of rendering indistinct. However, to gauge the value of Paulhan's rhetorical intervention in this question, let us turn again to Judith Butler's *The Psychic Life of Power*, in which *subjection* is figured, as in Paulhan, as a problem as much political as tropological. Butler faults most critical theories of the subject, power, and agency as operating within a reductive binary framework in which power is either exerted by a subject or imposed on that subject. A pervasive account of this double aspect of subjection holds that the subject performs a reflexive "turn" by which he or she internalizes norms and takes him or herself as the object of discipline and the self-beratements of conscience. However, the problem of subjection lies in a more difficult and elusive distinction, as indexed by the very ambiguity of the phrase "subject of power," in which the double genitive "of" conveys each of the two options. Moreover, this crucial difference is not so much the site of the subject's willful options or fateful submission as it is the locus of a "turn" that the subject enacts without realizing, and that escapes the logic of "turning" as self-reflexivity and internalization. This supplemental turn is, rather, a chiastic reversal that inheres in the unspoken difference between the objective and subjective genitive. This unaccountable "turn" indicates what Butler calls the subject's "primary complicity with subordination" (17); the subject can claim power only by submitting to it, but by the same token rearticulates power by taking it on. As such, Butler's claim that "agency is implicated in subordination" would seem to fulfill Mehlman's worst fears about the poststructuralist legacy of Paulhan. However, as Butler makes clear, her aim is to pursue the fruitful challenge of Foucault's post-liberatory theories of power and subjectivity, and thereby to avoid the deadlock of fatalism and naïve political optimism. To do so, however, is to confront what Butler calls a "tropological quandary": to posit a subject of discourse we must make a discursive "turn" that presupposes precisely what we aim to explain (4). Reflexivity seems to founder on this contradiction. As a result, Butler's formulations resonate with Paulhan's troubling *passages,* his *récits,* and his vexing turns of rhetoric: "Who or what is said to turn, and what is the object of such a turn? How is it that a subject is wrought from such an ontologically uncertain form of twisting? Perhaps with the advent of this figure, we are no longer in the business of 'giving an account of the formation of the subject.' We are, rather, confronted with the tropological presumption made by any such explanation, one that facilitates the explanation but also marks its limit" (4). Following Butler, critical agency must, then, vie with the conundrum that the subject presumes what it enacts, a performative gesture that undermines the subject's authority even as it exposes the lability of the terms it appropriates. Butler's "twisting" and "turning" speaks to the tropological presumptions of any claim to power, but is especially apt when applied to the chiastic interweaving of Paulhan's favored turns of rhetoric. Likewise, the *implication* of the subject in power is suggested by the double fold of Paulhan's chiastic formulae, which grant him discursive agency only at the cost of a fundamental dispossession: "Master of the word you will speak, slave of the word you have spoken."[91]

Such insights are inherently unstable, as they occupy the site of a tenuous middle ground that is never merely neutral. Moreover, as we have seen, Paulhan's supposed "impersonality" reflects neither passivity nor indifference but rather the highly cathected site of a traumatic eclipsing of the subject. Further, Paulhan's rhetorical arguments, so insistently chiastic, are not a secure place of enunciation but rather the site he aims to occupy by means of a reflexive turn back from the opposing sides of an argument to its decisive crux. In this sense, then, the chiasmus is only articulated secondarily, from out of an insistently binary confrontation of opposites. Paulhan's arguments are, as a result, marred by two significant failings: a "stubbornness" such as we have indicated above, and a penchant to lean to one side, preferably the one branded as erroneous, to voice a provocative contrarian's perspective.

In the postwar years Paulhan sharpened his polemical pen, provoking controversy and orchestrating arguments that often turned personal and acrimonious. Ever resistant to partiality, Paulhan attempted to maintain what Badré calls an "extreme middle" position from which to expose failings common to each side of a debate (*Paulhan le juste,* 170). This studied impartiality would, however, prove difficult to maintain in the face of the Algerian war. Indeed, colonial crisis would represent the ultimate test of what Barthes, less generously, would call Paulhan's "neither-nor criticism."[92] As a result of the fire drawn by his critique of the defenders of a free Algeria, Paulhan's pseudonymous *Chroniques* would abandon the political fray. As the personal embodiment of the NRF's centrist editorial policy, Paulhan attracted particular scrutiny for his political pronouncements. At such times, Paulhan took cover under the journal's centrist policy, claiming that its politics, by their very impartiality, exposed it to a dual illusion: "The Progressives generally see the NRF as a reactionary journal, but the Conservatives see it as revolutionary."[93] What would an "extreme middle" position be, however, but the very lack of a position, defined only by an unstable dividing line visible from one side or the other, or indeed, by its transgression? In this sense, the extreme middle is necessarily partial, not dividing but divided by ambivalence. I leave it to biographers to identify Paulhan's party loyalties and affiliations of the period. The fact that every debate in Paulhan recapitulates the issues at stake in the *hain-teny* suggests that politics in Paulhan is secondary to the ambivalence, guilt, and anxiety at the heart of his studies of language. Far from exposing error and passing judgment, Paulhan's political essays undergo error as with Malagasy proverbs. Indeed, Paulhan's efforts in politics seem nothing so much as the desire to be *in the wrong*, to occupy that crux of error at the heart of an argument.[94] To be in the wrong would be to practice indifference only to allow events to decide themselves. Paulhan's magisterial skepticism, his stubborn determination to expose the contradictions of others, finally yields up its purpose: to draw fire as a means to feed a ravening conscience. Paulhan was never averse, moreover, to putting his weight to one side in order to pitch into a more decisively wrong position, if only to provoke the other into a game of errors. Thus, for instance, his observation in *Of Chaff and Wheat* that Pétain's Vichy was "legal," only to counter his accusers that he did not thereby mean to claim its "legitimacy." Elusive, ambiguous and often contrarian, Paulhan's tactic seems to be a slippage between a general error and a personal wrong. This movement of slippage seems implied in the unlocatable crux of error of "L'Illusion des explorateurs," which could serve as the credo of Paulhan's entire corpus: "For proof that there exists, with regard to language, a crux of illusions and traps against which we have no defense, one need only draw out the point of error [*la pointe d'erreur*] introduced into the most serious of studies—be it the psychology of peoples, literary criticism or sociology—by any reflection concerning phrases and words."[95] This formulation, which seems deconstructive *avant la lettre*, posits a "pointe," a sticking point, that is also errant, or wandering.[96] As such, it seems to provide a key to Paulhan's paradoxical tropology: the transformation of slow progress or paralysis into unaccountable, and often unjustifiable transports (recall the motorcycle race in Madagascar). There is no defending oneself, Paulhan says, against such errors. And if all debates and arguments are matters of language, each party is indefensible in the face of this determining error. It is this indefensible position that Paulhan, in his poetic jousts and political debates, aims to occupy. Unlocatable as it is, this point may be indexed only through a personal error. Indeed, this very point, like the "tache" of "Aytré," may be the mobile and shifting trace of Paulhan's Orphic conscience, posited after the fact by way of alibi.

In 1955 Paulhan mediated a heated debate between Lévi-Strauss and Roger Caillois on the question of cultural relativism in anthropology.[97] In the context of this acerbic exchange Paulhan risked some statements in his correspondence that can only appear reactionary, and, indeed, racist. "Why shouldn't ethnology discover one day that black or yellow skin goes with physical or moral traits of some kind or other?"[98] Siding with Caillois's critique of Lévi-Strauss's supposed "moralism" in the matter of race, Paulhan's pronouncement claims impartiality only to err on the side of the immoral, the better to continue the argument. What is perhaps most interesting in this exchange is a subtext to the argument to which Paulhan and his interlocutor refer. This text is an essay on Jules Vallès, in which Paulhan defines what could be taken as his theory of polemic. "One may sometimes notice in one and the same man both the feeling he expresses and that which he suppresses," Paulhan says.[99] A man's argument, one might say, is primarily with himself. The very notion of polemic is consequently altered by Paulhan's definition: "A professional boxer caught up in a street brawl denies himself the skills that would let him knock out his opponent with the first blow. But he brings to the fight an art of dodging and retreating that comes from those skills. He must defend himself, in one and the same movement, from his adversary and himself" (62). As a fearsome rhetorician, Paulhan might well be compared to this unfairly endowed fighter whose means of aggression must be curtailed. The fighter is limited to parrying the blows of the other, seemingly aggressed on two fronts. What results is what we might call an *art de la défense*, in which the verb *se défendre* plays an ambiguous role. For the French verb signifies at once "to defend" or "justify" onself, and on the other hand, "to prohibit" or "to refuse" oneself, an ambiguity Lacan underscores in saying that the pervert "defends himself in his desire."[100] One's self-defense is consequently disarmed by an interdiction. What might this interdiction be but the *inter-dit* of the embattled subject prey to opposing sentiments, those of mastery and submission? These opposing sentiments, moreover, are expressed in that very language against which, Paulhan says, it is impossible to defend oneself. To the extent that Paulhan's sentiments pitch decisively to the side of the passive, the aggressor never wins out, or only at the price of guilt.

At the age of ten, when asked what his vocation was, Paulhan oddly replied, "being sick."[101] The older Paulhan would come to realize to what extent this prediction was apt. Paulhan had been a sickly child and would grow up to face many illnesses, the most serious of which would nearly kill him in Tarbes in 1918. This episode is the basis of "The Severe Recovery," a story that relates the somewhat magical delusions the narrator suffers at the height of his illness only to fall into a disenchanted convalescence. It is noteworthy that the narrator's reluctant recovery takes place at the expense of his wife who, at his bedside, suffers his reproaches and shares his hallucinations. Structured in three parts, with an enigmatic exchange of roles at its center, the story has striking parallels with "Aytré." The crime in this case is that of the narrator's infidelity, which he reveals in exchange for his wife's bearing the responsibility for his apparent wish to die. "What kind of recovery is mine, then," the narrator asks himself, "and what is there that is false about it?"[102] Something remains uncured in Paulhan, a traumatic kernel lodged in the tale as the X of a chiasmus. If the hallmark of trauma is its unspeakability, its figure for Paulhan would be that elusive singularity he seeks in the duplicitous proverb. Sickness delivers Paulhan from such duplicity: "This duplicity become unbearable for me during my illness."[103] One might say that illness resolves, at the cost of the body, the metaphysical contraries that beset him in his linguistic explorations. If Paulhan was given to a Bataillian joy in the face of death, the pleasure is tied to the former to masochism.[104]

In recent years, one of the longstanding mysteries of contemporary French literature was solved, that of the identity of the author of the pornographic novel *Story of O*. By the same stroke, it was revealed that the author hidden by the pseudonym Pauline Réage—Dominique Aury—had addressed the text to Paulhan as a love letter. The identity of the masochistic O, however, was not immediately clear. By way of clarification, we might turn to Paulhan's essay on Sade, which opens with the intimations of a "secret."[105] This secret, Paulhan says at the end of the essay, is that Justine is Sade himself. Deliberately coy, Paulhan tenders a final reversal, suggesting that the secret of Sade bears the name of another, whom Paulhan will not name as such: Masoch. Paulhan's reversals are true to the dynamic that Freud described in "A Child Is Being Beaten": that the sadistic fantasy of a child being beaten masks the unconscious masochistic fantasy of suffering the assault oneself.[106] If Paulhan is the sadistic addressee of *Story of O*, it is by role reversal that he enjoys it, identifying with the victim. Our reading of Paulhan shows that he had long been acquainted with such role reversals and ambiguity, his rhetorical penchants in particular pointing toward the "paradox of masochism" that Laplanche identifies with the figure of "a strange chiasmus."[107]

Paulhan's introduction to *Story of O*, entitled "Happiness in Slavery," opens with the evocation of a slave revolt in Barbados.[108] Having been recently liberated, the slaves appealed to their master to take them back, only to kill him when their demands are refused. Paulhan characterizes the slaves as being in love with their master, and thus masochistic. Paulhan wrote this conflation of psychology and servitude shortly after Octave Mannoni's work on the psychology of colonization in Madagascar, and the text echoes the latter's thesis of a "dependency complex" among the colonized.[109] "Happiness in Slavery" thus seconds the view that colonial revolt is a revolt against the threat of freedom. Whether sincere or not, Paulhan's colonial fable reinforces one of the most insidious negations of the claims of the subordinated. As a result, Paulhan's insights into paralysis revert into mere stubbornness, and subjection into the conservative discourse of subjugation. French national identity would soon be torn apart on the fault lines of this discourse. Published in 1954, at the start of the Algerian War of Independence and the height of the broader movement of decolonization, Paulhan's essay is as scandalous as the text it introduces. Not least of this scandal is its secret admission to a guilty mastery.

4. Frustration
Michel Leiris

Each will create his own Rite, — for the purpose of self-discovery. Art has no other aim than the magical evocation of inner demons. — Leiris

Of all learned discourse, the ethnological seems to come closest to a Fiction. — Barthes

Without Alibi

In 1931 Michel Leiris left France with the first major French ethnographic expedition across Africa, the Mission Dakar-Djibouti, for which Leiris served as secretary-archivist. Setting out, as he says in the introduction, on what he hoped to be "a test, a trial, a poetic experience and a change of scenery [*une épreuve, une poésie vécue et un dépaysement*]," Leiris finds his exotic impulses run headlong into disillusionment.[1] Africa proves a "phantom" by failing Leiris on at least two counts: travel as means of escape from his personal troubles only provides another stage for his inhibiting psychological problems, while the scientific nature of the mission frustrates his desire for real adventure. At the end of *Manhood* (*L'Age d'homme*), the first volume of his autobiography, Leiris delivers this summary judgment of his experience: "In 1933 I returned, having killed at least one myth: that of travel as a means of escape."[2] The bitter fruit of this disillusionment is a return to a psychoanalytic cure, the beginning of an interminable self-analysis in autobiography, and a career as ethnographer assumed upon his return to France. Leiris's dual career in literature and ethnography converge in the critique of travel as alibi, and his work as a whole can be seen as an exploration of the lures and disappointments of travel. Travel as exotic escape is replaced by the more sober business of ethnographic study, while Leiris's literary work turns away from fiction and fantasy and, foregoing all alibis, focuses on his own self-portrait in autobiography. No text of Leiris's stages the evolution of this consciousness more dramatically than his work of 1934, *L'Afrique fantôme* (Phantom Africa). This chapter will deal at some length with the account of Leiris's African travels, as it is in this text that we may locate the genesis of Leiris's autobiography and the distinctive tensions and interferences between his self-analysis, politics, and ethnography.

In keeping a journal of his trip with the Mission Dakar-Djibouti, Leiris followed the recommendation of Marcel Mauss that the ethnographer maintain a daily log with which research in the field could be cross-checked. As secretary-archivist, Leiris was also expected to provide notes toward an official history of the mission. However, Leiris went well beyond documenting noteworthy events of the mission by including his personal fantasies, dreams, and misgivings, as well as details of a compromising nature, such as thefts and extortions committed in the course of collecting artifacts. The publication of Leiris's unedited journal as *L'Afrique fantôme* in 1934 thus made public a darker face of the well-funded and highly publicized ethnographic mission. Mauss and Marcel Griaule, the leader of the expedition, would be among those who objected to the picture Leiris painted, and as Leiris notes in his preface, the consensus among the French ethnographic community was that the book could only damage future relations between field-workers and other Europeans in the colonies. Tellingly, though the first edition of *L'Afrique fantôme* was dedicated by Leiris "to my friend Marcel Griaule," by the time of its reissue in 1951 the dedication would be dropped.

Despite its apparent disservice to ethnography, Leiris in later years counted *L'Afrique fantôme* as his most significant contribution to the field—if indeed one considers the book to be a work of anthropology, he however adds.[3] This qualification is significant, as it points to the hybrid and unruly quality of the text, part literary, part ethnographic, and struggling against each generic definition. Leiris's journal is a text seeking out its own purpose, and this reflexive and troubled quest goes against the grain of his ostensible mission in Africa. What *L'Afrique fantôme* brings to anthropology is a subversion of its discursive mastery by mixing in other discourses and other subjects, including colonial economy and sexual politics. For these reasons Leiris's text has gained new attention in the field of cultural anthropology as critics, notably James Clifford, have turned their attention back on the discursive presumptions of the field and sought out cultural relays and contacts that challenge anthropology's unilateral thrust.[4] In the years following the publication of *L'Afrique fantôme*, Leiris's ethnographic missions would adopt an activist role in economic and race relations, and he would contribute a militant voice to the cause of decolonization in his essay "L'Ethnographe devant le colonialisme" ("The Ethnographer Faced with Colonialism"). In this essay of 1950, Leiris boldly asserts the coextensivity of ethnography with colonial authority and challenges what he calls the "myth" of objectivity in the scientific study of others.[5] From a frankly politicized viewpoint, the later Leiris sees the ethnographer's preference for the study and conservation of primitive cultures as conditioned by and unwittingly perpetuating unequal power relations. In so doing, Leiris reprises *L'Afrique fantôme*'s portrait of travel as failed escape in calling traditional ethnography an "alibi" denying more pressing problems of a political nature, problems implicating the scientist himself (124; 138). Foremost among these more pressing issues is the analysis of hybrid and developing cultures, societies caught at the intersection of colonial rule and native tradition. Leiris holds that such societies embody the overlooked reality of cross-cultural influence and rightly frustrate ethnography's claim to an authentic primitive. On the other hand, Leiris argues that despite development and the changes imposed by the colonizer, the colonized preserves traits of his cultural particularity that remain irreducible and thus warrant analysis. In this definition of a mobile and hybrid cultural predicament, Leiris theorizes an Other that is not utterly Other, determined not unto itself but in relation to a cultural exterior. For these reasons Leiris recognized that the fortunes of Antillean writers lay not in a reversion to a "native" tongue but in a contestatory claim to French, a position with which Fanon concurred.[6] Thus Leiris breaks with an entire tradition of ethnography, renouncing the "unilateral" direction of its research (127; 142) and proposing for the ethnographer an activist role in the other's culture: as advisor in matters of colonial rule, and as advocate of their self-determination.

The ethnographic position Leiris defines in "The Ethnographer Faced with Colonialism" ultimately depends on a political realignment with the other, a commitment that goes beyond principle to realize itself in the material struggle of liberation. Leiris's argument is to be situated in part within the perspective of his alignment at this time with Sartre and communism, and some might see in his argument a form of colonialism importing a Western humanism no less suspect than its counterparts. But this would be to misread an essential aspect of Leiris's text that undercuts the very authority of Western discourse on the Other, including, consequently, Leiris's own. The position of the ethnographer emerges in Leiris's essay as necessarily *partial* and thus politically engaged; his position is compromised on the one hand by an inescapable ideological power structure and by an object of study that is dynamic, relative, and in flux. One of the remarkable propositions of Leiris in these pages is that of the "colonized ethnographer," whose training would allow the native to cast an eye in turn on himself, his neighbors, and even—a possibility Leiris qualifies as utopic, or perhaps only premature—to return the gaze of the colonizer. What distinguishes Leiris's position from that of Lévi-Strauss, for instance—liberal and anticolonial as well—is his willingness to undermine ethnographic authority over others, and this scrupulous work of self-critique derives not so much from a political program as it does from an *ethical* insight into the contingency of knowledge and the illusion of mastery. It remains for us to define the source of this ethical insight and its discursive application in Leiris's work.

If the publication of *L'Afrique fantôme* was perceived by some as an overt "provocation" or insult to ethnography,[7] it would be premature, however, to attribute any concerted cause on the author's part. Leiris speaks to such a prematurity in the *prière d'insérer*, where he describes "the work the author would perhaps have written" had he not chosen to publish the text unedited.[8] With a retrospective glance, Leiris invites the reader to uncover the "germs" of a growing awareness implicit in the text: "It is up to the reader to discover the germs of a sudden awareness [*une prise de conscience*] achieved only well after the return from the trip" (47; 55). Reading the text is to see it in the light of what it *might have been*: whatever its failings and mistakes, the story of one man's loss of illusions. While the *prière d'insérer* reads backwards, at a crucial moment the African journal gets ahead of itself, anticipating what the text *will have been*. Thus, in the middle of *L'Afrique fantôme* we find the drafts of two "forewords," premature statements on the book-to-be. Leiris starts with a list of what the text is *not*: "This journal is neither an historical record of the Dakar-Djibouti Mission, nor what is commonly called 'a travel account.'"[9] Leiris justifies the project here in the terms in which he had earlier defined his *journal intime*, emphasizing the role of futility and the necessity of self-examination.[10] *L'Afrique fantôme*, Leiris flatly says, might just as well have been written in Paris. In these misplaced forewords, we see the author getting ahead of himself; Leiris himself points this out in a later footnote that indicates to what extent his self-involvement at the time of writing conflicts with his actual perspective upon his return (267).

The play of retrospection and anticipation of *L'Afrique fantôme* defines the peculiar disjunctive temporality of Leiris's journal, which, despite being written in a perpetual here and now, nevertheless escapes from the security of any present. Killing time during idle moments of the mission, Leiris attempts to write his way into this impossible present. But what returns to haunt him in the text's temporal confusions is the very passage of time that he hoped the mission would cancel. In the loose-leaf insert to his African journal, Leiris states his impossible aim as "arresting the process of aging by traveling through space in order to negate time."[11] The voyage will never go fast enough, consequently, to stop time, and for all his restlessness, Leiris will be under the impression that he is himself arrested, going nowhere. Writing for Leiris would be the art of the missed appointment; rather than filling out the present, it occupies the minimal interval in which his desire finds its play, as in the step of a dance that defines the "cadence" and "parade" of disappointment: "waiting and regret [*attente, regret*]."[12] The African journal, in its missed appointments, confirms the self-defeating project of filling one's date book with distractions: Leiris realizes eventually that far from dispatching time, it is, after all, "as though in the end I were making dates . . . with time itself."[13]

One aspect of this temporal dislocation is a failed engagement with political *actualité*. Leiris points up this situation in his preface to the second edition when, looking back, he judges the book to be outdated, outmoded, "dépassé par la situation."[14] Too early for political engagement, too late for adventure, *L'Afrique fantôme* occupies an interval between a legendary past and a political future. In 1950, the year of "The Ethnographer Faced with Colonialism," it is thus a more politicized introduction Leiris writes, evoking the text's suppression under the Occupation and the disservice it rendered to his fellow ethnographers. In the light of his espousal of the rights of the colonized, the journal is now seen as a "confession" of his blindness to the social issues of the colonies. Leiris's text is consequently suspended in a vacant interval: after adventure and before revolution, in the insecure period between two world wars. The trip across Africa constitutes an interval in Leiris's psychoanalytic treatment too, interrupted at the encouragement of his doctor and resumed again upon his return. Fleeing analysis, Leiris launches despite himself into the self-analysis of *L'Afrique fantôme*, fending off psychology even as he dramatically acts it out. As we will see, the distinctive dynamic and singular originality of *L'Afrique fantôme* lie in the conflicts and correspondences Leiris articulates between the heterogeneous but overlapping fields of psychoanalysis, ethnography, and literature. This makes Leiris, in his very disappointments, the prime witness to the compromises and missed appointments of the ethnographic mission.

Some of the most compelling passages in *L'Afrique fantôme* put the colonial situation dramatically into play, revealing the cultural and discursive contradictions of the mission. As the mission's program is to study traditional cultures and collect artifacts, the influence of colonial rule on native cultures constitutes an impediment to ethnographic analysis. A rhythm of anticipation and discouragement thus characterizes the progress of the mission as it passes through sites of varying levels of development. "Missionaries and salesmen go out of their way to spoil the country," Leiris complains. "Not a single man or woman who is not dressed in European style" (229). To encounter the authentic native, they must push beyond the zone of French influence and what Leiris calls the "annoyances of civilization" (241). A crucial paradox of such an ethnographic mission is that even as it seeks the unspoiled native, the team of ethnographers cannot but affect the primitive cultures they study. Such is the epistemological double bind of the research, tied both to colonial rule and the preservation of local custom. Everywhere, the mission plays catch-up with cultures in decline, justifying its incursions in the name of protecting artifacts and information. It does not escape Leiris's attention that the ethnographers themselves participate in this decline, although the clearest view of the predicament is reserved for his letters to his wife.[15] The most damning passages in the journal, as we will see, bear specifically on the abuses of authority to which the ethnographers succumb in the interest of study.

For Leiris himself, the disappointments of the mission carry a dividend of nostalgia that authenticates the voyage under the seal of disillusionment. Here we see a surreptitious turn in the discourse of disillusionment; if, on the one hand, the loss of illusions can foster a clearer view of things, on the other hand it can hold more firmly to its cherished losses in the mode of nostalgia. In a passage whose lyrical tone anticipates that of *Tristes tropiques*, he describes the demise of local custom under French colonial rule.

> They say that ever since French occupation the serpent no longer comes to lick the *hogon*, because there is no real *hogon* anymore. The myth has survived. What an admirable ending for a mythological serpent: it is not dead, it has not been diluted in any skepticism, it has merely hidden itself, for the times are no longer propitious. We are at the heart of this eclipse. (*L'Afrique fantôme*, 147)

The political situation Leiris describes here undermines the objectives of research, but the lyricism of the passage indicates that another object, this one not simply ethnographic, appeals to Leiris: an object of poetic nostalgia, inscribed within an eclipsed present that holds out for a future return. Leiris here is close to the romantic temperament of Nerval, who constitutes as much as the adventurous Arthur Rimbaud Leiris's literary precursor in Africa. It is worth recalling the lines from Nerval's "Delfica" that speak of the sleeping dragon: "They shall return, these gods you still bemoan! / Time will bring back the order of the ancient days."[16] Far from being a stylistic conceit, Leiris's writerly perspective allows for an approach to the object of research that undermines the mission's pretenses, exposing the reality of the mission in its missed appointment with native culture. But the echoes of Nerval suggest at the same time that "imperialist nostalgia," to adopt Renato Rosaldo's term, can maintain its contradictions in a poetic mode that enjoys its losses.[17] Leiris recognizes that between the ethnographers and the natives is interposed a political economy or an economy of tourism that undercuts any real contact. Taking stock of this falseness, Leiris is led to conclude, "The only bond we share is our common falsity" (*L'Afrique fantôme*, 131). This "common falsity" will reappear in Leiris's account of the theater of possession in Ethiopia, a vexed analysis that cannot settle accounts with the simulacrum.

An emblematic scene occurs in the middle of *L'Afrique fantôme*: "The sides of the road seem to be completely deserted, but you need only turn your head to see the people hidden in the bushes who come out again once the car has passed by" (180). This scene figures the elusiveness of Leiris's object, experienced only after the fact. Cursory and fragmentary, as befits a *journal de route*, it inscribes a temporal lag in which Leiris's trajectory coincides with nothing but its own passage: anticipation and backward glance with no present. In its brevity, it notes a situation in which the commentary is lacking; the latent schema requires an additional look back, that of the reader or another Leiris. What if Leiris's Africa were a "phantom" for the simple reason that its peoples were in *hiding* from the mission?[18] This scene thus condenses the experience of the voyage: both in terms of a personal predicament, symptom of a personal *décalage*, and in terms of a colonial situation that authorizes the mission even as it frustrates its objectives; a situation that, the time come, will *dépasse* in turn the journal and leave it behind.

Exotic Ethnography

The beginnings of Leiris's African journal date back to 1929, when Leiris contributed to Georges Bataille's magazine *Documents*. An unruly publication, *Documents* was a hybrid mixture of art, literature, philosophy, and ethnography, and it was at *Documents* that Leiris met Marcel Griaule, who, having just returned from an ethnographic expedition to Ethiopia, would invite Leiris to join a team of researchers on his next ethnographic mission. *Documents* sheds light on the cultural context in which the Mission Dakar-Djibouti was hatched, as well as on Leiris's mixed motives for joining it. In 1929 Leiris's career was in limbo. His literary output remained scant and the autobiographical project had not yet taken shape. Just broken from Breton's surrealist circle, Leiris was exploring his new affinities with Bataille in their shared fascination with the sacred. *Documents* provided a forum in which the surrealist dissidents could extend their aesthetic adventure in new directions, and in which ethnography played a major part. In ethnography, Leiris, Bataille, and their colleagues, frustrated with what they came to see as the idealizing and reductively aesthetic concerns of the surrealist group, discovered a field in which their interests could take on a more concrete form. The result, what James Clifford terms "surrealist ethnography," was an extraordinarily original and inventive laboratory in which cultural criticism and art cross-fertilized with a budding social science.[19] In the pages of the magazine, one found Carl Einstein's study on the relations between modern sculpture and African art; essays on jazz and popular cinema; poetry, literary criticism, and ethnographic research. The father of French ethnography, Marcel Mauss, contributed to an issue on Picasso. In an homage to his friend Bataille, Leiris would later qualify the man and his magazine as "impossible" by virtue of the journal's provocative tone and the heterodoxical nature of its material.[20] This impossible quality—extravagance allied with sober analysis, reason neighboring the absurd—would develop following the demise of *Documents* into Bataille's work in the Collège de Sociologie, whose primary program, inspired by "primitive" cultural forms, was the revival of the sacred in contemporary culture. But if *Documents* is termed impossible by Leiris, it is also because its utopian vision would be literally impossible to maintain. At the heart of its untenability is a double-edged exotic. Whatever Leiris's commitment to Bataille and to his other colleagues at *Documents*, the "impossibility" of Bataille's project would be the eventual cause of Leiris's break from the Collège, when, siding with responsible ethnography, he would take exception to Bataille's fast-and-loose application of ethnographic material to contemporary cultural analysis.[21] Leiris's exception to the Collège can be seen as a settling of scores with a certain exotic motive in the avant-garde, dating back to *Documents* and surrealism.

At the time of *Documents*, the exotic played a double role in the development of French ethnography. Sustained by colonial commerce and travel, exoticism in the metropole represented the culturally Other primarily in a reductive mode of fashion and fantasy, perpetuating the politics of empire in imaginary delights. At the same time, exotic fantasies laid bare, for those who could read them, a cultural unsettling in its ambivalent projection of monsters and paradises. To analyze the exotic during this period is thus to situate it within a political, economic, and discursive field coextensive with the reach of colonialism, but also to read into its contradictions an implicit critique. Exoticism, in this light, is not reducible merely to illusion, but is instead a field in which power and desire play out their imaginary contradictions. Leiris certainly represents one of the most interesting instances of this ambivalent exotic. His affection for jazz and African American variety shows betrays an escapism with links to contemporary negrophilia in high culture, manifested in the Parisian *style nègre* of the 1920s and a generalized fascination with Oceanic, African, and pre-Columbian art. The fact that jazz during this time was linked, even by Leiris, to African primitivism is an index of the exoticizing quality the music held for its public. At the same time, such cultural phenomena and artifacts from abroad made possible a radical estrangement of culture. In an essay on Gide, Michael Lucey shows the multivalent significance a Tuareg spear from Algeria could hold for a queer young Frenchman, representing both a trophy of colonial conquest and the sign of resistance in which Gide could be affectively invested. A "proliferation of fantasies" thus inheres in the artifact, settling in no coherent narrative of order and reinforcing Gide's wayward desire.[22] A similar ambivalence characterizes that vein of modern art tied to primitivism. In her account of aesthetic practice within the context of *Documents*, Rosalind Krauss usefully distinguishes two forms of primitivism in the arts: one content to import themes and forms from an exotic storehouse in order to aestheticize them; the other, exemplified by *Documents*, that integrates the primitive in a local critique of exoticism's home base through avant-garde invention and political and philosophical contestation.[23]

To the extent that such alternatives exist within a single field, then, the exotic can be seen as a discursive space in which heterogeneous options cohabit, as alternate tendencies and divided impulses of attraction and abjection, exclusion and overture. My analysis thus takes its distance from a reading of exoticism in primarily ideological terms, as if its representations were reducible to a unified discourse or political order. While I intend, in what follows, to engage a critique of exoticist domination and misrepresentation, I propose to maintain the exotic within this ambivalent overture. To do so is to follow on such work as Edward Said's *Orientalism*, which studied the alliance of cultural forms of exoticist representation with political ideology.[24] But whereas Said, particularly in his earlier work, tended to see such representations as totalizing and unified, I suggest that the cultural forms of exoticist consumption and production provide for a play of fantasy, invention, and critique that may go against the grain of colonial order.[25] This is to claim that art is never fully reducible to the conditions of its production and consumption; while necessarily informed by and informing social and cultural norms, art provides for the deconstruction of those cultural norms and forms.

The popularity of African exoticism would be a major enabling factor for *Documents* and the Mission Dakar-Djibouti, both generously funded by patrons of the arts. James Clifford highlights the productive nature of this exoticism, showing how the vogue was turned to profit by the founders of the Musée de l'Homme.[26] Despite the illusions on which it was based and the colonial order that made it possible, French ethnography would develop away from its exoticist beginnings to ultimately lay claim to scientific legitimacy as institution and practice. Leiris would be among the founding members of this new institution. Leiris's career at the time of *Documents* is thus the hinge between a surrealist-inspired "wild" ethnography and the official career as ethnographer he would assume upon his return from Africa. During this period, Leiris thus participated in the transformation of French ethnography from its early stages into a state-subsidized institution with field-workers stationed in a renovated Trocadéro, soon to be replaced itself by the Musée de l'Homme. In his account of this evolution, Clifford says that the history of French ethnography during this period can be resumed as the story of these two museums. Whereas the Orientalist-style Trocadéro museum housed an undisciplined collection of exotic curios, the modernist Musée de l'Homme, under the auspices of the Institut d'Ethnologie, would display a scientifically sanctioned portrait of humanity in its diversity. Leiris himself would express nostalgia for the old museum, being always more at home in a *jumble*. Moreover, the futures of French ethnography and anthropology would show to what extent the institutions subtly perpetuated exoticist motives, the progressivist humanism of the new museum being all too often linked to the "civilizing mission" of French colonialism. The liberal banner of a synthetic "Humanity" finds its ironic rejoinder in the totalizing grasp of colonial order. Thus, Paul Rivet, director of the Trocadéro, while a socialist, antiracist, and advocate of colonial reform, could comfortably speak of ethnographic museums as "instruments of colonial propaganda."[27] It would take Leiris's "The Ethnographer Faced with Colonialism" of 1950 to fully expose the political compromises of such liberal posturing. With the rise of the new museum, the hotbed of intellectual ferment of the period of *Documents* would be supplanted by the compromising politics of a state-endowed institution. In retrospect, the price paid for this authority seems very high. *Documents* and the odd context of the Trocadéro represent in Clifford's analysis a facet of cultural activity smoothed over by the accession of ethnography to scientific legitimacy. Clifford's aim is thus to reappraise ethnography's origins and revive the singular moment when ethnography, in its intersection with art, philosophy, and cultural critique, expressed a utopian opportunity of cross-cultural invention and disorientation, making strange the familiar and familiar the strange. Clifford thus sees the promise of ethnography to lie in such a context, where cultural practice is not limited to the consumption of otherness, but involves a questioning of the home culture and the very grounds of discursive authority. The exotic, in this analysis, is not simply overcome, but provides at once the means for overture and its very limits: a double-edged "dépaysement," as Leiris puts it in *L'Afrique fantôme*, whose transports are drawn toward the pleasures of the exotic, but thereby provoke a more unsettling disorientation.

Transports

One of Leiris's earliest texts, written in 1929 for *Documents*, is an article on metaphor. In the light of his ethnographic career and the travels it will occasion, it is striking that the figure Leiris critiques in his essay is that of *transport*. A slim text published under the rubric of a "Dictionary" entry, "Metaphor" appeared among regularly featured articles by Desnos, Limbour, Griaule, and Bataille in the pages of the magazine. These "Dictionary" entries included such scabrous and provocative topics as "Spittle" and "Materialism," and were calculated to shock. But beyond the gesture of provocation, the project of the "Dictionary" testifies to nothing less than an exhaustive effort of cultural redefinition on the part of Bataille and his colleagues. By means of cultural cross-referencing and conceptual debasement, *Documents*' definitions extend the reach of cultural analysis, plunging into the murky domains of primitivism, violence, and sexuality. Bataille's hand is evident throughout, as the dictionary tends less toward definition than *heterology*, according to a mode of inquiry whose characteristic movement is from knowing to not knowing. Accordingly, Bataille's entry "Formless" takes to task both the notion of definition itself and the conceptual ideology that would elevate "form" above the riot of the world's base materialism. The authors of the dictionary are civilization's malcontents, reversing humanity's presumed elevation with their insistence on sacred violence, primitivism, and all that "high" culture would suppress.[28]

In keeping with this disarticulation of form and meaning, Leiris's "Metaphor" does not serve as guarantor of sense. If, in the common definition, metaphor provides for the transfer of sense between abstract and concrete, proper and figural meanings, Leiris disputes the grounds of such a belief, claiming that "it is hard to know where metaphor begins and where it ends."[29] In metaphor, the transfer of meaning would ground itself in a "proper" sense that serves as base and reference point for a figural meaning. And yet, such a proper meaning does not exist, as it implies knowledge of its object's essence, which, Leiris asserts, is impossible:

> An abstract word is formed by the sublimation of a concrete word. A concrete word, which never designates an object by more than one of its qualities, is itself hardly more than a metaphor, or at the very least a figurative expression. Moreover, to designate an object by an expression that corresponds to it not figuratively but literally, one would need to know the very essence of that object, which is impossible, since we can know only phenomena, not things in themselves. (18; 25)

Any word, therefore, deprived of its grounding in proper meaning is consequently caught up in a figural "play of transpositions" without beginning or end: "all known objects are connected to one another by relations of interdependency. With any two of them, it is impossible to determine which is designated by the name proper to it and is not a metaphor of the other, and vice versa" (18; 25). The notion of metaphor is thus displaced to name instead a metonymic relay of figures.

This disavowal of metaphor implicitly critiques a certain definition of transport and translation that, denying the hazards of the trip, would guarantee safe passage, stable identity, and univocal meaning. Such precisely is the function of metaphor in philosophy as circumscribed by what Derrida calls "the law of the same."[30] In privileging identity over difference and laying claim to an illusory proper meaning, the trope of transport is above all for Derrida the figure of a *return*: a return to the fold of the home, as well as the return of profit. In the place of such transport, Leiris substitutes the work of metonymy, which, strung out on another axis, links terms not according to identity but contiguity, in a series of substitutive displacements without proper beginning or end. Travel becomes dislocation, accident, and wandering, rather than a speculative circuit of profit and return.[31] The rhetorical critique distilled in Leiris's "Metaphor" can thus be brought into relation with his disillusionment with travel and his political demystification of ethnography. As traveler and writer Leiris conducts an exploration of two axes of transport: one ordered according to identity and property, the other according to displacement and difference. We have seen how the critique of the ethnographic traveler operates an undermining of the proper in favor of what we might call a metonymy of social relations. Interestingly, such a formula seems coded in a late criticism by Leiris of French "assimilationist" policy in the colonies, to which he favorably contrasts the British "associative" policy.[32] Travel and rhetorical transport, for Leiris, are not governed by similitude or assimilation but by displacement and difference. Autobiography and ethnography thus converge for Leiris in this displacement of transport.

Put another way, Leiris's redefinition of metaphor in terms of metonymy coincides with what James Clifford identifies as the "surrealist moment in ethnography": the moment, exemplified by the cultural context of *Documents*, in which "the possibility of comparison exists in unmediated tension with sheer incongruity."[33] Within this epistemological context, cross-cultural comparison and hybrid discourses lose the common ground that would ensure their authority, like the "dangerous mixtures" and "unusual juxtapositions" famously invoked at the outset of Foucault's *The Order of Things*.[34] Likeness is not thought from the perspective of a singular, unified field, or from the vantage point of a dominant culture. Similitudes are reversible, and thus undermine and call into question the perspective from which identity may be thought.

Now, if metaphor becomes Leiris's target in his essay, one might say it is because of the hackneyed commonplaces it habitually serves. What Leiris objects to in metaphor is the propriety of civil language and common parlance that would shun semantic errancy. In an entry titled "Civilization," it is thus metaphor itself as much as civilization that provokes Leiris's disgust: "However little taste one might have for proposing metaphors as explanations, civilization may be compared without too much inexactness to the thin greenish layer—the living magma and the odd detritus—that forms on the surface of calm water and sometimes solidifies into a crust, until an eddy comes to break it up [*jusqu'à ce qu'un remous soit venu tout bouleverser*]."[35] If common language itself is repulsive, Leiris will be at pains to find the right words for his assault on culture, which is why another entry faults a litany of domesticated metaphors of catastrophe, false commonplaces, if ever there were: *coup de foudre* (love at first sight), *avalanche de compliments* (shower of compliments), and so forth. A single word, *débâcle*, appeals to Leiris, not for its metaphorical quality, but because of the resonances it carries for him as he disarticulates and glosses it, in the manner of a rebus: "However worn most of these images are, one of them is still capable of moving us because it is so brutally, implacably concise, one that is, in fact, *bâclé* [bungled], with the very haste that characterizes disasters—and this is the word *débâcle*" (36; 44). Here, despite Leiris's revolutionary affinities with his fellow contributors to *Documents*, it is clearly his own dictionary that Leiris is compiling, following the method of the ludic gloss begun with his *Glossary: My Glosses' Ossuary* (*Glossaire: J'y serre mes gloses*) and continuing through to the *Souple mantique*, in which selected words take on singular definitions through a process that, spurning etymology and common semantics, rearticulates them by the deformations of puns, anagrams, and chance associations, their "room for play [*le jeu*]" (61; 69). "Metaphor" and Leiris's other entries take their place, then, in a distinctively Leirisian project of linguistic disarticulation that will propel in later years the composition of his four-volume autobiography, *Rules of the Game* (*La Règle du jeu*). According to this method, homophonic elements serve to "explicate" word entries as more or less extended puns: in *débâcle*, then, Leiris reads *implacable*, *bâclé*, *hâte* (haste), and *désastre*. Similarly, his *Souple mantique* offers "métaphore, Orphée est maître de tes fards"; "métonymie—méthode pour que mes mots miment le mythe."[36]

What Leiris brings to *Documents*, then, is the project of a dictionary announced in the preface to his 1925 *Glossaire*, which stands at the head of Leiris's life work and could serve as its general introduction. Scorning the "usefulness" of dictionary definitions, Leiris dismisses both etymology and custom, the latter qualified as "the lowest criterion to which one could refer."[37] Leiris here lays claim to a private domain of language over which others have no hold. "The everyday meaning and the etymological meaning of a word can teach us nothing about ourselves, since they represent the collective part of language, which was made for all people and not for each of us individually." Only a subjective definition of words, without regard for their common sense can unveil their "hidden qualities," turning language into a personal "oracle." Leiris's *Glossaire* is thus the inverse but the correlative of Flaubert's *Dictionnaire des idées reçues*, excluding popular language to arrive at his intimate, subjective truth. If Leiris, following this lifelong method, is a *man of his word*, scrupulously honest in his confessions, it is in this paradoxical sense that his word seems as if without appeal and true only to himself.

In *Mimologiques*, Gérard Genette points out that "*Glossaire* is a Cratylist dictionary," placing Leiris's linguistic explorations within the tradition of Plato's Cratylus, who argued the mimetic correspondence between words and things.[38] What Genette says of Cratylus would, then, apply to Leiris: "He goes into exile and retreats into what he decides is the truth—"his" truth—of language and of the world. Henceforth a stranger to all common *communication*, he devotes himself to exploring his interior universe and his interior vocabulary" (*Mimologics*, 296). This tendency is particularly apparent in the preface to the *Glossaire*, where we read this apparent disavowal of communication: "A monstrous aberration causes people to believe that language came into being to facilitate their relations with one another."[39] In response to Genette, however, one might say that Leiris's objection bears less on communication itself than on its claim to *facility*; Leiris's linguistic exercises would then be a means of taking issue with the givenness of language, its self-apparent common sense. Accordingly, the apparently "subjective" nature of Leiris's glosses thus would point less toward his unique selfhood than to a field of linguistic difference in which he apprehends his linguistic and thus social nature. In structuralist terms, his dictionary entries exclude the *langue* to foreground *parole*, the metonymic syntagm in which the linguistic code is actualized. For all its uniqueness, Leiris's syntagm would then speak to the simple fact that every speaker must make language his own in order to transform the metaphoric code into metonymic speech. One might also ask what forms of address Leiris sets up in his writing, even as he carves out his own linguistic world. It remains to be seen, in short, what may be defined as communication in Leiris, and to what Other he addresses himself. To answer these questions, one would have to add to the stylistic, rhetorical, and linguistic analysis of Genette an account of Leiris's chosen form of address, confession, and auto-analysis. One would also need to broach the ethics of his prose and the politics it espouses. It is noteworthy, then, in the light of these political and ethical questions that in 1986 Leiris contributed one of his last "glosses" to a volume committed to the cause of Nelson Mandela. Leiris's short essay consists of nothing more than a Cratylist interpretation of the word "apartheid," which starts, in a style that remains utterly faithful to his literary beginnings:

"*Apartheid*: I know neither the exact pronunciation of this word nor its etymology." If the definition that follows is unmistakably Leirisian, it is also, however, one shared by his collaborators and borne out by postcolonial history. "When I read it I always think of the word 'hideous' because of its resemblance with the final syllable." Leiris's private lexicon thus performs a supplementary twist, linking an absolutely subjective definition of the word to a common world: "*Apartheid*: a harsh, mean word that resounds in one's ears like a trapdoor opening beneath a gallows."[40]

That Leiris's rhetoric, founded as it is on a vindication of the absolutely subjective, should lend itself to such political and ethical ends testifies to the transformations Leiris underwent in the course of his long career as writer and ethnographer. And yet, we can see even in the earliest form of Leiris's method an ambivalence that ties the private to an ethical overture. Indeed, I would argue that an account of Leiris's travels and politics cannot do without an account of the ambivalent figures at the heart of his writing practice. This ambivalence points to what are two main directions, impulses, or tendencies of Leiris's writing. The first of these corresponds to Leiris's retrospective quest, directed toward his personal origins; the other is the movement away from the origin, played out in a textual grappling with absence and lack. These two tendencies are narrated most concisely in the well-known opening pages of *Scratches* (*Biffures*), where Leiris dwells on the moment of his first conscious grasp of language. In this chapter, a toy soldier falls to the ground and the young Leiris, discovering to his relief that it has not broken, emits a single word of satisfaction: "reusement!" (i.e. *heureusement*, "happily, fortunately").[41] In the beginning, for Leiris, was *his word*, characterized "simply as an interjection" and "completely private." Notably, however, this origin is also a moment of departure and exile from imaginary self-sufficiency, for the opening chapter of *Scratches* emblematically relates a fall from grace in which Leiris's word leaves the charmed circle of childhood to connect with a larger world. Leiris recounts how the word misspoken by the young Leiris is corrected by one of his elders and made to conform to correct grammar. The quest for the self in Leiris's autobiography thus finds its tragic response in the recognition that his word is also the word of others, *socialized*, as Leiris says: "It had changed from something belonging to me [*propre à moi*] into something communal and open." Thus, the "lost linguistic paradise" Genette speaks of in regard to Leiris can never be the place to which he might return but provides instead for the reenactment of a trauma in which the subject is originally lost from himself.[42] Self-constitution in Leiris is inseparable from the self-division brought on by language or the apprehension of death. So if Leiris strives to revive his first words by returning to the past, it is only to rediscover this alienation, itself repeated in his wandering prose. Elsewhere Leiris succinctly sums up this predicament: "There is a paradox to this kind of memory: in it I find the purest expression of myself, to the very extent that it struck me by the strangeness it harbored within it."[43] This experience of strangeness or alienation corresponds, then, to the second direction in Leiris's writing: the digressive, impulsive proliferation of writing that spells out the realization there can be neither first nor last word. We might say that all of Leiris's innumerable glosses, so many "misspoken" words, stand at the place where these two trajectories diverge, repeating the experience of his primal encounter with the social symbolic. In this way, Leiris's childish play sets the stage for his interminable approach to manhood.

The toy soldier in *Scratches* is manifestly a metaphor for Leiris, a stand-in for the young subject insofar as it fails to stand, and falls. The "danger" faced by the soldier is analogous to that faced by the child Leiris under the threat of the law, just as Leiris's "vertigo" responds to the fall of the soldier. Leiris is careful to point out that the soldier does not represent, in the mind of the child he was at the time, a *soldier*, as he would have been ignorant of such a meaning. Rather, as a mere toy, it stands in a one-to-one relationship of belonging and attachment to Leiris. The vocabulary of attachment thus contrasts sharply with Leiris's vocabulary of breakage and cutting. The soldier is "within an inch of being broken [*sous le coup d'avoir été cassé*]," while Leiris is interpellated by the word of another that, as he says, "cut short my joy" (5; 11). This violent cutting is prefigured, however, by the toy *itself*, which belongs to the category of things, Leiris says, that represent the real world only in their division from it. Such objects "contrast so strongly with the real world [*tranchent sur le monde réel*], at the same time that they represent perhaps its sharpest features" (4; 11). This formulation would suggest, then, that the narrative of the fall is secondary to what in the story of Leiris's life is not of the order of an event or a primal scene that can be remembered, but belongs to the order of representation. The scene Leiris narrates at the beginning of *Scratches* can only be a stand-in for a prior castration, properly unnamable. But the "vertigo" provoked by the experience that left him "dazed [*interdit*]" (6; 12) persists and remains the motor of Leiris's searching prose. It thus becomes particularly suggestive that the fall of the toy is obsessively repeated, not merely twice but eight times in the course of the telling. This repetition signals the echo of the trauma that remains, despite Leiris's reformulations, corrections, and precisions, unassimilable to the Leiris who writes and remembers. It thus gives form to what is not unique to the event, the fact that this *singular* moment in Leiris's life is itself but the echo of an earlier fall that recedes to the limits of memory.

The repetition, the quest for the origin and the experience of a fall suggest that *Scratches*, the first volume of *Rules of the Game*, opens under the sign of allegory. These thematic elements are borne out by the structural ordering of the narrative. For if allegory, in its simplest structural definition, is defined as metaphor strung out in a series, that is, on the metonymic axis, the metaphor of the soldier becomes allegorical by means of the repetition that alters, rephrases, and attempts to re-member what is dismembered in the beginning. As such, Leiris's allegory would be an allegory of castration, understood in the Lacanian sense as the cut introduced in the subject upon entry into the Symbolic. And as allegory, it links up etymologically with Lacan's definition of the Symbolic as the *discourse of the Other*, that discourse Leiris speaks only against his will, under pain of confession.

The beginning of *Scratches* makes legible the stakes of Leiris's linguistic play specifically as it relates to self-expression, desire, and symbolic law. *Rules of the Game* thus breaks with the self-portrait of the earlier autobiographical volume *Manhood* to the extent that it pitches decisively into the domain of allegory. To be more precise, the allegorical dimension of *Rules of the Game* is explored in a closer attention to a process of writing and self-reading, as distinct from *Manhood*'s obsessive catalogue of myths and classical themes. The two tendencies of Leiris's prose that we have outlined thus far converge in allegory as the conjunction of metaphor and metonymy. These two tropes, as we have seen, provide the rhetorical axes that correspond to the articulation of the private and the social, identity and difference. To the extent that these plot out an allegory, it is an allegory of order, of law, and thus they decide in favor of a social necessity that, in Lacanian discourse, goes under the name of castration. This order is in keeping with the structure of allegory, to the extent that this rhetorical mode, in its common acceptance, is a hierarchizing mode that appeals to a transcendent signification, typically, in Western tradition, in a Christian form. And yet, in recent years, critics and rhetoricians have come to break with this tradition, seeing in allegory a mode of discourse that lends itself to no such determinate order. It is noteworthy that this perspective develops as a challenge to structural linguistics, to which of course Lacan is particularly indebted. Allegory stands in a distinctive place in this system, as the fundamental binary articulation of structural linguistics, metaphor and metonymy, are conjoined within it. This conjunction, however, is not without its difficulties. Jakobson himself points out that within allegory each of the two terms is implicated in the other, thereby indicating a structural instability at the root of the system itself. This instability bears on the system's inability to justify its first principles, or, to invoke the allegorical motif, its origin. In a far-reaching essay on the structure of allegory, Joel Fineman concludes that "Every metaphor is a metonymy of its own origins," thus condemning structure and identity to an abyssal displacement from out of the source. What results is allegory, understood not restrictively as style or genre, but as the ironic condition to which language is bound in its quest for meaning: "Distanced at the beginning from its source, allegory will set out on an increasingly futile search for a signifier with which to recuperate the fracture of and at its source, and with each successive signifier the fracture and the search begin again: a structure of continual yearning, the insatiable desire of allegory."[44] As we saw in chapter 1, this formula resonates with Leiris's restless textual practice, providing a key to his retrospective quest and his obsessive, repetitive play with language. It also anticipates the futile search of Leiris's ethnographic mission as rendered in the frustrated and yet driven force of his African journal. Within this optic, it would thus be less than apt to reduce Leiris's textual adventure to the order of castration, or the rule of the signifier. What may pertain, instead, is a play with symbolic structure, the *jeu* in the *règle*, rather than the rule *of* the game: a systematic disequilibrium that is legible in Leiris's early definition of metaphor, where he approached the structural incompletion of the master trope and its restless origin.

In this way, the symbolic unsettling of allegory provides a means to read the tensions and impulses of Leiris's self-account in the text of his travels. Leiris's travels in Africa will take on a distinctive topology already prefigured in his rhetorical practice and in the essay on metaphor. What is repeatedly at stake in the text of *L'Afrique fantôme* is an inability of Leiris to *situate* himself; this predicament bears at once on a symbolic positioning and the desires of Leiris as they are stimulated and thwarted by the adventures of the mission. Our reading of Leiris's travels will show how the practice of writing, his symbolic play, dislocates him from the social symbolic and provides for an unsettling of its fundamental terms. Denis Hollier has aptly spoken of Leiris as a "déséquilibriste," showing how his writing tends above all to unsettle the writer through a linguistic exercise in instability.[45] Such instability reveals its stakes when it problematizes Leiris's political stance, personal affiliations, and sexual rapports. Indeed, one may argue that a political field or sexual problematic may be unapproachable without the articulation of such instabilities. This is to argue that "the political" is not reducible to a unified field or to a set of stances, just as the politics of gender is best cornered not in roles, identities, or postures, but in their performative tropes. This performative dimension is suggested in the complex turns of Leiris's phrase that describes dance as "traduire en parade judicieusement réglée les orages sensuels."[46] Leiris's ostentatious *parade* is one that, while under the purview of the *règle*, is no less a *parrying* of the rule than a self-display—and that, as we have seen, tends stubbornly toward the paralysis of a halt. In this last sense, "traduire en parade" is the expression of an antinomy of movement and stasis. It is, however, more precisely *paralyzing* to the extent that it expresses the inextricable linkage of the master-trope of metaphor (suggested by *traduire*) with the metonymic slide of *parade*'s glossemantic complexities.

Just as "Metaphor" bears on a certain negation of transport, *L'Afrique fantôme* is defined by Leiris above all by a repudiation of the genre of literary travel.[47] Indeed, Leiris's African adventure speaks to nothing so much as the experience of *getting nowhere*. This restless stasis is played out in fantasies of self-discovery, primitive wholeness, and African Edens, perpetually invoked and just as often dispelled. Such themes of primitive origins can be tied, as we have seen, to the motivating force of allegory, its appeal to beginnings played out in symbolic displacement. And if, on a structural graph, metaphor and metonymy plot out the space of symbolic positionings, Leiris's prose tends irresistibly toward the point of their convergence in what, mathematically speaking, is named the origin. This is a point that defies any access or account, and it drives the rhythm of Leiris's paralyzed travelogue.

Getting Nowhere

Rather than composing a developmental narrative, Leiris's African journal is a series of false starts, anticipations, and retractions. For every step forward, Leiris takes a step back; the voyage consequently never seems to get underway: "July 4. The life we lead here is basically very monotonous, like that of circus folk who move around all the time but always put on the same show. I'm having a great deal of trouble adapting to discipline and can hardly resign myself to suppressing this equation: traveling = lounging about [*voyager = flâner*]" (*L'Afrique fantôme*, 56). The town of Bamako revives him: "August 5. . . . The whole route from Dakar to here sinks into the past. . . . A feeling not of arrival but of departure, strength and renewal" (81); "November 27. . . . Sudden change of mood again: indifference at traveling, stupidity of working for a museum. I can't wait to be . . . where? I wonder!" (164); "January 26. . . . You quickly grow weary of traveling and, with few exceptions, the sequence of things and events soon becomes tiresome, as if we were not moving at all" (210); "February 19. . . . No more tourism. We are going to travel now and get much closer to things and men" (227). Finally, nearly a year into the trip, and with the better part of travel behind them, Abyssinia provokes hope for a new beginning: "How many miles has it taken for us to feel that we are finally on the threshold of exoticism!" (281).

In this way, the exotic remains a threshold never crossed, a horizon endlessly receding before Leiris's desire. Abyssinia in particular stages the disappointments of this threshold. While the mission is held up for weeks at customs, the exotic disintegrates into bureaucratic tangles and political turmoil. Finally settled in Gondar for an extended stay in Ethiopia, the mission is hosted on Italian soil at the "consulate"—in fact unrecognized by the local government—whose extraterritoriality serves as protection for the ethnographers' thefts and requisitions. The mission's objectives in French colonial Africa and in Ethiopia are unthinkable without this protective extraterritoriality, arrogated unilaterally in the interests of research and trade. The mission's stay in Ethiopia, more than anywhere else, lays bare the political conflict that underlies its very presence on African soil. Hosted by the Italians, the ethnographers find themselves implicated in an Italian political adventure that soon after their departure would lead to the invasion of Ethiopia.[48] Such is one of the latent political schemas that would be fully readable only in retrospect, shortly after the publication of Leiris's book.

The value of *L'Afrique fantôme* is not that of a political critique, unless, as we have seen, it be a latent critique, unknown to its author. The seeds of this critique are to be seen in Leiris's personal frustrations and in his unwillingness to fully identify with a mission that would be exclusively scientific. This frustration of Leiris's extends to all representatives of French culture in Africa. Upon arrival in Dakar, Leiris does not hide his disgust at the influence of the French on Senegalese culture. His disapprobation is greatest for the French colonial bureaucrat, whom Leiris faults for carrying on a life hardly different from the one he might lead in Paris: "the same petty existence, the same vulgarity, the same monotony, the same systematic destruction of beauty. . . . I'm anxious to leave for the bush" (*L'Afrique fantôme*, 28). Outside of the French influence, Leiris revels in the local color: "Now at last I love Africa" (34). He is enthusiastic upon first contact with a sacrificial custom: "I'm beginning to see what is fascinating about scientific research: going from one piece of evidence to the next, from enigma to enigma, following the trail of the truth [*poursuivre la vérité comme à la piste*]" (66). But a month later, still early in the trip, we find another picture of this research, in which Leiris is transformed into the very thing he had hoped to flee: "I keep on with my work of supervisor, magistrate, or bureaucrat. In France I was never as sedentary as this" (93). The demands of the mission cut off Leiris's desire for exotic encounter: "The life we lead could not be more dull and bourgeois. The work no different, basically, than factory or office work. Why has ethnographic investigation often made me think of police interrogations?" (260). Moreover, whatever the limitations posed by his official role, Leiris himself provides ample cause for disappointment, since his colonial and bureaucratic identity seems to assert itself against his own will. This tendency sheds light on Leiris's "colonial depression" at the end of the voyage. "Awful depression in the morning. . . . Then salvation, by plunging into bureaucratic duties and the writing of this journal" (62). Despite himself, Leiris finds the role of the writer and researcher all too easy to assume. It is in such terms that Vincent Kaufmann underscores the "principal paradox" of *L'Afrique fantôme*: wishing to break with his sedentary literary existence in the metropole, Leiris composes a journal whose publication will, upon his return, cause him to be recognized as a writer.[49] In a telling moment of discouragement, Leiris notes, "It's almost as if I had come up with the idea of traveling just so as to write it down."[50] Far from being an escape from his ills, the voyage across Africa becomes Leiris's initiation into writing, and in so doing puts into play, as Kaufmann says, a *décalage* (gap, discrepancy, time-lag) that characterizes his future writing.[51]

This *décalage* provides for the black comedy of Leiris's frustrations and exposes the discrepancy between his personal desires and the objectives of the mission. Leiris's restlessness and frustrations make legible what for his fellow ethnographers must go unacknowledged, including exoticist motivations, a hypocritical humanism, false claims to objectivity and the legal extraterritoriality that undercuts the very illusion of transport. Between Leiris's account and the intentions of the mission we thus see defined two distinct *objects*: the object of desire and the object of ethnography. One of the main purposes of the Mission Dakar-Djibouti was the collection of objects and artifacts; some 3,600 found their way back to the holdings of the Musée de l'Homme. Leiris himself helped draw up the principles and objectives of ethnographic collection in a brochure published just prior to the departure of the mission, the *Instructions sommaires pour les collecteurs d'objets ethnographiques*.[52] No such objects, however, catalogued for research alone, could motivate or satisfy Leiris's desire for travel.[53] Leiris's dissatisfaction points out another dimension of the mission in which the very object of travel is dramatically called into question. This indicates a point at which the object of desire diverges from the object of acquisition, a point helpfully indexed by the psychoanalytic notion of the *drive*. Lacan provides for a reading of this predicament in his clarification of the relation of the drives to their object, using English terminology to make a crucial distinction between *aim* and *goal*. Lacan could well be speaking of Leiris and his frustrating mission: "When you entrust someone with a mission, the *aim* is not what he brings back, but the itinerary he must take. The *aim* is the way taken [The aim, *c'est le trajet*]."[54] The *goal*, as distinct from the *aim*, is the objective of this trajectory insofar as its motive aims for satisfaction. But the goal does not constitute an object for Lacan any more than does the aim. Indeed, the goal is the place of a lack that no object can fill, and the aim, in its restless and repetitive strivings, simply marks out the contours of this irreparable absence. Slavoj Žižek provides the following explanation of Lacan's formula: "The goal is the final destination, while the aim is what we intend to do, i.e. the way itself. . . . [T]he real purpose of the drive is not its goal (full satisfaction) but its aim: the drive's ultimate aim is simply to reproduce itself as drive, to return to its circular path, to continue its path to and from the goal. The real source of enjoyment is the repetitive movement of this closed circuit."[55] Given the misdirection of the drive in relation to any goal, Lacan suggests it could go under the name of *dérive*, or "drift."⁵⁶ Further, in a formula that resonates with the paradoxes of transport in Leiris's African journal, Lacan characterizes the drive not in terms of motion but rather as "a stationary tension."⁵⁷

In these terms, one might read *L'Afrique fantôme* as misunderstanding its own mission. The paradox of desire's quest is that it aims not for absolute satisfaction but repetition, deferral, and delay. Such would be the dilemma characteristic of the drive, whose motives, whatever goal the subject sets for himself, run counter to any project of acquisition or any exotic ambition. In Žižek's words, "we mistake for postponement of the "thing itself" what is already the "thing itself," we mistake for the searching and indecision proper to desire what is, in fact, the realization of desire" (*Looking Awry*, 7). True to such a delayed and deferred desire, Leiris painstakingly records the drudgery and boredom of the Mission Dakar-Djibouti. Even the deflating picture he paints of the scientific project is true to Lacan's definition of the *aim*. *L'Afrique fantôme*, we might say, is the ambiguous *waylaying* of Leiris's desire: foundational for his life and work by virtue of the derailing of transport to its goal. This waylaying, in its ambiguity, explains the two facets of Leiris's failure, of the journey as *acte manqué*. And yet this *waylaying* may also challenge the Lacanian model we have invoked so far. In what follows, then, I will bring out the points at which Leiris's predicament diverges from the Lacanian account of desire, all too often supporting the normative order of a structural Symbolic, or even a moral discourse of renunciation. In so doing, I will inflect Leiris's *waylaying* with the sense Laplanche gives to "going astray": *le fourvoiement*, for Laplanche, is not so much an error as it is the expression of fertile yet intractable impasses of self-analysis.⁵⁸ Accordingly, the subject is less at grips with the symbolic Other than he is with an intimate otherness that, congealed into a stubborn and unconscious *thing*, imposes the paralyzing injunction to *translate* what cannot be translated, or only by deviations and allegorical misreadings.

In Leiris's autobiography, the chapter "The Trumpet-Drum" ("Tambour-trompette") provides the most sustained inquiry into the *object* of his literary quest. The story Leiris tells is a simple one: "the search for a known object that had been lost for awhile and that I ardently wanted to recover."[59] What Leiris discovers in the course of the search is less any *thing*, however, than the "pure desire" of his dream of fulfillment. His insatiability only underscores the single lack hidden behind endless stand-ins, and he sees his obsessional behavior reduced to "handling objects because I hadn't found *the object* [*faute d'avoir trouvé l'*objet]" (224; 264). In the absence of this absolute object, the literary quest is a quest of the same order as the one he undertakes in daily life: "All of this leads back to a rudimentary notion of exile, or being cut off, of a fault [*faille*] opening between myself and what I apprehend" (228; 267). In this reflexive analysis of desire, the supposed object itself disappears, outdistanced by the quest itself. "Research itself," Leiris says elsewhere, "overrides the object of the research."[60] Leiris will suggest later that the symbolic cornering of the lack will provide the solution he has been seeking, that "this writing, which for me is fundamentally a response to a lack, reaches the point where expressing that lack is worth as much as the possession of what is lacking."[61] Leiris here lends support to the Lacanian recognition that the object as such is out of reach, and presents itself only by becoming symbolized; the phallus is the linchpin of this symbolic order of lack that dictates the castration of the speaking subject. Thus, Leiris's obsessional quest for the Thing, then, ultimately reveals the force of an interdiction that he upholds despite himself in his symptoms: "What in its various advances and byways the behavior of the obsessional reveals and signifies is that he regulates his behavior so as to avoid . . . the goal and end of his desire."[62] And yet regulation and interdiction vie constantly with transgression, suggestively linked by Leiris to the gesture of a *theft*: "A childish gesture, the greedy movement of my hand toward an object whose rightful use I am not considering but which my hand is determined to appropriate [*que ma main tient à s'approprier*]" (*Scratches*, 227; *Biffures*, 265). Indeed, as the object itself fades away, in its place a "token" of presence is established by means of an intimate transgression: "I expect a complicity to form between things and myself—fleetingly, stealthily—as though now, instead of the lucky find in the guise of a "gift from heaven," the pure and simple fact of my passing encounter with a world in league with me, for the time being, assumed in my eyes the value of a magical conquest" (222; 260).

Lacan provides a means to read the convergence here of the *Thing* and transgression. For if, as Lacan asserts, the Thing as lost object is modeled on the mother, appropriation by Leiris of "what I had been originally looking for [*ce que j'avais primitivement cherché*]" (*Scratches*, 226; *Biffures*, 264) points to an act of primal transgression. As we will see, the fateful lure of such a "primitive" object takes a monstrous turn in Leiris's African travels. In the ethics seminar, Lacan formulates the moral consequence of this desire. For if, as ultimate satisfaction and supreme good, the Thing is off limits, moral law finds itself turned on its head: the desirable good is stricken down by the primordial interdiction of incest. And if the goal of desire is the place of the Thing, that Thing, then, is a utopic goal; psychoanalysis thus provides a novel elucidation of the dual meaning of the term "Utopia." To the extent that Leiris is oriented toward the primal Thing as reparation of his sense of lack, his restlessness and linguistic child's play would be symptomatic of a failed symbolic positioning. *L'Afrique fantôme*, then, dramatically stages the difference between the ethnological object and the object of psychoanalysis. Through his dissatisfaction Leiris skews the aim of his fieldwork, pitching ethnology into an economy of lack. In so doing, he anticipates Bataille's outline for a sacred sociology that holds that "[t]he absence of need [is] more wretched than the absence of satisfaction."[63] It is satisfaction, in Bataille's analysis—as in Lacan's—that must be held at bay, and his appeal to sacred myth, festival, and transgressive action serves to place desire at the top of the sociological agenda.

Now, it is precisely by means of transgression that Leiris truly rises to the occasion in Africa, sealing the elusive *complicity* between himself and his objects of choice. That these objects are *sacred* marks them at once as ethnographic artifacts and as objects of libidinal investment. Leiris here reenacts the mythic anthropology of Freud's *Totem and Taboo*, which posits the primitive origin of desire in a primal transgression. I refer to the notorious thefts committed by the Mission that Leiris recounts in some detail, not without pleasure.[64] A decisive moment occurs three months into the trip, in the course of a visit to a village where the ethnographers visit a hut containing the sacred *kono*. The team is requested to fulfill a ritual sacrifice of chickens before entering, but following a number of delays they interpret as willful stalling or obstruction on the part of the locals, Griaule, exasperated, cuts short the negotiations by announcing that the sacred *kono* will be confiscated in the name of the colonial administration. By means of this *coup de théâtre*, which humiliates the chief and the entire village, Leiris is transformed: "the fumes of sacrilege really start to go to our heads and . . . we find ourselves thrown onto a level far superior to ourselves."[65] No small part of Leiris's excitement, no doubt, is the very *imposture* of his stance, underscored by a "theatrical gesture" with which he insults the village chief before Griaule and he make off with the object. Indeed, this imposture magnetizes elements indispensable to the staging of Leiris's desire: the suspension of belief, the act indissociable from artifice, equivocalities condensed in that ambivalent phenomenon par excellence, the sacred. Lofty and wretched at the same time, such is the object that the thieves capture: "an enormous mask with a vaguely animal shape, unfortunately deteriorated, but entirely covered with a crust of dried blood that confers on it the majesty that blood confers on all things" (104).

The next day another theft is committed. "My heart is beating very fast because, after yesterday's scandal, I am more acutely aware of the enormity of the act we are committing" (Leiris, *L'Afrique fantôme*, 105). This awareness does not prevent Leiris from following up the theft with yet another, this time single-handedly, although he admits to a touch of shame: "When I notice that two men—not menacing at all, to be frank—have entered behind me, I realize with an astonishment that only later turns into disgust, that you feel mighty sure of yourself when you are white and you are holding a knife in your hand" (105). Leiris's misgivings here would seem to bear less on morality than on his own imposture of virility, an equivocal masquerade that pitches him from heady surprise to self-loathing. As for the object of his desire, it remains unmoved even as the mission moves on, leaving behind the world of the *kono*: "Griaule and I are sorry that there are no more *Konos* in this region. But not for the same reasons; what drives me [*ce qui me pousse quant à moi*] is the idea of profanation" (106). Here Leiris unflinchingly gives name to his suspect *drive*, for which no mere object and no form of exchange can substitute.[66] Griaule, less anxious than Leiris, is free to dilate in a colonial context that legitimates his ethnographic inquests and requisitions; his mode of operation is characteristically modeled on the police interrogation.[67] Thus Griaule the professional feels authorized to role-play in the aim of garnering scientific data, while Leiris characteristically acts out the symptoms of his guilty desire. If Leiris's perspective is no more responsible than that of Griaule, his imposture makes room for an unsettling of authority that remains foreign to Griaule. What the colonial world would represent for Leiris is the stage of an imposture on which he acts out guilty desires amid the trappings of a generalized cultural culpability.[68]

In this way, Leiris's "participant-observation" in the field dramatically puts his own troubled desires into play. In profaning sacred objects, he attempts to take the stage in the sacred world of the other. The patent irony or imposture involved, however, is that his profanation flouts local custom, and thus corresponds to an entirely *personal* sacred. As such, it anticipates the telling question with which Leiris broaches the question of the sacred in his statement for the Collège de Sociologie: "What, for me, is the *sacred*? To be more exact: what does *my* sacred consist of?"[69] The paradox of a personal sacred is that it aspires to a *domesticated* sacred: confined to the symbolic space of the household, and with the aim of staging the transgression of that very space. A "sacred in everyday life" is then a crucial aspect of the "philosophy of moving [*philosophie du déménagement*]" that Leiris advances in his autobiography: a symbolic *ménage* that includes its very transgression and sets the terms of his symbolic restlessness.[70] Leiris's ambivalence in the matter of love thus finds its privileged object in the equivocal nature of the sacred, and profanation provides the means for Leiris of sealing the guilty complicity of love and betrayal: "Love—the only possibility of a coincidence between subject and object, the only means of acceding to the sacred, as represented by the desired object insofar as it is exterior and alien to us—implies its own negation because to possess the sacred is at the same time to profane it and finally to destroy it by gradually robbing it of its alien character [*son caractère d'étrangeté*]."[71]

The paradox of a love that kills is not in itself novel, having been artfully treated in Wilde's *The Ballad of Reading Gaol*, for instance. Leiris goes so far as to characterize lovemaking as "asocial," following the duplicitous features of his favored "glosses."[72] Under the influence of Bataille's reflections on eroticism, Leiris reads love and death as expressions of a dialectical impasse and impossible transgression. In this light, the "negation" Leiris invokes above is inadequate to the paralyzing problem his own passage raises. This more paralyzing problem is suggested in the phrase "son caractère d'étrangeté," which anticipates the conundrum explored in "Mors," to which we devoted our attention in chapter 1. At the limit, the "caractère d'étrangeté" is betrayed even before it undergoes domestication or profanation;

to the extent that it has a *character* at all, the alienness of *étrangeté* is already betrayed. This may seem a fine distinction, but it is one to which Leiris's "Mors," like all of the *Rules of the Game*, is irresistibly drawn. The *character*, then, is already pregnant with the implications of the paralyzing *trace*, minimal marker of the always-effaced other that the text presumes and inevitably betrays. As such, *Manhood*'s moral and melodramatic discourse of a necessary killing opens up a dimension of radical ethics to which Leiris's later work is more finely attuned; in quest of an otherness that defies representation, seeking out its singular trace, Leiris finds himself engaged in the responsibility for its fateful duplicity.

Following on *Manhood*, *Scratches* will name this trace a *biffure*: the *crossing out* of a word, but also a *bifur*, the bifurcation and deviation leading into the autobiographer's digressions. What is *crossed out* is thus also "a fork in the road or a crossroads," Leiris says. The occasion for such a crossing out may be a *lapsus* or error of speech "no sooner blurted out than corrected [*sitôt lâché et sitôt raturé*]," which then provokes a new textual deviation or digression (*Scratches*, 239; *Biffures*, 279). We recognize here a basic Freudian insight into everyday psychopathology, a key to Leiris's self-analysis. However, the word crossed out is not only a guilty *lapsus*, calling for rectification and the order of the *rule*, but a more intricate reflection on the problem of the trace. For the *biffure* comes into focus in the course of an inquiry into "a mysterious doubling that challenged the very basis of identity" and "the troubling conjunction of two things in one" (240; 280). Here the *lapsus* is less a *fault* than a duplicity of the thing itself, as in Leiris's description of "objects that were supposedly *one and the same*," but contrasting in a strange temporality, "one when there was still a visible tear, and the other when all trace of it had been obliterated" (240; 281). The problem of such "infinitesimal cracks" (242; 283) is that, while they seem to lie at the very origin of Leiris's quest, he can only betray them by "connecting, cementing, knotting, causing things to converge," thereby obliterating the "trace" or the "tear" in a work he insistently compares to making "knots" (244; 285). In their very duplicity, *biffure* and *bifur* attempt to remain faithful to this singular trace: the *biffure* by marking with an X the place of the thing "under erasure," as Derrida puts it; the *bifur* by indicating the necessary deviation from the origin.[73] The rhythm of this inquiry transfers into the work of writing the troubled transports of Leiris's journeys: "bogged down [*enlisé*]" at every step of his unrelenting bifurcations (245; 287). The ethnography that follows *L'Afrique fantôme* will bear the fruit of this tormented analysis.

In an essay that cites the above passage from *Manhood*, Michèle Richman characterizes the sacred in Leiris as a means to overcome social alienation and as a key to his overture to ethics and politics.[74] In Richman's account, transgression and the sacred are broadly tied to a Bataillian project of social renewal and the contestation of bourgeois order through the disruptive forces of death and eroticism. To link Leiris too closely to Bataille is, however, to discount Leiris's claim to a personal exemption from a communal sacred. It is, further, to misread the motives that tie Leiris's sacred, as distinct from Bataille's, to the experience of a primordial transgression and an unresolved accession to the Symbolic. To frame the issue psychoanalytically is not, however, to simply pathologize Leiris's experience and contain it within a private symptomology. What is at stake, rather, is a social rapport to be located at the level of the writing subject, in which Leiris defines himself in a distinctive ethical relationship to the other. The sacred, as we have seen, appeals to Leiris because it mobilizes the affective energies that mark his rapport to the object of desire under the sign of ambivalence. Transgression would be a dramatic response to the experience of symbolic displacement or im-position legible in Leiris as of his earliest texts and memories. As such, a personal sacred, attained in profanation, sacrilege, and transgression, speaks precisely to the waning of sacred ritual in Leiris's modern life-world that the Collège aimed to revive. But

Leiris's work does not so much support its social revival as it does its displacement into the modern realm of personal psychology. Indeed, Leiris's "everyday sacred" could hardly express better Freud's definition of neurotic desire in *Totem and Taboo*: "to achieve by private means what is effected in society by collective effort."[75] Pursuit of a private sacred thus fosters the dubious pleasures of Leiris's sacred thefts and transgressions in Africa. But Leiris's ongoing self-critique, only just begun in *L'Afrique fantôme*, will provide the means for a more responsible alignment of neurotic desire and ethnography, and it is to this that we now turn.

Magical Belief

As we have seen, it is one of the ironies of *L'Afrique fantôme* that the author's aspiration to escape from his literary world into genuine adventure should launch his autobiography. Likewise, the voyage would end in a resumption of psychoanalytic treatment upon his return to Paris. In this light, one might read Leiris's African episode in terms of the psychoanalytic concept of "acting out," defined as "an attempt to *break off* the analytic relationship."[76] Performed by a subject blind to his own motivations, and bearing in its compulsion to repeat on an unconscious content, what is acted out is by definition misplaced and subject to suspicion. The subject who acts out *performs* what he refuses to *say*, so his overly dramatic gestures are inherently lacking in sincerity.[77] We have seen aspects of such theatrical artifice in Leiris's dubious colonial masquerade among the Dogon. Toward the end of the journey, the most sustained fieldwork of Leiris concerns rites of spirit possession in Ethiopia, which alternately fascinate and disappoint Leiris for their theatrical artifice. The monograph Leiris subsequently devotes to the cult of possession emphasizes this theatrical dimension of possession. It is tempting, then, to bring *acting out* and ethnographic artifice together here on the colonial stage, to see Leiris's fascination with the extravagant actions of the possessed Ethiopians as an attempt to solve the riddle of his own bent for melodrama and violent outbursts. *La Possession et ses aspects théâtraux chez les Ethiopiens de Gondar* (Possession and Its Theatrical Aspects among the Ethiopians of Gondar) would represent yet another means by which Leiris explores his "démons intérieurs" and the theatrical aspects of his presence in Africa.[78]

It is clear in *L'Afrique fantôme* that Leiris invests more than an objective interest in the study of the cult of possession in Ethiopia. During the course of his fieldwork Leiris was sexually obsessed with Emawayish, the daughter of the healer who presided over the *zar* cult in Gondar, and in whom, as he later relates in *Manhood*, he saw the embodiment of his archetypal loves, Judith and Lucrecia. James Clifford has highlighted the apprentice ethnographer's frustration with the role of spectator dictated by his research.[79] Worse yet than this objective distance is the evidence of inauthenticity and playacting that Leiris detects in the cult of spirit possession. Leiris's account of his research in Ethiopia is consequently marked by moments of high exhilaration and bouts of despair as sacred activities give way to profane simulation, contaminated by the ethnographer's colonial presence, his obsession with Emawayish, and the mundane self-interest of the adepts of the cult. And yet, if theatricality is the stumbling block of Leiris's analysis, it is no mere obstacle to authenticity, providing as it does the only scene on which Leiris's fantasies can be played out. As a result, Leiris is prone to express contradictory attitudes toward theater: "I love even the deceitfulness [*la fausseté*] of their possession, these dear girls who introduce a bit of tawdry fantasy into their lives."[80] Leiris's contradictions indicate the extent to which his trouble with theater overlaps with the conflicted scene of his imaginary desire, to which a dose of mystification is necessary. "I've always more or less considered coitus as a magical act, expected from certain women what one may expect from oracles, treated prostitutes as prophetesses" (578), he says. Later, though, on the way home from his stay in Gondar, a disenchanted Leiris sees the abandonment of his morbid attachment to theater as the only road to recovery: "I dream of a marvelous peacefulness upon my return. To obtain it, one thing must be eliminated at all costs: my dramatic attitude toward coitus" (839). Twenty-five years later, Leiris's *La Possession* attests to the unresolved conflicts such theatricality poses for Leiris. Theater is not eliminated from the equation in his analysis, but rather divides into two facets of his contradicted belief, into a "played theater [*théâtre joué*]" and a more genuine "lived theater [*théâtre vécu*]." This amalgam of "lived theater" recalls the stakes of the *corrida* evoked in *Manhood*, and the link to Leiris's autobiography is confirmed by the terms by which Leiris defines this form of theater in "La Croyance aux génies *zar*" (The Belief in *Zar* Spirits): as a kind of expiation and an appeal for forgiveness.[81] Possession, in other words, as confession. Based on this correspondence, might we not speak of Leiris's "manhood" itself as a mode of spirit possession?

Confession implies belief, and the question of belief traces the fissure of a defining contradiction in Leiris's work, one that is only exacerbated by the fact of his determined atheism. It is worth noting that the confessional nature of Leiris's literary undertaking dooms his writing to a miming of Roman Catholic behaviors and beliefs, as Leiris himself acknowledges in *Manhood*. Thus, Leiris says of his Catholic education that it "still obsesses me, however certain I am of having broken intellectually with this kind of prejudice."[82] With the same force that he disavows Christian ideology, Leiris pursues occult, sacred, and mystical forms of belief: "no beliefs but superstitions."[83] This latter tendency, originally allied with his surrealist activity, contributed as well to his espousal of ethnography as a career and to his fellow travels with Bataille. His study of spirit possession in Ethiopia reflects this longstanding interest in magic and superstition, and it dramatically puts Leiris's belief to the test.

While properly speaking an ethnographic study, and deriving primarily from the fieldwork described in *L'Afrique fantôme*, Leiris's *La Possession* is the product of a personal obsession, showing the extent to which his professional career carries on the symptomatics of his life and autobiography. Spirit possession, as Leiris says, is located "midway between life and theater" and as such is part and parcel of Leiris's affective investment in theater as lived experience.[84] But this "mi-chemin" is less a resolution of contraries than a neither-nor state, and in his examination of what he calls the "ambiguous states" of spirit possession Leiris is at pains to determine the quantity of simulation and falsity that goes into their manifestation.[85] Leiris's quote from another scholar at the beginning of his text sets out the terms of the study: "A shaman in effect does not behave at random in his frenzy; it is as if he plays like an actor the role of a deranged person whose sequence of acts and words were made up ahead of time. But this fact does not contradict the existence of a genuine state of possession" (957). True to his aestheticist penchants, Leiris posits here a principle of noncontradiction between artifice and authenticity. And while such a principle may be fully congruent with the disillusioned gaze of another ethnographer, for whom as an objectively inclined social scientist the "customs" and "beliefs" of others are in a sense equivalent, in the case of Leiris it points to nothing so much as the troubled scene of his own desire as structured by the magic of belief. It would seem that all evidence to the contrary—the bad faith of the *zar* adepts, the patently bogus playacting Leiris witnesses—only serves to reinforce his conviction in "a true state of possession." Consequently, as the ethnographer repeatedly weighs in against the aficionado, the terms of Leiris's disavowal are reiterated, both negating and sustaining his conflicted belief. Leiris's aim, then, seems less to determine which feature predominates in the phenomenon of possession than to locate the middle ground where artifice and reality strike a tenuous balance. This is implied in the central equivocation with which Leiris names the topic of his study. The *zar* cult, Leiris says, "comprises a feature equally discrediting and appealing: its theatrical aspects" (957). Never stated as such in his ethnographic text, Leiris's belief is faithfully rendered by such equivocations and ambiguities, so many aspects of the author's affective mystification.

If Leiris's initial motives for traveling across Africa were the desire for adventure and escape, his subsequent work consists in a slow and difficult weaning from such exoticism. *La Possession* is exemplary in this regard, as it undoes what Mary Douglas has identified as one of the most abusive myths of anthropology: namely, the imputation of utter credulity in magic among traditional peoples and the absolute dominion of religion in their societies.[86] Leiris's work rejects such convenient exorcisms, whether as an autobiographer exploring his dreams and fantasies, or as an ethnographer contributing to the revival of sacred forms in contemporary society. Here Leiris homes in on a defining aporia of ethnographic knowledge, and carried on in the disillusionment of the tourist faced with the "spectacle" of cultural displays. In so doing, Leiris anticipates Glissant's postcolonial insight into culture as paradoxically authentic "diversion" from an identity to which there is no simple "reversion."[87]

It is therefore striking that several readers of *La Possession* have recently faulted Leiris precisely for an overly aesthetic analysis at the expense of the more violent and passionate aspects of the *zar* cult. Jacques Mercier, pointing to what he sees as the lack of passion in Leiris's 1958 text, considers it as amounting in its disillusionment to "a theory of the aestheticization of the everyday without genuine transgression."[88] Sylvère Lotringer, for his part, assesses Leiris's late writings on the theater as "a step backward toward the very kind of bourgeois art and artifice he had dismissed from the start."[89] One might well concede that *La Possession* attests to a certain disillusionment, and point, for instance, to the near-absence of Emawayish in the text. And yet disillusionment breeds ever-new beliefs, less exotic and closer to home, perhaps, but for all that no less extraordinary. I would argue that in its analysis of the theatrical aspects of the *zar* cult, *La Possession* does not constitute a betrayal of Leiris's desire but rather a refinement of its essential terms. That the text tends repeatedly toward impasse and ambiguity is a measure of the author's resolve not to cheat with the analysis and, in a manner faithful to his autobiography, to take it to the point where his own motives and desires may be opaque to himself. The "imprecise boundary" between simulation and authenticity—that blind spot of Leiris's analysis—is itself a figure for the author's desire, caught in the vacillation of belief and the suspect motives underlying his adventurous acting out.[90] *Autocritique* and theater thus converge for Leiris in a perpetual unmasking of his own impostures of mastery.

To the extent that Leiris's autobiography is a confession, we might say it is a confession of his impostures and *parades*. The major imposture is his own masculinity, as Leiris casts himself throughout his autobiography in the humiliated role of the castrated. The other is that of the phallic woman, in whose imposture, however, Leiris insistently believes. Accordingly, all of Leiris's favorite female figures of the theater play the role of a phallic woman. The Lacanian psychoanalyst Octave Mannoni offers an analysis of the function of belief that sheds light on Leiris's fascination with sexual theater. The object of Mannoni's analysis is a formulation common to neurotics, and that consists of the contradictory statement, "I know very well, and yet . . . [*Je sais bien, mais quand même . . .*]." Following Freud's study of fetishism, Mannoni sees this structure of divided belief as deriving from a primal source, namely, the repudiation or disavowal (*Verleugnung*) of the mother's lack of a penis. According to Freud, upon the child's traumatic discovery of sexual difference, the maternal phallus is installed as the object of a newfound belief, giving rise among some to fetishism. But this belief, founded in disavowal, bears the mark of its indelible trauma, and the subject's compromise is to maintain "a divided attitude" in which his belief is "both abandoned and conserved."[91] Now, Mannoni's interest is less in the fetishist proper than in the neurotic, that is, in the everyday subject whose ordinary symptoms reflect a fundamental denial of castration. For the fetishist, after all, the conservation of belief seems settled once and for all in an object of fixation. The neurotic, however, lacking this unshakable evidence, is compelled to express a "mais quand même" with regard to various other beliefs.[92] The latter is closer to Leiris's predicament. The magical phallus, conjured up out of a physical absence, thus makes possible all other forms of mystification, from magic and superstition to religion. As a result, Mannoni suggests, "there isn't at first a belief in magic, but first a magic of belief [*il n'y a pas d'abord une croyance à la magie, mais d'abord une magie de la croyance*]."[93]

La Possession testifies to this neurotic belief at the source of Leiris's ethnographic analysis. And yet, as we will see, Leiris may not so much reflect the reversal of priorities Mannoni describes as dwell in the chiasmus of their interrelation. Should *La Possession* represent a certain failure, then, such failure must be linked to the unique resourcefulness of Leiris's frustrated *autocritique*, his bid for veracity that will never have done with the disenchantment of literature and artifice. What autobiographer has felt more keenly than Leiris the double edge of his own self-evidence, that subjecthood given only in so far as it is given up, or given away? All of Leiris's writing attests to an unresolved tension between artifice and authenticity, between frivolous wordplay and the lyrical evocation of his innermost self, a tension implied in the title of *Rules of the Game*. How can the autobiographer be sure of a rule that is only approached by means of so much playacting and histrionics? "Liturgy or sequence of moves in a ballet?" Leiris characteristically wonders of the rituals he imposes on his prose in the quest of an elusive *règle* by which to live his life.[94] "Motions performed more for show [*Gestes, à vrai dire, de parade*]," he is forced to concede (236; 276). *La Possession* presents the same problem for Leiris, and in nearly identical terms: how distinguish between the *rite* and the *jeu*, when the one may lead to the other, and vice versa, without any clear demarcation? "It seems that here, between play and rite, there is no solution of continuity," Leiris confesses.[95] There is finally no resolving the antinomies presented in the course of Leiris's text on possession. But Leiris's frustrations lend the very movement to the text, here as elsewhere. The import of *La Possession* lies precisely in the patient, indeed paralyzed, quest for the point where the opposite terms are suspended and conflated. This irresolution corresponds to the suspension of disbelief that both vexes and motivates Leiris's desire. Implicit then in *La Possession* is the pursuit of that impossible quarry Leiris defines in his notes on the sacred in everyday life. Tellingly, it is on the same page evoking a "Magic of words" that Leiris advances the notion of rites that, he says, "tend toward the rite but are not rites, that is to say not yet cold and stiff [*pas encore refroidis et figés*]."[96] Such "improvised rites" defy the artifice of consecrated rituals (and their attendant beliefs), but they also elude any formulation and any present. "The sacred can only be a flying spark: a moment when the gesture becomes ritual (before cooling down as rite)" (130). It is consistent with the problem of belief I have been tracing here that in a lyrical passage defining his aesthetic credo Leiris formulates the "geste" of writing in mystified terms, where the final form of his writing and, perhaps, his elusive *règle* is established outside of all time, in the shape of destiny. "Every line, however polished, traced by a pen must be open to chiromancy, and in every motion of every hand that breaks the new ground of the paper, one can probably read the whole of this person who allows his destiny to be mirrored in the calm or troubled surface of a gesture."[97] Tellingly, "gesture" (*geste*), is a term that conveys the key ambiguities of theater as rendered by Leiris, for it hesitates between the alternatives of signification and action, and voluntary and involuntary movement. *Geste*, then, aptly renders the motivating aporia of Leiris's every *act*, in writing as in travel, as well as the ironic interplay between dramatic exploit and deflating *jest*. The tensions here cannot be resolved into clear distinctions or oppositions; rather, they trace out what Allan Stoekl has termed the "figure of the unknowable yet necessary mechanism behind Leiris's autobiographical project."[98] Leiris suggests that only a mystical reader—the palm reader invoked above—could resolve these ambiguities to confer an identity on Leiris's writing. No reader, perhaps, might assume this oracular role but a prophetess such as Emawayish, the meaning of whose name haunts the text of Leiris's entire confessional autobiography: "I entrust you with my troubles [*Je te confie mes peines*]."[99]

Like the *geste* of self-authoring, and like the "improvised rites" that magically suspend the alternatives of life and theater, Leiris's analysis of the cult of possession ultimately approaches a *performative* dimension of sexuality: those "imaginary sexual relations"[100] that he discovered in the trance-states of the possessed that make up a theater that "can never avow its theatrical nature."[101] Such a performative dimension is differently paralyzing than the fixations, dramas of castration and Medusa-inspired fears of Leiris's early *Manhood*. It points, rather, to an intuition into the paradox of a sexuality that enacts and thus brings about what it purports to merely show. Performative sexuality is thus the site of a claim that undermines itself, reiterating the unknowing enactment of a performative bind that escapes the logic of "true" and "false" theater. The performative invokes the norms of sexuality, but its surreptitious *geste* escapes both the scene of performance and the acts of the subject. Indeed, as Judith Butler argues, theatricality is always a *dissimulation* of the more subtle work of the performative, whose acts "are not, strictly speaking, performed by a subject."[102] It is this performative within the theatrical performance that, to adopt Leiris's words, "can never avow its theatrical nature." All of Leiris's writings on the theater, whether that of Gondar or the Paris Opera, should be considered an effort to make the actor "sing" like the accused, and *avow* the trace of a performative dissimulated by their performance.[103] As we have seen, Leiris's own autobiographical confessions bear the insistent mark of such a problematic trace. If we add, finally, that in the *zar* cult women are held to be possessed in the main by masculine spirits, one may easily judge that the will to believe is very strong in Leiris—if no stronger than the evidence to the contrary. The role of magic, as Leiris indicates at the conclusion of *La Possession*, is precisely to allow for belief to persist in the face of disproof: "It would seem that one touches here on what gives such great force to magic in spite of the constant contradictions inflicted on it by experience: the affective elements it mobilizes."[104] Such also would be the magical force of Leiris's desire as it seemingly transmutes these pages of ethnographic analysis into another volume of his autobiography.

The Masochistic Ethnographer

This chapter has dealt at length with *L'Afrique fantôme*, which, I have argued, contains the germ of Leiris's work, and I have employed a psychoanalytic vocabulary to examine the psychic dimension of Leiris's motives, acts, and beliefs in his ethnographic travels. The stakes of this approach are summed up in Freud's *Totem and Taboo*, whose subtitle, it is worth recalling, is *Some Points of Agreement between the Mental Lives of Savages and Neurotics*. Here, at the intersection of psychoanalysis and anthropology, Leiris holds an eminent position, though one that is always partial, conflicted, and shifting. Leiris's self-analysis and ethnography do not conclude in a general system, and he remains foreign to Lacan's and Lévi-Strauss's claims to structural order. As such, Leiris represents better than each what Foucault saw as the fundamental epistemic challenge posed by the twin fields of ethnology and psychoanalysis to the human sciences.[105] For this reason Leiris's work has been a touchstone for poststructuralist anthropology and its studies of the epistemological tensions between social-scientific fieldwork and colonial and sexual politics.[106] I have shown that the convergence of psychoanalysis and ethnography in Leiris's work led both to fruitful contacts and fateful misunderstandings in the course of his mission. And while this tension continues throughout Leiris's later work, we see an important shift to political engagement and ethical reflection on

Leiris's part, though neurotic symptoms persist, defying any cure or attenuation. In closing I will indicate how Leiris's symptoms present an implicit challenge to normative codings of gender and desire, to argue that it is precisely in this sexual dissidence—and not on the basis of a common structural order—that Leiris communicates across cultures.

As we saw at the beginning of this chapter, *L'Afrique fantôme* occupies the temporality of a *contretemps*, and the later Leiris would work to correct his missed appointment with history. In *Scraps* (*Fourbis*), Leiris relates how a mission to Africa in 1945 to study labor conditions changed his perspective from that of a "romantic" anthropologist to one more attuned to the economic realities of the colonies. Leiris found himself again in Dakar—the starting point of his first African mission—on the day Berlin fell to the Allies. "I was doubly happy," Leiris says, "first because the great news had reached me in Dakar and second because the population with which I would be fraternizing in the joy aroused by such an event would be the black population of an African town."[107] Leiris does not find this fraternity at a cocktail party and heads toward the center of town, intending "to blast through the barriers, to abolish the distances that separated me from other people" (167). Leiris goes from one bar to the next, finally running into a group of three Africans, and wandering drunk with them, Leiris says, "I affirmed my desire for greater understanding between the races, my love for Africa, and the very great esteem I had for Africans, who were closer to real life than Europeans" (170). Soon afterward he is felled by a punch and robbed. A white naval officer appears on the scene to help Leiris, only to accuse him of having let himself be sodomized by the men. Leiris insults the officer and is promptly felled again. When Leiris comes to, he is furious, but not at the first assaulters, only at the officer who, he says, "was so convinced at the lack of common measure between the black and white races that he couldn't conceive of someone going out at night with negroes except for reasons having to do with sex, and this on a day when people were celebrating the fact that Hitlerism had been crushed!" (172).

Colonial history is full of such historical *contretemps*; on May 8 of that same year, the surrender of Germany coincided with the French massacre of Algerian civilians in Sétif. Leiris's aim in relating his episode in Dakar is to highlight this discrepant colonial history, as well as his own fitful, belated, and frustrated attempts to heal its wounds. If Leiris's first journey in Africa was a "buffoonery,"[108] this later journey, more practical, more politically engaged, nonetheless ends on a similar note. A common thread links these very different texts, each of which, like all of Leiris's *autocritiques*, exhibit his manhood as castrated and self-castigating, while he seeks justification in his own debasement. It is thus as a "grieving moralist" that Leiris proceeds to the police station in Dakar,[109] fully aware of the absurdity of lodging his complaint to a colonial bureaucrat as if to "a supreme judge" (173). He was not sodomized, though he holds nothing against homosexuals; he has no complaint against the Africans, only against the officer; Leiris's torturous accusations and self-justifications fall on deaf ears. Inevitably, it seems, Leiris's misadventure leads him to reflect on the theatrical artifice of his behavior: "[W]hat was motivated by an authentically heartfelt impulse had been translated into action in the facile guise of a theatrical attitude: to fraternize with the population of color" (175). In this colonial theater where Leiris's politics are put to the test, he seems to occupy the in-between state of the theater of possession. And as in the case of possession, everything hinges on a stubborn kernel of belief: the faith in a supreme judge, now no longer a cop, but sublimated into "some unknown administrator of justice" Leiris imagines to be punishing him for his artifice. And here, once again, Leiris reprises the bullfight as metaphor of his autobiography, evoking the bravado moves of the *torero* that shadow his heroic acts with mere artifice. "To do and to pantomime, to be and to appear" (176), these distinctions motivate all of Leiris's writings and travels, yet paralyze them, as he said of spirit possession, "midway between life and theater."

Leiris's critique of racism and his anticolonial commitment, though supported by liberal convictions and a communist commitment to liberation, have their wellspring in a poignant self-critique, deriving from a masochistic sensibility, which allows for an identification with the suffering of others and a refusal to align himself with forces of domination. It is important to distinguish this position from a Christian morality of renunciation and compassion, often prone to cruel turns of judgment both against the self and the other. Leiris's is instead a politics of affinity in injury. Another text by Leiris clarifies this masochistic politics by exploring the meaning of fraternity in the context of decolonization. Like Césaire, with whom he made common cause in decolonization, Leiris would belong among those who, as he puts it, "sing under torture."[110] But an asymmetry mars this common accord of Leiris with the colonized, which he explores by means of an inquiry into the meaning of pity. "If I was moved to such an extent," Leiris speculates, "isn't it because of the guilt that colored . . . my pity?" (63). Insincerity, in other words, threatens once again to alter Leiris's genuine feelings. But why? The *duplicity* of Leiris's pity would seem to reflect the surreptitious turn by which pity for the oppressed is authorized by a judging power to which Leiris himself submits. Pity thus depends on a guilty identification with power. In this way, Leiris corroborates Freud's observation that sadism and masochism are interchangeable in fantasy. And indeed, there is something of the fantastic in the *double* beating of Leiris in Dakar, one to which he submits, and the other to which he objects. Interestingly, such a double beating reappears in these reflections on postcolonial fraternity in the cryptic message Leiris recounts from a dream: "He was beaten, beaten" (62). It is precisely the combination of guilt and pity that seems to duplicate the beating in the dream.

How, then, can the dream of fraternity avoid the duplicity of pity and guilt? Is there no way out of the conflict that pits action against theater and sincerity against artifice? Leiris's entire work would devote itself to the literary and political consequences of these conundrums. And throughout his work the bullfighter remains an insistent model of Leiris's dilemmas, staging masculinity in the problematic space where act and art meet and divide. The "supreme judge" of the *corrida* is nothing other than death itself, incarnated in the phallic threat of a castrating horn, and which Leiris would like to invoke on every page of his risky autobiography. Transgression and the sacred, then, take place for Leiris under the rule of the Symbolic, which dictates the necessary translation of Leiris's every affect, however sincere, into the realm of language and artifice. Castration and the Symbolic thereby authenticate the truth of language's necessary artifice. But what if the horn Leiris dreams of is merely conjured to repair the duplicity of language? What if the phallus were itself a fiction designed to rule over the distinction between fact and fiction? This would be to argue that the impostures of the actor and bullfighter were settled only by invoking a supplementary imposture. Indeed, the phallus would be that imposture, hard to dislodge precisely due to its supplementarity: both equated with the reality of the male member and an abstract symbol, it is alternately a profitable addition to male privilege and its sheer replacement.[111] Yet this duplicity is commonly overcome by magical belief in the impostures of the phallic man. Leiris is finely attuned to this duplicity, and, much as he fails to dispel the fearsome judge, phallus, and castrating horn, we may see in his masochism a defiance of the *rule*, one that condemns him to perpetually reenact what Deleuze calls the characteristic "suspense" of the masochistic scenario.[112] This paralyzing suspense and its passing insights define all of Leiris's travels and writings, whose transports are always frustrated, "in movement even if one is fixed."[113]

At the conclusion of *Rules of the Game*, Leiris sees his golden rule as connected to the essential problem of restlessness, the frustrating negotiation of *here* and *there*. Far from arriving at a *rule*, however, Leiris's last words conclude in favor of *play*: a play of movement, alternately means and end, the unfinished resolution of Leiris's literary technique. Tellingly, Leiris's very invocation of movement cannot help pairing it with a figure of stasis, thus reiterating the paralyzing problematic of the *biffure* with which *Rules of the Game* began: "isn't my only recourse [*ma seule ressource*] to try to hitch myself to [*m'accrocher à*] that which is movement itself and that presents itself as both affirmation and negation?"[114] Glossing the verb *accrocher* brings out the impediments, accidents, hitches, and snags that accompany the sense of desperate clinging Leiris invokes here. But *accroc* also means infringement, breach, and bending of a rule, including even the rule of noncontradiction broken by Leiris's suggestive formula. Perhaps such a breach can only be penned at the risk of a blot or stain (*accroc*) to the author's reputation, though it traces as well the mark of a *geste* that defies any choice or act of confession.[115]

Leiris may never have settled scores with the "ambiguous states" that defined spirit possession, and indeed all art, with a dose of imposture. For good reason: the *rule* of the game always proved lacking, even if he could not help fearing and desiring its judgment. But behind his fears of imposture and artifice lies the imposture of the masculine phallus itself, which he dreamed belonged instead to his fascinating women. Leiris's imposture, then, goes further than a mere symptom or pathology, posing a challenge to the colonial order in Africa, where, as Achille Mbembe has pointedly argued, "phallic domination" was the abiding form of power and knowledge.[116] And if the belief in the masculine phallus is the "dominant fiction" of societal order, as Kaja Silverman claims, Leiris's marginal masculinity served as a constant resistance to that fiction both at home and abroad in his long labor of decolonization.[117] Within the terms of Leiris's study of spirit possession, artifice is never clearly distinct from the sincerity of affect. In this sense, then, Leiris's literary self is never a mere imposture, but a more equivocal *parade*, the perpetual quest for an "ambiguous state" where sincerity and imposture meet. Only phallic mastery is truly an imposture, and in refusing to assume its privileges Leiris undermined the hold of the dominant fiction in the discourse of ethnography and colonialism.

5. Atopia
Roland Barthes

No progress in pleasures, *nothing but mutations.*
— Barthes

Excursus

On the occasion of his entry into the Collège de France in 1977, Roland Barthes delivered an inaugural lecture at once deeply personal and highly elusive. Speaking of his intellectual career and interests, ranging from the critique of ideology to structuralism and the theory of the Text, Barthes characterized himself as "a patently impure fellow [*un sujet impur*]" with contradictory attributes, and one whose qualifications lay less in academic rigor and discipline than in the displacements and eccentricities he brought to bear on his fields of study.[1] In this way, Barthes turned the occasion of his entry into the Collège into a discourse on not belonging. A new member of the Collège de France, the most prestigious French institution of higher learning, might well pride himself on having *arrived*; Barthes, instead, leaning on the literal sense of *chercher*, reserved the right to look elsewhere, to teach what he didn't himself know and, further, to "unlearn" (478; 814).

Barthes's pursuits, following chance and subjective passions, will carry him always elsewhere; his institutional place will be one of perpetual displacement. This would seem to place Barthes in a deeply contradictory position. So if Barthes could see occupying a Chair of Literary Semiology, it is insofar as the Collège de France would represent an institution "*outside the bounds of power [hors-pouvoir]*" ("Inaugural Lecture," 458; *Leçon*, 802) where he might pursue research free of any claim to mastery or authority: "it seems to me that the intention behind the establishment of a chair at the Collège de France is not so much the consecration of a discipline as the allowing for the continuance of a certain labor, the adventure of a certain subject [*à l'aventure d'un certain sujet*]" (471; 810). Here, the idea of a *discipline* evokes a strong sense of control and punishment, and Barthes's unruly pursuits and resistance to classification constitute so many strategies by which he resists and evades the hold of power. In Barthes's "Inaugural Lecture" discipline thus carries all the weight it does in the work of Michel Foucault who, himself a new member of the Collège, had presented Barthes's candidacy and proposed the chair he would be called to occupy. Indeed, in its focus on the questions of language, power, and the institution, Barthes's "Inaugural Lecture" reads as an homage and an improvisation on Foucault's own *Leçon inaugurale*, presented six years earlier.[2] Thus Barthes, seconding Foucault's critique of the sovereign model of power, affirms that "power is present in the most delicate mechanisms of social exchange . . . and even in the liberating impulses which attempt to counteract it" (459; 802). Further, in a formula with explicit ties to Foucault's "Discourse on Language," Barthes sees power's most pervasive and insidious operations as lying in language, both object and agent of "classification" and order: "This object in which power is inscribed, for all of human eternity, is language, or to be more precise, its necessary expression [*son expression obligée*]: the language we speak and write [*la langue*]" (460; 803). The irreducible condition of the speaking subject is that of his *subjection*, the double-edged condition in which he assumes the power of speech only to submit to the order of discourse. "In speech, then," Barthes says, "servility and power are inescapably intermingled" (461; 804). Barthes goes on to posit a means of escape from this troublesome bind via literature, whose "utopian function" offers the possibility of subtracting language from the regime of power (466; 806).

In its emphasis on utopia Barthes's "Inaugural Lecture" hearkens back to his earliest writings, notably *Writing Degree Zero*, whose political theory of literature memorably concludes with a reference to "l'utopie du langage." Utopia, as we will see, is among the most persistent themes in Barthes's corpus, and reflects not only the imperative for social critique but also the pressing need to locate the space of his personal desires. In the "Inaugural Lecture," however, Barthes submits the notion of utopia to important qualifications: "Utopia, of course, does not save us from power. The utopia of language is salvaged [*récupérée*] as the language of utopia." ("Inaugural Lecture," 467; *Leçon*, 807). Tellingly, the intermingling of power and servility takes the form here of a stubborn chiasmus. Such a chiasmus, as we have seen, is always paralyzing, and accordingly Barthes casts himself as *persistent, waiting* at the crossroads defined by its problematic interlacing: "A writer ... must have the persistence of a watcher [*l'entêtement du guetteur*] who stands at the crossroads of all other discourses, in a position that is *trivial* in relation to the purity of doctrine (*trivialis* is the etymological attribute of the prostitute who waits at the threshold of three roads)." As an "impure subject," Barthes willingly admits to the prostitution entailed by the imbrication of servility and power. Such a prostitution is, of course, no simple submission to power, discipline, and authority, but rather an affective and intellectual exploration of its complex and ambiguous agency. Indeed, Barthes sees his entire career as the passionate and perpetually renewed conflict between his strategic *paradoxa* and the force of *Doxa*, the rule of common opinion; each *paradoxa* Barthes advances is inevitably caught again in the rule of *ordo*. Interestingly, at the time of the "Inaugural Lecture" this is seen to pose the danger of *paralysis*: "the Text risks paralysis: it repeats itself, counterfeits itself in lusterless texts, testimonies to a demand for readers, not for a desire to please: the Text tends to degenerate into prattle [*Babil*]. Where to go next?" Barthes asks. "That is where I am now."[3] Much as he celebrates innovation and change, at every point in his life Barthes's next step seems to be at cross-purposes with itself, reiterating a stubborn chiasmus. As such, Barthes's progress defies either the option of stasis or motion, just as it does the metaphor of a *career*. I will give what Barthes calls "paralysis" a different inflection, then, to name the paradoxical transports that occur at his crossroads of servility and power.

Neither *Doxa* nor *paradoxa*, paralysis is the elusive site of Barthes's most searching questions and intractable passions.

In the face of the threat of classification, of the recuperation of utopia as theme or topos, Barthes's "Inaugural Lecture" advances the notion of *atopia*, a change that corresponds to the shift in Barthes's thought from literature—classifiable and thematizable— to the broader notion of the text: "The Text contains in itself the strength to elude gregarious speech (the speech which incorporates [*s'agrège*]), even when that speech seeks to reconstitute itself in the Text.... The Text procrastinates elsewhere, toward an unclassified, atopic site, so to speak, far from the topoi of politicized culture" ("Inaugural Lecture" 472; *Leçon*, 810). The theoretician of the Text presents himself as similarly unclassifiable, as seen in his autobiography: "*Pigeonholed* [*Fiché*]: I am pigeonholed, assigned to an (intellectual) site, to a residence in a caste (if not in a class). Against which there is only one internal doctrine: that of *atopia* (of a drifting habitation). Atopia is superior to utopia (utopia is reactive, tactical, literary, it proceeds from meaning and governs it)."[4] The atopia of the Text corresponds, then, to the placelessness and unclassifiability of Barthes himself, who emerges as *atopos*, a term that, Barthes points out, had been applied to Socrates by his interlocutors.[5] In response to an interviewer in 1977 who remarks that he has become "less and less localizable," Barthes invites the comparison with Socrates: "They said that Socrates was *atopos*, that is to say 'without a place,' unclassifiable."[6] As Barthes notes, he had employed the figure of *atopos* in *A Lover's Discourse* to characterize the love object, insofar as he defies categorization. In this figure, then, many of the key themes of Barthes's thought converge: resistance to the stereotype, the ethical relation to the other, the primacy of desire, and the failure of metalanguage. Moreover, as *atopos*, Barthes would place himself in the position of the love object. "Being atopic, the other makes language indecisive [*fait trembler le langage*]: one cannot speak *of* the other, *about* the other; every attribute is false, painful, erroneous, awkward: the other is *unqualifiable* (this would be the true meaning of *atopos*)."[7] Even as he appeals to unconditional recognition, then, Barthes withdraws, seemingly unlocatable and indefinable.

"[O]ne writes in order to be loved," Barthes states in his autobiography. At the same time, and as if to underscore his own unqualifiability, Barthes notes the objection of one reader who found the remark "imbecilic [*idiot*]."[8] While the sarcasm is unfortunate, the objection seems warranted, given that Barthes in his earlier structuralist phase had advocated the sacrifice of the author—that figment of humanist myths of identity and creation—by the hand of the reader. At that time, the death of the author was seen to liberate the impersonal agency of *écriture*, forerunner of what Barthes would come to name the Text. Contradicting such pronouncements as "The Death of the Author," Barthes's later work marks a turn toward a more personal style of writing in which the author returns, implicating himself in his analyses. In another sense, then, the above charge against Barthes is apt, if one recalls the pejorative term's derivation from the Greek *idios*, meaning "private" and "peculiar." *Idios*, then, would be the correlative of *atopos*, insofar as the absolute particularity of the atopic other entails an impossibility of expression. We have seen how Barthes's "Inaugural Lecture" calls for such an impossible acknowledgment on the part of his auditors. Likewise, Barthes characterizes his own desire in terms of a failure of naming: "[T]he more I experience the specialty of my desire, the less I can give it a name; to the precision of the target corresponds a wavering of the name [*un tremblement du nom*]; what is characteristic of desire, proper to desire, can produce only an impropriety of the utterance."[9] The lover's idiom is condemned to failure, its impropriety a factor of the *atopic* object. What results is what one might call an ethics of misunderstanding that, beyond the incidental improprieties of classification and naming, points toward a more fundamentally necessary inadequation of language and desire. This ascendancy of desire over all qualification is succinctly formalized in Barthes's "Inaugural Lecture": "desire is stronger than its interpretation" (469).

By the time of his entry to the Collège de France, then, Barthes exasperates all definition, and it is a common feature of his commentators to point to this unclassifiability. Jonathan Culler, for instance, speaks of Barthes as a "man of parts"; Bernard Comment of a "plural" Barthes; while Réda Bensmaïa considers the late Barthes to be writing within an "unclassifiable" and indeed "impossible" genre.[10] A recurrent figure among such commentators is that of constant movement, as indexed by the title of Stephen Heath's *Vertige du déplacement*. Barthes's "perpetual movement," for Culler as for others, prevents the reader from attributing a single face to the heterogeneous and complex author.[11] And yet, one might seek Barthes's character and style precisely in his figures of movement. Such an approach would not necessarily defy Barthes's own pronouncements on atopia by abusively identifying, as Culler puts it, "a unifying, underlying desire" to the man and his work (16). This is the aim of my examination of Barthes, which will show that all of Barthes's work is marked by a sustained exploration of the figures of travel.

Serge Doubrovsky, in an essay that dwells on the restless figures of Barthes's prose, provides the means to consider his affective attachments in terms of the movements of the text. Doubrovsky's analysis, focusing on the figures of "drift," "atopia," and "displacement," has the merit of seeing Barthes's identity in terms of a dynamic of alternating postures, rather than as a reductive essence. Interestingly, for Doubrovsky this results in a reading that contradicts Culler's perhaps too faithful account of Barthes's plurality: "Under the seeming 'progress' or 'caprice' of the work's general arc, there is, in reality, only one single *textual motor*: oscillation between contradictory terms, simultaneous affirmation of an antinomy, reversal of for and against, in a word (which comes from Barthes himself) a *coming-and-going* [*le va-et-vient*]."[12] Doubrovsky's analysis goes some way toward offering an account of Barthes's *style*, that intimate feature of an author's writing theorized in *Writing Degree Zero*, which, born of the body and foreign to language, betrays itself in stubborn automatisms. A crucial contradiction of Barthes's writing, Doubrovsky points out, is the tension between a stated desire for fluid and free signification and the propensity for an aphoristic mode of expression. This tension is familiar to any reader of Barthes's searching, elastic phrases interrupted by parenthetical pauses. On the level of the sentence, then, Barthes's style plays out the struggle of his life's work: contesting the concretion of meaning with the free rein of *signifiance*. Beyond such vicious antinomies, however, Barthes would increasingly seek out a third alternative, the *neutral*, a space of play between opposing terms, and a means of affirming difference over opposition. *S/Z* is no doubt the key moment in this evolution, for at this juncture between the structuralist paradigm's machine of oppositions and the late Barthes's explorations in post-structural textuality, the figure of the castrato Zambinella opens up a neutral alternative to the symbolic order and its sexual norms. Neither-nor, *ne-uter*, the sexually neutral would be that categorically atopic subject of Barthes's seductive and elusive style.

To the threat of language as classification and order, Barthes responds with the elusive tactics of drifting, displacement, and atopic neutrality. Sexual classification is a dominant threat, not only because its fundamental opposition rules over structural accounts of symbolic norms, but because it fails to make room for homosexuality as an alternative to the structuring binarisms of social discourse. Such an alternative is a utopian possibility both in that it is without proper *place*, and also in that homosexuality does not so much constitute an identity for Barthes as a horizon of possibility. If the Barthes of the "Inaugural Lecture" shares with Foucault the theory of sexuality as object of discursive order, he diverges, however, from the historian in his utopian insistence on the liberatory possibility of a "sexuality outside discourse."[13] Thus, while Barthes falls short of sexual militancy, and has been faulted for an unnecessary discretion with respect to his own sexuality, his critique may be seen to anticipate the limitations of what later came to be known as identity politics. This is perhaps nowhere clearer than in his preface to Renaud Camus's *Tricks*, a sexually explicit gay text that would seem to call for a *prise de position* on Barthes's part. Barthes pointedly refuses such a call: "to proclaim oneself something is always to speak at the behest of a vengeful Other [*un Autre vengeur*], to enter into his discourse, to argue with him, to seek from him a scrap of identity: 'You are . . .' 'Yes, I am . . .'"[14] Camus's text seems to accomplish an *atopic* writing, whose principle would be, as Barthes says, "never to invoke, not to let Names into language—Names, the source of dispute, of arrogance, and of moralizing" (292; 1018). Likewise, in refusing to name himself, Barthes looks beyond his own sexual identity to the abusive order of classification in general: "Ultimately, the attribute is of no importance; what society will not tolerate is that I should be . . . *nothing*, or, more precisely, that the *something* that I am should be openly expressed as provisional, revocable, insignificant, inessential, in a word irrelevant [*en un mot: impertinent*]" (291–92; 1017). At stake in queer desire for Barthes is nothing less than a resistance to discursive order in general, and as such, he holds open homosexuality as a space of possibility beyond interpellation. Barthes's seductive prose, his rich and yet elusive figurations may render homosexuality discursive, but without presuming those figures to fully constitute or name their object. Atopia, then, would be the way in which Barthes militates for the "sense of desire as a limit to referentiality," as Judith Butler puts it.[15] What Butler diagnoses as "the gap between the performative and the referential" is the fruitful enunciatory space that must remain open in order that the discourse of homosexuality escape the paranoid complex of contagion and injury, or what Barthes felt to be the fascism of language.[16]

Barthesian criticism has shown itself to be remarkably resistant to a queer engagement with Barthes's writing, a tendency that has seen change only in recent years. This resistance is no doubt partly due to Barthes's own refusal to assume homosexuality as a name or identity for the reasons we have briefly outlined. Ostensibly respecting Barthes's own refusal to be classified, such critics however unwittingly reinforce two of the main modalities of the discursive control of homosexuality: a panicked profession of ignorance, and a symbolic embargo on its name and various forms, along the wide spectrum of suppression and tolerance. This is perhaps nowhere clearer than in Bernard Comment's work, which, much as it focuses on the "neutral" in Barthes, nevertheless makes no inquiry into the sexually neutral, thus failing to answer a question that he himself poses: "[I]t is advisable to ask oneself beforehand what might be the reasons that would impel an individual to flee from meaning, *our* meaning, to want to except himself or exempt himself from it."[17] For his part, Jonathan Culler's apparent negation of the question of homosexuality awkwardly performs its reification as "a unifying, underlying desire," as if Barthes's queer constitution were a simplifying rather than complicating factor in his affective motives. As such critical responses make amply apparent, classification is not so easily dispensed with, even by those who profess a liberal stance. Further, what one seems to see here is a failure of classification, but one that, rather than pursue its own undoing, slyly reappropriates failure itself in the service of a presumed norm. In this sense, then, Barthes's queer drifts appear in these texts as a failure put back to work, and back in their place, if only at the dubious margins of the analysis. To inquire into Barthes's sexuality need not be to pigeonhole him against his will; it is, more importantly, to see his desire as bound up with and resisting other desiring norms. The marginal status of Barthes's sexuality no doubt affords him a critical stance that informs his various critiques, and his allergy to classification is one of the significant ways in which sexuality operates a subtle but far-reaching critique of the normalizing forces of social discourse. As we will see, the call of discourse, as ideological interpellation or as the thrall of rhetoric are so many modalities in which Barthes explores his relation to normative desire, and to which he responds with the queer transports and paralyses of the neutral, *dérive*, and atopia.

Alibis

Barthes made a name for himself, so to speak, with the critical essays collected in 1957 under the title of *Mythologies*. At this time Barthes was called to identify himself, and was subsequently drawn into a polemic with none other than Jean Paulhan. Taking to task Barthes's broad assault on the mythologies of contemporary life, Paulhan asked that Barthes declare his critical doctrine: "After all, perhaps Mr. Barthes is simply a Marxist. Why doesn't he say so?"[18] Paulhan's red-baiting question (MacCarthyist, as Barthes retorts) seems an early instance of that "vengeful Other" Barthes later conjures with respect to homosexual identification. With his talent for arguments, Paulhan deftly targets the ambiguous enunciatory posture that, already in *Mythologies*, lends a subtly atopic quality to even Barthes's most overtly politicized pronouncements. If Paulhan's motives are politically suspect, he nonetheless brings out an interesting feature of *Mythologies*, one that anticipates the writing practice of the mature Barthes. Notably, Paulhan cites from Barthes's essay on the flooding of Paris, a text on which one critic comments at length for its "drifting" quality and "subversive complicity" with the myths it supposedly debunks.[19] This confrontation between Paulhan and Barthes is striking in that the misunderstanding—according to a dynamic familiar to Paulhan's readers—masks a deeper accord between the two writers, as Michael Syrotinski has noted.[20] In the following years, Barthes would increasingly see literature as a tragic condition pitting fatal constraints against the desire for free expression, as in this phrase that might well have come from Paulhan's *Flowers of Tarbes*: "look at my words, I am language; look at my meaning, I am literature."[21] As Barthes often says, to escape from literature is to be fatally reabsorbed into its fold. By the time of his "Inaugural Lecture," when language is held to be "fascist," Barthes's means of reconciling the tragic condition of literature would be, in a Paulhanian vein, to assume the burden of language's inherited store of figures as a neutral compromise between Terror and Rhetoric.

Perhaps Barthes took Paulhan too simply at his word, as Syrotinski suggests, and did not recognize an occasion to participate in an exchange on the role of ideology in criticism. In retrospect, what this exchange seems to dramatize above all is Barthes's vexed relationship to the vengeful Other without whom he would have no means to speak. In later years Barthes would acknowledge that the call of the Other inhabits the entirety of his writing, as seen in an interview from 1971: "In sum, I've always written in response to someone's urging."[22] Despite himself, Barthes seemingly has no proper voice, and is condemned to write only under orders: "Writing in response to a request (or to an order) is a 'task,'" Barthes says, with the result that whatever his pleasure in writing, he inevitably gives expression to what he calls "the desire of the Other." Barthes's missed appointment with Paulhan, then, can be seen as a symptom of his ongoing negotiation with the "absolutely terrorist character of language,"[23] voiced over the course of his career in the various forms of mythology, the Symbolic, and rhetoric. Reading with an eye to interpellation, we will attempt to see how the episodes in Barthes's career represent so many ways in which the labor of criticism constitutes the phases of a latent and emergent autobiography.

The essays that make up the text of *Mythologies* were written over the course of two years, from 1954 to 1956, and published on a monthly basis in various journals and magazines. Many of the essays deal with current events and stick close to the news of the hour; others deal with broader aspects of modern French mass culture. These two aspects of Barthes's subject matter—the *quotidien* and the broader *ethos* of culture—converge in modern myth, which imbues the transitory phenomena of everyday life with a stock repertoire of phantasms and stereotypes. In *Mythologies*, Barthes says, modern France is "ethnographed."[24] One of the dominant features of modern myth is the transformation of historical phenomena into static and timeless essences; myth is a temporal aberration that arrests the flow of history, its historical function being to replace historical consciousness with the reassuring impression of a timeless, natural present. As analyzed by Barthes, the strategies of popular mythic representations—naturalizing artifice, essentializing the contingent—are the means by which mass culture remakes history in its own image, as ideology.

The elimination of temporal history by myth is matched by an eradication of space. Among the recurrent terms in Barthes's essays is that of *alibi*, "a spatial term," Barthes reminds us, and a term in which he retains the double meaning of "elsewhere" and "justification."[25] The role of alibi in modern mythical representations is exemplified in *Mythologies* by touristic consciousness and its exoticizing and phantasmatic images of other lands. The stock in trade of such exotic elsewheres are the picturesque and the stereotype, so many conventional representations that reduce the culturally other to a consumable object of recognition. What is thus "recognized" in the other, however, are typologies rooted in petty-bourgeois consciousness and disseminated in such venues as the *Guide Bleu*, the French tourist guide to which Barthes devotes an essay in *Mythologies*. The "elsewhere" of other lands thus serves as a veiled "justification" of the tourist's native culture, reinforcing his local values through convenient images of illusory others. Barthes shows that travel as alibi runs a continuous spectrum from benign but insidious exoticism to outright colonial exploitation. The representations of the *Guide Bleu* are of the same order as the entries in Barthes's collection of Africanisms, "African Grammar," a sort of dictionary of received colonial ideas. Tourism and colonialism dilate in the same sphere of mythic representations, one that arrogates the world to its own universalizing myths. Just as myth serves to arrest history, then, so it halts travel, which, confined to its own representations and without overture to the other, vainly pronounces its ideological alibis.

A false alibi calls for an arrest, and in many of the essays in *Mythologies* Barthes takes to task ideological instances of travel and brings them to a halt. His essay "The Jet-man," for instance, lingers on the paradox that extreme speed results in apparent stasis. "[W]hat strikes one first in the mythology of the *jet-man* is the elimination of speed" (Eng., 71; Fr., 619). Similarly, Jules Verne's science fiction Nautilus represents for Barthes the antithesis of travel. "Imagination about travel corresponds in Verne to an exploration of closure," Barthes says (65; 611). Assimilating Verne to a general "bourgeois posture of appropriation," he sees the Nautilus as a domestic fantasy of comfort and seclusion rather than a means of adventure: "a ship is a habitat before being a means of transport" (66; 612). To the Nautilus as bourgeois dream and infantile locus of private enclosure Barthes opposes Arthur Rimbaud's "Drunken Boat," which he sees as representing "a genuine poetics of exploration" (67; 612). In Barthes's celebrated essay on the new Citroën, the DS 19, he compares the car to the Nautilus, seeing in it "a kind of control exercised over motion, which is henceforth conceived as comfort rather than performance" (89; 656). Petty-bourgeois "advancement" through consumerism as represented by the desire to own a state-of-the-art DS is thus ironized by Barthes as an unwitting stasis.

An insistent feature of Barthes's *Mythologies*, then, is its focus on questions of travel. In "The Jet-man" and "The New Citroën," progress itself is ironized as illusory, sustained only by its fantastical alibis. Other essays, such as "The Writer on Holiday," "The 'Blue Blood' Cruise," and "The *Blue Guide*" target vacations and cruises, while others, including "Bichon and the Blacks," "African Grammar," and "*The Lost Continent*," undertake a critique of exoticism and colonialism. The crucial link between Barthes's critique of everyday domestic life and its illusory elsewheres is the French empire, the colonial economy of domination that ties every aspect of the domestic sphere to possessions abroad. Thus, while Barthes's Marxist framework of analysis takes economics and class division as the ground of social critique, the critique is also displaced onto another scene, that of the emergent scene of decolonization. A footnote to *Mythologies* speaks to this displacement of French politics in the 1950s: "Today it is the colonized peoples who assume to the full the ethical and political condition described by Marx as being that of the proletariat" (148; 859).[26] Alienated from history, the French petty-bourgeois is also blind to the other and his historical imperative of liberation. As a result, what travel stages in French mythological discourse is a double ignorance of self and other, exemplified, for Barthes, by the ideology of Poujade: "the whole petit-bourgeois mythology implies the refusal of alterity, the negation of the different, the euphoria of identity and the exaltation of 'kind' [*l'exaltation du semblable*]."[27] Thus, in a recurrent formulation, Barthes characterizes mythology in its broadest sense as an "impotence to imagine the Other" (29; 588). And yet, travel still holds out the means of approach to others, but only on the condition that it goes beyond the touristic consumption of high culture and artifacts to reintegrate the traveler with history and with the specificity of other societies: "It is unquestionable that travel has become (or become again) a method of approach based on human realities rather than 'culture': once again (as in the eighteenth century, perhaps) it is everyday life which is the main object of travel, and it is social geography, town-planning, sociology, economics which outline the framework of the actual questions asked today even by the merest layman."[28] Progress, for the Barthes of *Mythologies*, is thus conceived either in terms of scientific materialism or the human sciences, whereas myth is condemned to regression and stasis: "Science proceeds rapidly on its way [*La science va vite et droit en son chemin*], but the collective representations do not follow, they are centuries behind, kept stagnant in their errors by power, the press, and the values of order."²⁹ Curiously, Barthes's invocation of the *speed* and *directness* of scientific knowledge betrays an almost positivist faith in the progress of knowledge. A contradiction arises here, since applied science as represented by the jet-man, for instance, is cast as anything but progressive. Barthes's polemical stance and its dialectical play of contraries leads him into these contradictions, though, as we will see, the import of *Mythologies* lies precisely in its tampering with such oppositions, including that of speed and stasis.

Myth for Barthes is retrograde, even when attached to novelty, high-tech, and science fiction, and this tension between apparent advances and sluggish representations underlies all the critiques delivered in *Mythologies*. The "neomania" that surrounds such new consumer products as the DS 19 is amalgamated with deep-seated beliefs and mystifications. Likewise, the "technocracy" of journalism sustains backward illusions about human nature in such venues as advice and astrology columns. Barthes's essays "Celle qui voit clair ['Agony Columns']" and "Astrologie" thus target the same material treated by Adorno in his *The Stars Down to Earth*, which examines the role of neo-occultism and superstition in modern society.³⁰ Like Adorno, Barthes does not limit his critique of astrology to a simple debunking of its blatant illusions; demystification in *Mythologies* also aims at an analysis of the function of mystification in contemporary society. In this way, his materialist scope of inquiry shares with Adorno's the attempt to theorize mystification as a function of social alienation, and thus as revelatory index of opaque social relations. Like Barthes, then, for Adorno astrology represents "a symptom of retrogression of society as a whole which allows some insight into the illness itself" (123). Backward and deluded as it might be, occultism brings out essential features smoothed out by modern social life. Whereas Adorno's emphasis is on "pseudo-superstition," Barthes's attention in *Mythologies* is focused on "semi-alienation," a virtual state of awareness that indexes a lived state of social contradiction.

Astrology, a form of modern "sorcery," represents a "semi-alienation (or semi-liberation)" that intervenes in real life but is incapable of going so far as demystifying reality.³¹ Similarly, advice columns market a kind of vicarious freedom without providing the means for genuine social liberation: "The apparent freedom of the advice makes unnecessary any real freedom of conduct: morality seems to be loosened a little, only to tighten a little more securely the constitutive dogmas of society [*on semble lâcher un peu sur la morale pour tenir bon plus sûrement sur les dogmes constitutifs de la société*]."³² The tightening hold of dogma is thus akin to the unwitting stasis of the deluded traveler. But the paradox of a loosening that tightens anticipates the chiastic double bind of power and servility in Barthes's "Inaugural Lecture." Indeed, Barthes's paradox seems almost to gloss the ambiguity of the term *paralysis* itself: while commonly conceived as an immobilizing *rigor*, paralysis in its etymological sense conveys instead a *loosening*, though one that is *aside* and *amiss*. The paralyzing logic of this twisted stricture accompanies all of Barthes's critiques of transport from *Mythologies* on.

The characteristically retrograde and innovative aspects of myth and its objects reflect the economic period to which Barthes's devotes his mythological analyses: the period of rapid and unprecedented modernization in French history that followed the second world war. The thirty-year economic boom that would come to be known as *Les trente glorieuses* had just begun when Barthes voiced his reservations about the shape of progress in France. Barthes was, of course, not alone in his suspicions, nor in his focus on the ephemera of contemporary mass culture. During this same period other critics, most notably Henri Lefebvre, turned their attention to "everyday life," arguing that the decisive issues of economics, social policy, and demography were realized in the seemingly innocent sphere of neobourgeois advancement. Kristin Ross provides a useful account of the rise of modern consumer culture in France and the emergence of everyday life as a field of critical analysis. What Ross calls the "French lurch into modernization" was characterized by the suddenness of material progress and a concurrent anxiety about change on the part of its critics.[33] One might add, however, that such anxiety is legible not only among its overt critics but also in the myths to which Barthes devotes his analyses. For modern myths may well serve to justify petty-bourgeois values, but they habitually do so in regressive and mystified forms. As in the case of occultism as analyzed by Adorno and Barthes, mythology's retrograde character may be seen as testifying to a latent resistance to the very progress it celebrates. Ross speaks of a "cargo-cult-like" invasion of modern appliances and products in the devastated France of the postwar years, and takes the American car's arrival in France during this period as emblematic of the ambivalent reception of modern products and the changes they effect on social life (4). The Citroën DS 19, much as it is a domestic product, is tellingly rendered by Barthes as an alien object, "fallen from the sky," "supernatural" and partaking of the qualities of science fiction spaceships. Like the Melanesians confronted with alien cultural forces beyond their reckoning, the French assimilate their new objects with a mixture of enthusiasm and resentment. French mythology of the period studied by Barthes would be the means by which progress is arrested even as it is rapturously embraced.

In the years immediately following the publication of *Mythologies*, popular consciousness and mass media would find their anxiety concerning progress confirmed in the spectacle of car crashes. As Ross demonstrates, the glamorization of high-speed driving during the 1950s by such figures as Françoise Sagan had already been accompanied by sensational accounts of crashes, but by the beginning of the 1960s a slew of fatal accidents, most notably that of Albert Camus and Michel Gallimard, confirmed the worst fears. In the frozen images of car wrecks the public saw the traumatic impact of modernization on French life. Such images are, of course, endemic to automobile cultures, but what Ross rightly underscores in the

French example is the friction resulting from the sheer speed of progress. If car crashes focus anxiety concerning the future of progress, however, an equally important aspect of this anxiety is turned backward to the traumatic past. French modernization during this period may be characterized as part of a generalized project of historical forgetting, and the spectacle of wrecks can be seen to bring back the memory of the disasters of war. A quote from François Maspero speaks to this anxiety: "For a long time ... the child of the war that he once was had lodged inside of him a tiny tenacious fear: the haunting worry, anchored in a corner of his memory, that once again everything might *come to a stop*."[34] A mythology of transport during this period must account for the dual anxiety that sees speed to be threatened by sudden immobilization. One of the features of modern mythology is to articulate such contradictions, even if it remains unable to theorize them. Thus, as Barthes says in his essay on the jet-man, popular discourse provides a telling paradox of transport that escapes its own understanding: "We must here accept a paradox, which is in fact admitted by everyone with the greatest of ease, and even consumed as a proof of modernity. This paradox is that an excess of speed turns into repose."[35]

As mythologist of modern life Barthes arrests the complacent movement of progress, suspecting its motives and disqualifying its ideological alibis. The critique of transport, as we have seen, allows for a bracing demystification of the economies of travel and colonialism. The broadest scope of this critique is an ethical objection to the economy of appropriation: the reign of "le mythe de l'Identique" in which the Other represents the alibi of a self incapable of imagining alterity.[36] This ethical dimension of Barthes's critique also inflects his theory of mythic signification as developed in "Myth Today," the theoretical text that concludes *Mythologies*. Barthes's semiological analysis sees the mythic signifier as depending on the functioning of an *alibi*. Barthes defines myth as a second-order sign whose ideological meaning is parasitically grafted onto a prior sign. This prior sign, composed of signifier and signified, becomes the signifier in turn of the ideological sign, a process Barthes characterizes as an "abuse" and a "deformation." The resulting mythic signifier is duplicitous, drawing both on a form and a content, alternately, in support of its ideological claims. It is this alternation that makes up the evasiveness proper to the functioning of the mythic signifier, and which allows ideological meaning to establish itself in what Barthes calls "a perpetual alibi" (Eng., 123; Fr., 693). The mythologist, confronted with the dizzying movement of the mythic signifier, goes against this dynamic and applies "a static method" of interpretation, in short, an arrest.

Curiously, however, Barthes goes on to characterize himself, in turn, as arrested by myth. In a formulation that anticipates Althusser's theory of ideology, Barthes describes the force of myth as an *interpellation*.[37] "Myth has an imperative, buttonholing character [*un caractère impératif, interpellatoire*]: stemming from an historical concept, directly springing from contingency . . . , it is *I* whom it has come to seek. It is turned towards me, I am subjected to its intentional force, it summons me to receive its expansive ambiguity" (*Mythologies,* Eng., 124; Fr. 694). Barthes thus makes clear that myth is not only an abuse of the sign, or of a larger social reality; it strikes closer to home as an abuse of the subject. The myth's signification goes beyond mere message to assault Barthes in his person, obligating him to recognize it and thereby establishing his "complicity." Here interpellation seems to carry the full sense with which Althusser later invests the term: the insidious force of an ideological state apparatus that enjoins the subject to recognize *himself* in the call of ideology. Althusser's well-known illustration of the "call" of ideology consists of an ordinary scene in which a police officer calls out, "Hey you there!" and someone turns around. This "someone" is the ideological subject, paradoxically constituted in the mere act of receiving the call. The example Barthes gives of such an interpellation might seem odd to the reader of *Mythologies*:

a phony Basque chalet incongruously located in the heart of Paris, and whose stereotypical features advertise what Barthes awkwardly calls its *basquité*. Such an object, as Barthes shows, is guilty of the essentializing inherent to any stereotype; isolated from its context, it loses the features that tie it to local custom, and presents itself as an ensemble of signifying elements that appeal to the viewer with "an imperious injunction" to lend it a name and an identity. "I feel this chalet has been created on the spot, *for me*, like a magical object springing up in my present life without any trace of the history which has caused it" (125; 695). Now the region, of course, in which such imitative architecture predominates is the area surrounding Barthes's own native Bayonne. This alerts the reader to the presence of Barthes himself in the example he stages: the *moi* emphasized here is connected to the Barthes of his upbringing. This would be a mere biographical curiosity did it not open up significant questions pertaining to the position from which the critiques in *Mythologies* are delivered. Anticipating the issues of classification that mark his later works, Barthes's particularity emerges here as the object of an abusive identification. The crisis of identity staged in Barthes's scene of interpellation is literally a locating of the subject, assigning him to his native *topos*. For Barthes to refuse to recognize the Basque chalet is to refuse at the same time the ideological identity conferred by the mythic sign. Rather than speaking in the name of a more genuine Basque identity hailing from Bayonne, however, Barthes pointedly distinguishes the French Basque country from the Spanish region, since "in France, petit-bourgeois advancement has caused a whole 'mythical' architecture of the Basque chalet to flourish" (124; 694). The genuine Basque has no place in France, absorbed as it is by spurious imitation. And if Barthes locates the Basque country in Spain, it is perhaps to underscore the homelessness of the Basque, who, a people without a nation, were at the time of *Mythologies* the object of a concerted program of ethnic erasure on the part of Franco in the aftermath of the Spanish civil war. As a "cultural alibi," the

Basque house in Paris partakes of the same touristic mentality that Barthes had critiqued with respect to the *Guide Bleu*'s tourist guide of Spain: ignorant of history, delighting in stereotypical "essences" and complicitous with a reactionary political regime.

The reader of *Mythologies* may be surprised, then, to turn to Barthes's autobiography and find among the first photos that illustrate the text an image of Bayonne with a Basque-style house dead center. The name of the establishment is boldly advertised in capital letters on the façade: "A la Maison Basque."[38] Although Barthes had not abandoned his Marxist and Brechtian convictions by the time of the autobiography, a significant shift has occurred in the interim. Ideology is no longer polemically assaulted but diverted and played with in the later Barthes. A larger space of play is accorded to the subject of Barthes's autobiography as he delves into the *imaginary* of his bourgeois childhood. Interpellation, echoed in the verbs *enthrall*, *fascinate*, and *rivet* (*Roland Barthes by Roland Barthes*, 3; *Roland Barthes par Roland Barthes*, 85), is replaced by the appeal of the image in which Barthes recognizes the immutability of his social person, which, however, does not cohere in a unified identity. Much as his self-reflection may be "egotistical," as he readily admits, Barthes suggests that the true object of his fascination escapes the image and lies in the "disturbing familiarity" of his bodily self. The autobiographer thus takes pleasure in simultaneously calling up an identity and exposing the "fissure of the subject."

Barthes's scene of interpellation points us in the direction of the *subject* of *Mythologies*. Behind the figures of arrested transport and the critique of tourism lies a subject who is similarly arrested. Is there something suspect in the voice that delivers his critique of ideology? What transports of the subject would call for such a paralysis? Barthes's arrest dramatizes an impasse in his critique of mythology, an *aporia* expressed at the conclusion of "Myth Today." "Wine is objectively good," Barthes says, "and *at the same time*, the goodness of wine is a myth: here is the aporia" (158; 718). Much as he may wish to escape them, the critic is nonetheless susceptible to capture by mythic representations. Faced with a seemingly inescapable aporia, Barthes sees himself as caught between two impossible alternatives: grasping at a reality supposedly free of representation, or reducing all reality to ideology: "We constantly drift [*nous voguons sans cesse*] between the object and its demystification, powerless to render its wholeness [*impuissants à rendre sa totalité*]" (159; 719). And yet this very impasse, as expressed by Barthes, gives room for a certain space of play, and this in-between space of an alternating *drift*, anticipating the *neutral* and the *atopic*, is the means by which Barthes eludes the thrall of interpellation.

The emergence of the figures of drift and displacement in Barthes's work are linked, then, to the threat of stasis and the insurmountable obstacle. In what follows, as we trace the emergence of these figures we must be attentive to the way in which drift and stasis form a dynamic bond, and not a simple opposition. This dynamic relationship elucidates the ambiguous nature of Barthes's "attachments," so to speak, which seek a space of play within their very arrest. A key feature of this ambiguity as expressed in *Mythologies* is the figure of drift, of which Andrew Brown has offered the most sustained analysis to date: "Drift, a paradoxical mixture of stasis and movement, of collusion and distance, is one way Barthes figures writing as a solution to (or dissolution of) the antinomies of his culture. It can include fragmentation and dissemination among its tactics, since drift is a complication of, rather than an escape from, the binary opposites of ideology: it consists of finding pockets of resistance within that ideology rather than attempting to leap outside it."[39] In this way, Barthes's attachments play out a dynamic of desire as subjection: called to order by normative discourse, Barthes's desire drifts among its figures, alternately captured and released. Barthes's *Mythologies* displays what Brown terms a "duplicity of response" with respect to myth, miming its language the better to unmask its purpose.[40] Further, this "subversive complicity" entails an enunciatory ambiguity in which the critic risks losing his critical voice, seemingly *spoken by* ideology even as he attempts to address it. As an example of drift, Brown comments on the essay "Paris Not Flooded," which concerns the Paris flood of 1955, and whose paradoxical result in the popular press was that it was greeted more as a festival than a disaster. Barthes's objection to the popular reception of the flood is that it domesticates the dramatic nature of the city's aquatic transformation: "The flood convulsed normal optics without invoking the fantastic [*sans pourtant la dériver vers le fantastique*]; objects were partially obliterated, not distorted: the spectacle was singular but reasonable."[41] However, even as he puts forward an objection to the sense of festival, Barthes's own account of the flood tends—or drifts—into agreement with it. His prose lingers on what he calls "a whole euphoric myth of movement [*glissement*]" in which others indulge, such as the newspaper reader who, Barthes says, "feels himself conveyed by proxy [*se sent glisser par procuration*]" (32; 600). Beneath Barthes's criticism of the myth is a certain *glissement de sens*, or a shift in meaning. It is, as a result, difficult to catch Barthes's drift when he describes the flooded cityscape as follows: "no more paths, no more banks, no more directions [*plus de voies, plus de rives, plus de directions*]; a flat substance which goes nowhere and which thereby suspends man's process, detaches him from reason, from a utensility of sites" (32; 599). Myth or demystification? Barthes's description seems to partake of both, since, if this image of the flood suspends the narrow purposes of reason and practicality, it also falls short of rendering what Barthes calls its "horror." After this interesting and complex effusion, Barthes's remark that the press overlooked the blunt reality that people's cellars were flooded seems to sacrifice too much pleasure to the cause of critique. Indeed, Barthes seems somewhat at pains to distinguish his own analysis from the "mythe heureux" he criticizes, and consequently the true interest of the essay becomes its own critical drift, a movement of ambiguous attachment and contradiction in which the position of the critic becomes strangely unmoored from his own project. Drift, here, would be the surreptitious movement of pleasure in the text: an attachment to myth betrayed by a drifting of writing.

Barthes's ambiguous position with respect to the pleasures of the flood would seem to result from an inability to fully account for the drift of his own pleasure. In this light, one might read this text as staging the ambiguous relation between *plaisir* and *jouissance* developed in his later *The Pleasure of the Text*. Mythology, in the essay on the flood, would largely be situated on the side of *pleasure*, that paler, more secure domain of desire, to which Barthes contrasts the disruptive force of all-consuming *jouissance*. As pleasure, Barthes characterizes the flood in terms of "infantile" enjoyment, such as "the great mythic and infantile dream of walking-on-water" (*The Eiffel Tower*, 32; *Mythologies*, Fr., 600). This connection of myth with childhood suggests, however, that a certain unavowed or guilty pleasure has infiltrated Barthes's critique. "Paradoxically, the flood has created a more accessible world, manipulable with the kind of pleasure a child takes in wielding his toys, exploring and enjoying them [*en jouir*]" (33; 600). The most suspect of such toys is the *boat*, in which the reader may recognize Barthes's critique of the Nautilus: "[T]he little boat, the superlative toy of the childhood universe, which has become the possessive mode of this arranged, outspread, and no longer rooted space." If, as we have seen, Barthes holds up the *bateau ivre* as the contrary of such bourgeois pleasure, he seems to forget, however, that Rimbaud's tumultuous poem of oceanic *jouissance* itself concludes by regretfully evoking childhood and a toy boat.[42] Would the claims of *jouissance* be built upon the denial of pleasure? Is Rimbaud's "genuine poetics of exploration" simply Barthes's alibi for a more sedentary enjoyment? The later Barthes accommodates himself to another figure of transport: in the "Inaugural Lecture," the atopic "drifting habitation" conjoins, in a single figure, both features of dwelling and displacement. Already prefigured by the ambiguous transports of *Mythologies*, Barthes's "habitacle en dérive" speaks to the drift of pleasure that finds its space of play only in and through the constraints of normative discourse, or within, one might say, what the French call *bateau* forms of expression. This implicit pleasure of the mythologist is frankly assumed by the time of Barthes's autobiography: "Might it not be possible to take one's pleasure [*jouir*] in bourgeois (deformed) culture *as a kind of exoticism?*"[43] This exoticism of the familiar makes room for a certain play, or drift, within the confines of ideology, which the later Barthes no longer sees as possible to fully escape.

An entire history of postwar Marxist French thought is summed up in the space of play between Barthes's two drifts. This history, of course, is more than that of the death of Marxism or an accommodation to ideology, but rather a reckoning with the limitations of the ideology-critique exemplified by *Mythologies*. In 2007, on the fiftieth anniversary of Barthes's book, there appeared a volume of essays under the title *Nouvelles Mythologies*, authored by a wide range of critics and writers. At best a nostalgic homage, and at worst a regressive imitation, *Nouvelles Mythologies* displays the outworn critical optic that has become an ingrained feature of French cultural critique. Thus Jacques-Alain Miller: Google is "stupid"; Google is "big brother."[44] Jacques Rancière, one of the most incisive critics of the tradition of ideology-critique in France, sees such demystifying claims as laboring under the presumption of the image-as-illusion, itself a classical motif of metaphysical lineage. Against the presumptions of the alienating image and passive spectatorship, Rancière posits that the image is always fabricated, and thus material, while the spectator is always engaged in a work of creative interpretation. In this way, Rancière wrests critique from the authority of the teacher and critic, and portrays contemporary society as a web of contesting visions, a "dissensus" without overarching order. One of Rancière's chief targets in his critique is Barthes and his *Mythologies*, which he sees as emblematic of the impasse of critique that led, after May '68, to the decline of radical critical theory. Curiously, Rancière's critique of Barthes tends to view his entire *oeuvre* in the light of *Mythologies*, such that even Barthes's *Camera Lucida* is seen as working within the framework of demystificatory analysis.[45] Rancière thus gives little credit to the evolution of Barthes's thought, and notably fails to account for the queering of theory that inflects all of his late writings with a subversive drift. Moreover, as we have seen, Barthes's drift in *Mythologies* already contains aspects of this subversion of its own masterful critique, and we will now turn to a fuller account of the development, or mutation, of Barthes's critical thinking.

Idios

The methodological failure expressed at the conclusion of "Myth Today" signals a key feature of Barthes's critical work to come, namely the abandonment of metalinguistic discourse, or the presumption of critical exteriority from the symbolic phenomena under analysis. Thus, the foreword to the 1957 publication of *Mythologies* already speaks of "demystification" as a virtually outmoded term, and the prefatory note of 1970 points to a shift of methodology from the analysis of collective representations to the critique of the linguistic sign. This "semioclasty," which the Barthes of 1970 shares with his colleagues of the Tel quel group, draws on structural analysis in order to expose the determining role of linguistic structure in ordering the larger symbolic domain, and proceeds to a militant "liberation" of the signifier. The abiding interest of Barthes's *Mythologies*—aside from its status as a major document of French intellectual history—lies in its ambiguous and contradicted stance of "demystification," performed in the course of Barthes's critiques as discrepancies, contradictions, or ambivalent attachments to the objects of critique. Laying claim equally to the objectivity of a *savant* and the subjectivity of a writer, Barthes wills his text to expressing the "contradiction" that the combination may entail, be it, as he flatly states, by means of "sarcasm."[46] Here, Flaubert is a subtext to Barthes's critical approach, particularly the Flaubert of *Bouvard et*

Pécuchet and the *Dictionnaire des idées reçues*. Beyond the controlled irony of a sarcastic posture, however, Flaubert points toward a less identifiable ironic agency: the *style indirect libre*, what Barthes calls "an admirable instrument for demystification" in "Myth Today" (136; 703). The Barthes of *Mythologies* shares with Flaubert a biting critique that nevertheless has no clear source, and which shades in and out of ironic distance and sympathy. Often mistakenly attributed to an "omniscient" perspective, Flaubertian irony is, rather, a feature of a dispersed and contradicted subjectivity. The rhetorical devices of satire and parody are casualties of such *atopic* discourse; Barthes comes to see them as so many ways in which an illusory mastery is asserted over discourse. In *S/Z* Barthes lays out his critique of restricted irony and sketches out a program for his own works: "Employed in behalf of a subject that puts its imaginary elements at the distance it pretends to take with regard to the language of others, thereby making itself even more securely a subject of the discourse, parody, or irony at work, is always *classic* language. What would a parody be that did not advertise itself as such? This is the problem facing modern writing."[47]

Critical *distance*, then, is not only a ruse but a self-deception on the part of the parodic writer, who constitutes himself as subject to discourse even in claiming an illusory mastery. Barthes's own writing tactics will elude the alternatives of distance and attachment in a drifting attitude that neither assumes nor rejects the language of others, be it even of the order of the *bêtise* (stupidity). Indeed, Barthes shares with Flaubert a certain attachment to the *bêtise*, an attraction to and a complicity with received ideas. This affinity with Flaubert is shown in an interview in which Barthes turns, notably, to *Bouvard et Pécuchet*, that ironic monument to received knowledge. While rejecting what he calls Flaubert's political *bêtise*, his reactive attack on petty-bourgeois ideology, Barthes also speaks of a certain necessity of stupidity, or the stubbornly "intraitable" (intractable). Barthes thus identifies Flaubert's reactionary *bêtise* with his own stubbornness: "It is because there is a certain Intractability in me that I am obliged to turn toward semifictional forms of writing."[48] Barthes's turn toward figuration and autobiography in his late works can be seen, then, as an attempt to account for what remains intractably resistant to earlier analyses, and this turn toward a more explicit self-examination involves a return to stereotypic discourse, as shown in *A Lover's Discourse: Fragments*.

Just as the political *Mythologies* suggests a theory of desire, the hedonistic *Lover's Discourse* suggests a theory of the political. Organized as a catalogue, with entries placed in alphabetical order, *Fragments* offers itself as a guidebook or encyclopedia for the reader's use. In this way, *A Lover's Discourse* would seem to answer Barthes's call in *S/Z* for a "writerly" text, one that allows for the reader's active intervention in the text's composition. In another sense, however, the coded nature of *A Lover's Discourse* makes it something of a dictionary of received ideas, and this relation between personal desire and social codes is a feature of the text's tension and pathos. *A Lover's Discourse* thus articulates a double movement of categorization and dispersal, an unsettling play in which the lover's singular *idios* negotiates with ever-inadequate discursive expressions shared with others: "Most of my injuries come from the stereotype: I am obliged [*contraint*] to make myself a lover, like everyone else: to be jealous, neglected, frustrated, like everyone else" (*Lover's Discourse*, 35–36; *Fragments*, 494). In its focus on what Barthes calls the subject's "affective contagion" by society (136; 587), *A Lover's Discourse* illuminates the affective stakes we have drawn out of the critique of ideology.

"Mass culture," Barthes states in *A Lover's Discourse*, "is a machine for showing desire" (136; *Fragments*, 587). Against this interpellation of the desiring subject, Barthes asserts the lover's privilege to embrace "envers et contre tout" the value of love, subtracted from the ends and means of social existence: "I accept and I affirm, beyond truth and falsehood, beyond success and failure" (23; 479). Barthes thus characterizes the lover's resistance as a stubbornness in the face of disproof or better judgment, immune to demystification or critical distance: "Though I listen to all the arguments which the most divergent systems employ to demystify, to limit, to erase, in short to depreciate love, I persist: 'I know, I know, but all the same . . .' [*je m'obstine: 'Je sais bien, mais quand même . . .'*]" (22; 479). This stubborn attachment to the figures of love, Barthes says, is the lover's *bêtise*. "What is stupider than a lover? [*Quoi de plus bête qu'un amoureux?*]" Barthes asks, only to add, however, that *bêtise* is his own *daïmôn* (177; 624). *Bêtise* holds the subject paralyzed in the grip of fascination: "[A]bout stupidity, I am entitled to say no more than this: *that it fascinates me*. Fascination is the *correct* feeling stupidity must inspire me with (if we reach the point of speaking its name): it grips me [*elle m'étreint*] (it is intractable, nothing prevails over it, it takes you in an endless hand-over-hand race)."[49] *Bêtise*, then, is the lover's protest against reason and his defiance of social good grace. Ironically, however, this stubborn defiance is also a submission to stereotypic figures and to their host of conventional *phrases*: "[I]s it not on the level of the sentence that the subject seeks his place—and fails to find it—or finds a false place imposed on him by language?" (*A Lover's Discourse*, 6; *Fragments*, 463). As we have seen, such interpellation of the subject signaled the failure of demystification in *Mythologies*. In *A Lover's Discourse*, as in *Mythologies*, this failure hinges on Barthes's pleasure as it surreptitiously attaches to the figures it aims to contest. In *A Lover's Discourse*, however, this stubborn *bêtise* is embraced as such, and the resulting text presents a subversion of discourse from within. Thus, the figures of love are presented at the level of the amorous subject's enunciation, and not from the perspective of analysis; as stated at the outset, "no metalangage" is the principle of Barthes's exposition (3; 461). One may relate this breakdown of analytic perspective to the *texte de jouissance* introduced by *The Pleasure of the Text*: "you cannot speak 'on' such a text, you can only speak 'in' it, *in its fashion* [*à sa manière*]."[50] No metalanguage, no critical alibis: pleasure and desire find their transports only in and through the figures of discourse. As a result, Barthes's transports vie constantly with the figures of paralysis and fixation.

This sense of fixation is reinforced in the introduction to *A Lover's Discourse*, where Barthes defines the notion of the lover's *figures* as a kind of paralysis:

> These fragments of discourse can be called *figures*. The word is to be understood, not in its rhetorical sense, but rather in its gymnastic or choreographic acceptation; in short, in the Greek meaning: σχημα is not the "schema," but, in a much livelier way, the body's gesture caught in action and not contemplated in repose: the body of athletes, orators, statues: what in the straining body can be immobilized. (*Lover's Discourse*, 3–4; *Fragments*, 461)

If the lover's *figures* are defined in terms of action and not repose, it is only the better to freeze that motion, such that the visible body as a whole, so to speak, grimaces. This straining body is the object of an act of recognition on the part of the lover: "'*I recognize that scene of language*,'" Barthes renders him as saying (*Lover's Discourse*, 4; *Fragments*, 462). An implicit contrast is set up, then, between *dis-cursus*, or "the action of running here and there" and the subject's entrapment in a paralyzed *figure* (3; 461). In the figures of the lover's discourse, in other words, lies the lure and the threat of his imaginary identification: "Whence the emotion of every figure: even the mildest bears within it the terror of a *suspense*: in it I hear the tempestuous, Neptunian *quos ego*" (6; 463).

This paralyzed lover is characterized by Barthes as "sedentary, motionless, at hand, in expectation, nailed to the spot, *in suspense* [*en souffrance*]—like a package in some forgotten corner of a railway station" (*Lover's Discourse*, 13; *Fragments*, 471). By contrast, it is always the loved *other* who is in movement: "The other is in a condition of perpetual departure, of journeying; the other is, by vocation, migrant, fugitive." Further, this sedentary subject is defined as feminized: "in any man who utters the other's absence *something feminine* is declared: this man who waits and who suffers from his waiting is miraculously feminized. A man is not feminized because he is inverted but because he is in love. (Myth and utopia: the origins have belonged, the future will belong to the subjects *in whom there is something feminine*)" (14; 472). Barthes's ethics of desire thus entails a rejection of the heroism of travel and adventure in favor of a more feminine posture. This confirms a general feature of *A Lover's Discourse*: while seemingly exhaustive in its catalogue of figures, little place is given in the book to the conventionally heroic aspects of romance. Love as conquest, romance as adventure give way to susceptibility without appropriation and overture to an always absent other. In a telling inversion, Barthes asserts that the classical *subject* (agent of a story or drama) has been replaced in our time by the *object* of desire, the "immobile," "ravished," "wounded," and "feminized" lover (188–89; 633). The amorous *transports* of this queer subject go some way, then, toward illuminating Barthes's critique of travel and suspicion of narrative. A lover's discourse does not amount to a story; it has no development; at most, it is a rhythm of alternation that expresses the presence and absence of the loved object. Proust and Freud are among Barthes's most frequent intertexts here, as the absent other is persistently figured as the mother, and the amorous subject a stubborn and demanding child. What Barthes retains from Freud in this context is not the child's Oedipal predicament—an eventuality that he suspends, as it were—but specifically the scene from *Beyond the Pleasure Principle* in which Freud's grandson, coming to terms with the painful fact of his mother's periodic absence, plays with a bobbin and thread to mimic her comings and goings. This play of alternation persists in Barthes's amorous subject, whose love story, in a sense, is always already over: having once loved and lost, he forever and repeatedly compensates in playing with his "perpetual calendar" and "encyclopedia" of figures that are "non-syntagmatic, non-narrative [*hors récit*]" (7; 463). Barthes's emotive transports thus entail a different dynamic of mobility, alternately arrested and displaced, stubborn and restless, without the convenient option of a self-serving alibi. The ethical dimension of *Mythologies* may thus be closely linked to the ethics of desire elaborated in Barthes's *Lover's Discourse*. As we will see in Barthes's *Empire of Signs*, the resulting transports yield an entirely novel form of travel account.

Jonathan Culler has noted that for a critic of literature "Barthes is surprisingly uninterested in story."[51] While Barthes's readers may be familiar with his commitment to avant-gardist prose and its dismantling of narrative conventions, in *A Lover's Discourse* this disinterest in narrative reveals its underlying affective causes. Narrative, here, is another instance of that "vengeful Other" which would show Barthes his place in the social order. The lover's discourse rebels against the demands of what Barthes terms the "grand Autre narratif"; indeed, narrative is characterized as a kind of extortion levied against the lover: "the love story (the 'episode,' the 'adventure') is the tribute the lover must pay to the world in order to be reconciled with it" (*Lover's Discourse*, 7; *Fragments*, 463). *A Lover's Discourse* thus pits the social order—Lacan's *grand Autre*—against the intractable pre-Oedipal child, and in staging a conflict between the two, Barthes militates against the normalizing claims of the Symbolic in favor of the Imaginary. It is worth underscoring that in Lacanian psychoanalysis, Imaginary and Symbolic desire are not seen as *phases* in a developmental history, but as separate *registers* of desiring identification. At best, the Lacanian subject is bound to accommodate his persistent imaginary attachments to the demands of society. Barthes's lover, however, refuses even such accommodation; his intractable attachment defies any substitution or attenuation. Another word for this intractable attachment is the "unreal," the "inactuel," as Barthes states at the beginning of *A Lover's Discourse* (3; 461). *Inactuel* speaks both to the outmoded nature of romantic figures, their virtual banishment from contemporary social discourse, as well as to the subject's prehistory and its temporal dislocation from any discursive *present*. Tellingly, *inactuel* also connotes a lack of *action*; the lover's figures are frozen poses that convey his affective paralysis.

In its focus on themes of stubbornness, *A Lover's Discourse* may be seen as a continuation of Barthes's fragmented autobiography. In each text the reader comes up against Barthes's *intractability*, a term with which we might finally qualify the author, were it not, as with all his favored qualifications, fundamentally ambiguous: for intractability suggests at once a stubborn identity and a resistance to identification. Failing any definition, it is this very ambiguity or equivocation that defines the *subject* of Barthes's quasi-autobiographies. As we have seen, the crux of this equivocation lies in the figures of transport in which the author's motives and drives are put into play. The stubbornness of pleasure goes against the grain of history; thus, speaking of his childhood, Barthes says, "it is not the irreversible I discover in my childhood, it is the irreducible: everything which is still in me, by fits and starts [*par accès*]."[52] The stubborn persistence of his childhood traits lends a distinctive dynamic to Barthes's writing style: "Discourse advances by little fates, by amorous fits. (The cunning of language: in French the word for this infatuation is *engouement*, which means an *obstruction*)" (110; 179). How does the notion of the intractable combine the two senses of identity and resistance to identification? One key to this equivocation lies in the dual function of the Lacanian Imaginary, conceived as what is both most proper and most alienating to the desiring subject. For Lacan, the "mirror stage" inaugurates the subject's ideal self as an image of wholeness with which he can never coincide. Following Lacan, Barthes characterizes the attachment to the image as fundamentally alienating, in that the subject seizes upon himself only as another. To the extent that the subject's love is modeled on this image, the loved other is conflated with the ideal self. The inherent frustration of the image is compensated by the lover's rapturous assumption of this other as his own, as the unique image of his desire, as, Barthes puts it in *A Lover's Discourse*, "the singular Image which has miraculously come to correspond to the specialty of my desire" (34; *Fragments*, 493). This figure, Barthes says, is *atopos*, unqualifiable, and resistant to any stereotype. No sooner is its singularity asserted, however, than it is cast into doubt. Despite its singularity, the lover realizes that the image may correspond to an invariable *type*, and is consequently alienated in the larger social domain: "Does this mean that my desire is classifiable?" (34; 493). According to a dynamic that should be by now familiar, Barthes finds his own desiring idiom contaminated by the social. Such splits, reversals, and contradictions are the hallmark of the Imaginary, as identity purchased by means of reflection is condemned to frustrating duality.

Much as Barthes insists upon the lure of a certain *fusion* in the Imaginary, as represented by the exclusive bond of the mother and child, this "infantile embrace [*dyade enfantine*]" (*Lover's Discourse*, 104; *Fragments*, 566) can only perpetuate the subject's painful division. In this way, Barthes confirms the Lacanian proposition that the Imaginary, in its self-alienating structure, already anticipates the alienation of the subject in the Symbolic.[53] According to a developmental model, the subject's successful negotiation with his imaginary other thus provides the means for his eventual integration into the Oedipal matrix. Barthes's own itinerary is somewhat different, however; indeed, it defies the very notion of development and persists instead in an alternating rhythm of attachment and detachment, frustration and plenitude. Without conforming to Lacan's symbolic Law, Barthes nonetheless makes the Imaginary a site in which an illusory self, "the *I*, proud organ of misapprehension [*méconnaissance*]" is necessarily *both* unique and stereotyped.[54] This painful division is nothing other than the space of love, or the subject's wounded attachments. If on the one hand the lover embraces the absolutely singular nature of his love, he also wishes to put that love into words: "I struggle [*je m'épuise*] to put 'into other words' the ipseity of my Image, to express improperly the propriety of my desire" (20–21; 477). Such an effort, however, is bound to fail, and the lover falls back on the virtually solipsistic expression "adorable" in qualifying his love. Further, as Barthes says, this failure of nomination entails a tautology: "*The adorable is what is adorable* [*Est adorable ce qui est adorable*]" (21; 477). This last formula is particularly striking if one recalls that *Mythologies* had characterized tautology as one of ideology's most pernicious ways of asserting its purported self-evidence. Once again, a link suggests itself between Barthes's critique of ideology and his theory of desire; *A Lover's Discourse*'s dream of fusion is related to the subject's capture by ideology. If this is so, how then can the desiring subject, in his attachment to *bêtise*, avoid conforming to socially sanctioned desire? Further, what alternative is there to Barthes's painful splits and vicious antinomies?

In his autobiography Barthes confesses to his affection for binarisms and dualities. This systematizing impulse, inherited from structuralist methodology, increasingly comes under critical attack in the later Barthes, where the regime of oppositions is displaced by such figures as the *neutral* and *différance*. Thus, *The Pleasure of the Text* presents a paradigm of *plaisir* and *jouissance*, only to render the difference between them highly undecidable. This very undecidability is the "subject" of the text, so to speak: contradicted, inconsistent, partaking both of ideological *pleasure* and the rapture of asocial *jouissance*. While Barthes's desiring subject cannot help but fall in with normative *plaisir*, that very pleasure is inevitably subverted by *jouissance*; in this way, Barthes frees desire from its conflicting alternatives, allowing for the transport he names *dérive*:

> *Drifting* occurs whenever *I do not respect the whole*, and whenever, by dint of seeming driven about by language's

illusions, seductions, and intimidations, like a cork on the waves, I remain motionless, pivoting on the *intractable* bliss that binds me to the text (to the world). Drifting occurs whenever social language, the sociolect, *fails me* [*me manque*] (as we say: *my courage fails me*). Thus another name for drifting would be: the *Intractable*—or perhaps even: Stupidity.⁵⁵

Characteristically, this evocation of emotive transport risks incoherence in combining figures of motion and immobility. Drift is an aimless wandering within social language, but a wandering that stubbornly attaches itself to *something else* within that language: not its structure, but the vacillation of structure; not meaning, but the matter of signification: its very sounds, sensual forms, and erotic texture. Keeping in mind *Mythologies*' contradicted critique of vessels of transport, as well as his ambiguous "habitacle en dérive," one might characterize Barthes's description of drift here as a rocking motion, as of a boat on the water or a child in his mother's arms, moving and yet attached. This figure elucidates a crucial aspect of Barthes's transports in *The Pleasure of the Text*: *jouissance* is linked to a maternal aspect of language, as opposed to symbolic law and the reign of meaning. This maternal aspect, suggested as well by Barthes's "ici et là," returns us to the child playing with spool and thread in his mother's absence, as narrated in *Beyond the Pleasure Principle*. For Lacan, the child's alternating play of *fort* and *da*, or *here* and *away*, represents the child's entry into language: his game of presence and absence stages the foundational role of absence and lack in the Symbolic order. More importantly, as regards Barthes, this child's play is linked to something that cannot be integrated into the Symbolic, and this is the intractability of the Real. The Real, in a sense, is the motor of symbolization, the force of desire in language. At the same time, it is an object of *jouissance* that remains intractable to the subject's lesser pleasures. As the very failure of symbolization, the Real is manifested as a restless striving to capture an object that cannot be represented. As Lacan says, the child's toy does not *represent* the mother and thus cannot compensate for her. The child's game aims at "what, essentially, is not there, *qua* represented."[56] The toy instead indicates that a part of the child has split off from himself in response to his trauma, an object Lacan terms the *objet petit a*. No longer corresponding to symbolic mastery, and aiming beyond the function of an appeal or demand, the game simply indicates a gap in the subject that cannot be healed. The game thus goes beyond the pleasure principle in repeating without mastering a trauma that brings him into being as subject to a decisive split (*Spaltung*). As Lacan says, "It is the repetition of the mother's departure as cause of a *Spaltung* in the subject—overcome by the alternating game, *fort-da*, which is a *here or there*, and whose aim, in its alternation, is simply that of being the *fort* of a *da*, and the *da* of a *fort*." This properly *aimless* thrust of symbolization is nothing other than the *drive*, which Barthes, in agreement with Lacan, characterizes as *dérive*.[57]

In the Real, then, converge some of the key features of the work of the late Barthes: resistance to the Symbolic, drifting pleasure, and intractability. Barthes's *jouissance*, his paradoxical transports, connect with the Lacanian theory of the drive, and the recurrent theme of the *atopic* other in the work of the late Barthes can be seen as an elaboration on the question of the unattainable *objet a*, fascinating, unique, and resistant to symbolic definition. The dimension of the Real illuminates the ethical dimension of Barthes's work: beyond imaginary frustration and symbolic conformity, drift entails a nonappropriative relation to the *atopic* object of desire in and through the very failure of representation. As we have seen, for Barthes the failure of nomination gives rise to further nominations; rather than escaping all categorization, the *objet a* elicits endless qualifications. It is, then, *intraitable*: frustrating all definition, and stubbornly persistent. In this, Barthes is close to the notion of the "object-cause of desire" in Lacanian theory, whose paradoxical property is to be *produced* by the very effort of *searching* for it. This crucial equivocation would go some way toward explaining Barthes's comment in the context of remarks on Flaubert that Lacan's dictum "there is no metalanguage" is in a sense identical to "there is nothing but metalanguage."[58] The denial of metalanguage in Lacanian psychoanalysis reflects the insight that no position can be taken up in language that would be external to that language, no position of mastery by which a subject might regard his language as an object, an assertion that Barthes's comments on irony amply confirm. How, then, might Barthes consider the reverse to be valid as well? "I *see* language," Barthes confesses in his autobiography, voicing an estrangement from his linguistic medium even as he appropriates it as an imaginary object.[59] This imaginary relation to language cannot be reduced to a function of commentary, given that the subject himself is staged within the scene of figures and poses. What results for Barthes the critic is a role that is neither one of commentary nor unreflective figuration, an *untenable* position rendered as a dynamic of restlessness and fixation. Barthes's discourse, we might say, stages an *impossible* metalanguage, neither external nor absorbed in its figures. All language is a metalanguage, that is, an object language, on condition that one define that object as the *objet petit a*; metalanguage is the position of mastery (illusory as it may be) that the intractable subject occupies in voicing his imaginary desire. At least one Lacanian critic, in unwitting agreement with Barthes, confirms this definition of metalanguage.[60]

While the Real as theme only appears in the work of the late Barthes, due to a belated engagement with the work of Lacan, we have seen how Barthes's paradoxical drift undermined his early critique of ideology. Earlier yet, in *Writing Degree Zero* Barthes had already posited a domain of *style* that resonates with *engouement*, with the *intraitable*, and with the seemingly endless figures by which Barthes renders the equivocal motives of his attachments. Certainly the most compelling passages of *Writing Degree Zero* concern this function of *style*, "the writer's 'thing,'" alien to history as to art, and which is rooted in the biology of the writer.[61] "Whatever its refinement, style has always something crude about it [*le style a toujours quelque chose de brut*]: it is a form with no clear destination, the product of a thrust, not an intention, and, as it were, a vertical and lonely dimension of thought. Its frame of reference is biological or biographical, not historical." One of the tasks of *Writing Degree Zero* is to accommodate this recalcitrant function of style to the writer's task, which the Barthes of this period—Sartrian and Brechtian—conceives in terms of historical responsibility, or *engagement*. In Barthes's tripartite distinction, the writer's *langue*, that abstract medium that he inherits and shares with others, is opposed to his personal *style*; *écriture* mediates these two and represents "an act of historical solidarity" (14; 147). Over the course of his argument Barthes's history of writing turns to the modern period, in which literature bears the indelible mark of its historical "impasse." At the same time as bourgeois writing in its alienation begins to represent the political conscience of its class, that writing develops a certain stubbornness characteristic of literary modernity: "Fixed connections being abolished, the word is left only with a vertical project, it is like a monolith [*un bloc*], or a pillar which plunges into a totality of meanings, reflexes and recollections: it is a sign which stands [*il est un signe debout*]" (47; 164). The modern political condition of the writer is equated, in other words, with the question of *style*, and it is as if Barthes's excursion into politics is compelled, despite the urgency of the historical imperative, to founder on the *intractable*. And yet, Barthes's analysis does not conclude with this intractable style, which is confined to the separate domain of poetic writing. In this, Barthes's argument shares something with Sartre's *Qu'est-ce que la littérature?* whose theory of engagement required an exclusion of the poetic from the field of literary responsibility.[62] Following his elaboration on modern poetic practice, the second half of Barthes's argument offers an analysis of the means by which the modern prose writer reflects the historical imperative, be it only by the illusion of a "zero degree" of writing that would resolve the alienation of the writer from his world, heralding a utopic world through "the Utopia of language" (88; 186).

This brief retrospective reading of *Writing Degree Zero* suggests an alternate understanding of the role such utopia might play in the early Barthes. Moreover, this does not consist so much of a backward reading as an attunement to what is present, yet only implicit, in the early work. Beyond the historical argument, and yet functioning as the very motive force of Barthes's historical sensibility are a number of dynamic figures which illustrate a familiar play of motion and stasis. Thus, as "a matter of density," style is opposed to "a matter of speed" (12; *Degré zéro*, 146), reducing the syntagm of discourse to "words as static things [*des stations de mots*]" (49; 165). Barthes characterizes modernity in literature as a progressive concretion of form in the face of the "objectified Form that the writer fatefully encounters on his path."[63] Barthes's own argument seemingly stumbles on this hard kernel of form that remains intractable to his historical argument. This is particularly so in the case of modern poetry, which Barthes globally defines as "une poésie objective," and as such is deprived of the mediating function of *écriture*, the writer's only means of social engagement. Barthes's weakest claims in *Writing Degree Zero* concern objective poetry, with regard to which he assumes the unlikely posture of a humanist; and these claims are only the more striking given that the things to which he objects take on a positive value in his work to come. In defiance of "socialized discourse," Barthes says, objective poetry seems to assault the reader by reason of its associative plurality of significations, akin to an "encyclopedia" or a "dictionary" (48; 165).

It is fitting, perhaps, that Barthes's early writing on objective poetry constitutes something of a *bêtise*, that it *objects*, so to speak, to his own pronouncements. Barthes's subsequent work, from the studies of "objective literature" through "The Reality Effect" attest to an unfinished confrontation with "la chose de l'écrivain." The case of Robbe-Grillet is particularly striking, as the author Barthes praised in several essays for his rigorously objective descriptions would eventually be taken to task for his humanism. In a reversal of opinion, what Barthes calls the "notorious *Dasein* (being-there) of the object" in his last essay on Robbe-Grillet is shown to be hopelessly contaminated by signification.[64] During this period of his structuralist adventure Barthes's objects are fully supplanted by the semiotician's exhaustive analysis of systems of signification, but even Barthes's most assertive claims to this effect seem to pose an anxious question: "Is everything in narrative significant?"[65] Even the most realist prose, Barthes argues, fails to achieve simple denotation, its supposedly factual data, even the most *useless*, always doomed to *signify* reality. What Barthes calls "this mixture—this interweaving—of constraints" (145; 481) reprises a pervasive figure of a paralyzing bind, and conveys nothing so much as a stifling reign of signification and the evaporation of the real described in *Mythologies*. Tellingly, "The Reality Effect" relegates to a mere footnote the question of "insignificant" notations to which his later work would be more attuned, as we saw in the case of his preface to *Tricks*. In his "Inaugural Lecture" at the Collège de France Barthes offers a new perspective: "literature is categorically realist, in that it never has anything but the real as object of desire."[66] By this time, Barthes's *real* has taken on the sense with which Lacan invests the term, as "impossible" yet inscribed in and as the subject's intractable *jouissance*. As we will see, Barthes's own journeys of this period reflect the attempt to narrate the unnarratable transports of the subject of drift and *jouissance*.

Atopos

One of the key elements contributing to the shift in values we have sketched above is Barthes's encounter with Japan, as rendered in his *Empire of Signs*. The experience of Japan represents an overturning of Barthes's critical values and a means of looking beyond the structuralist optic and its symbolic norms. Barthes's account of Japan opens with a disclaimer of "reality," positing instead this country as the author's "fiction" and "dream."[67] As phantasm, however, Japan is no less *real*, as the "Empire of Signs" accomplishes for Barthes an "exemption from meaning" and an exemplary capture of the literary object in the poetic haiku. We need hardly note the irony of Barthes's espousal of the haiku in contradiction to his pronouncements on poetry in *Writing Degree Zero*. But the experience of travel confirms the latent drift of Barthes's desire and the quest not for reality but the real. Japan exposes Barthes to a radically unfamiliar language, and this dislocation realizes the utopian dream of a language free of the burdens of myth and stereotype. To *know* without *understanding* this foreign language, Barthes says, is to return to the maternal tongue, which Barthes renders as sensuous and enveloping: "The murmuring mass [*la masse bruissante*] of an unknown language constitutes a delicious protection, envelops the foreigner . . . in an auditory film which halts at his ears all the alienations of the mother tongue."[68] Barthes's utopic Japan is a release from the paternal Symbolic: "Hence, in foreign countries, what a respite! [*quel repos!*]." Barthes's phrase slyly mimes the *far niente* of the vacationer, but in order to accede instead to a vacancy of the signifier. This resting or respite is, then, not without its transports, which promise an unsettling of all familiar values: "to descend into the untranslatable, to experience its shock without ever muffling it, until everything Occidental in us totters and the rights of the 'father tongue' vacillate" (6; 748). Barthes's *Empire of Signs* thus aims not so much at Japan as at the very experience of estrangement, which thereby promises a healing of a more primary alienation, be it only through the experience of the "untranslatable." We might object that this evacuation of the actual Japan—including, as Barthes himself notes, the recent history of capitalism, Americanization, and technical development—in favor of traditional culture, shares something with the mythology of travel Barthes had critiqued in his early work. Unlike such exoticisms, however, Barthes's intent is not to compare or oppose customs and values, but to effect an estrangement from the Symbolic itself, a de-patriation without return.

For Barthes haiku is the most important of the estranging features of Japanese culture; estranging, moreover, because it troubles the very distinction between the familiar and the unfamiliar: "[T]o our eyes the haiku is neither eccentric nor familiar: it resembles nothing at all [*il ressemble à rien et à tout*]" (*Empire of Signs*, 81; *L'Empire des signes*, 802). This uncanny familiarity of haiku makes up the largest topic of Barthes's account of Japan, as he sees haiku as presenting a challenge to the most fundamental ideas of representation. Neither description nor definition of the world, haiku seemingly reduces writing to mere designation, as Barthes says, like a child pointing his finger. In haiku "meaning is denied to reality [*au réel*]; furthermore, reality no longer commands even the meaning of reality" (83; 803). Moreover, Barthes says, "it makes impossible the most ordinary exercise of our language, which is commentary" (81; 802). Thus, by his own admission Barthes's lengthy developments on haiku attempt the impossible in attempting to give an account of the real. The child's gesture, then, evokes the trajectory of the Lacanian drive, "shunted [*dérivée*] toward a kind of inessential—eccentric—efflorescence of the object" (83; 803), and like this child, Barthes's text on Japan aims at what can be rendered only in the very failure of representation. "What I am saying here about the haiku I might also say about everything that *happens* [*tout ce qui advient*] when one travels in that country I am calling Japan" (79; 801). Modeled on an impossible task of commentary, the travel account founders on its "infinitesimal adventures [*aventures infimes*]," transports without object, the vicissitudes of Barthes's drift. But in so doing, the travel account attempts to resolve the vicious antinomies that mark Barthes's earlier work of the structuralist period. Further, as the written trace of an occurrence, the brief, modest and unassuming haiku, like the "incidents" Barthes notes in passing, seem to carry the force and promise of the unaccountable "events" of May '68, which, in "Writing the Event," Barthes saw as escaping the logic of history and bridging act and discourse, event and testimony.[69] As "a kind of faint gash inscribed upon time,"[70] haiku reflects both the exigency of a new historical temporality and the impact on Barthes's thinking of Derrida's theory of the *trace*.[71]

At times Barthes's travels in Japan seem to mime the tropes of conventional Orientalism, regressing in this way from his earlier critiques of colonial and touristic travel. And yet Barthes's seeming regression accords with the traces of his drifting attachments in *Mythologies*. To understand the political stakes of travel in the late Barthes, we must pursue the political transformations that accompany his shift to a poststructuralist methodology. "What would be the narrative of a journey," Barthes asks in *S/Z*, "in which it was said that one stays somewhere without having arrived, that one travels without having departed—in which it was never said that, having departed, one arrives or fails to arrive?"[72] Such a "scandalous" story, the very despair of narrative, would be the text of *dérive*. Much as it permits of displacements and stopping points, Barthes's voyage would not conform to an overarching and continuous tale. In this, Barthes's theory of the text clearly responds to the drift of his own desire. "*No progress in pleasures*," as Barthes says in his autobiography, "nothing but mutations."[73] Desire, modeled on the ludic play of repetition and oscillation, is the *suspension* of a story, of which it is the dubious task of narrative to ultimately *put to an end*.[74] Narrative, progress, and continuity would be, then, the price desire pays in conforming to the Symbolic; as Barthes reminds us in *The Pleasure of the Text*, "every narrative . . . is a staging of the (absent, hidden, or hypostasized) father."[75] In *S/Z*, the "step by step" breakdown of narrative yields a dispersed and "discontinuous" text of multiple codes.[76] While Balzac's tale itself may fall short of the journey Barthes calls for in *S/Z*, this role would be filled by the reader, whose decomposition of the text allows for a critical drift that takes the text beyond the confines of structure and the overarching Symbolic.

To stay without having arrived; to travel without having left; to leave without destination: such would also be the paradoxical transports of Pierre Loti's *Aziyadé*, the subject of one of Barthes's late critical essays. Loti's atmospheric and sentimental tale, published in 1892, concerns the romantic escapades of an Englishman in Ottoman Turkey. This somewhat minor and middlebrow text of French Orientalism seems an unlikely exemplar of Barthes's "scandalous" voyage and all that such a voyage might promise of resistance to ideology, subversion of the Symbolic, and hedonistic ethics. And yet Barthes characterizes Loti's *Aziyadé* as "the novel of Drift."[77] Loti's novel realizes a form of drifting habitation, a neutral term to the alternatives of tourism and residence which Barthes names the *sojourn*: "The *sojourn* has its own substance: it makes the country of residence ... an element in which the subject can *dive*: that is, sink, hide, slip away, intoxicate himself, vanish, absent himself, die to everything which is not his desire" (118; 1409). One recognizes here the figure of fluid that persistently recurs in Barthes's evocations of drifting desire. As the medium of the desiring subject, language too is a fluid in which the subject is dissolved, or better, *suspended*. Such a fluid, however, must be distinguished from the detested *filé* of discourse and its regime of meaning. As opposed to any masterful grasp of language, translated into the false *flumen orationis* of commentary and narration, the desiring subject plunges with abandon into the fluid medium of language, as into the text of pleasure. The sojourn, or drift, Barthes says, is an "intermediary" position (117; 1409), and this untenability confirms once again the notion of metalanguage as an *impossible* discourse. There is no holding forth in language, only drift and dissolution: "the text liquidates all metalanguage."[78] Barthes's figure of fluid aptly conveys the notion of an object language, the *objet petit a* of the drifting subject, in that it posits a materiality without consistency. The materiality of language is a medium in which the subject's ludic play perpetuates the comings and goings of the drive in the pursuit of its impossible object.

For Barthes, the emblem of this drift in Loti's *Aziyadé* is a romantic scene on a boat that Loti himself describes as "a bed that drifts." "Is there a more voluptuous image than this one of a drifting bed?" Barthes asks. "A profound image, for it unites three ideas: that of love, that of floating, and the notion that desire is a force adrift" ("Pierre Loti," Eng., 119; Fr., 1410). Drifting bed, drunken boat: Barthes's favored figurations of drift insistently invoke queer transports of desire. Perhaps in writing on Loti Barthes also had in mind the reverie of Gide in his *Travels in the Congo*, the first page of which oddly drifts into a meditation on the beds of his childhood as Gide connects his "sea sickness [*mal de mer*]" to the fixed, rather than rocking beds his mother imposed on him as a child.[79] Gide's seasickness would seem to rehearse the dynamic of attachment and separation that inaugurates the *Real* of the Lacanian divided subject. Equally importantly, his inarticulable desire points to a queer modality of transport resistant to heterosexual narrative and symbolic norms. As Michael Lucey writes with respect to this passage: "That relation provides the structure of frustration at a pleasure glimpsed, but never understood, or to the extent that it is understood, understood to involve a dispersal impossible to confront, impossible to enact."[80] Coming as it does after the book's dedication to Conrad, Gide's queering of the narrative of travel is especially striking. And yet, reading back with Barthes to Gide, Loti, and beyond, one may trace a longer lineage of such painful separations and gender politics; *Perceval* itself, the ur-text of grail narratives, recounts Perceval's enforced repudiation of his mother's upbringing in his failed journey into masculine knighthood.[81] Narratives of adventure, however, unlike the queer texts Barthes favors, tend to resolve their sacrifices in appeals to order and mystified rewards. Queer drifts resist such narrative closure and in so doing expose the stubborn insistence of the drive passed over by the demand for progress, development, and redemptive meaning. Accordingly, Barthes's *atopic* prospect of a journey without origin or end can be understood as an assault on narrative, conceived as the discursive hegemony of heterosexual identities.

In spite of *Aziyadé*'s experimental and innovative tendencies, Barthes's essay insists, however, on figures of *regression* and *return*. Barthes notes that Loti's Turkish exoticism is turned toward the archaic, and thus colludes with a certain "political regression" ("Pierre Loti," Eng., 117; Fr., 1408). Moreover, Barthes characterizes this imperious tendency toward archaism as a feature of desire itself: "desire is always feudal," Barthes contends. Barthes ties this backward tendency of desire to the *phantasm* and the open possibility of signification, divorced from the demands of reality, praxis, and political responsibility. The freedom of desire as expressed in Barthes's essay thus seems to place Loti within the "retrograde" ideology of travel and tourism that Barthes had targeted in such essays as *Mythologies*' "The *Blue Guide*." Consequently, Barthes's accommodation of Loti's phantasm seems complicit with some of the dominant traits of Orientalist discourse, namely the representation of the Oriental other as a static essence, outside of history, whose horrifying and compelling desires dilate in the primal sphere of a fascinating despotism.[82] Barthes's essay on Loti has thus been seen as effecting a "remystification" of previously discarded ideological alibis.[83] If true, such an Orientalizing remystification is all the more striking given that Barthes subtly places himself in Loti's phantasmatic realm, the better to identify with it. "In our day, what would have been Lieutenant Loti's Oriental fantasy?" Barthes asks, then evokes modern Egypt and "some young professor"—no doubt the Barthes who taught at the University of Alexandria from 1949 to 1950 (116; 1408). Like Loti the Oriental transvestite passing for native in Istanbul, Barthes betrays himself as "'the one who belongs to the tableau,'" a phantasmatic operation that he characterizes as "the passage from the body into a collective writing," and which entails the self's very *dissolution* (115; 1407). On the basis of this transvestism, or *transcription*, as he names it, Barthes makes the case for Loti's literary modernism: "to write only insofar as one is written: that abolition of passive and active, of expresser and expressed, of subject and statement, in which modern writing precisely seeks to discover itself" (116; 1408). Here, we may usefully compare *phantasm* to *myth*, in that Barthes's approach to each involves a complicity with discursive order that undermines the ideological subject himself. We have seen how *Mythologies* provides insight into the desiring subject's interpellation by the figments of ideology, and how the generalized irony of this subject's equivocal drift allows for an unsettling of ideological discourse. Barthes's apparent "remystification" in his essay on Loti is, then, not unlike the subversive drift of his *Mythologies*: rather than dispensing with illusion, Barthes exposes the libidinal function of "the sublime object of ideology" in the mystified subject, without which its affective dominion cannot be shaken. Loti's drift aims at just such an impossible object, and in its compromised archaism expresses a phantasm whose very cause can be delineated: "Desire always proceeds toward an extreme archaism, where the greatest historical distance assures the greatest unreality, there where desire finds its pure form: that of an impossible return, that of the Impossible (but in writing it, this regression will disappear)" (117; 1408). To the question Barthes poses with regard to *Aziyadé*, "But where is the Orient?" the response would seem to be nowhere but the Imaginary. Barthes thus subtracts the Orient as phantasm from the regime of discourse and what he calls the "tyranny" of the signified. The Orient would be the vanishing point of the subject *en dérive*; neither a place, nor an object, but rather the "temptation" of an imaginary alternative to the West. As an indeterminate "autre chose" for the traveler, an *atopic* alterity, Barthes's Orient motivates an ethics of drift, beyond appropriation or domination.

What I have called the vanishing point of the subject may well risk mere pointlessness, however, as seen in Barthes's *Incidents*.[84] In a finely nuanced reading of these two parallel texts of Barthes—his brief accounts of cruising in Paris and sexual tourism in Morocco—Ross Chambers shows how each text contains what is missing in the other; the "pointless" stories of an everyday Paris complement the contextless, abstracted and thus "storyless" points of his Moroccan travels.[85] In this way, Chambers's essay shows how Barthes's refusal of narrative can be complicit with a denial of the context and history of the episodes he sketches. Indeed, as Chambers argues, the poignant and exotic "points" of encounter and cruising in Morocco are sustained only by the denial of the postcolonial context of Barthes's travel. It is the missing context of colonial history that makes Barthes's Paris "pointless" and his Morocco "storyless." Chambers avoids the moralizing tone with which many greeted Barthes's posthumous text, and gives a measured, though quite devastating picture of a traveling Barthes complacent in his colonial stereotypes while pursuing the illusion of innocent pleasures. But if the key to Barthes's texts is their missing context—"a historical and global framework," as Chambers says (269)—it is difficult, to say the least, to set the limits of that framework. Surely, that context includes Barthes's own ideological critiques, which thus implicitly shadow his own colonial travel. It would also include the context of Barthes's readers, to whom Barthes exposes (albeit posthumously) his self-deflating image to criticism. And in an additional twist, that context would include critics indebted to Barthes, who use Barthes's own narrative theory to critique his travels. Multiple facets of Barthes thus populate the context of his *journal intime*. This is not to dismiss the charge that Barthes's erotic drift may have led him to suspend his own critical judgment. It is, however, to resist the moralizing temptation to simply identify Barthes and to call him to account.

Barthes's question, "where is the Orient?" anticipates that of his essay "Well, and China?" written following his trip to Maoist China with the Tel quel group in 1974, including Philippe Sollers, Julia

Kristeva, and François Wahl. As part of a group of leftist intellectual ambassadors Barthes was expected to answer many "urgent questions" relative to contemporary Chinese politics and culture upon his return.[86] Barthes's essay is a gentle yet firm refusal to answer to such expectations, which he casts as "im-pertinent" (117; 32). "Alors, la Chine?" ("Well, and China?"), the general form of this interpellation, thus calls to mind what Barthes considers the burdensome "tâche" of writing at the incitation of others, or indeed, of that "vengeful Other" to which he refuses accountability. Barthes's response to his questioners is that he returned from China with "nothing." In assigning a certain *inscrutability* to the Chinese, Barthes would seem to fall in with one of the major tropes of Orientalist discourse, which casts the other as impenetrable and absolutely alien. And yet, by a supplementary twist, Barthes claims that the notion of the "impenetrable" always serves a hermeneutics of "penetration" and "decipherment." For Barthes, then, the challenge China poses to the West is nothing less than "the end of hermeneutics" (117; 32). The experience of China defies any account, as it undoes the very symbolic and ideological terms by which such an account might be constructed. The alterity of China results in an estrangement from Barthes's own culture, and in this way he attempts an *alteration* of his native culture and its reigning discursive order.

For Barthes, travel accounts have an imperious narrative thrust that his drift and discretion aim to resist. The discursive capital of travel accounts—epitomized in journeys of discovery—lies in their textual exploitation of an unfamiliar other, to which oneself and the implied reader are distinguished and opposed. One may situate Barthes's text on China within a different "heterological tradition," as defined by Michel de Certeau, "in which the discourse about the other is a means of constructing a discourse authorized by the other."[87] What de Certeau names the "text as witness of the other" unsettles the fundamental terms of cultural intelligibility—such as the familiar versus the strange—and effects a displacement of the boundaries between cultures. De Certeau's description of this critical domain resonates with the spatial figures we have been tracing in Barthes's work. The text as witness of the other, de Certeau says, creates "a space of interplay" or an "interspace" that negotiates between self and other, with the possibility of altering and redistributing cultural topology. Similarly, Barthes seeks out a *median* position with respect to the alternatives of affirming or negating, according to the binary constraints of dogmatic political discourse. This is a perspective with which Kristeva's *About Chinese Women* concurs, in positing the simple evidence that "there are others [*il y a des autres*]," and maintaining that alterity as a challenge to the totalizing vision of Western humanism and in distinction to political options.[88] "To write 'for' or 'against': the old trick of a militant," Kristeva says (12; 15). Characteristically, Barthes's tactic in approaching the Chinese as other inflects political discourse with "a slight deviation [*une dérive légère*]," or the drift of desire ("Well, and China?" 120; "Alors, la Chine?" 35). Like Kristeva, then, Barthes seeks an alternative to the seemingly inescapable options of *affirming* or *denying*. "But cannot the human subject have another desire: to *suspend* its enunciation without at the same time abolishing it?" Barthes asks. This "other desire," an alteration of the speaking subject, is voiced in Barthes's text as "an assent [*un assentiment*]," an *ethical* relation within the terms of political discourse. This notion of an assent to the other reprises the drift of an essay of *Mythologies* dealing with a French soldier's altered loyalties in Korea: "we are in the presence of neither a choice nor a conversion nor a desertion, but rather of a gradual *assent* [*un* assentiment *progressif*]."[89] In his assent, then, Barthes gives himself over to the other; further, this assent is an alteration of the discursive terms of an encounter, conceived as a stabilizing regime of oppositions and subordinations. Barthes's *other desire* is no less China than the language in which he aims to render it, and this ambiguity goes to the heart of his hedonistic ethics. Language as the medium of desire is not an instrumental relation to an other, as to an object, but an atopic interspace in which self and other are both bound and severed. Barthes's travel account, in other words, aims at transports outside the phallic domain: "I wanted to bring together in a single movement the infinite feminine (maternal?) of the object itself, that extraordinary way China, in my eyes, had of overflowing the boundaries of meaning, peacefully and powerfully, and the right to a special discourse, that of a slight deviation [*une dérive légère*]" (120; 35).

The postface to "Well, and China?" was written in response to the negative reactions elicited by Barthes's initial text, and takes pains to justify the figures of suspension and acquiescence with which he renders his impressions of China. This double feature of the text is telling: just as Barthes's self-portraits go by way of estrangement, the picture of the other partakes of autobiography. Not surprisingly, Barthes's travel account ends with an evocation of the writer's atopia: "The intellectual (or the writer) has no place [*n'a pas de lieu*]." Like de Certeau's "interspace," the writer's atopic text neither completes the discovery of the other, nor returns within the symbolic fold. It accomplishes, in other words, the "scandalous" voyage Barthes called for in *S/Z*: neither arriving nor departing, but suspending all ends in the continuous play of desire, and stubbornly refusing to be called to order: "*no comment*," Barthes provocatively concludes his essay on China ("Well, and China?" 120; "Alors, la Chine?" 35). Thirty-five years later, Barthes's travel notebook has finally been published as *Carnets du voyage en Chine*. Interestingly, the *Carnets* suggest somewhat different reasons for Barthes's resistance to a fuller account of his journeys. As distinct from Japan, as Barthes himself admits, he recognizes "la faillite, en ce pays, de mon écriture" (April 18). The Tel quel group's travels are strictly managed by the Chinese authorities, and discouraged like them by party dogmatism and social regimentation, Barthes is frustrated, often bored, and finally impatient to leave.[90] Upon returning to Paris, the Tel quel group would soon admit to disillusionment in the promise of the Chinese Cultural Revolution, ending the Maoist phase of the group and indeed, as Eric Hayot pointedly asserts, "the last moment (in Europe) of pure faith in a simultaneously cultural and political revolution."[91]

Barthes's scandalous travels continue to raise objections, as seen for instance in Lisa Lowe's *Critical Terrains*. Lowe characterizes Barthes's "poetics of escape" as less *atopic* than *utopic*, that is, according to the distinction Barthes makes in his autobiography, as "reactive, tactical, literary."[92] Lowe's view of Barthes's Oriental travels is that they operate fully within a binary logic: "The desire to escape his own subjectivity, history, and language," Lowe contends, "is quite evidently an oppositional desire, still caught within the binary logic he seeks to avoid." This "logic of opposition" (163), reiterated throughout Lowe's analysis, is, however, more a feature of her critical optic than of Barthes's text. In this, Lowe's work falls in with one of the pervasive features of postcolonial criticism, as diagnosed by Robert Young: a nostalgic temptation to assert a "straightforward oppositional structure" of analysis on the apparently Manichaean world of intercultural relations.[93] Given the exchange of ideas between the Western left and the Chinese Cultural Revolution—inevitably marred by the dogmatisms both Kristeva and Barthes amply register—must one conclude with Lowe that Barthes's interest in the Chinese example "relegates China to a position of serving the interests of the Occident"?[94] Further, in her apparent attempt to widen the cultural divide, Lowe dismisses psychoanalysis as a means of approach to China (169). Not surprisingly, she renders the stakes of Barthes's psychoanalysis in binary terms, as a war of the Imaginary and the Symbolic. This is not only to refuse what Barthes sees as the subversive relation of the Imaginary to the Symbolic, but also to elide the role of the Real, that third term in which Barthes's *dérive* finds its atopic space of play.

In this way, Lowe's critique wants to bring Barthes to account, insisting on an answer to her charges of political irresponsibility on

Barthes's part. In so doing, she seems to demand a travel account of Barthes as well, not unlike the critics he specifically tries to hold at bay. Lowe's political charges thereby miss the true political stakes of Barthes's journeys and drifting prose. Chela Sandoval offers us a different Barthes in her *Methodology of the Oppressed*, in which she sees Barthes as a postcolonial critic and fellow traveler of Frantz Fanon.[95] And yet, Sandoval's reading of Barthes is too reliant, to my mind, on the early *Mythologies* as handbook for a "methodology of the oppressed." Moreover, Sandoval specifically faults Barthes for his inability to fully extricate himself from the lure of ideology. My interest here has been different: I have argued that it is precisely in the drift of Barthes's critique, his lack of mastery of critical metalanguage, and his complicity with the cultural artifacts he aims to deconstruct that we find the subversive force of his wayward texts. To make this argument is to inflect the political angle of critique—shared by Lowe and Sandoval alike—toward the *ethical*. An ethical bent is evident in all of Barthes's work; its trace may be read in the paradoxical drifts and paralyses from his earliest to his latest works. Were we to unify Barthes's oeuvre, then, we might well do so under the name of the ethical. Barthes suggests this himself in his autobiography, where he asserts that his only claim to intelligence lies in an ethical intelligence.[96] Disavowing methodological mastery, political wiles and philosophical depth, and thereby exasperating many of his critics, Barthes thus brings ethics close to the stubborn intractability of a *bêtise*. Barthes's final book, *Camera Lucida*, would insist on such a *bêtise* in going against the grain of his generation to claim the simple, mute, and self-evident reality of the photographic *referent*. As Derrida shows, however, this claim of Barthes's is far from simple; it is, moreover, the implicit ground of all bids for meaning, which only a seemingly naïve critic can perceive and thereby deconstruct.[97] This ethical optic is oriented in a stubborn faithfulness to the fixed, static, and paralyzing image of the other.[98] Derrida himself, beginning with his essay on Barthes, would subsequently undertake a long project of his own on the ethics of mourning.

To call Barthes to account, as Lowe and even Sandoval do, is to miss his ethical bent, which we might call the *precondition* of politics. It is also to deny Barthes the drift of a text that refuses, as in *S/Z*, the account of any journey. Ethics might be located precisely at the place where accounting fails, where both the account of oneself and the travel account are paralyzed. Judith Butler makes such an argument in her *Giving an Account of Oneself*, where she insists on the "non-narrativizable" aspects of the self that escape conventional frameworks of selfhood, agency, responsibility, and address.[99] Ethics, Butler argues, must be rethought on the basis of a self that cannot fully know or narrate itself, and not on the basis of an "ethical violence" that assumes, or demands, that one conform to self-identity and coherence (42). We have seen the various ways in which Barthes suffered such "ethical violence" and skirted its dominating call. Against the moralizing demand for *accountability* Butler says that the self is and must be "interrupted" in its account of itself, and this interruption is the place in which the ethical relation must be sought. "[W]e are, from the start, interrupted by alterity," Butler asserts; "our 'incoherence' establishes the way in which we are constituted in relationality: implicated, beholden, derived, sustained by a social world that is beyond us and before us" (64).

The moralizing demand for *accountability* thus makes common cause with the demand for narrative coherence, but at the expense of the very texture of the self's complex *implication* with the other. We have seen the trace of such implication in Barthes's drift in *Mythologies*, his estrangement in Japan, his acquiescence in China. And just as morality and narrative share a common aim in the moral *account*, our readings have shown that narrative and travel too find common cause in delivering an account of the self's transports. Barthes insists, however, that such transports must escape the regimentation of desire. They will not be arrested; they may, however, be paralyzed. They drift, and always at the risk of interrupting both travel and narrative. In *Camera Lucida*, a final pose of Barthes's—in which *pose* has the meanings we have explored in *A Lover's Discourse*—casts Barthes as wounded, pierced, and fixated by the other's image. Such amorous poses convey the ethical bent of Barthes's travels, transports, and postcolonial critique. These poses share something with the traveling predicaments of postcolonial and immigrant writers as well, and it is to such fellow travelers that we turn in the following chapter.

6. The Wake of Ulysses

Time and again, walking and always in place, another country, other cities, other routes, the same country.— Blanchot

Economies of Travel

Zygmunt Bauman argues that globalization has stratified and polarized the world into two populations: *global* subjects with the privilege to travel and *local* subjects confined by borders, immigration controls, and lack of resources to a more static existence. "The mark of the excluded in the era of time/space compression is *immobility*," Bauman says.[1] At its most exclusionary, control over the underprivileged takes the form of prisons, which function as "factories of immobility" (106). If global subjects enjoy the benefits of travel, Bauman argues that this should be understood as a privilege gained through the forceful denial of immigrant others. Thus, travel and immobilization are two faces of a global economic system that grants freedom of movement to some at the expense of others. Global travelers are, however, not simply willful agents of travel; rather, as economic subjects they reap the advantages of a system of consumerism and flexible accumulation that *requires* their permanent displacement and perpetual consumption. These privileged "tourists," as Bauman names them, are *compelled* to travel, not unlike the unfortunate "vagabonds," who "are on the move because they have been pushed from behind—having first been spiritually uprooted from the place that holds no promise, by a force of seduction or propulsion too powerful, and often too mysterious, to resist" (92). It is precisely this *common* displacement in a precarious economic world system that is denied in the separation of tourists from vagabonds: "*Green light for the tourists, red light for the vagabonds*" (93). This separation often occurs through roadblocks and fortified borders, but also through violent acts of disavowal: "the vagabond is the tourist's nightmare; the tourist's 'inner demon' that has to be exorcised,"

Bauman says. (97). "The vagabond . . . is the *alter ego* of the tourist. The line which divides them is tenuous and not always clearly drawn. One can easily cross it without noticing" (96).

Bauman's "tenuous line" should give us pause here. Indeed, we might say the sociologist has reached the *end of the line* in his analysis, a point where his crucial distinctions, buttressed with walls and borders, break down into a minimal differentiation. This tenuous line shares something with the paralyzed figures we have explored so far in my readings of Fromentin, Paulhan, Leiris, and Barthes. At stake here is a border and a crossing Bauman's analysis cannot fully account for, and which seems to defy figuration. The perplexity of Bauman speaks to the paradoxes of transport in an age of virtual voyages, telecommuting, and the Internet, an age of "space/time compression" that disrupts the traditional coordinates of travel. But by disrupting these coordinates, the age of "space/time compression" may in fact aid in undoing the metaphysical certainties that serve to guarantee safe passage and profit in travel. Indeed, such critique is needed more than ever at a time when the disruptions of travel's coordinates can provoke the reflexes of denial and exclusion Bauman describes. To undertake such an analysis is to go beyond Bauman's sociological framework in order to analyze the subtle tropes and transports that ground our understanding of travel. In this light, Bauman's "space/time compression" and "tenuous line" are suggestive of what Derrida calls "*spacing*, the becoming-space of time and the becoming-time of space."[2] This spacing, or *différance*, makes displacement the condition of any claim to presence or belonging. All journeys, whether that of the tourist or the immigrant, draw their source in this original displacement that they seek at all cost to deny. Against this recuperative impulse Derrida tells us "we must think this without *nostalgia*, that is, outside of the myth of . . . a lost native country" (27). Derrida's reference to nostalgia alerts us to the pervasive aim of travel and transport to cut their costs, eliminate risk, and guarantee a safe return. In this way, a deconstruction of the figures of travel offers a political critique of travel's metaphysical economy, always oriented in its nostalgia toward the profitable return home.

In what follows, I will turn my attention to narratives of immigration, combining a deconstruction of travel with a critique of the political economy of contemporary immigration. In Bauman's terms, this would seem to entail a shift of perspective from *tourist*—the focus of the preceding chapters—to *vagabond*, from mobile subjects to their immobilized alter egos. And yet, as I have shown, mobile tourists also share in the vagabonds' predicaments of immobilization. To draw this parallel is of course not to equate the two, nor is it to diminish the difference in the privilege and fortunes of the tourist and vagabond. It is to suggest, however, that paralyses are a point of contact between the two; by calling into question the motives and aims of the privileged traveler, paralyses may bring his political and economic position into crisis. At such moments a tenuous line divides the traveler from his others, linking his fortunes, often unwittingly, to those traveling the opposite way. In addition to the difference between tourist and vagabond, then, paralyses reveal the difference *within* each pathway.[3] Literary journeys are particularly important in this respect, for they tend to undermine the ideological claims other travelers may take for granted. Accordingly, I have argued that the paralyses of mobile subjects are symptoms of the politics of French travel, and reflect doubts and suspicions as to the progress of history, the colonial enterprise, and the authority and privilege of the Western observer. The latent traces of paralysis may be found in all travel literature; indeed, the cultural estrangement provoked by any journey makes its narrative prone to self-reflection and doubt. It is only in the modern period, however, and most markedly in France, that literature turns consistently against narratives of adventure and forgoes the staple themes of discovery and conquest. This literary transformation reflects major shifts in modern French culture: democratic and republican values find themselves at odds with colonial ideology, while class affiliations conflict with mercantile projects and leisure travel; the rise of secular society throws into doubt hallowed notions of the beyond and redemptive purpose; finally, post-exotic travelogues come to terms with others who are no longer monstrous, primitive, and alien, but who challenge the traveler's authority and purpose. These former objects of colonization become subjects of their own journeys homeward and to the metropole.

Anthropology and colonialism have played a large role in this book, as empire and the study of native cultures provide the modern French traveler with the two main avenues of the outward thrust of power, knowledge, and desire. If, however, anthropology and empire sought objects of profit abroad, each would experience similar mutations in the status of their respective objects. Anthropology, born of an exoticist interest in primitive and alien others, first submitted its human subjects to an objectifying and rationalistic gaze, only to find that gaze reversed and its privilege undermined. The reflexive and post-exotic turn in postmodern anthropology exemplified by such authors as Asad, Fabian, and Clifford is the fruit of the discipline's belated acknowledgment of its illusory mastery over the cultural other. Similarly, empire sought profit in the political and economic exploitation of its quasi-citizens and colonial subjects, but bred resistance that constantly challenged the forces of colonization. Moreover, the increasingly hybrid subject of colonization did not merely oppose the forces of empire but, in a complex negotiation that both drew on and contested imperial culture, gave birth to a postcolonial world that continues, as Chakrabarty says, to "provincialize Europe."[4] As Chakrabarty's expression indicates, the questions raised here exceed the French context, and include all European powers and the colonies they brought under their spheres of control. In what follows, therefore, I will broaden the question of paralysis to engage with a larger modernity and the recent postcolonial context.

As befits the conclusion of an account of travels, the motif I explore here is that of the return *home*. "Happy the man who, like Ulysses, has traveled well," Du Bellay says in his *Regrets*, "and has then returned."[5] Du Bellay's poem of travel sings the preference of the poet for his native land over knowledge gained abroad. Even the most adventurous journey aims, of course, for this return and its profits. And yet such an economy of return may cancel out the journey itself; to the extent that the journey aims homeward, its travel may be negated from the start. Du Bellay's poem incorporates this self-defeating insight as an unresolved tension between the benefits gained abroad and the desire for the native French soil.[6] Such a tension is a common feature of travelogues and their tropes. In *Travel as Metaphor*, Georges Van Den Abbeele has shown how travel and metaphor, the master trope of transport, share a common aim: acknowledging difference yet reabsorbing that difference into similitude, both travel and metaphor make circular transits that guarantee a safe return home. Travel and the language of the travel narrative thus manifest a perpetual conflict between identity and otherness, travel and return, profit and loss.[7] Van Den Abeeele's book builds on Derrida's argument that philosophy stakes its claims on metaphors it employs yet denies. Folding the texts of philosophy back into literature and rhetoric, Derrida shows how the turns and tropes of metaphor are complicit with a surreptitious backward turn that allows for a metaphysical recuperation of philosophy's textual losses. This recuperation thus claims a *usurious* profit that is enabled only by an effacement, or *usure*, of metaphor.[8] The metaphysical gesture thus guarantees, in spite of all losses and against all reason, the journey's circular voyage.

The homeward journey of Ulysses exemplifies Derrida's argument that Western metaphysics habitually frames travel and its metaphors within the circular scope of the return home. This profitable return is *economy* itself: the Greek *oikonomia* derives from *oikos* (house) and *nemein* (to manage). As Derrida argues, the claim for profitable returns can only be made through a metaphysical gesture that masks the true costs of the journey; what lies outside the circular return are the stubborn remainders, the *restes* that defy transport home. The journey and its account are thus littered with the remains of these untransported, unmetaphorized elements, so many testaments to the journey's unwitting paralyses. In this way, Derrida makes common cause with the critique of the political economy of adventure in such works as Michael Nerlich's *Ideology of Adventure*, discussed in my introduction, as well as with Horkheimer and Adorno's *Dialectic of Enlightenment*. Horkheimer and Adorno's scathing indictment of Ulysses focuses on the scene in *The Odyssey* in which the adventurer has himself bound and tied to the mast of the ship, in order to enjoy the sirens' song without risking temptation and danger. Horkheimer and Adorno see this rapturous and immobile adventurer as the figure of the bourgeois aesthete, ferried homeward only by virtue of his laborers, whose ears are stopped up, deaf to the beauty of the sirens' call.[9] The Marxist indictment of Ulysses draws on Hegel's dialectic of master and slave, and is politically committed to those excluded from the adventurer's profits and enjoyment. Derrida, more broadly, is committed to expose whatever and whoever is excluded from the cycle of return. For Derrida, unlike the Marxists, exclusion bears crucially on an unassimilable other, the stubborn remainder of a *general economy* that cannot be enclosed within the dialectic, but which opens only onto sheer loss and expenditure. In this, then, Derrida is closer to Blanchot, who, in his seminal essay "The Sirens' Song," sees Ulysses at the mast as exposing himself to nothing less than the lure of death, and suffering, in his suspended trespass, the experience of a mortal limit never crossed.[10] For Blanchot as for Derrida, death is the ultimate figure of the unassimilable other; this radical otherness defies the Marxist dialectic, which attempts to harness death as negation, and so shares with metaphysical thought the attempt to contain the general economy and profit from the return voyage.

Ulysses's homeward journey leaves a wake that all tourists and travelogues are tempted to ply. As deconstructed by Derrida, *The Odyssey* reveals a pattern constitutive of Western thought: much as they aim outward, travelogues tend to short-circuit their trajectory to guarantee a safe return. Similarly, Foucault speaks of Don Quixote's journeys as bound within a circuit of identity, comparison, and resemblance: Quixote, Foucault says, is "the hero of the Same."[11] The round trips, *allers-retour*, and "circular tickets" of tourism are the modern inheritors of this tradition. This return may well be one of profit gained and risk avoided, as the Marxists have it. For Derrida, however, the economy of travel makes short shrift of the journey's others, and of otherness as such, whether through exclusion or assimilation. For this reason, deconstruction provides powerful tools to examine the blind spots, silences, and constitutive exclusions of Western literature and thought, and has also provided new models with which to think about travel and transports. Aporia, chiasmus, and the nonarrival are among the figures that I have employed here in my readings. These are maps, of a sort, of paralyzed travel.

Samuel Beckett provides such a map in his short text "The Way," a manuscript I indexed in the introduction. A distillation of all Beckett's paralyzed journeys, the miniscule text of "The Way" embroiders on two images of a figure eight, one upright and one on its side. In its looping circuit, Beckett's "one-way way" seems to echo the ever-returning trajectory of the journey of Ulysses.[12] And yet, this "one-way way" is not single but double: two versions of the journey echo each other without coinciding. Moreover, each circuit doubles itself, between the single "way" and the plural "ways" of each figure eight, and hesitates between the alternatives of repetition and singularity: "No retracing the way back down," the text says, and leads us "down another way." As in *Worstward Ho*, a chiastic play of "no" and "on" echoes throughout Beckett's spare language: "on," "no," "not," "another," "down," "nor," "one," "none," "once," "long," "second," "ignorance," "known," "no one." The two texts

"8" and "∞" both end with the elliptical line, "No one ever before so—." It is tempting to see this last line as a claim on Beckett's part for the originality of his singular vision of a new path of travel.[13] And yet, as we have seen in this book, others have traveled this path as well. Speaking of the "*retrait* of metaphor," Derrida has argued that metaphor, as trope of transport, masks a simultaneous *tracing* and *retraction* of its figure.[14] To uncover the trace of this *retrait* is to challenge the economy of metaphor as return of the same. This duplicitous trace is always paralyzing; it does not present two alternatives or a choice of contraries. Rather, as in Beckett, it traces an asymmetrical difference whose two faces are chiastically intertwined. Beckett insists, moreover, on this asymmetry in "The Way": "The ways crossed midway more and less. A little more and less than midway up and down." It would be wrong to take this "more and less" too literally as the stable distinction between the different sized loops of each figure eight.[15] Rather, the "more and less" defies both the economy of profit and loss in a trajectory that is always "midway," always alternately poised between "no" and "on," in a "standstill" and "at rest."

"The Way" may be seen as a late instance of Beckett's rivalry with Joyce and an attempt to plot other literary journeys. It is well known that Beckett suffered the burden of Joyce's literary legacy. This burden and debt are strikingly rendered in *Molloy*, where Beckett casts himself as a "sadly rejoicing slave" on the deck of Ulysses's boat. Beckett thus claims for himself a less "pioneering spirit" than Joyce, opting instead to crawl along the deck, in the manner familiar to Molloy.[16] Beckett's reference is, of course, a nod to Joyce's *Ulysses*, in which the adventures of *The Odyssey* are allegorized in the prosaic urban wanderings of Leopold Bloom in Dublin. The high-water mark of literary modernism, Joyce's novel deflates the pretensions of adventure narratives and the picaresque, and confirms Ortega y Gasset's definition of the modern novel as "a sluggish genre."[17] Joyce's deflation of the adventurer is, however, the apotheosis of a new modernist literary subject, whose interior life weaves literature, myth, and history into the fabric of an everyday present haunted by antiquity.

In recent years, a different subject has detached itself from Bloom, Joyce's modernist alter ego. Recent critics have made the case that *Ulysses* is a postcolonial novel, the fictional reflection of Joyce's political positions regarding the cause of Irish nationalism under the British Empire.[18] Such readings challenge the traditional heroic trope of exile and modernist cosmopolitanism, drawing Joyce into another modern canon, that of the immigrant narrative and postcolonial displacement. Joyce's predicament, and that of Bloom, indeed resonates with the politics of language and identity in many subsequent postcolonial narratives. One may detect in *Ulysses* the features of a hybrid subjecthood caught between the rival claims of native identity and foreign rule, and the ambivalence of a speech act that borrows the terms of native resistance from imperial discourse itself. Such a "subaltern Joyce" would, then, share as much with W. E. B. Du Bois's "double-consciousness" and Naipaul's "mimic men" as he would with the exilic identities of James, Pound, and Eliot; his return home would be the fellow traveler of such textual journeys as Césaire's *Notebook of a Return to the Native Land*. One might, indeed, include the cosmopolitan *Ulysses* among the literature of Gilroy's Black Atlantic; British racializing discourse of the nineteenth century made overt comparisons between black Africans and the Irish. Such a reading of Joyce's *Ulysses* has only been made possible, however, by the recent emergence of a field of postcolonial studies, a field inspired by texts that largely postdate Joyce, and which derive from more far-flung outposts of empire. This is not to discount the pertinence of such rereadings of Joyce; it is, rather, to say that the emergence of immigrant and postcolonial voices has had a retroactive impact on modernism. This retroaction is, of course, one of the crucial stakes of postcolonial writing, which aims not only to forge new subjects and futures, but to write counterhistories of empire. Rather than make Joyce the forebear of the postcolonial, then, we might instead credit his immigrant followers with our insights into Joyce's latent subaltern identity.

Postcolonial writing traces what I have been calling, after Derrida, a *counterpath* in literature: a twin project that, on the one hand, gives voice to subaltern subjects and their histories and, on the other, challenges Western history and its travels. This postcolonial challenge entails a dramatic overturning of the politics of travel, though it always risks reinscribing the polarities of the colonial difference even when contesting them. To radicalize the colonial difference would be to bring out what is incomplete in metropolitan identity—an inadequation marked by the colonial other, as structurally necessary counterpart or alter ego—and to foster, on the side of the colonized, insight into a colonial differential that *generates* identity. This differential belongs to neither side; indeed, each identity is secondary to and produced from out of a difference that is invoked yet habitually denied. The secondariness of metropolitan identity, its origin in difference, is precisely what is disavowed in its opposition to the colonial other, denigrated as lack or reified as (negative) object of comparison and translation. It is consequently with the colonized and his postcolonial inheritor that one best gauges the instability of the colonial difference and its generative force, provided that the subaltern lays claim not simply to a pregiven identity but to the in-betweenness from which it derives. The "subaltern betwixt," to adopt Tullio Maranhão's expression,[19] stands in the way of conventional tropes of translation, transfer, and conversion, rediscovering instead a subversive *displacement* that not only contests the asymmetry of the colonial difference and its polarized identities, but adopts that displacement as the generative terrain for the construction of identity-in-process. Accordingly, travel too becomes displacement, no longer following the trails blazed by the colonizer, but shadowing his failed translations and finding in that counterpath the trace of identity as subaltern *différance*.

This is not to overlook the fact that, for postcolonial travelers, the stakes of travel often present themselves starkly as the choice of life over death and freedom over servitude. Thus Paul Robeson, communist, cosmopolitan, and anticolonialist activist, states, "the concept of *travel* has been inseparably linked in the minds of our people with the concept of *freedom*."[20] And yet, behind the history of black militancy and colonial liberation lies a longer story of colonial resistance, survival, and persistence that extends from the discovery of the New World through the slave trade and postcolonial times. This story is not merely one of revolt or submission, but a more complex one of accommodation *and* resistance, of tactical acceptance and sly subversion. This long story of colonialism is one that nurtured the mixed, hybrid, and complex identities of the culturally marginalized, whose survival involved borrowing both from the master discourse and a disparate native heritage. Thus, for instance, when Fanon argues that the colonized black must adopt the language of the master, he makes the Hegelian argument that the slave accepts his mediation through the other to perform a dialectical revolt. Colonial resistance has found in the dialectic a particularly apt model of liberation, as the subjects of colonization were often slaves themselves.[21] At the same time, however, Fanon sees race as an intractable condition that defies the dialectics of recognition and identification. A black man confronting a white world, Fanon experienced the stubbornness of white racism as well as the intractability of his own black identification, unsublatable into the synthesis of a common liberation. This interruption of the dialectic of self and other would stymie Fanon's colonial journeys.[22] Fanon concludes that Negritude's nativist journeys to Africa, to the colony, or to the metropole will never simply lead to a return home.[23]

Narratives of immigration confirm Fanon's account of the difficulty of the colonized's homeward journey. In the case of the fatherland, mother country, or metropole, that home is a place to which the colonized is purported to belong, but in which he experiences mainly exclusion and alienation. In *Culture and Imperialism* Edward Said shows that for the better part of the nineteenth century, empire appears only as a "shadowy presence" in metropolitan culture; accordingly, the colonized tends to emerge from a site of exclusion as an "unwelcome appearance."[24] As an example, Said refers to Dickens's *Great Expectations*, in which Magwitch, returned illegally from Australia, confronts Pip like a monstrous ghost or the return of the colonial repressed. If the colonial immigrant appears as monstrous and alien, however, it is not because he is *alien*, but because he has been "alienated," as Freud says, by repression.[25] The immigrant thus imports the alienated truth of imperial culture, making the metropole into an uncanny home peopled by guests who are *unheimlich*, strangely familiar.

This predicament is strikingly captured in Sam Selvon's *The Lonely Londoners*, which narrates the story of Jamaican immigrants seeking opportunity in the mother country in the 1950s. Like Joyce's *Ulysses*, Selvon's novel makes the story of the return home an allegory of classic voyages of the past. And as allegory, this evocation is not so much one of metaphoric comparison as it is of difference, distance, and disjunction. The protagonist, Moses, serves as guide and go-between for newer Jamaican arrivals in London but, disenchanted with the immigrant's life, resents the epic role his name seems to confer on him. Just off the boat, his friend Galahad, for his part, is no chivalrous hero but an opportunistic dandy and seducer. And just as the characters fall short of their epic namesakes, the narrative is fragmentary and episodic; the storyline reflects the exclusion of the characters from the plot-generating conditions of the standard *Bildungsroman*. Romance leads not to social networks and marriage, but only to one-night stands; work is a sequence of odd jobs and dead-end toil. At the end of ten years in London, Moses reflects, "I ain't get no place at all, I still the same way, neither forward nor backward."[26] Moses thus finds himself stuck, paralyzed, and motionless in the midst of a world of opportunities: "he could see a great aimlessness, a great restless, swaying movement that leaving you standing in the same spot" (141). Moses stands on the banks of the Thames at night, "the thoughts so heavy like he unable to move his body," reflecting on his life and what he sees mirrored in the water: "As if, on the surface, things don't look so bad, but when you go down a little, you bounce up a kind of misery and pathos and a kind of frightening—what?" (142). If Dublin was "the center of paralysis," as Joyce put it,[27] Selvon's London is a place of dynamic movement from which his characters are excluded.

It would be worthwhile comparing this scene in *The Lonely Londoners* to a crucial moment in Flaubert's *Sentimental Education*, the consummate, though ironic *Bildungsroman*, in which Frédéric is caught in a moment of similar ambiguous rapture at the water's edge at night. Both scenes culminate in the discovery of an artistic vocation; Selvon's Moses imagines himself as a novelist, Frédéric decides on painting. Neil Hertz brings out the way Flaubert's scene leads the reader, as he says, "to the end of the line." In the scene from Flaubert, Frédéric's moment of reflection at the banks of the Seine draws the reader in to share with the protagonist a fascination with a pattern of symmetrically paired details of the landscape. In the course of the description, as Hertz demonstrates, these paired details converge in the barest trace of difference, "reduced to the minimal difference between black and black."[28] Reflexive moments such as these bring the reader and the character to a momentary halt as the text arrives at a point of near-indetermination, and Hertz argues that such moments betray the work of art's tendency to reflect on its own activity and the very limits of representation. They also motivate in the reader, through his identification with the character, a feeling of "blockage" in the face of the unrepresentable. As Hertz says, "looking down at the river at those *redoublements d'obscurité* . . . can be read as a figure for end-of-the-line opacity" (221). Moments of opacity tend to resolve themselves, as Hertz shows, in a recoil from indetermination that results in violent scapegoating. In Selvon's novel, however, these issues are more politically pointed: "he could see the black faces bobbing up and down in the millions of white, strained faces, everybody hustling along the Strand, the spades jostling in the crowd, bewildered, hopeless." If Hertz's privileged examples are those near-opacities of "double darkness" (229), and "the minimal difference between black and black," Selvon renders his distinctions more starkly as black and white. Issues of representation, likewise, are more political, having to do with those who have representation and those who have none. Moses's dawning awareness that he could write a novel is a realization that he could, in fact, represent those black faces lost in the crowd. Indeed, Moses reflects that in France immigrant voices are getting published: "Taxi-driver, porter, road-sweeper—it didn't matter." But behind the inspiring example of these new immigrant voices seems to lie Flaubert's novel as well, which Selvon has appropriated to make his own claim to represent the unrepresented.[29]

Adopting Hertz's model of the end of the line for postcolonial critique, we may see how such characteristic scenes of reflection are differently paralyzing in postcolonial, as opposed to metropolitan, narratives. Selvon's *Lonely Londoners* does not display the mechanism of scapegoating, occupying as it does the very place of the excluded and marginalized. And yet, in an effective play on readers' expectations and fears, Selvon mobilizes stereotypes of criminal, illicit, and questionable behavior in his characters, all of whom are imperfect. Moses himself, in spite of his compassion and generosity, plays the role of a malevolent trickster at times. In so doing, Selvon clearly shows the causes of these failings in the characters' social alienation. This abjection, which often turns to farce, thus confronts the reader as the truth of the Mother Country's alienating exclusion of the immigrant other. Moreover, Moses, the reluctant immigrant guide and mentor, resists and denies the wide-eyed optimism of the newcomer Galahad. This tension between Moses and Galahad contains then, in an attenuated form, the larger conflict of immigrant and metropolitan. Indeed, Moses finds himself repeating to Galahad—though with Galahad's best interests at heart—the sentiments of anti-immigrant Londoners in suggesting he "hustle back to Trinidad" (129). Two parallel stories thus run the course of *The Lonely Londoners*, with Moses's steady disillusionment doubled by Galahad's irrepressible optimism. It is only in the final pages, and specifically in the scene by the Thames, that the reader comes to recognize that a new narrator takes shape in Moses, the surrogate of Selvon himself, who merges the two opposed characters in the discovery of a postcolonial writer's vocation.

Selvon's novel intersects with some of the high texts of modernism, while charting a course for postcolonial immigrant literature. *The Lonely Londoners* counters modernism's formal equivocations with the more social narrative of a divided character, who blends his voice with that of the foreclosed. The final lines of the novel have the narrator saying, "He watch a tugboat on the Thames, wondering if he could ever write a book like that." Perhaps, in an uncanny colonial echo, Conrad's *Heart of Darkness* lies in the offing here. But unlike his modernist forebears, Selvon does not dwell so much on the unrepresentable—often freighted, as in Conrad, with the weight of a foreclosed other—as he does on the unrepresented, the former objects of colonization, cargo of involuntary journeys, and agents, finally, of the counter-voyages of immigration.[30]

The Postcolonial Arrivant

I now turn to a novel by Rachid Boudjedra, *Topographie idéale pour une agression caractérisée* (Ideal Topography for a Specific Aggression), which relates the nightmarish journey of an Algerian immigrant lost in the bowels of the Paris metro.[31] *Topographie* dramatically captures the stakes of the French politics of immigration; I will argue, further, that it serves as a prime source-text for a politics of postcolonial hospitality. As we will see, echoes of *Ulysses* resonate in the corridors of Boudjedra's metro. Like Joyce's novel, *Topographie* is restricted to the time span of a single day; in *Topographie* the day is a fateful September 26, 1973. Unlike Bloom, however, Boudjedra's protagonist is unnamed and anonymous, variously referred to as the "the traveler," and more pejoratively as the "fakir" and the "idiot." This nameless immigrant thus stands as a representative sample of a larger North African immigrant population in Paris. *Topographie* makes specific references to *The Odyssey* as well, ironizing in this way heroic narratives of adventure, discovery, and return. Further, *Topographie* poses a challenge to narrative as such; conflicting and contradictory versions of events impede the progress of the story, and while long, labyrinthine sentences, often lacking punctuation, weave in and out of different angles of perspective, an insistence on descriptions of seemingly incidental objects obstructs the story's development. The reader's disorientation thus matches the traveler's bewilderment and confusion. The traveler's perspective is further complicated by the voice of an investigating officer who, hapless, irate, and racist, attempts to organize the testimony of a number of witnesses to the traveler's journey, which ends in the racially motivated murder foretold by the book's title.

Published in 1975, Boudjedra's novel draws significantly on narrative techniques of the Nouveau Roman. This stylistic influence is evident in the use of flat, detailed description, the complication of narrative perspective, and the defiance of chronology, sequence, and coherence. In the works of Boudjedra's precursors Sarraute, Robbe-Grillet, Simon, and Butor, among others, these narrative techniques launched a challenge to realist literature as well as broader conventions of representation and storytelling. Writing in a critical and analytical spirit, the Nouveau Roman advanced not merely a new *style* of narrative, but dismantled pervasive and intractable *norms* of narrative representation. And while critics of the Nouveau Roman may have faulted the authors' supposed lack of political *engagement*, Barthes would recognize in the Nouveau Roman a challenge to narrative norms whose assumed lifelikeness, in their very realism and self-evidence, lends credence to bourgeois ideology and its representations. This technique of "defamiliarization," as Stephen Heath points out, thus makes the reader of the Nouveau Roman an active semiotic interpreter of the social construction of reality.[32] Interestingly, Robbe-Grillet's work of defamiliarization would go so far as to banish the use of *metaphor* from his writing, insisting instead on objective descriptions that defy recuperation into anthropomorphic and ideological expectations. The absence of metaphor has the effect of suspending the delivery of meaning through the trope of comparison and transport. And indeed, most Nouveaux Romans are characteristically *static*: Sarraute would reduce movement to the minimal "tropisms" of consciousness and experience; Claude Simon's *Flanders Road*, as we saw in my introduction, would freeze time in the near immobility of "glacial" movement. In Boudjedra's hands, however, these narrative techniques have a strikingly different political aim. In *Topographie*, the protagonist's paralyses, impeded progress, and violent end are the symptoms, specifically, of racism and exclusion. The fateful day of his journey is located within a particular historical moment, that of a vicious spate of anti-Arab murders in metropolitan France.

The "labyrinth" of Boudjedra's metro may be seen as a nod to Robbe-Grillet's *Dans le labyrinthe*; both stories are disjointed and contradictory narratives of a wandering character, and each story ends in their death. Another textual reference for Boudjedra, no doubt, is Robbe-Grillet's *Snapshots* (*Instantanés*), and more specifically the short texts "Dans les couloirs du métropolitain" ("In the Corridors of the Métro"). The first of these texts describes a group of people on an escalator; Robbe-Grillet insists on the stasis of these travelers: "a motionless group, standing on the bottommost steps, having barely left the bottom platform, has suddenly become frozen for the duration of the mechanical ascent, has come to a stop suddenly, in the midst of its agitation, of its haste, as if the act of stepping on the moving stairs had immediately paralyzed their bodies."[33] The text seems to offer nothing more than the description of this motionless group on the moving staircase. And yet, in a mirroring *mise en abyme*, the perspective of the describing eye is reproduced in one of the characters in the group, who looks down to see another group—probably the same one—at the point of departure. An exercise in description, "The Escalator" thus abolishes what it purports to describe, since what is seen exists only as a textual mirror-play of reading. The paradoxical moving immobility of the scene reinforces the narrative's logical impossibility, that of a *metalepsis*, in the substitution of a cause for an effect: the viewer of the scene turns to look down the escalator, in reaction to the backward look of the person in front of him, who, paradoxically, is himself viewed, at the beginning of the narrative, by the backward look of the former.

Boudjedra's *Topographie* has a similar scene on an escalator, though the problems of perspective and interpretation are not merely of a formal nature, as in Robbe-Grillet, but reflect the bafflement and fear of the immigrant. Boudjedra's traveler makes the same backward look on the escalator: "What puzzles him [*ce qui l'intrigue*] ... is that on the departure platform that grows further and further away, no one else appears, as if the group had an exclusive right to the escalator. . . . He wonders whether he has not made a mistake and whether he is not traveling with a particular group, which he has no right to do. . . . But he is soon reassured since down below, at the bottom of the steps, far away now, a noisy group of rowdy youngsters takes its place on the escalator" (102–3). In Boudjedra's Nouveau Roman, defamiliarization is caused by cultural estrangement, one that the reader is made to experience in turn. Perspective is no less complicated than in Robbe-Grillet, since this description on the escalator is that of a man presumably dead, and whose version of events cannot be extricated from the Babel of witnesses who contribute to the narrative. And in insisting, like Robbe-Grillet, on the paradox of motion in stasis, Boudjedra, however, makes that paradox a source of the immigrant's fear: "the traveler, suitcase in hand, silently watches the group that intimidates him with its vertiginous fixedness (101). The paradoxical and impossible perspective of Robbe-Grillet's story becomes, in *Topographie*, that of a character who struggles to make himself known, and this voice of the excluded is one that the reader, like the traveling companions on the escalator, may well fail to hear or respond to: "having nearly arrived at the top of the incline, the people composing the group keep silent, as if on purpose, in order to frighten him, to refuse and reject him" (103). What I called the metalepsis of cause and effect in Robbe-Grillet is here a confusion as to the source of the immigrant's fear, a presumed hostility that anticipates the actual murder at the end of the story. And just as the scene on the escalator anticipates the book's conclusion, the murder itself is emblematic of a broader context of anti-immigrant violence. One might say that such violence is the cultural symptom of a persistent metalepsis, according to which the *cause* of violence is blamed on an *effect*. Thus, in racist discourse, naming the North African an "invader" substitutes the cause of immigration—the invasion and colonization of Algeria, and the disruption of its economy—for its effect—the search for economic security. Boudjedra indicates this violent substitution in the scene of murder itself: "living history in reverse [*vivant l'histoire à reculons*]," Boudjedra says, the immigrant's assailants throw themselves on him "as if they were not the assassins . . . but the victims" (154).

In *Lettres algériennes*, Boudjedra reminds us that for the Algerian immigrant, "one goes *up* to Paris."[34] This supposed upward mobility is ironized in the escalator scene and in the immigrant's long journey in the metro's labyrinth, "les dédales de la mythologie assimilationniste" (*Topographie*, 145). Boudjedra's critique of French anti-immigration attitudes and policies thus targets both the myths of travel, including *The Odyssey*, and mythology in the Barthesian sense, as collective delusion of consumer culture. Boudjedra's illiterate immigrant is indeed an apt figure for the modern subject of consumerist ideology, fascinated as he is by the lure of subway advertisements, and fatally drawn toward dreams of wealth. Similarly, in Barthes's *Mythologies*, the consumerist subject is unable to decipher the hieroglyph of ideological meanings hidden within the signs of popular culture. Boudjedra's immigrant is thus often engaged in a difficult activity of semiotic interpretation: "The break [*La brisure*] occurs within by the addition of all these strange mixtures, combinations, imbrications, pilings-up, and various accumulations of a single and unique phenomenon that is beyond him, of course, and of which he has a vague but implicit awareness, knowing that the entire mystery of the environment of which he is the victim has its secret in this diabolical conjunction between things, objects, and beings caught in a code of connections he cannot manage to decipher" (76). Surrounded by "this deluge of words, signs that remain more than cabalistic" (234), the only message the immigrant manages to formulate himself is a short telegram home: "ARRIVED. STOP. ALIVE. STOP. WELL. STOP" (77). In a wicked irony, his friends back home—actually malicious accomplices to his journey's failure—make a point of ridiculing the fact that he paid money for each of those needless "stops" (83).

Though illiterate, the immigrant engages in detailed study of several advertising posters that fascinate, disturb, and shock him for their sexuality and indecency. The passages devoted to the description of these posters draw effectively on the techniques of *mise-en-abyme* in the Nouveau Roman as well as on Barthesian mythological critique. One of these is none other than a picture of a baby on a toilet seat, playing with a roll of toilet paper. The poster vaunts its product with the line "Lotus is soft as a baby's skin" (167). Since the letter O is replaced with a stylized lotus flower, the immigrant is able to identify the object the name refers to, but remains perplexed as to its purpose in the advertisement. And yet this failure of reading, which impedes his reception of the sign's mythic signification, allows for a sophisticated critique of camera angle, color, lighting, and props, and even speculation on the equipment outside the frame of the image, all of which, the immigrant reflects, serve to make the viewer overlook the scatological and "incongruous" aspects of the scene (165). This insight is more than the product of prudish offense; it is, rather, a failure of ideological interpellation, and exemplifies the postcolonial inheritance of the Nouveau Roman's formal defamiliarization. The demystification of the poster also leads the immigrant into speculation on the Homeric implications of the lotus: as the text indicates, in chapter 9 of *The Odyssey* the lotus-eaters served lotus to Ulysses's companions, so that they would "forget the way home" (167). The mythological story of the lotus-eaters thus resonates with the risks the immigrant runs in leaving the native country and succumbing to the lure of the metropole. At the same time, however, the immigrant recognizes the lotus as a plant belonging not to France but to his own native region; as a result, the text's reference to *The Odyssey* does not simply sing the praise of home and the fatal lure of the other. The immigrant's journey lacks the stable referents of home and abroad, as conveyed in another poster: "Be like Ulysses! Sail off to the island of the Lotus-Eaters!" (169). Instead, the postcolonial immigrant travels *between* homes, between the "bad reintegration [*mauvaise réinsertion*]" of a return to the postcolony (121) and failed integration into the metropole, voyaging both within and against the myths and mythologies of travel. This predicament is characteristic of postcolonial authors: straddling different worlds and perpetually displaced, they give the lie to the Odyssean narrative of adventure, profit, and return. Seth Graebner argues that Boudjedra's protagonist is not an *immigrant* but an *emigrant*: "Kept perpetually outside, the protagonist never manages to become an *im*migrant anywhere; he is always the *e*migrant, the one who has left his old place, but never arrived in a new one."[35] The point deserves some refinement; as I will argue in what follows, Boudjedra's protagonist is an *arrivant*: neither inside nor outside, and tampering with the boundaries that define their imbricated topographies.

Disoriented as he is, over the course of the day Boudjedra's immigrant shows some progress in his interpretation of the signs that surround him. This change in perspective, however, is due to retrospective thoughts that may come to him only at the end; the entire narrative, it seems, is the phantasmagoria of his mind at the moment of death. One poster in particular undergoes a dramatic reevaluation in the course of his harrowing narrative. The poster shows a radiant woman and child that he first takes as a sign meant to "extend a welcome to all the miscreants of the earth" (215), without realizing, however, that it is simply an advertisement for a tampon. He blames himself later for taking this picture for "a sign of hospitality [*une marque d'hospitalité*]" (221), and its ambiguous message of welcome reappears in his dying thoughts in the novel's final paragraph. Interestingly, this poster reappears twenty-five years later in Boudjedra's more recent novel, *Fascination*. The protagonist Lam, like the immigrant in *Topographie*, takes the picture as a sign of welcome, then reconsiders its message as something other than "une marque d'hospitalité."[36] In a technique of cross-textual borrowing characteristic of Boudjedra, *Fascination* cites verbatim from the earlier text, and it also reprises the "Lotus" advertisement as well as the references to Homer and Joyce's *Ulysses*. This textual play adds an additional disorientation to the narrative of *Topographie*, as the evidence of the racist crime risks being lost in the process of rewriting. And yet this textual play might point to an alternative to the strict opposition of hospitality and inhospitality, an alternative no less political than the narrative of *Topographie*. *Fascination*, after all, is a political story of war and colonial resistance, traveling from colonial Algeria through the war of independence, with journeys to Russia, China, Vietnam, Spain, and finally Paris, where Lam is briefly arrested for his revolutionary activities. Boudjedra's madcap narrative of postcolonial resistance avoids, however, a "pretentious and heroic narrative" (111), delivering instead an "impotent epic," to borrow Emily Apter's term, of postcolonial Algeria.[37] The father in *Fascination* is, indeed, literally impotent, and dies shortly after independence; Lam, his adopted son, fears as much for himself, and is tormented by guilt following his incest with his lesbian sister. As in Boudjedra's groundbreaking *La Répudiation*, a critique of the early postcolonial Algerian state, politics in *Fascination* involves an exploration of queer, marginal, and dissident sexualities that challenge patriarchy and gender normativity in the postcolony. Similarly, the queer narrative in *Timimoun* provides an indictment of the terrorist violence of the Algerian civil war of the 1990s. Elsewhere, I have argued that *Timimoun*'s paralyzed narrator is subject to gender melancholia, and his dawning awareness of an internal sexual repudiation leads him to discover the "trace of the other" in his psychic torment.[38] *Topographie*'s narrative thus shares with all Boudjedra's texts a concern for those suffering social marginalization. The immigrant protagonist of *Topographie* is, then, a figure of the marginal: neither inside nor outside the metropole, but the uncanny trace of the other in the margins of French culture. We might say that the immigrant thus traces a *marque d'hospitalité*, a problematic mark or margin *between* hospitality and inhospitality, integration and exclusion, assimilation and alterity. Can this margin be assimilated? What politics of hospitality can recognize the marginal?

Leïla Sebbar's recent *Métro: Instantanés* adds a striking new intertext to the weave of narratives we have followed here. With a title evocative of Robbe-Grillet's short fictions, Sebbar's *Métro* updates the postcolonial perplexities of Boudjedra's traveler in a collection of short episodes and portraits evocative of a contemporary multicultural and multiethnic Paris. A recurrent motif in these short texts, as in Boudjedra, are posters; here the ads feature Laetitia Casta, photographed in suggestive poses, and who Sebbar invokes as well as the new Marianne, allegorical symbol of republican France. This "mystical muse" of advertising and national identity contrasts with the many Muslim women and girls Sebbar describes wearing the hijab in the metro, discussing the law against the veil, and militating for freedom of cultural identification.[39] Turning right-wing discourse against itself, these "Mariannes musulmanes" invoke a veiled Marianne as ambiguous rallying cry for an identity both French and culturally distinct.[40] Whereas Boudjedra's traveler is engaged in a seemingly impossible labor of decipherment, by the time of Sebbar's *Métro* the posters that confront the commuter are routinely tagged, defaced, and contested by a heteroglot population in the "Babel" of the postcolonial metro (11). Commenting on the image of the "Marianne voilée," Chiara Bottici has argued that Islamophobia is most entrenched in images that convey stubborn mythic symbols of identity and otherness, whether through caricatures of Muslims or cherished national emblems.[41] Sebbar's *Métro*, however, shows that such images are not merely disseminated from on high and passively consumed, but are cited, contested, and reworked in a practice of what Jacques Rancière calls "dissensus." In Sebbar's gallery of snapshots, the multiethnic population of the metro is itself a collection of images, but no longer ordered under a single dominating or exoticizing gaze, even when evoking the "Scènes et types" of colonial photography (43). "Photographers traveled the Empire beyond the seas; their images live here, in the metro," Sebbar says (12). These practices of estrangement and dislocation are implicit in Boudjedra's tragic tale, but its challenge bears its fruits only after a long history of *beur* activism and cultural mutation. Like Sebbar's post-exotic snapshots, ethnography, as we will see, also turns homeward to study the urban milieus of the new immigrant populations, the postcolonial legacy of modern French travel.

Postcolonial Haunts

Boudjedra's *Topographie* was written after a wave of murders of North Africans in 1973.[42] Ten years later, after another wave of attacks, the Marche pour l'égalité et contre le racisme, popularly named

La Marche des beurs, proved a watershed in immigrant political organization and public advocacy for civil rights. The following year Tahar Ben Jelloun published *Hospitalité française*, arguing that French anti-Arab racism is the violent symptom of a failed reckoning with the colonial past. Ben Jelloun shows that two dominant myths constrain the immigrant: the "myth of return" to the postcolony, which casts the immigrant as a temporary visitor, and the myth of French hospitality itself, cruelly negated in the exclusion of the immigrant.[43] In the years since *Hospitalité française* was published, the French state has taken an increasingly repressive approach to the immigrant, with immigration quotas, forced expulsions, and limits on access to citizenship. During the same period, the *affaire du foulard* tested the limits of French tolerance of cultural difference within the abstract framework of republican and secular citizenship. Meanwhile, state housing projects in the suburbs have continued to widen the economic rift between immigrants and the native French. The myth of French hospitality was exploded in the fall of 2005, when riots broke out in suburbs all over France in the wake of the death of two immigrant youths in an altercation with the police. Images broadcast night after night showed cars burning; for three weeks the French woke up to the grim spectacle of charred hulks of automobiles. Azouz Begag underscores the irony of the rioting youth targeting symbols of mobility in their frustrated rage. In a practice they name a "rodeo," youths steal cars, go on a joyride, and finally smash and set them on fire.[44] There is indeed a bitter irony in this attack on the automobile, Barthes's mythological object par excellence. Among the poorest of French citizens, the suburban youths belong to families for whom a car is often an impossible luxury. At the same time, as François Maspero showed in his *Roissy Express*, residents of the suburbs lack good access to public transit, and their housing projects are stranded in zones of administrative neglect.[45] Similarly, Paul Silverstein points out that the *banlieusard* today views "the transportation system as a space of harassment, racism and alienation."[46] This spatial segregation of the poor suburbs, for Silverstein, amounts to a form of endo-colonization: "[M]artial imperatives to maintain colonial state security," he says, "served as an example for parallel processes within the metropole" (85).[47] And in an uncanny return of colonial history, the state responded to the 2005 riots with emergency measures not used since the Algerian War.[48]

Car burnings and "rodeos" are only the most extreme responses to social alienation, at one end of a spectrum of resistant acts designed "to take possession of spaces defined violently."[49] Silverstein mentions the idiom *se faire un métro* ("doing a *métro*"), to name petty thievery in the anonymous crowds of underground transit (114). Drawing on Michel de Certeau, Silverstein sees these as "spatial practices" and "tactics" that take advantage of the contradictions of the lived reality of the *banlieue*. De Certeau's "tactics" provide a useful way to account for lived behaviors that escape the neat divisions of illicit and legal acts, and whose subversions of discipline express the promise of other mobilities. His tactics are, then, eminently suited to the practices of resistance and survival of such marginal groups as immigrants. A tactic, moreover, might be framed as a practice of *hospitality*. "The place of a tactic," de Certeau says, "belongs to the other. A tactic insinuates itself into the other's place, fragmentarily, without taking it over in its entirety, without being able to keep it at a distance."[50] De Certeau's prime example of such tactics is outlined in his "Walking in the City," an essay on "the ordinary man," the "anonymous hero" that resonates with Leopold Bloom in Dublin, Selvon in London and Boudjedra's nameless immigrant in Paris (v). "To practice space is . . . *to be other and to move toward the other*" (110). The mere act of walking, in its improvisations, wanderings and weaving of links, defies the city's regimentation and surveillance. And yet it is not *opposed* to a structuring order; rather, walkers "elude discipline without being outside the field in which it is exercised" (96). Similarly, place-names in the city serve not simply as official designations, but as nodes of "semantic tropisms" (103) that secretly orient the walker "just as they can haunt dreams" (104). As de Certeau says, "These names create a nowhere in places; they change them into passages."

Such a haunting displacement was felt by Walter Benjamin in the Place du Maroc in Paris, which, he says, "became for me, when I happened on it one Sunday afternoon, not only a Moroccan desert but also, and at the same time, a monument of colonial imperialism; topographic vision was entwined with allegorical meaning, yet not for an instant did it lose its place in the heart of Belleville."[51] What Benjamin calls the "evocative power" of street names creates an "intertwining" of places that does not simply *transport* the *flâneur*, but ensnares him, brings him to a "standstill."[52] Indeed, topographic vision turns him into a sick patient, or perhaps the nameless victim of *Topographie*: "the patient who wanders the city at night for hours on end and forgets the way home is perhaps in the grip of this power." Proper names thus "haunt urban space like superfluous or additional inhabitants," as de Certeau says (106); "they create in the place itself that erosion or nowhere that the law of the other carves out within it" (105). In Benjamin's case, such haunting is specifically a colonial haunting; a migrant himself, he sensed the uncanny presence of "superfluous or additional inhabitants" summoned to Paris by the name of Morocco. These ghostly inhabitants, following the logic of the *supplement*, transform familiar places into familiar *haunts*. Indeed, de Certeau says, "Haunted places are the only ones people can live in" (108).

Why this emphasis on *haunting* in de Certeau's "Walking in the City"? What ghosts are shadowing his anonymous pedestrian?[53] Given that de Certeau's essay is based on dense urban pedestrian spaces, one might say it betrays a certain nostalgia in a time of increasing suburbanization and automotive transport. Reading with and against de Certeau's model of pedestrian mobility, a different anonymous subject profiles itself, that of the marginal immigrant, relegated to suburban enclaves and struggling for *droit de cité*.[54] Similarly, the immigrant is a more apt figure for Marc Augé's anonymous "Monsieur Dupont," who travels the "non-places" of an alienating postmodern metropole. If, as Augé says, "non-places are the real measure of our time,"[55] the immigrant would be the primary subject of this experience of uprooting and displacement. Likewise, the paradoxical "ethnology of solitude" Augé proposes (120) finds its appropriate subject less in the postmodern traveler than in the alienated immigrant of Ben Jelloun's *La Plus haute des solitudes*.[56] The haunts of de Certeau and Augé sketch out a spectral logic of urban space and the trace of an uncanny hospitality. The immigrant other appears here, in the margins of their texts, as an other summoned yet invisible, crucial to their arguments but relegated to the periphery. As the marginal, the immigrant exposes the margins of lived space, perhaps the very threshold of the proper home, tampering with the boundaries of the here and the now. This uncanny hospitality is powerfully rendered in Michael Haneke's film *Caché*, in which a Parisian couple suffers the threat of a home invasion, and uncovers over the course of the narrative the guilty memory of inhospitality to an Algerian boy whose parents died in the Parisian massacre of 1961.[57] *Caché* dramatizes the devastating costs of inhospitality and repressed history, and calls for a politics of mourning and an historical reckoning with the events of 1961.[58] Sebbar, Jean-Luc Einaudi, and Ben Jelloun, among others, have contributed to this belated anamnesis.[59] Similarly, Mehdi Charef's *Le Harki de Meriem* begins with the racist murder of the son of Algerian immigrants, and takes the reader on a mournful journey back to the distant sources of that violent act in the Algerian War.[60] A politics of mourning, however, need not be that of a settling of scores or a final reckoning with the dead. Neither should it accept the negative symptoms of a fearsome uncanniness. Rather, the city as *haunt* unsettles the defensive proprieties of familiar spaces, opening

Moroccan deserts in the heart of Paris, raising unexpected monuments, revealing the global in the local.

Derrida provides the basis for such a politics of mourning, and his focus in recent years on specters, immigration, and hospitality draws together the all the themes raised by our reading of Boudjedra's novel. Derrida asserts that "there is no politics . . . without an open hospitality to the guest as *ghost*."[61] As such, a politics of mourning raises the challenge of hospitality in its most unconditionally ethical dimension, as a welcome to the absolutely other. Derrida shows, however, that mourning is constrained by a number of paradoxes: is it more faithful to welcome and absorb the dead other, at the cost, however, of denying their very death? Or is it more faithful to acknowledge their absolute otherness, at the cost of abandoning them? The former would amount to a contradictory assimilation of the other; the latter, a recognition that excludes. Mourning and hospitality are thus constrained by "two infidelities" and "an impossible choice."[62] The specter is itself the sign of this impossibility: what the ghost manifests is an intimate other, the "other in the same" (42). Indeed, *whatever* appears bears the trace of this spectrality, by which it *returns*, repeats, and supplements itself.[63] The spectral, then, is what in any given event and location "takes place"; but it is also, by the same token, what "takes the place" in a surreptitious supplementarity (55). An uncanny and duplicitous *taking place* is thus inscribed in every proper place as its spectral margin. This is what Derrida calls "the ghostly power of the supplement": "it is never inscribed in the homogeneous objectivity of the framed space but instead inhabits or, rather, haunts it" (41). A politics of mourning for Derrida departs from the recognition of the uncanniness of the proper, and indeed of the home. Derrida thus speaks of "the rootlessness of place, the dis-location of the house, the infraction of the home" as features of this uncanny home, altered before any traveler's departure or return, before any immigrant.[64] To practice hospitality to the immigrant is to give room to the other where hospitality has already, unknowingly, *taken place*.

Deconstruction requires that we orient our thinking toward the other. A political critique of travel will, then, depart from an espousal of the excluded; gender, sexuality, and race are among the most important zones of exclusion and repression. Paradoxically, however, this reorientation cannot take the form merely of a call for more inclusiveness, if that inclusiveness entails another totalizing and assimilating grasp. The French politics of colonial assimilation is a vivid reminder of the violence, denial, and hypocrisy that may accompany such an appropriation of the other. Likewise, a postcolonial politics of integration will fail to the extent that it reduces the alterity of the immigrant. In its ethical orientation toward radical alterity, deconstructive politics is particularly sensitive to the pitfalls of assimilation and recognition. Deconstruction thus advocates neither exclusion nor assimilation, and would suspect any simple call for the recognition of the other. For these reasons the politics of deconstruction remain obscure to liberal and leftist politics alike. And yet deconstruction is very hospitable to the ambiguities of immigrant identity, which inhabits a marginal status between identification and rivalry, assimilation and difference, self and other. And if hospitality always entails a welcoming into the *home*, Derrida refigures that home not as Ulysses's destination, but as an uncanny—unhomely—site of encounter with the other. Home economics, then, is a practice of uncanny hospitality, a reckoning with the otherness that always already disrupts the security and self-identity of the presumed home. This is the predicament facing the French couple in *Caché*: while their reflexes of panic try to reassert the boundaries of the residence, hidden guilt and unconscious mourning speak the deeper truth of their uncanny home. In this way the film speaks to a broader historical haunting by 1961 and the Algerian War; the haunted space of the home in *Caché* extends to Paris and France as a whole.

The Algerian war has left the persistent trace of a disparity in grieving in France. Thus, the mournful plaints of *nostalgérie* dwell on French losses but deny those of the Algerian victims, and the heritage of this division of the grieved and the ungrieved continues in the attacks on immigrants that followed. Part of the work of mourning requires a social and political correcting of this disparity in grieving, or what Ben Jelloun calls "selective indignation."[65] A more difficult work, however, lies beyond the alternatives of losses avowed and unavowed. Paradoxically, this work of mourning lies not in repairing losses but in submitting to the *ungrievable*. For if mourning implies a recognition of loss, to what extent is that recognition a recuperation of loss? And can we fully know *what* we have lost when we lose something? Even supposedly successful mourning can thus serve as a denial of loss. Building on the work of Derrida, Judith Butler has shown how the politics of mourning tends to divide groups into the "grieved" and the "ungrieved." There are those whose loss is granted recognition and mourning, and others—the victims of AIDS or enemy casualties—whose deaths go ungrieved. In contrast, Butler says, "mourning would be maintained by its enigmatic dimension, by the experience of not knowing incited by losing what we cannot fully fathom."[66] This experience of the ungrievable would entail an ethical reorientation that can inform political life. Far from condoning the denial of grief, the ungrievable thus makes mourning an infinite task. This has been the work of Assia Djebar, whose commitment to the memory of the Algerian dead has taken the paradoxical form of a refusal to submit to official mourning.[67] Djebar relates that walking the street one haunted night in Paris, she found herself voicing, against her will, a terrible cry of the dead. A Frenchman on the sidewalk begs her to stop.[68] As this episode from Djebar shows, her unofficial mourning is not a private but a social one. She makes a scene, if only to confront the other with his incomprehension. Further, she expresses what may defy narrative, what interrupts her telling of the tale. As Butler says, "the very 'I' who seeks to tell the story is stopped in the midst of the telling; the very 'I' is called into question by its relation to the Other, a relation that does not precisely reduce me to speechlessness, but does nevertheless clutter my speech with signs of its undoing."[69] In fact, Djebar's scene binds together two "relations to the other" in the scene: the relation to the haunting dead, and the relation to the French other, ambiguous figure of rival and addressee of her text. This social relation is implicit in mourning itself for, as Butler argues, the loss of the other may be seen as revealing relationality in its minimal form, and doing so, precisely, by calling the autonomy of the self into question. To account for loss is to open communication, but also to communicate the unaccountable; in the thrall of grief, Butler says, "narrative falters, as it must."[70]

Hospitality too opens up a fundamental relationality by means of a similar faltering and interruption. Derrida argues that hospitality follows two contradictory imperatives: the *law* of unconditional hospitality, enshrined by ethics as the principle of "a welcome without reservations or calculation," and the plural *laws* of hospitality that put hospitality into practice, and thereby, whether intentionally or not, set conditional limits.[71] Derrida makes this conflictual relationship itself, rather than the hospitable "ideal," the place of ethical choices. This displacement of ethics has the advantage of making the ethical always political; accordingly, Derrida has contributed a good deal of reflection to the politics of immigration in contemporary France. By the same token, the political must always relate to ethical ideals, and not merely to pragmatism and laws. But if the hospitable ideal and hospitable practices are necessarily linked, that link is deeply problematic. For if the hospitable ideal never exists apart from concrete practices, those practices, however, inevitably betray the hospitable ideal. As Derrida says, "These two regimes of law, of *the* law and the laws, are thus both contradictory, antinomic, *and* inseparable. They both imply and exclude each other, simultaneously."[72] What is at stake in hospitality is not, then, a distinction or an opposition between two imperatives, but rather a margin and a difference. And if this problematic difference threatens to paralyze us in a double bind, it does, however, cause us to dwell at the very site of encounter and welcome, the threshold itself. As Derrida says, it is "a difference both subtle and fundamental, a question that arises on the threshold of "home," and on the threshold between two inflections."[73]

How is such hospitality put into practice? In 1983 Ben Jelloun suggested that a North African should be placed in a ministerial post. Twenty years later, Azouz Begag took up such a post as minister for equal opportunities (Ministre délégué à la Promotion de l'Egalité des Chances). In a terrible historical irony, Begag's early tenure as minister would coincide with the riots of the fall of 2005. Begag's efforts at integration and support of the immigrant underclass placed him in conflict with the government's repressive police actions as well as with a general French consensus of Islamophobia. Begag's work up to the events of 2005 had criticized the assimilationist model of immigration, arguing instead for an integration that allowed for ethnic difference. His critiques address a familiar paradox of hospitality: according to the secular republican model of French citizenship, for others to accede to citizenship, they must abandon their very identity. In this sense, French hospitality amounts to a paradoxical denial of otherness, a "repressive tolerance," to borrow Spivak's term.[74] In a similar paradox, immigrant claims to ethnic identification are denigrated as a divisive *communautarisme* by secularists who themselves enjoy the benefits of religious, racial, and cultural identification that go without saying. In this light, the cultural and political challenge of immigrants is not so much a confrontation with French "national character" and *laïcité* as it is the symptom of the double standards and tacit exclusions of French identity itself.

Begag's *Ethnicity and Equality*, written immediately prior to the riots of 2005, has been seen as a prescient diagnosis of the failures of French integration.[75] Begag's book advocates for a multicultural recognition of ethnic diversity in France, and outlines new employment initiatives and programs for improved educational access for immigrant youths, which he divides into three categories, the *rouilleurs*, the *dérouilleurs,* and the *intermédiaires*. *Ethnicity and Equality* emphasizes the positive role played by the economically and socially successful *dérouilleurs*, the "movers," as opposed to the delinquent *rouilleurs*, the "rusters," those who remain stuck in place; the *intermédiaires* lie between the two. As these names show, Begag's sociology relies on metaphors of movement and stasis. "Mobility," Begag says, "best corresponds to the new outlook that France needs" (92); he encourages the young ethnics to take "the elevator of social mobility" (120), to "get moving" (125). While he is deeply concerned with the exclusions suffered by the young immigrants, Begag faults the *rouilleurs* for their sense of victimhood and resentment against society, and especially their resentment of the *dérouilleurs* who succeed, who "get out" of the neighborhood. "Why are those who get out rejected in this way?" Begag asks. "One of the reasons is that those who succeed, those who gain personal autonomy, make brutally and unmistakably visible the immobility of those who rust where they are" (81). This is perhaps true, though not in the sense that Begag intends. Bauman, as we have seen, argues that the immobility of the underprivileged, or at best their vagabondage, is the price they pay for the mobility of others. Begag, however, writing from a position of privilege, and accused of being an "Uncle Tom" (80), casts himself as "attacked," "suspect" and "spurned," though, in an ambiguous reversal, he also says that it is the movers who "make brutally . . . visible the immobility of those who rust."

Begag would no doubt admit that not everyone can climb the social elevator, and that a certain resentment of the privileged is perhaps inevitable. His argument, then, would simply be that young Arabs in France should not arbitrarily bear the brunt of economic and social exclusion, or defeat their own chances for success. However, despite their best intentions, Begag's policies fail to account for what Immanuel Wallerstein calls the "social-structural" nature of the *rouilleurs*' "institutional marginalization."[76] Further, the term "marginalization" may be unable to capture what is at stake in the debate over integration; as Samir Amin argues, the underclass is neither unintegrated nor marginalized, but is rather fully integrated within a system of exploitation that requires their impoverishment and dispossession.[77] At best, Begag's policies may open up opportunities to an enterprising few, without however addressing the root causes of precarity. Indeed, what the "immobile" *rouilleurs* and rioters manifest above all is the *systematic* nature of their marginalization, which improved opportunities for the few cannot resolve. This is to suggest that the sociologist of integration may have failed to identify the social group to which he has devoted his work. The *rouilleurs* and rioters of 2005 are not only members of an ethnic minority, but belong to a more amorphous group voicing their exclusion on a broader economic and cultural scene. Radical sociologists and political theorists increasingly emphasize the *global* affiliation of this disparate group: the "multitude," in Hardt and Negri's term, the "post-communal citizen," in Balibar's.[78] The fault-lines of economic exploitation, once located more securely beyond the borders of the European states, increasingly lie within the bounds of the metropole, as globalization and neoliberal economic policies spread their instabilities into the domestic territory. The immigrant suburban youth in France are the primary economic victims of the deregulation, privatization, welfare cuts, and unemployment that have opened a widening gulf between the successful and those left behind by globalization. Begag largely skirts this victimhood and exclusion in the name of personal initiative. Likewise, his discourse of tolerance and inclusiveness cannot encompass the larger group of economically excluded who loom behind the suburban rioters, those displaced and uprooted by the turbulence of the global market, Bauman's "vagabonds" of globalization. In what seems a willful reversal of such concerns, Begag's book ends not with immigration but *emigration*, rhapsodizing on the ambitions of a new "beurgeoisie," the "megamovers" who have left the French suburbs to strike out into a world of opportunities: "These pioneers are now all over the world, in Australia, in America, in the Caribbean, in New Caledonia, in Guyana, echoing the voyages of their parents or grandparents when they fled the poverty of their native lands" (127). The neoliberalism of Begag's policies betrays itself here in an exuberance that disavows its motivating contradiction.[79] Elsewhere in the text, however, such a contradiction is more pointedly paralyzing. In spite of himself, Begag comes close here to expressing the disorientation and paralysis of Boudjedra's nameless immigrant.

> [W]e're sitting in a train in a station next to another train and suddenly our train starts to move. We feel an unpleasant, dizzy sensation, for the train is moving, but we can't hear it moving, and everything in the compartment is motionless. Then, as we look through the window, we suddenly realize that it's the other train that's leaving, not ours. For a few seconds we were convinced our train was leaving, and we had a strange, dislocated feeling, with our bodies separated from our minds. (66–67)

Presumably, Begag's intertext here is Einstein's illustration of the theory of relativity with the metaphor of trains in motion, or perhaps Lévi-Strauss's invocation of that metaphor in the course of his discussion of "mobile cultures" and "immobile cultures" in the essay "Race and History."[80] For his part, Begag's anecdote is meant to illustrate the perspectival illusion to which *beur* youths may fall prey in their social aspirations. In retrospect, however, it seems to speak as well to the illusions of Begag's own ministerial career, marked by his differences with the Minister of the Interior, Nicolas Sarkozy, and with the conservative UMP government's repressive police policies. The aggressive language of Sarkozy played a large part in fueling the rage of the rioters, and his election as president in 2007 may be credited to the posture he adopted during the crisis, which rallied the public to his brand of a new nationalism with strict security policies against threats both at home and abroad.[81] Begag resigned from his post as minister due to his differences with Sarkozy and the government's repressive policies. In spite of these differences, however, Begag made common cause with the controversial CPE law, vaunted by the UMP as a measure to promote youth employment, but which provoked a fresh wave of riots and demonstrations in March 2006.[82] Demonstrations against the CPE law have been called one of the most significant mass actions since May '68, joining university students, labor unions, high school students, and suburban youths in protests that led to the government's abandonment of the proposed law.[83] In spite of their tactical success, however, the anti-CPE demonstrations in Paris were marred by violence and disorder: bands of suburban youths turned on their fellow demonstrators in violent assaults that laid bare the racial and class cleavages between the participating groups. In response, the French media revived the specter of irrational violence, or worse, "anti-white racism" on the part of the rioting suburban youths. It has been the mission of sociologists such as Michel Kokoreff to account for the social causes of such violence and to articulate the latent voice within the rioters' problematic actions. To do so is to challenge the criminal-justice approach of the French state as well as its discrediting of suburban sociologists as apologists for civil unrest, an attitude summed up in Sarkozy's dictum, "L'inexcusable est inexplicable."[84] In contrast, Kokoreff asserts that the riots merely reflect the concrete "topography of the zones of social disqualification" in which the socioeconomic conflicts of French society as a whole are most manifest.[85] "By calling civil and social order into question," Kokoreff says, "the rioters mobilize the resources at their disposal to exist and make themselves known. Riots are in keeping with a strategy of social protest that goes by way of a desire for visibility and recognition" (98). In the context of the anti-CPE movement, the suburban youths' violence would go so far as to challenge the Parisian tradition of street protest and to alienate them from leftist groups and their political representatives, all too slow to espouse their cause. If, as Kokoreff says, the youths rebel against their spatial segregation and claim a right to "mobility in the city" (279), that right finds its expression not in the traditional mode of political petition and passive street demonstrations, but in violent confrontation with the forces of order, the dominant presence of the state in their social world. Taking to the street in Paris, the rioting youths thus brought with them the "topographie des zones de disqualification sociale" of the suburban *cités*.

The young ethnics of France are a diverse and complex population, as Begag shows. But as targets of anti-immigrant attitudes and Islamophobia, they are habitually grouped as a threat to French culture and public security. To confront the hegemony of French racism one must address the ways in which that population is habitually singled out as a group. The point here is not to assign a single identity to this grouping; rather, it is to point out that the grouping is a factor of "a unified response," as Talal Asad says, by a dominant population bent on the denigration of a convenient ethnic population.[86] Asad's comment was made in the context of the controversy surrounding Salman Rushdie's *The Satanic Verses*. And whereas Muslim responses to Rushdie were varied and multiple, the consensus of the British majority was to cast those offended by Rushdie's anti-Muslim humor as a homogeneous, barbarous other, and to focus only on the most violent reactions to the book. More recently, in the wake of the Muslim headscarf controversy, Asad has shown how the arguments for the defense of French secularism mask the violence of the French state's purported liberality. The example is instructive, as it shows how policies of inclusiveness—here, under the banner of *laïcité*—can support the secular state's tacit role in what Asad calls the "distribution of pain."[87] Asad demonstrates how secularism today bears the contradictory heritage of its colonial history. "Anti-clerical schooling at home, unequal agreements with the Church, and imperial expansion abroad were the pillars on which *laïcité* was established" (499). In Algeria, however, religious schooling and conversion were the norm, which only perpetuated a religious schism between France and its Algerian subjects, delaying their accession to full citizenship. The French secular project has inherited these contradictions, Asad says, "to promote a certain kind of national subject who is held to be essentially incompatible with an 'Islamic subject'" (510).

What Asad calls a "unified response" to a perceived Muslim threat bears some resemblance to what René Girard calls the sacrificial logic of "unanimous violence."[88] The unified response to immigrants constitutes a new and disturbing consensus of metropolitan populations, binding together an imagined community of natives in a sacrificial logic. Citizens of post-9/11 security states today override their internal differences in this vindictive logic of exclusion. But an account of such violence must go beyond the structural model of Girard to account for the more complex political and economic roots of this ostensibly religious hostility. The lines of exclusion are clearly defined, as we have seen, by colonial history. Today, the state seems increasingly unable to manage the economic disorders and inequalities that have developed in the wake of colonization and globalization. But in a show of force, the security state manages the distribution of pain to the detriment of its internal others; French Arabs and Muslims thereby become surrogate victims of the security state. The true target of this hostility, however, is neither alien, strange or other; it is the return of the colonized *subject* in the segregated quarters of a recolonialized metropole. In a striking phrase, Balibar says that this *subject* is the "shadow cast by the citizen."[89] The subject, appearing only as ghost, monster, or shadow, is the dark side of the citizen's privilege and welfare, a postcolonial reminder that the birth of the secular, democratic citizen went hand in hand with the *subjugation* of colonized others. In the post- and neocolonial era, the *subject* of power, as opposed to the citizen with guaranteed rights, is located more squarely within the borders of the state, or challenging those borders through immigration. This neocolonial subject, the shadow of the citizen, bears the repressive and exclusionary force of the state, and few of its benefits, in the social wastelands of the *banlieues*. Balibar's political solution is to extend a *droit de cité*, a "right to the city" to immigrants (47), and in so doing he invokes an old principle of hospitality. This is a difficult, and well-nigh impossible task, as we have seen; it implies the unlearning of privilege and a reckoning with the dead, and with the shadows we cast, but should not cast out, in the haunted spaces we share. To do so, as Homi Bhabha suggests, would be to take "the complex, often incommensurable fate of the migrant as the basis for a redefinition of the metropolitan public sphere."[90] This is the right claimed by immigrant narratives such as Boudjedra's *Topographie*, which invite us to share the hopes and fears of our shadow selves.

To Balibar's hospitable *droit de cité* we might also add a *droit de citer*—a right to citation, provided, however, that citation is understood not as a simple copying, but rather as a subversive resignification of the original. In this sense, following Judith Butler's notion of the "insubordination" of the copy, citation mimes subjugation, the better to claim the unsaid in the original and to voice the more complex agency of speech as *subjection*. Butler calls on us to consider citation "not as enslavement or simple reiteration of the original, but as an insubordination that appears to take place within the very terms of the original, and which calls into question the power of origination" in the presumed source text.[91] We have seen such insubordination in the unlikely form of a prostrate Molloy, "sadly rejoicing slave" on Ulysses's deck. Similarly, Césaire's homeward journey in the *Notebook*'s slave ship, Fanon's torturous back talk, and Selvon and Kincaid's countervoyages all speak to the promise of resistance from within the most crippling verbal and social constraints. Likewise, Boudjedra's immigrant takes on without taking over his voyaging precursors, miming their travels in spatial and textual tactics of resignification. Postcolonial citation occurs where the source text seems to *admit* nothing, yet betrays an opening where the specter can make its appearance. Here, hospitality is not generously extended or gratefully accepted, but is *claimed* without being fully owned, and on the basis of prior claims that admit more than they avow. In this way, much as the specter may call for a settling of scores, its legacy is incalculable and, indeed, points not so much to the past as to the future. Glossing the notion of the *revenant* as that which *returns*, Derrida asserts that "the specter is the future, it is always to come, it presents itself only as that which could come or come back."[92] Homeward bound, yet always caught in a paralyzing double bind, the immigrant claims the metropole as his familiar haunt, and wills to the future the spectral legacies of postcolonial travel.

Notes

Introduction

1. Clastres, *Archeology of Violence*, 9 (translation modified); *Recherches d'anthropologie politique*, 7.

2. Lévi-Strauss, *Tristes Tropiques*, 414. Fellow structuralist Jacques Lacan anticipates Lévi-Strauss on this point in speaking of a modern "barbarism" that involves "the relativization of our sociology by the scientific collection of cultural forms that we are destroying in the world" (Lacan, "Aggressivity in Psychoanalysis," in *Ecrits: A Selection*, 26).

3. Clastres's self-deflating invocation of Beckett's Molloy raises the stakes of a narrative trope that was already, by the time of *Archeology of Violence*, long established in anthropology; the opening line of Malinowski's 1922 *Argonauts*, for instance, sets a similarly entropological tone by referring to the "ludicrous, not to say tragic, position" of the ethnologist, condemned to study what was disappearing before his eyes (Malinowski, *Argonauts of the Western Pacific*, xv). Following Patrick Brantlinger's analysis of the modern discourse of extinction, we might call this mournful trope a prolepsis; Brantlinger argues that even in their most humane expressions, Western portrayals of so-called primitive peoples are marked by the persistent genre of "proleptic elegy" that tends to confirm, if not promote, the passing of what they paradoxically mourn in advance (Brantlinger, *Dark Vanishings*, 3). In what follows, however, I will take issue with such models of "imperialist nostalgia" (5), which raise the problem of a temporal predicament more complicated and paralyzing than that of a "self-fulfilling prophecy" (3).

4. The watershed publication in this debate is Talal Asad's edited volume *Anthropology and the Colonial Encounter*.

5. Clastres, *Archeology of Violence*, 140, 50. In a striking political extrapolation on Lévi-Strauss's distinction between modern, "cumulative" societies and primitive, "static" ones, Clastres developed the influential theory of primitive societies

as fundamentally violent, anarchic, and homeostatic "societies against the state." Reframed as such, primitive societies appear as the living embodiment of an "impossible" political other haunting all of Western political philosophy and statecraft. See Clastres, *Archeology of Violence*, 139–67, and *Society against the State*.

    6. Fabian, *Time and the Other*, 61.

    7. Baudelaire, *Painter of Modern Life and Other Essays*, 99.

    8. Flaubert, *Sentimental Education*, 324.

    9. Conrad, *Heart of Darkness*, 107.

    10. Echenoz, *Courir*, 49.

    11. Savin, "La Saga Le Clézio," 37.

    12. Borer, "Note de l'éditeur," 8. Michel Le Bris, contributor to the manifesto, editor of the journal *Gulliver*, and director of Etonnants Voyageurs, is the most active and vocal proponent of a revived travel writing in France. His neoromantic exoticism disowns not only the French avant-garde but also intellectuals, the Nouveau Roman, and what he calls "structuralist terrorism." Le Bris, "Fragments du royaume," 138–39. More recently, Le Bris spearheaded the manifesto "Pour une littérature-monde en français," itself modeled on Anglophone world literature and aiming to challenge the perceived confines of the category of Francophone literature. See Le Bris et al., "Pour une littérature-monde en français," *Le Monde*, March 16, 2007; and Le Bris and Rouaud, *Pour une littérature-monde*.

    13. Forsdick, *Travel in Twentieth-Century French and Francophone Cultures*, 13.

    14. De Certeau, *The Practice of Everyday Life*, 115.

    15. Fabian, *Anthropology with an Attitude*, 141–42, 146.

    16. Fabian, *Out of Our Minds*, 44, 46, 5.

    17. Skeat, *A Concise Etymological Dictionary*, 569.

    18. On *paralyse*, see Derrida, *Parages*, 74, and *The Post Card*. "Paralysis" in French is *paralysie*; as noun, Derrida's *paralyse* is a neologism evoking both paralysis and *analyse*, or analysis. Ana-lysis (deriving from the Greek for "back" and "loosen") aims to *undo* and *resolve* an object, breaking it down into its component parts; similarly, para-lysis (from "beside" and "loosen") conveys an *untying* and *coming loose*. But the Greek *para-* means also "faulty," "amiss," and "improper," and is most often found in terms that define ailments, infirmities, and irregularities. Derrida's *paralyse* seems to welcome such perversities, indeed accentuates them by combining the movement *beside* and *beyond* with stubborn stasis. Accordingly, paralysis is not the *opposite* of analysis but that which troubles, sidelines and perverts its analytic claims. Further, Derrida stakes his claims for *paralyse* not in a single etymology, of course, but in a more complex play of puns and semantic slippage. *Para-* thus also evokes a sense deriving from the Latin *parare*, and conveying a

warding-off or protection; *paralyse*, due to its strong resonance with the French *parer*, would thus suggest *both* a loosening *and* a defense against it. Below we will develop this double and paradoxical character of paralysis in terms of a twisted logic of knotting and untying. More recently, Derrida suggested that "paralysis is the negative symptom of aporia," and that the task of thought is to "transform the paralysis into aporia" (*Without Alibi*, xvii).

19. Derrida, *Aporias*, 19.

20. "Si une science ou une théorie de la lecture de ces récits devait se constituer et en venir à son nom, je l'appelerais la *paralyse*" (Derrida, *Parages*, 74).

21. Putting a term "under erasure" is an important motif in Derrida's early work, deriving from Heidegger's typographic crossing out of the word "Being." In Heidegger, as in Derrida, the crossing out is not a simple negation, but, as Spivak puts it, "lets both deletion and word stand" ("Translator's Preface," xv). In this way, crossing out a term indicates that it is both necessary and inadequate: "Since the word is inaccurate, it is crossed out. Since it is necessary, it remains legible" (xiv). The tactic of placing a word under erasure reflects a general strategy of deconstruction: to challenge a metaphysical inheritance in the vocabulary of that inheritance itself. "Our very language is twisted and bent even as it guides us. Writing 'under erasure' is the mark of this contorsion" (xiv). The contorted X is paralyzing, then, in more than one way; if it guides our thought, it does so only by twists and turns. Further, its "twisting" evokes a crosswise weave that loosens as much as it tightens, as we will see below.

22. See Malabou and Derrida, *Counterpath*, 5.

23. It is striking that this orphan term of Derrida's is implicitly invoked in the final interview before his death. Indeed, in a discussion that ranges widely over his life's work, "Pas" is the last text Derrida mentions. And while one might hesitate to place undue emphasis on it for this reason, the reference appears in a paragraph that explicitly addresses finality and in which Derrida makes a moving farewell to life: "Everything I say—at least from 'Pas' (in *Parages*) on—about survival as a complication of the opposition life/death proceeds in me from an unconditional affirmation of life" (Derrida, *Learning to Live Finally*, 51–52).

24. Quoted in Foucault, "The Discourse on Language," 215.

25. See Katz, *Saying I No More*, 176.

26. Hill, *Beckett's Fiction*, 77, 78, 60, 61.

27. Bersani and Dutoit, *Arts of Impoverishment*, 87.

28. The most influential volume in this epistemological shift is Clifford and Marcus's collection, *Writing Culture*. See also Maranhão and Streck, *Translation and Ethnography*.

29. Bermann, introduction, 6, 4, 2.

30. Spivak, "Translating into English," 95, 99.

31. Judith Butler argues that a certain unnarratability of oneself is the condition of ethics and responsibility. "My account of myself breaks down," Butler says, and this "non-narrativizable" account of oneself is what ties the self to the other. "I find that my very formation implicates the other in me, that my own foreignness to myself is, paradoxically, the source of my ethical connection with others" (*Giving an Account of Oneself*, 83–84).

32. Barthes, *S/Z*, 105.

33. Virilio, *Open Sky*, 16, 64, 23, 65.

34. Enda Duffy's *The Speed Notebook* is the most recent contribution to the topic of velocity in modernity, delivering a paean to an "adrenaline aesthetics" (9) that counters the supposedly "unbearable languor" and "dreary dawdlings" of much modernist literature (7). For Duffy, speed has the advantage of "refusing critical distance" by promoting an entirely new sensorium of embodied experience, thereby challenging theories of alienation, moralizing discourse, ideology-critique, and what he sweepingly calls "Western post-Cartesian consciousness" (10). But the claim to a new embodied vitality is not without its own nostalgic tropes: "What we need to recapture is the excitement of those who drove the first cars or saw one raise the dust on a village street, for whom twenty-five miles an hour was intensely fast" (5).

35. Chambers, *Loiterature*, 89.

36. On Bataille and Blanchot's shared notion of transgression as impossibility, see Gregg, *Maurice Blanchot*, esp. 10–17.

37. Derrida, *The Truth in Painting*, 270 (translation modified); *La Vérité en peinture*, 309.

38. Derrida, *The Truth in Painting*, 276 (translation modified; Derrida's translators suggest the term "paralys" for *paralyse*).

39. Chiasmus, essentially a rhetorical figure of inverted parallelism, has a long history deriving from classical scripture, rhetoric, and literature. As invoked by Derrida, chiasmus is no mere rhetorical ornament, but reflects instead the more important role it plays as a structuring principle of thought and composition. As Rodolphe Gasché puts it, "the chiasm is a form through which differences are installed, preserved, and overcome in one grounding unity of totality." In this sense, chiasmus represents the very "matrix of dialectics" ("Reading Chiasms," 274) that Derrida sets out to challenge. Accordingly, Derrida sees chiasmus not as a harmonious and symmetrical structure, but rather as fundamentally asymmetrical, and its crisscross structure as the figure of a differential *trace* hidden

within its apparently polarized structure. As Gasché says, quoting Derrida, "this asymmetry becomes visible . . . only if one understands the chiasm's making of cross-connections—and the double participation that it implies—no longer as the mixing of previously separate elements . . . but rather as a *referral back* (*renvoi*) 'to a *same* that is not the identical, to the common element or medium of any possible dissociation.'" Read this way, chiasmus is not a figure of self-reflexive totality or doubled identity, but betrays a prior difference that *crosses out* the identity of each term. "No unity engendered chiastically includes within itself the play of difference to which it must refer in order to constitute itself" (275). See also Bennington, "X." Derrida provides a diagram of what he calls the "double chiasmatic invagination of edges" in his essay "The Law of Genre." See Derrida, "The Law of Genre," 71. Several different manuscript versions of this image are housed in the Jacques Derrida Archive at the University of California, Irvine. My thanks to Amelia Acker for informing me of these images.

40. Derrida, *The Truth in Painting*, 376 (translation modified). "Le piège marche toujours dans l'entrelacs, soit qu'il fasse marcher, laisse marcher ou qu'il paralyse" (Derrida, *La Vérité en peinture*, 430).

41. Derrida, *Of Grammatology*, 107, 108.

42. In a striking case of cultural translation, the English word "trace" retains its obsolete meaning as "path" via a French word used to designate Native American trails in North America, such as the Natchez Trace. Spivak's own translation of Derrida's French "trace" as "track" and "trace" extends this secondary derivation of the "aboriginal" pathway.

43. Rosaldo, *Culture and Truth*, 69.

44. Derrida, *Mémoires*, 132.

45. See Lévi-Strauss, "Jean-Jacques Rousseau," 35.

46. See *Of Grammatology*, 141–316. In light of the paralyzing logic we have been pursuing here, it is striking that the text where Lévi-Strauss claims Rousseau as the father of ethnology focuses on the scene in the perambulatory *Reveries* in which Rousseau is struck down and knocked unconscious. The scene from the "Second Walk" is justly famous and has provoked innumerable commentaries. Todorov faults Lévi-Strauss for presenting a portrait of Rousseau that hardly resembles him (Todorov, *On Human Diversity*, 77). Lévi-Strauss, of course, is not unaware of the paradox of choosing the scene of the fall as emblematic of Rousseau's promenades, nor is he blind to the contradictions of the philosopher's torturous and conflicted work, which attempts to ground a claim to society from the position of absolute alienation. But in pointing to the "dilemma" of the author's position, Lévi-Strauss formulates it in the somewhat pat and reassuring

form of chiastic symmetry: "man can at least reverse the poles of the dilemma and *seek the society of nature to meditate there on the nature of society*" (Lévi-Strauss, "Jean-Jacques Rousseau," 40). This "indissoluble message," as Lévi-Strauss puts it, seems to gloss the bind of his chiastic formula, as "indissoluble" is linked to the common etymological root of "solve" and "loosen." But following the logic of these figures of weaving, the implications of Rousseau's text are otherwise paralyzing. Indeed, the *Reveries* pursue a complex—if symptomatic—inquiry into the figures of the social *bond* that offer no resolution, but instead weave the insistent figure of a paralyzing *stricture*. Thus, the *Reveries* begin by claiming that men have "broken all the threads [*les liens*] that bound me to them" (Rousseau, *Reveries of the Solitary Walker*, 27; *Les Rêveries du promeneur solitaire*, 55), and Rousseau struggles to account for the contradiction that if he is happy "in spite of them [*malgré eux*]" (34; 63), it is also *thanks to them* that he has found his beneficent solitude; as Rousseau himself admits, his pleasant walks are "joys I owed to my persecutors [*des jouissances que je devais à mes persécuteurs*]" (36; 65). Consequently, even as Rousseau looks back on his former life, in which "I only enmeshed myself further [*m'enlacer d'avantage*] in my efforts to be free" (28; 56), his writing betrays a constant reiteration of a bind he cannot account for: "even in the midst of my suffering," Rousseau says, "I feel a sort of relief [*même au milieu de ma souffrance je ne laisse pas de me sentir soulagé*]" (29; 58). It is precisely such a relief in suffering that is recounted in the narrative of the fall. But Rousseau's willfully paradoxical formulation here invokes by connotation a "laisse" (leash) that persistently re-enlaces what Rousseau would loosen, and vice versa. Similarly, Rousseau says, "By stripping me of everything, they have left themselves unarmed [*en ne me laissant rien ils se sont tout ôté à eux-mêmes*]" (29; 57). Significantly enough, a *leash* is a tie that binds, but loosely—which perhaps invites a rereading of the opening line of *The Social Contract*. All of Rousseau's promenades bear the trace of this "laisse" that ties him to the other, not, as Lévi-Strauss has it, as a moral philosopher, or "founder of the sciences of man," but as an author enmeshed in alterity beyond figuration, and whose paralyses are allegorized in the theme of the fall.

47. Clifford, *The Predicament of Culture*, 343.

48. Toussaint's "vacillations" and "hesitations" lend his revolutionary story its truly "tragic" dimension, as James argues. Caught between his allegiance to French ideals of liberty and his war against French slavery, Toussaint acutely felt the "impossible position" in which his people were placed (James, *The Black Jacobins*, 267). As a result, Toussaint lost the faith of his followers and hampered his own revolutionary actions; he "became the embodiment of vacillation" (290). But, as James argues, "His very hesitations were a sign of the superior cast of his mind"; indeed, they raise Toussaint to the status of the tragic heroes of literature (281).

49. Kincaid, "In History," 6.

50. Spivak, *A Critique of Postcolonial Reason*, xi.

51. Spivak's running footnote mimes a persistent textual technique in Derrida. In *Aporias*, for instance, Derrida relegates to an impossible footnote what is nothing less than his entire intellectual career: "I would like to situate, from very far away and very high up, in the most abstract way, in a few sentences, and in the form of an index or a long footnote at the bottom of the page, the places of aporia in which I have found myself, let us say, regularly tied up, indeed, paralyzed" (13).

52. Following Derrida's model of "arche-violence," the problematic "appearance" of Kincaid in Columbus's history would reflect the insight that Antigua is "incapable of appearing to itself except in its own disappearance." See Derrida, *Of Grammatology*, 112.

53. Spivak, *In Other Worlds*, 263.

54. Glissant, *Caribbean Discourse*, 26, 9.

55. Caruth, "Trauma and Experience," 10.

56. Kincaid, *A Small Place*, 32.

57. I draw here on Dina Al-Kassim's theorization of the *rant* in *On Pain of Speech* as a "voice of enmity and embrace, which makes of its own misfiring the claiming of a new subjectivity" (8). Inflected by a Foucauldian analysis of speech as subjection, Al-Kassim's theorization of resistant address challenges the presumptions of sovereignty, autonomy, and interlocutive transparency on which political speech conventionally relies. "As resistant speech, the rant must invent its own terms from a censored encyclopedia of experience and social naming, which is to say that the rant materializes a speaking subject at the limit of intelligibility where none is authorized.... Radically dependent upon a particular history of injury, the rant's abject appeal flows from and indeed fosters the singularity of a speech that is imbricated and embedded in subjection" (10).

58. Cited in Laplanche, *Essays on Otherness*, 157.

59. I provide a more extensive account of Laplanche in chapter 1. Here, let me indicate the near convergence of Derrida and Laplanche on the question of translation. For Laplanche, the primary task of the patient is to translate messages deposited in the unconscious. These messages, however, are always already translations themselves of an otherness that remains out of reach of the patient. The "primacy of the other" in the psychoanalytic subject thus condemns him to *retranslate* and *detranslate* an original translation that is always secondary and belated, and thus foreign to him even in his most intimate fantasies. Derrida similarly undoes the possibility of an original translation, insisting on the foreignness of the proper, such that language is always already a translation of itself:

"translation does not pass among various languages. It separates translation from itself, it separates translatability within one and the same language" (*Aporias*, 10). For Derrida, this foreignness of the proper will always bear the traits of *paralysis*. Laplanche, for his part, claims the model of *analysis*, which, interestingly enough, he allies with deconstruction: "Analysis," Laplanche says, "is first and foremost a method of deconstruction (ana-lysis)" ("Interpretation," in *Essays on Otherness*, 165). Laplanche and Derrida converge and diverge in these different models of binding and unbinding. One may usefully compare Derrida's discussion of Freud's "knots" in *Resistances* to Laplanche's discussion of "unweaving" as analysis in "Time and the Other" (in *Essays on Otherness*, 234–59).

60. Ortega y Gasset, *The Dehumanization of Art*, 65.

61. This quality is already present in Conrad's first novel, *Almayer's Folly*. As Conrad's editor remarks, "In Almayer's story, . . . adventure- or quest-movement is replaced by a frustratingly static and motionless condition of waiting" (Knowles, introduction, xxiii).

62. Lyotard, *The Postmodern Condition*, xxiv. It should be pointed out that Lyotard's oft-quoted formulation is prefaced with an important qualification; as he says, "Simplifying to the extreme, I define *postmodern* as incredulity toward metanarratives."

63. Nerlich, *Ideology of Adventure*, 59.

64. Jon Krakauer's international bestseller *Into Thin Air* is a recent exemplar of this tradition, and it owes its success not only to its bracing narrative of a deadly catastrophe on Mount Everest, but also to its portrait of adventure threatened by the corruptions of commercialism, mass tourism and technology. What the author calls the "paralyzing force" of his trauma (319) culminates in the scene describing his guide, frozen in place near the summit, dying yet connected by satellite phone to his wife half a world away. *Into Thin Air* demonstrates that adventure persists—indeed thrives—on its own obsolescence. Fittingly, the book begins with an epigraph from Ortega y Gassett. Sherry Ortner's ethnographic study *Life and Death on Mt. Everest* is an excellent counterpoint to the adventure narrative, providing a rich account of the power and politics at play in the cultural encounter between mountaineers and Sherpas. A short bibliography of this field might also include Laplanche's *Life and Death in Psychoanalysis* to unpack the ramifications of one of Ortner's quotes: "a climber on the upper part of Everest is like a sick man climbing in a dream" (9).

65. Simon, *The Flanders Road*, 308.

66. Zweig, *The Adventurer*, 3.

67. See Freud, "Notes on a Case of Obsessional Neurosis."

68. See Sarraute, *Tropismes*, in *Oeuvres complètes*.

69. Paul Morand's *Eloge du repos* (In Praise of Rest) is characteristic of this Freudian turn in French literature: "We are beginning to realize—thanks in part to psychoanalysis—that if an entire continent is in this way a victim of speed, it is because it is fleeing itself and seeks, more than money, speed as such, as a means not to think and to avoid a certain number of painful problems and hidden complexes. *Délit de fuite*" (121).

70. Leiris, *Manhood*, 155.

71. Lacan, "Aggressivity in Psychoanalysis," in *Ecrits: A Selection*, 17.

72. Lacan, "Aggressivity in Psychoanalysis," 22.

73. Mannoni, *Prospero and Caliban*, 21.

74. Mannoni's account of the psychology of colonization is nonetheless marred by his own claims to mastery, notably in attributing a pathological "dependency complex" to the colonized. Mannoni would later renounce the notion of "dependence" in an essay that critically revisits his book. See "The Decolonization of Myself," in *Clefs pour l'Imaginaire*, 291. Frantz Fanon's *Black Skin, White Masks* would level the most famous objections to this aspect of Mannoni's work. Interestingly, Fanon's polemic against Mannoni, by failing to give the latter's analysis its due, unwittingly stages its own dynamic of misrecognition and rivalry, as Emily Apter has argued (*Continental Drift*, 77–95).

75. MacCannell, *The Tourist*, 3.

76. Culler, "The Semiotics of Tourism," 165.

77. See Alloula, *The Colonial Harem*.

78. The role of disavowal in the colonial postcard brings out the insecurity on which its desiring thrust is founded. These complacent stereotypes of France's golden age of colonialism thus bear witness, despite themselves, to a certain disillusionment. For this very reason, however, the stereotypes are fundamentally intractable; the logic of disavowal holds that the compensation must be able to stand up to the loss of belief. In the Imaginary, any threat to the integrity of the self is matched by a more imperious image, and in this way, disillusionment may ultimately serve only to foster grander illusions. It is suggestive then, that travel in the modern period is ostensibly characterized by disenchantment and the waning of the exotic. We have seen how this phenomenon defines touristic consciousness in its frustrated bid for authenticity. In his very disillusionment, the Orientalist traveler would hold firm to his image of the exotic other. The expression of a disappearing exotic would be the means by which he disavows the culture at hand to relegate his phantasm to a protected sphere in the past, or to a perpetual elsewhere. As such, disillusionment is a ruse—a disavowal—by which the traveler

maintains his exotic beliefs in the face of their refutation. This may clarify the ironic fact that the traveler often mourns the passing of what he may never have experienced. Lured by exotic images that hold out the promise of fulfillment, the Orientalist traveler arrives to take the measure of his disappointment, thus mourning not the place of his travels but his imaginary destination. This, then, would be the sense in which his travels are always "belated," and that he shares with touristic consciousness in general: the experience of dislocation resolves by means of a temporal alibi a split inherent to his imaginary desire.

79. The dream experience of running in place is itself mentioned in the scene from which Zeno's paradox derives in *The Iliad* of Homer. On the relation between Zeno and his literary sources, see Milner, "La Technique littéraire des paradoxes de Zénon."

80. Joan Copjec, *Read My Desire*, 52.

81. Lacan, *Encore*, 13. Cited in Copjec, *Read My Desire*, 60.

82. Milner, "La Technique littéraire des paradoxes de Zénon," 59.

83. Copjec, *Read My Desire*, 60–61.

84. See Derrida, *The Post Card*.

85. See Derrida, *Parages*, 55.

86. See Brooks, *Reading for the Plot*, 90–112.

87. One such theory is provided by Jurij Lotman, whose morphological analysis postulates a primordial mythic plot structure that doubles, significantly enough, as a travel story. In Lotman's account, the basic plot structure is generated by the binary articulation of two terms, boundary and entrance, yielding the elementary story of a subject who enters or exits a given space. Lotman's account affirms a fundamental sexual distinction that differentiates between subjects who are active and mobile, and passive and immobile: "characters can be divided into those who are mobile, who enjoy freedom with regard to plot-space, who can change their place in the structure of the artistic world and cross the frontier, the basic topological feature of this space, and those who are immobile, who represent, in fact, a function of this space" ("The Origin of Plot in the Light of Typology," 167). In this account, "woman," Lotman specifies, is assimilated to "house," "cave" and "grave," as function of the space penetrated by the masculine agent (168). Several critics have questioned the grounds for this presumption of difference and its arrogation of agency to a male subject. See, for example, Killick, "The Penetrating Intellect," 76–106; de Lauretis, "Desire in Narrative," 103–57.

88. Barthes, *A Lover's Discourse*, 13; Barthes, *Fragments d'un discours amoureux*, 471.

89. Barthes, *S/Z*, 105.

90. Derrida, *Parages*, 63.
91. On the "non-arrival," see Malabou and Derrida, *Counterpath*, 61.
92. Flaubert, *Sentimental Education*, 451.
93. Clifford, *The Predicament of Culture*, 270, cited in Jay, *Downcast Eyes*, 16.
94. Clifford, *Routes*, 26.
95. See Terdiman, *Discourse/Counter-Discourse*. Terdiman's book includes an excellent study of Flaubert's travels in the Orient. See his chapter "Ideological Voyages: On a Flaubertian Dis-orient-ation," 227–57.
96. Beckett, "The Way," 173.

1. The Muse of Paralysis

1. Barthes, *Mythologies*, Engl., 96.
2. See Gilroy, *The Black Atlantic*. For an account of the formative years of negritude and black diasporic modernism between the world wars, see Edwards, *The Practice of Diaspora*. Christopher Miller's *The French Atlantic Triangle* provides the fullest single account of the history and postcolonial legacy of the French slave trade.
3. Césaire, *Notebook of a Return to the Native Land*, 32.
4. Miller, *The French Atlantic Triangle*, 6.
5. Genet, *The Thief's Journal*, 11.
6. Foucault, "A Preface to Transgression," 35.
7. Fanon, *Black Skin, White Masks*, 133, 120, 140. Markmann's translation of Fanon's essay "L'Expérience vécue du Noir" as "The Fact of Blackness" is somewhat unfaithful to the phenomenological and psychoanalytic framework of Fanon's critical optic, though it does convey the object-like status he argues is imposed on the black by the racist white gaze.
8. Butler, *Subjects of Desire*, 9. The motif of the journey is a consistent thread in Butler's reading of Hegel. However, as she argues, the French encounter with Hegel calls that journey radically into question, to the point of undoing the premise of the traveler himself: "as Hegel's subject makes his way across the border into France, and into the twentieth century, we will see that the question of historical agency and historical experience will come to challenge that subject's well-planned itinerary. Indeed, without his progressive journey, it will become unclear whether the traveler himself can survive" (59).
9. Mellah, *Clandestin en Méditerranée*, 18.
10. Cf. Breton, "A Great Black Poet," ix–xviii.
11. Leiris, *Brisées*, 127.
12. The consolidation of this critique dates to Asad, ed., *Anthropology and the Colonial Encounter*.

13. See Clifford, *The Predicament of Culture*.
14. See Killick, "The Penetrating Intellect," 76–106.
15. Clifford, *The Predicament of Culture*, 14.
16. Fabian, *Anthropology with an Attitude*, 12.
17. Clifford, "Partial Truths," 11.
18. Clifford, *On the Edges of Anthropology*, 19.
19. Cf. Clifford, *The Predicament of Culture*.
20. Leiris, *Scraps*, 4.
21. Derrida, *Aporias*, 73–74.
22. As Derrida says, "Such is perhaps the case for every work worthy of its name: there, what puts thinking into operation exceeds its own borders or what thinking itself intends to present of these borders. The work exceeds itself, it surpasses the limits of the concept of itself that it claims to have properly while presenting itself. But if the event of this work thus exceeds its own borders . . . , then it would do so precisely at this locus where it *experiences the aporia*" (*Aporias*, 32).
23. Fineman, "The Structure of Allegorical Desire," 49.
24. See Derrida, "Tympan," in *Margins of Philosophy*, ix–xxix.
25. Derrida, *The Work of Mourning*, 34, 39.
26. Laplanche, "The Drive and the Source-Object," in *Essays on Otherness*, 132.
27. Laplanche, "A Short Treatise on the Unconscious," in *Essays on Otherness*, 92.
28. Laplanche, "The Drive and the Source-Object," in *Essays on Otherness*, 132.
29. Fletcher, "Introduction," 30.
30. Hertz, *The End of the Line*, 53, 229.
31. Laplanche, "Time and the Other," in *Essays on Otherness*, 247.
32. Fletcher, "Introduction," 14.
33. See especially Laplanche and Pontalis, "Fantasy and the Origins of Sexuality."
34. Hertz, Foreword, xx, xvii.
35. See Hertz, *The End of the Line*, 161–93.
36. For a virtually exhaustive account of how Freud's theory of the uncanny both constrains and disseminates its definition, see Royle, *The Uncanny*.
37. Derrida, "Différance," in *Margins of Philosophy*, 20.
38. Kofman, *Freud and Fiction*, 116.
39. Deleuze, "Coldness and Cruelty," 34.
40. Jensen, *Gradiva*, 107.

41. Barthes, *Fragments d'un discours amoureux*, 148.
42. Freud, "Delusions and Dreams in Jensen's *Gradiva*," 45.
43. Cited in Derrida, *Mémoires*, 61.
44. Baudelaire, *The Flowers of Evil*, 189.
45. Derrida, *Archive Fever*, 98.
46. Gautier's *Le Roman de la momie* (1858) anticipates Jensen here, and indeed outdoes him in describing a footprint in the dust that, dating back more than three thousand years into Egyptian antiquity, is found by archeologists in a newly discovered tomb. Gautier embroiders on the Baudelairean contrast between the singular *moment* and eternal presence: it is exactly "au moment de franchir le seuil" (28) that the "miraculeuse empreinte" (29) is discovered: "cette trace légère, qu'un soufflé eût balayée, a duré plus longtemps que les civilisations, que des empires, que les religions mêmes." On noting the footprint as he crosses the threshold, "prenant garde toutefois d'effacer la miraculeuse empreinte," Lord Evandale experiences, as Gautier says, "une impression singulière." The litotic *singular impression* aptly conveys the *archive fever* of the archeologist in his quest for the absolute trace that here, like the ab-original footprint in Defoe's *Robinson Crusoe*, is cast as a *singular* print, thus denying the duplicity of its printing as well as the *other* foot, unmentioned and seemingly under erasure, that would risk carrying off the trace into seriality and dissemination. In this way, the theme of sacred trespass, partaking of an imperial imaginary, nonetheless speaks to a paralyzing "pas" and an impossible transgression: an always-erased singularity crossed over and crossed out in the journey and the narrative quest.
47. Derrida, *Mémoires*, 58.
48. Gautier, "Arria Marcella," Engl., 238; "Arria Marcella," Fr., 237. Citations will be to the English edition unless otherwise noted.
49. Gautier, *Emaux et camées*, 149. This poem, as Gautier says, "résume l'idée" of the collection as a whole (221n.3).
50. On this equivocal nature of sculptural desire, see North, *The Final Sculpture*, esp. 62–82.
51. Laplanche, "Time and the Other," in *Essays on Otherness*, 234.
52. Laplanche, "Interpretation between Determinism and Hermeneutics," in *Essays on Otherness*, 152.
53. Laplanche, "Time and the Other," in *Essays on Otherness*, 258.
54. Freud, *Civilization and Its Discontents*, 18, 16.
55. Fletcher, "Introduction," 14.
56. Fineman, "The Structure of Allegorical Desire," 45.
57. The first version of "Octavie" appeared in 1842, and was later revised and

included in *Les Filles du Feu* in 1854. Gautier's "Arria Marcella" was first published in 1852.

58. "Octavie," Chambers points out, "se trouve associée, dès le début de la nouvelle, aux arrêts, aux retards, à la lenteur" (*Gérard de Nerval*, 230).

59. Nerval, *Selected Writings*, 198.

60. Jensen, *Gradiva*, 92 (my emphasis).

61. See Goethe, *Wilhelm Meister's Years*, 127. Here I must relegate to a footnote another paralyzed inheritor of Goethe's Mignon. Beckett makes an oblique reference to the song of Mignon in *Premier amour*, the first of his texts in French, and which anticipates in style and theme the great period of his first trilogy of novels. Beckett's Mignon is, however, a prostitute, and the narrator lovingly inscribes her name in cow shit, though we cannot know what exactly he writes, as her name alternates between the infantile "Lulu" and the chiastic "Anna." What might seem a willfully scatological deflation of the poetic Mignon—the object of a virtual cult in the arts of the nineteenth century—is in fact, as in Goethe, a searching meditation on memory, national identity, and exile, though challenging the structuring and developmental role of *Bildung* in narrative. See Beckett, "First Love," and *Premier amour*. In a brilliant reading of *Premier amour*, David Lloyd argues that the text prefigures the stakes of postcolonial writing, understood as a means of unworking alienation, but without opting for the consolations of identity and the dangerous lure of native autonomy: "Beckett's own oeuvre, as inaugurated by *First Love/Premier Amour*, stands as the most exhaustive dismantling of the logic of identity that at every level structures and maintains the post-colonial moment" (Lloyd, *Anomalous States*, 56).

62. Nerval, *Selected Writings*, 36. 7 (translation modified). "Reconnais-tu le TEMPLE, au péristyle immense, / Et les citrons amers où s'imprimaient tes dents, / Et la grotte, fatale aux hôtes imprudents, / Où du dragon vaincu dort l'antique semence?"

63. Nerval, "Isis," 1:327.

64. Doane aptly points to a *disseminating* power of the femme fatale: "The power accorded to the femme fatale is a function of fears linked to the notions of uncontrollable drives, the fading of subjectivity, and the loss of conscious agency—all themes of the emergent theories of psychoanalysis. But the femme fatale is situated as evil and is frequently punished or killed. Her textual eradication involves a desperate reassertion of control on the part of a threatened male subject.... Nevertheless, the representation—like any representation—is not totally under the control of its producers and, once disseminated, comes to take on a life of its own" (*Femmes Fatales*, 2–3).

65. Sieburth, "Introductory Note," 64.

66. Gradiva is an obsessive reference for the surrealists, Dalì in particular. Robbe-Grillet, for his part, has devoted several works to reimagining Jensen's story, including *Topology of a Phantom City* (1976), the screenplay *C'est Gradiva qui vous appelle* (2002), and the film *Gradiva* (2006).

67. Echoes of Nerval's paralyzing impression are very strong in Bonnefoy's spellbinding *L'Arrière-pays*, a text that is part travel narrative, autobiography, and aesthetic theory. *L'Arrière-pays* not only follows in the wake of Bonnefoy's Romantic predecessor, but also in the wake of his own abandoned text *Le Voyageur*. Destroyed but not forgotten, *Le Voyageur* haunts *L'Arrière-pays* as its missing origin. And in an abyssal Nervalian fashion, that absence covers another: the unwritten first page of *Le Voyageur*, in which, Bonnefoy says, he failed to pen "les origines du voyageur" (*L'Arrière-pays*, 86). It is insistently toward such missing "origins" that Bonnefoy's *L'Arrière-pays* is oriented, and in so doing he reprises many of the themes of our Pompeian fictions. One such origin is the poet's memory of a story he read in childhood, and which he imagines to be, like his *Voyageur*, lost forever. (The text is in fact Léon Lambry's *Dans les sables rouges*). The story recounts the journey of an archeologist in the Gobi desert, following the traces of a lost culture, which turns out to be a forgotten outpost of the Roman Empire whose residents survived millennia by going underground. The survival of the past is embodied, as in Nerval, Gautier, and Jensen, in a young girl, "vêtue comme on l'était à Rome," before whom the archeologist is "paralysé par l'étonnement" (*L'Arrière-pays*, 38). But the truly paralyzing implications of Bonnefoy's journey back in time are realized only later in *L'Arrière-pays*, under the influence of nothing other than the statue of the Sphinx of Naxos. Bonnefoy carries the enigma of the Sphinx's face back with him from Greece to Italy, where he imagines writing, under the cover of fiction, the theory of a mysterious "sentiment inconnu," evidenced in the faces of the art of antiquity and the renaissance. What Bonnefoy calls "ce texte continu, signifiant, paralysant, que j'imaginais d'écrire" (148) seems to be, no less than Hanold's, under the sway of a powerful delusion. But it is also for that reason a haunting testimony to the motivating force of primal fantasy in poetic art. The classic figure of the enigmatic Sphinx gives way, in Bonnefoy's "sentiment inconnu," to that of a Laplanchian enigma from childhood, motor of the drives and wellspring of the poet's yearning, exile and nostalgia, "ce besoin de l'ailleurs, que rien ne comble" (57).

68. Jacques Derrida, *Parages*, 109.

69. Nerval, "Isis," 321.

70. Nerval, "Isis," 322.

71. See Behdad, *Belated Travelers*.

72. Prosper Mérimée combines these two threads in his fantastic tale of 1837, "La Vénus d'Ille" (The Venus of Ille). In the story, a recently unearthed statue of Venus apparently comes to life to crush a man in his bed on his wedding night. The tale is narrated by an archaeologist from Paris, in whom one recognizes features of the author. Appointed Inspector of National Monuments, Mérimée inherits the preservationist project championed by Hugo, and shares with Gautier a taste for the fantastic theme of the living statue.

73. On the role of archaeology in defining a postrevolutionary "secular theology of memory," see Blix, *Paris to Pompeii*.

74. Al-Kassim, *On Pain of Speech*, 151.

75. This is a case made forcefully by Madeleine Dobie who, indicating Nerval and Gautier in particular, states that "writers who took an oppositional stance on domestic matters actively *advocated* colonial expansion into the Orient" (*Foreign Bodies*, 135.

76. Sieburth, "Leiris/Nerval," 56.

77. Gradhiva is the anagram of *Groupe de Recherches et d'Analyses Documentaires sur l'Histoire et les Variations de l'Anthropologie*. On the founding of the journal and its name, see Jamin, "Les Chemins de la Gradiva," 1–6.

78. Cf. Clifford, *The Predicament of Culture*, 117–51.

79. Leiris, *Scraps*, 49.

2. Horizon of Conquest

1. Deleuze and Parnet, *Dialogues*, 37.

2. Nizan, *Aden, Arabie*, 158.

3. Maupassant, *Bel-Ami*, 5–6.

4. Indeed, this demystification that negates the adventurous traveler seems a feminizing castration. There is, then, a misogynistic reflex in the deflation of Bel-Ami at the hands of a woman, as if the novel's critique of the adventurer found compensation in blaming the other sex. It is tempting, then, to link Bel-Ami's ultimate betrayal of the editor's wife to this misogynistic reflex. As author of his fictional *arriviste*, bound to the norms of adventurous storytelling he seeks to ironize, Maupassant himself cannot settle accounts with the masculine thrust of narrative. If to negate travel is to tamper with the basic coordinates of narrative, Maupassant wins back his story through his hero's ultimate victory over the editor's wife and by his grotesque Parisian apotheosis. Colonial travel, as a result, is not so much negated as disavowed, its denial compensated by the hero's story of vindication.

5. Fromentin, *Between Sea and Sahara*, 114; *Une Année dans le Sahel*, 294. Anne-Marie Christin begins her excellent book on Fromentin with this quote, and the paradox of a traveler who denies travel has interested many of Fromentin's readers (*Fromentin conteur d'espace*). Barbara Wright's otherwise useful book is too hasty in ascribing a "harmony of opposites" and a "synthesis" of travel and stasis in Fromentin's work (*Eugène Fromentin*, 14).

6. See Rosaldo, *Culture and Truth*, 68–87.

7. Fromentin, *Between Sea and Sahara*, 1.

8. Fromentin, *Un Été dans le Sahara*, 176.

9. Fromentin, *Between Sea and Sahara*, 43; *Une Année dans le Sahel*, 228.

10. Fromentin, *Correspondance*, 1:684.

11. Sagnes, "Les Voyages de Fromentin en Algérie," 1265.

12. Fromentin, *Un Été dans le Sahara*, 181.

13. Quoted in Cardonne, introduction, 11.

14. Djebar, *Fantasia*, 226. On intertextual links between Djebar and Fromentin, see also Donadey, *Recasting Postcolonialism*, esp. 63–94.

15. Derrida, *Aporias*, 33, 34.

16. Jacques Derrida, "Faith and Knowledge," 7.

17. Fromentin himself makes a clear distinction between the journeying form of *A Summer in the Sahara* and the more domestic *Between Sea and Sahara* at the outset of the latter text: "I want to try to be *at home* on this bit of foreign soil where up to now I've only passed through" (*Between Sea and Sahara*, 4).

18. Fromentin, *Correspondance*, 1:689.

19. For an account of the solidarity of literary "adventure" with capitalist ideology, see Nerlich, *Ideology of Adventure*.

20. Sagnes, "Les Voyages de Fromentin en Algérie," 1265.

21. Fromentin, *Correspondance*, 1:688.

22. Said, *Culture and Imperialism*, 23.

23. Barthes, "The Death of the Author," 142.

24. Memmi, *The Colonizer and the Colonized*, 17.

25. Laplanche and Pontalis, "Fantasy and the Origins of Sexuality," 26.

26. The story of Haoûa in *Une Année dans le Sahel* derives from Du Mesnil's manuscript for "Zorr," reproduced in Fromentin's *Oeuvres complètes*, 1229–48. See editor's notes on 1358.

27. See editor's notes to "Zorr," in Fromentin, *Oeuvres complètes*, 1735.

28. Fromentin, *Between Sea and Sahara*, 94.

29. Barthes, "The Death of the Author," 142.

30. Fromentin, *Correspondance*, 1:595.

31. One might cite in this respect André Gide's sharing of the prostitute Mériem with a friend in *Si le grain ne meurt*, the telling of which would, in turn, inspire friends at home to set out to find her. See Gide, *Si le grain ne meurt*, 573–74.

32. Fromentin, *Un Eté dans le Sahara*, 176, 110.

33. Fromentin's colonial perspective displays an interesting tension between the masterful view from on high and the pleasures of an interior space coded as feminine. The harem and the elevated view converge in Fromentin's letters, where, describing the architecture of the houses of Algiers, he evokes a room "right at the very summit of these houses" (*Correspondance*, 1:607). Fromentin indulges in a reverie of Oriental pleasures as he imagines the interior décor, as well as the perspective from this elevated space: "And from within this charming nest where it is always dark and cool, somebody, *Zuleika* perhaps, watches" (1:608). Fromentin asks his friend, "Have you never, as a child, dreamt of the secret pleasures of such sheltered spots?" These *jouissances furtives* are further developed: "Singular pleasure," Fromentin says, "mixing together the joys of hiding, of sensuality and a good deal of indolence" (1:608). What Fromentin conveys in this passage is an identification with the pleasure of captivity, a pleasure both infantile and feminine: "During my previous stay in Algiers, I was with a woman, in her little room high up at the top of a Moorish house in the highest neighborhood in town, such that, from her little window, invisible to those who, down in the port or in the square, might have looked our way, we could, however, see and take in with one look all the animation of the city, the port, and the harbor.—I felt then the pleasure I have spoken of" (1:608). What is perhaps most insidious here is how Fromentin's passive spectatorship nonetheless accords with, while dissimulating, the power of the gaze of surveillance and appropriation.

34. Fromentin, *Une Année dans le Sahel*, 294 (my translation).

35. Fromentin, *Un Eté dans le Sahara*, 67.

36. Lorcin, *Imperial Identities*, 132.

37. Daumas, *Le Grand désert*, xii.

38. For an account of this military history, see Porch, *The Conquest of the Sahara*. A broader historical record is provided in Durou, *L'Exploration du Sahara*. Peter Bloom gives a fascinating account of the role of French automotive companies in promoting trans-Saharan transport in "Trans-Saharan Automotive Cinema," 139–56.

39. Lafouge, *Etude sur l'orientalisme d'Eugène Fromentin*, 97.

40. Fromentin, *Un Eté dans le Sahara*, 164.

41. Fromentin, *Correspondance*, 1:963.

42. Barthes, *The Eiffel Tower and Other Mythologies*, 15; "La Tour Eiffel," 1390.

43. Barthes, *The Eiffel Tower and Other Mythologies*, 45.

44. The narrative potential of such digressive and wandering "loiterature" in Barthes and others are extensively explored by Ross Chambers. See Chambers, *Loiterature*.

45. Barthes, "Fromentin: *Dominique*," 98; "Fromentin: «Dominique»," 163.

46. Fromentin, *Dominique*, Engl., 148; *Dominique*, Fr., 484.

47. Richard, *Littérature et sensation*, 247.

48. Loutfi, *Littérature et Colonialisme*, 47.

49. Foucault, "Questions on Geography," 68.

50. Derrida, *Writing and Difference*, 95.

51. Pratt, *Imperial Eyes*, 61.

52. Fromentin, *Correspondance*, 1:957.

53. Caillié, *Travels through Central Africa to Timbuktoo*, 1:1. Caillié was the first European to travel to Timbuktu and return safely; he was also one of the first to cross the Sahara, traveling north from Timbuktu to Morocco in 1828. The Société Géographique de Paris awarded him ten thousand francs upon his return, a prize indicative of the commercial interests behind his pathbreaking discoveries.

54. Waberi, *Aux Etats-Unis d'Afrique*, 29. Waberi's citation alters Caillié's text slightly; whereas Caillié says that Timbuktu is the "objet des recherches des nations civilisées de l'Europe" (Caillié, *Journal de Voyage à Temboctou et à Jenné*, 206), Waberi has him say that it is the "objet de convoitise des nations indigentes d'Europe" (29). *Convoitise* (lust) might well be seen as a valid gloss of Caillié's euphemistic *recherches*, while the replacement of *civilisées* by *indigentes* (destitute), with its sly connotation of *indigène*, carries the full force of Waberi's satirical reversal of values. And yet, *indigentes* is faithful to Caillié in that it casts him and his culture in the very guise the explorer adopted in order to penetrate unnoticed into the African interior: that of an indigent Egyptian trying to make his way home.

55. Caillié, *Travels through Central Africa to Timbuktoo*, 2:49.

56. See Saint-Exupéry, *Terre des hommes*. The romance of this ordeal of travel continues to have a hold on contemporary "adventure" discourse; *Outside* magazine ranks *Terre des hommes* first among the travelogues of our time (Wieners, "The 25 (Essential) Books").

57. See Fromentin, "Notes et variantes," 1308.

58. Fromentin, *Un Eté dans le Sahara*, 86.

59. Fromentin, "Notes et variantes," 1308.

60. Fromentin, *Correspondance*, 1:957, 1332.

61. Cited in Thompson and Wright, *La Vie et l'oeuvre d'Eugène Fromentin*, 302.

62. Fromentin, *Un Eté dans le Sahara*, 183.

63. Fromentin, *Between Sea and Sahara*, 39 (translation modified); *Une Année dans le Sahel*, 224.

64. Fromentin, *Un Eté dans le Sahara*, 126.

65. Fromentin, *Correspondance*, 1:312.

66. Fromentin, *Between Sea and Sahara*, 67.

67. Fromentin, *Un Eté dans le Sahara*, 65.

68. Fromentin, *Between Sea and Sahara*, 128.

69. Sagnes, "Les Voyages de Fromentin en Algérie," 1253.

70. Bhabha, *The Location of Culture*, 129, 132, 125.

71. Fromentin, *Un Eté dans le Sahara*, 14.

72. Fromentin, *Correspondance*, 1:713.

73. Fromentin, *Lettres de jeunesse*, 333.

74. Fromentin, *Between Sea and Sahara*, 130; *Une Année dans le Sahel*, 308.

75. Barthèlemy, *Fromentin et l'écriture du désert*, 13.

76. Fromentin, "Notes et variantes," 1288.

77. Fromentin, *Un Eté dans le Sahara*, 40.

78. Thompson and Wright, *La Vie et l'oeuvre d'Eugène Fromentin*, 87.

79. Freud, *Beyond the Pleasure Principle*, 35.

80. Kant, *Critique of Judgment*, 115.

81. See Žižek, *The Sublime Object of Ideology*, esp. 201–31.

82. Lyotard, *Lessons on the Analytic of the Sublime*, 150.

83. As Richard Boothby puts it, "Freud is continually drawn toward the very threshold of representation, that outer boundary of the thinkable at which the structures of psychic life trail off into a reservoir of forces that remain active but relatively devoid of form" (*Death and Desire*, 102).

84. Derrida, *The Truth in Painting*, 42.

85. Derrida, *Aporias*, 32.

86. Hertz, *The End of the Line*, 53.

87. Hertz finds confirmation of this insistent and pervasive predicament in Julia Kristeva's theorization of the pre-Oedipal. Before the drama of Oedipal identification and rivalry, Kristeva argues, the subject would have enacted an initial differentiation between itself and the mother's body, in a double gesture that acknowledges difference and denies separation. What Kristeva calls "the archaic modality of the paternal function" (cited in Hertz, *The End of the Line*, 232) would continue to bear its duplicitous trace beneath and before the stabilizing function of subsequent lines of demarcation that assure the self of its illusory integrity. As Hertz makes clear, the passage beyond the problematic limit, for the

child and for the adult who reenacts it, usually entails a violent reflex of abjection and scapegoating, and this serves Kristeva in a feminist project of retrieving the abjected feminine. Fromentin's transgression of the harem and his portrayal of Hawa bear the marks of this abjecting reflex.

88. Levinas, "Philosophy and the Idea of Infinity," 50.

89. Coetzee, *White Writing*, 61–62. In a nice rhetorical turn, Coetzee figures this crucial political/aesthetic distinction as *chiastic*: his inverted clauses cross each other in a pairing that is not simply oppositional or symmetrical. The distinction, in other words, is both *crossed over* and *crossed out*. The paralyzing consequences of such a limit are compellingly rendered in *Waiting for the Barbarians*, which offers a searching postcolonial development on "the limits of the Empire" and the receding frontier. See Coetzee, *Waiting for the Barbarians*, 70.

90. Derrida, *Archive Fever*, 91.

91. Christin, *Fromentin conteur d'espace*, 156.

92. See Wright, *Eugène Fromentin*, 21.

93. We have seen in chapter 1 how the motif of Gradiva's footprint serves to explain the paralyzing logic of a number of traveling stories, and we might add *Dominique*'s Madeleine to our host of paralyzing muses. In a key scene in the novel, Madeleine leaves her footprints as she walks in the wet soil, and Dominique is transfixed by this "delicate trail [*cette trace fragile*]." Here the motif of the "impression" is insistent: "Madeleine walked lightly on the sodden roads, leaving the print of her narrow shoes on the soft earth at every step [*A chaque pas, elle y laissait dans la terre molle la forme imprimée de sa chaussure étroite à talons saillants*]." This trace is both fixating and motivating: "My eyes followed this delicate trail [*Je regardais cette trace fragile, je la suivais*]." A characteristic desire to fix what is transitory is expressed in this "wake [*sillage*]" of his beloved in "the very soil where I was born." A sign of what is unique in his beloved, the footprint, like a character of typeface, also prints a series of iterations. The fixating trace is thus also a trail that defies the stasis of a present: "I should have liked it to stay fixed forever, so that . . . it might bear witness to her presence [*J'aurais souhaité qu'elle restât toujours incrustée, comme des témoignages de présence*]" (Fromentin, *Dominique*, Engl., 153; *Dominique*, Fr., 488. Jean-Pierre Richard sees this scene as emblematic of what he calls Fromentin's morose "poésie du sillon." However, Derrida's trace as *impression* allows us to read, beneath the novel's narrative of masochism, abnegation, and nostalgia, a more complex logic of archive fever in *Dominique*. It will take Beckett's *Premier amour* to mine the irony of such a mark of the beloved in the muck. See chapter 1, note 61.

94. See Apter, *Continental Drift*, 195–211.

95. Fromentin, *Un Eté dans le Sahara*, 164.

96. Derrida, *Aporias*, 33.

97. To trace the exigency of this idea of experience one may go back to Derrida's first essay on Levinas in *Writing and Difference*, where he faults Levinas for a certain "empiricism" in the notion of the experience of alterity. For Derrida, alterity is undergone in and as the very interruption of experience. Significantly, this essay, one of Derrida's most important, concludes in the entanglement of a paralyzing chiasmus. See Derrida, "Violence and Metaphysics," in *Writing and Difference*, 152–53.

98. Fabian, *Time and the Other*, x.

99. See Clancy-Smith, *Rebel and Saint*, 91.

100. See Fromentin, "La Fin du ramadan," 866–67.

101. Behdad, *Belated Travelers*, 15.

102. Coetzee, *Waiting for the Barbarians*, 70.

103. Edmond de Goncourt gives an account of this power of Fromentin's recollection. See Thompson and Wright, *La Vie et l'oeuvre d'Eugène Fromentin*, 258.

104. Pratt, *Imperial Eyes*, 7.

105. Djebar, *Fantasia*, 46, 45.

106. Derrida, *Mémoires*, 60.

107. Nancy, "The Sublime Offering," 44.

108. Maupassant, *Au soleil*, 87.

109. Augé, *L'Impossible voyage*.

110. Maupassant, *Selected Short Stories*, 314.

111. Fromentin, *Between Sea and Sahara*, 69.

112. Rosello, *Postcolonial Hospitality*, 176. On the "interchangeability" of guest and host, see chapter 4.

113. One passage in particular uncannily anticipates its author's fate. "I . . . struggle madly," the protagonist says, "hampered by that terrible helplessness which paralyses us in dreams" (Maupassant, *Selected Short Stories*, 316).

114. Djebar, *Women of Algiers in Their Apartment*, 137.

3. Slow Progress

1. Blanchot, "The Ease of Dying," 122.

2. In the time since this essay first appeared, several important English translations of Paulhan have been released, as well as a number of significant critical volumes. See especially Syrotinski, *Defying Gravity*; Syrotinski, "The Power of Rhetoric"; Milne, *The Extreme In-Between*.

3. Paulhan joined the *Nouvelle Revue Française* in 1920 as secretary, then served as editor-in-chief and director from 1925 to 1940, and from 1953 to 1963.

4. Hollier, *The College of Sociology*, 304.

5. Although drafted as early as 1910, "Aytré qui perd l'habitude" was not published until 1921 in *Nouvelle Revue Française* 89 (February 1921), and was subsequently published separately (Brussels: Editions de la Nouvelle Revue Belgique, 1943).

6. Paulhan, *La Vie est pleine de choses redoutables*, 135.

7. Paulhan, "Aytré Who Gets Out of the Habit," in *Progress in Love*, 80.

8. Miller, *Theories of Africans*, 24.

9. Blanchot, "The Paradox of Aytré," 68.

10. It seems fitting that a recent French edition of "Aytré" includes Blanchot's essay within the binding, as if it were a belated chapter to this tale of complicity and failed detection. See Paulhan, *Aytré qui perd l'habitude*.

11. The motif of this reflexive turn finds its exemplary formulation in "Orpheus' Gaze." See Blanchot, *The Space of Literature*, 171–76.

12. Blanchot, "The Ease of Dying," 127.

13. Blanchot, *The Space of Literature*, 54.

14. De Man, *Blindness and Insight*, 63.

15. See, for example, "The Most Profound Question."

16. Paulhan, "Progress in Love on the Slow Side," in *Progress in Love*, 8.

17. See Blanchot, "How Is Literature Possible?" Blanchot's "Comment la littérature est-elle possible?" was originally published in the *Journal des débats* in 1941 and later included in *Faux Pas*.

18. See Paulhan, *The Flowers of Tarbes*; Paulhan, *Les Fleurs de Tarbes*.

19. Blanchot, "The Paradox of Aytré," 72.

20. On the relation of possibility and impossibility in Blanchot, see Gasché, "The Felicities of Paradox," 34–69.

21. Blanchot, "Mystery in Literature," in *The Work of Fire*, 56.

22. Derrida has explored this "paralyzing" logic in his essay on Blanchot, titled "Pas." See Derrida, *Parages*. See also the discussion in my introduction.

23. Paulhan, *The Flowers of Tarbes*, 62.

24. Paulhan, "Progress in Love on the Slow Side," in *Progress in Love*, 33.

25. Paulhan, "Le Guerrier appliqué," 192.

26. Paulhan, *La Vie est pleine de choses redoutables*, 244.

27. Michael Syrotinski, introduction, xiv.

28. Blanchot, "Mystery in Literature," in *The Work of Fire*, 45.

29. Smock, *What Is There to Say?* 37.

30. See Blanchot, *The Step Not Beyond*. The *pas* in the title of *Le Pas au-delà* conveys the non-dialectical pairing of transgression with its negation; *pas* means both "step" and "not." For an extensive and illuminating study of the figure of transgression in Blanchot, see Gregg, *Maurice Blanchot*.

31. In Blanchot, *The Work of Fire*, 300–344; *La Part du feu*, 291–331.
32. De Man, *Blindness and Insight*, 68.
33. See, for instance, Mehlman, *Genealogies of the Text*; Ungar, *Scandal and Aftereffect*. Leslie Hill has objected to such characterizations of Blanchot's convictions, though his detailed account of Blanchot's prewar and wartime writings makes clear that Blanchot was, at the very least, willing to have his name associated with fascist and collaborationist authors. See Hill, *Blanchot*.
34. See Blanchot, *The Instant of My Death*.
35. Blanchot, "The Ease of Dying," 134.
36. Paulhan, "Progress in Love on the Slow Side," in *Progress in Love*, 33.
37. Syrotinski, *Defying Gravity*, 61.
38. Freud, *Moses and Monotheism*, 84.
39. See Freud, "Some Points in a Comparative Study of Organic Hysterical Paralyses."
40. Freud, "Fixation to Traumas," 273.
41. For a more extended analysis of this question of fixation in Laplanche, see my chapter 1. In *The Language of Psycho-Analysis*, Laplanche and Pontalis challenge the "genetic" model of fixation, bringing out what I would call a more paralyzing logic of primal repression. Interestingly, "fixation" is given pride of place in the authors' citation from what they call "the most complete presentation of the theory of repression that Freud ever gave." See Laplanche and Pontalis, *The Language of Psychoanalysis*, 164.
42. See especially Caruth, *Trauma*; Caruth, *Unclaimed Experience*.
43. Lacan, *The Four Fundamental Concepts of Psycho-Analysis*, 55.
44. Blanchot, "The Sirens' Song," 65. Blanchot's best-known definition of the *récit* evokes nothing so much as the *return of the event* of trauma, belated with regard to the presumed cause, yet actual: "Narration [*Le récit*] is not the account of an event but the event itself" (62). See also Blanchot, *The Writing of the Disaster*. On the question of trauma in Blanchot, see also Newman, "The Trace of Trauma," 153–73.
45. Freud, *Beyond the Pleasure Principle*, 6; Benjamin, *Illuminations*, 6.
46. Paulhan, *The Flowers of Tarbes*, 6; *Les Fleurs de Tarbes*, 35.
47. Cited in Ungar, *Scandal and Aftereffect*, 162.
48. In the context of Occupation, Paulhan's notion of terror in literature could not fail to carry a contemporary political charge. It would also seem to be freighted with the legacy of Blanchot's prewar texts, in which he asserted that "terrorism seems to us at present a method of public safety." See Blanchot, "Le Terrorisme, méthode de salut publique," 106; republished in *Gramma* 5 (1976): 61–63 (cited in Ungar, *Scandal and Aftereffect*, 124; see also Hill, *Blanchot*, 34).

49. Caruth, "Trauma and Experience," 10.

50. Blanchot, "The Ease of Dying," 123 (cited in Syrotinski, introduction, vii).

51. Mannoni, *Prospero and Caliban*, 31. Mannoni's book, which focuses on colonial Madagascar, itself opens with a *hain-teny*, the emblem, for Paulhan, of misunderstanding.

52. Although no documents have been found to substantiate the story, Louis Chevasson and André Malraux claim to have learned of the event directly from Paulhan. See the notes to "Aytré," in Paulhan, *Oeuvres complètes*, 502.

53. Belaval, présentation, 15.

54. See Paulhan, *L'Innocence utile*.

55. A telling entry in the pages of the NRF corrects the view that "je m'excuse" signifies "I excuse myself," pointing out that the phrase is in fact no different than "excusez-moi." There is no excusing oneself, one might say, only the appeal for the other's pardon. See Paulhan, *Chroniques de Jean Guérin*, 98.

56. Paulhan, "The Experience of the Proverb," in *On Poetry and Politics*, 5. "Avant de m'appliquer à connaître le langage proverbial, j'ai éprouvé de façon particulièrement vive son existence par la gêne, et, si je puis dire, le tort qu'il m'apportait" (Paulhan, "L'Expérience du proverbe," 101). These opening words are repeated in "D'un langage sacré," a talk delivered May 16, 1939, before the Collège de Sociologie, and found in *Cahiers Jean Paulhan* 2, 251–356, as well in Denis Hollier's anthology of the Collège (Hollier, *The College of Sociology*, 304–21). The English translations notably render "le tort qu'il m'apportait" as "the harm it caused me," thus failing to capture the sense of incrimination and self-doubt in the original; Paulhan's subtle turn of phrase suggests the additional sense of "the wrong it put me in."

57. Paulhan, "La Mentalité primitive," 152.

58. Paulhan, "Anarchie," 454.

59. Jean Paulhan, "Young Lady with Mirrors," in *On Poetry and Politics*, 60. In French, the question is "Qui sait au juste ce qu'il pense?" (Paulhan, "La Demoiselle aux miroirs," 174).

60. Paulhan, *Les Hain-teny merina*; *Les Hain-tenys*.

61. Yeshua, "Jean Paulhan et les hain-teny," 338–56.

62. Cited in Yeshua, "Jean Paulhan et les hain-teny," 341.

63. See especially Lévy-Bruhl, *Les Fonctions mentales dans les sociétés inférieures*, and *La Mentalité primitive*.

64. Paulhan, "Sacred Language," 317.

65. Paulhan, "La Mentalité primitive," 143–53. Paulhan's argument with Lévy-

Bruhl strikingly anticipates the argument with which Lévi-Strauss opens *The Savage Mind*, regarding the purported lack of abstraction among traditional societies. Derrida, in turn, would level against Lévi-Strauss a similar critique, assigning him an "ethnocentric" bias regarding the language of the Nambikwara (Derrida, *Of Grammatology*, 122). Paulhan would no doubt characterize this dispute as yet another rehearsal of the roles of Rhetorician and Terrorist.

66. Chemama, "L'Expérience du proverbe," 43–55.

67. Paulhan, "Sémantique du proverbe," 310.

68. Lacan, *On Feminine Sexuality*, 14; Lacan, *Encore*, 19.

69. Paulhan, "Progress in Love on the Slow Side," in *Progress in Love*, 47.

70. Paulhan, "The Experience of the Proverb," in *On Poetry and Politics*, 15.

71. Paulhan, "Sacred Language," 317.

72. Paulhan, "The Experience of the Proverb," in *On Poetry and Politics*, 19–20; *L'Expérience du proverbe*, 44.

73. Paulhan, "Entretien avec Robert Mallet," 311. In the context of this story, Paulhan evokes one of his favorite examples of progress in reverse. The Malagasy, Paulhan claims, were suitably impressed with the automobiles the French brought to the colony, but much more so by the horse-drawn carriages that followed. "C'est de ce jour qu'ils ont commencé à croire au progrès," Paulhan says (310). During World War I, however, Paulhan would teach driving lessons to Malagasy soldiers in France.

74. On Zeno's paradoxes of motion, see my introduction.

75. Butler, *The Psychic Life of Power*, 45.

76. Lacan, *Ecrits: A Selection*, 299; Lacan, *Ecrits II*, 159–60.

77. Paulhan, *Les Fleurs de Tarbes*, 278.

78. Paulhan, "Cours de malgache," 179.

79. Paulhan, "Les Hain-tenys" (1939), 92.

80. Paulhan, "Les Hain-tenys," 93.

81. Paulhan, "Progress in Love on the Slow Side," in *Progress in Love*, 21.

82. "Elle lui plut pour cette image exacte qu'elle lui offrait de sa méfiance à son propre égard" (Paulhan, *La Vie est pleine de choses redoutables*, 181). The citation is drawn from Paulhan's private journal. In cross-citing fiction and personal journals I do not believe I am falsely conflating Paulhan and his narrator. The journals reveal to what extent "Progress in Love," like all of Paulhan's stories, matches the events of his life. This citation specifically corresponds to the period from which the events of "Progress" derive, in which he met his second wife, Germaine Pascal, the "Simone" of "Progress in Love" and "The Severe Recovery."

83. Paulhan, "The Experience of the Proverb," in *On Poetry and Politics*, 19.

84. Paulhan, *Of Chaff and Wheat*, 65; "De la paille et du grain," 370.

85. The linguistic basis for Paulhan's political critique—exposing the contested and divisive nature of the so-called "commonplace"—thus approaches Lyotard's analyses in *The Differend*: "The *vicus*, the *home*, the *Heim* is a zone in which the differend between genres of discourse is suspended. An 'internal' peace is bought at the price of perpetual differends on the outskirts." Interestingly, with regard to this affinity with Paulhan, Lyotard adds, "The same arrangement goes for the ego, that of self-identification" (*The Differend*, 151).

86. See Badré, *Paulhan le juste*.

87. Paulhan, *Of Chaff and Wheat*, 25; "De la paille et du grain," 331.

88. The formula is Blanchot's ("The Ease of Dying," 140). While discreet as regards politics, Blanchot's essay is essential to a reading of transgression in Paulhan.

89. See Mehlman, *Genealogies of the Text*, 97–112.

90. For a critique of Mehlman's arguments, see Smock, "More on Writing and Deference," 158–62.

91. Paulhan, "Rhetoric Rises from Its Ashes," in *On Poetry and Politics*, 47–48 (translation modified). The original reads: "Maître du mot que tu vas dire, esclave du mot que tu as dit" (Paulhan, "La Rhétorique renaît de ses cendres," 159).

92. Barthes, *Mythologies*, Engl., 81–83.

93. Paulhan, *Chroniques de Jean Guérin*, 91.

94. The editor of Paulhan's *Chroniques* makes a similar suggestion: "On croirait que par un souci de précision et de mesure, il cherche à se placer lui-même en situation périlleuse" (Segonds, "Le Retour de Jean Guérin," 19).

95. "Qu'il existe, à l'endroit du langage, un nœud d'illusions et de pièges contre lesquels nous ne sommes pas défendus, il suffit, pour s'en assurer, de dégager la pointe d'erreur qu'introduit dans l'étude la plus sérieuse—soit psychologie des peuples, critique littéraire ou sociologie—toute réflexion portant sur les phrases et les mots" (Paulhan, "La Mentalité primitive," 143).

96. Compare to the incipit in Blanchot's *The Space of Literature*: "A book, even a fragmentary one, has a center which attracts it. This center is not fixed, but is displaced by the pressure of the book and circumstances of its composition. Yet it is also a fixed center which, if genuine, displaces itself, while remaining the same and becoming always more central, more uncertain and more imperious" (unpag.).

97. For an account of Paulhan's role in this debate, launched by Caillois in response to Lévi-Strauss's *Race et histoire*, see Massonet, "Quelques lettres à propos du relativisme culturel," 97–114.

98. "Pourquoi l'ethnologie ne découvrirait-elle pas un jour que la peau noire ou jaune s'accompagne de tels et tels traits physiques, ou moraux?" Cited in Massonet, "Quelques lettres à propos du relativisme culturel," 105.

99. "Il arrive que nous ne soyons pas moins sensibles, dans le même homme, au sentiment qu'il exprime qu'à celui dont il se défend" (Paulhan, "Jules Vallès," 62).

100. "For desire is a defense [*une défense*], a prohibition [*une défense*] against going beyond a certain limit in *jouissance*" (Lacan, *Ecrits: A Selection*, 322).

101. Paulhan, *La Vie est pleine de choses redoutables*, 312.

102. Paulhan, "The Severe Recovery," in *Progress in Love*, 53.

103. Paulhan, *La Vie est pleine de choses redoutables*, 190.

104. Speaking of his brushes with death, Paulhan says, "I had the feeling on each occasion of being at last on the brink of rapture such as I had never known—a rapture that I was perhaps not able to contain, that I would die precisely so as not to contain it" (*La Vie est pleine de choses redoutables*, 294).

105. Paulhan, "Le Marquis de Sade et sa complice," 11.

106. See Freud, *Sexuality and the Psychology of Love*, 107–32. This reversible dynamic may be seen as of Paulhan's very earliest writings, most strikingly in a story titled "Supplices" (Torture) recently published in Paulhan, *Le Fruit dans la forêt*, 53–56.

107. Laplanche, *Life and Death in Psychoanalysis*, 124.

108. Paulhan, "Happiness in Slavery," xxi–xxxvi.

109. On Paulhan and Mannoni, see Apter, *Continental Drift*, 77–95.

4. Frustration

1. Leiris, *L'Afrique fantôme*, 1981, 14. Unless otherwise noted, references to *L'Afrique fantôme* will be to this edition.

2. Leiris, *Manhood*, 140; *L'Age d'homme*, 201.

3. "Je crois que l'ouvrage de moi qui a le plus compté à cet égard, c'est *L'Afrique fantôme*, si on le considère comme un ouvrage anthropologique" (Price and Jamin, "Entretien avec Michel Leiris," 48).

4. See Clifford, *The Predicament of Culture*, 165–74.

5. Leiris, "The Ethnographer Faced with Colonialism," in *Brisées: Broken Branches*, 114; *Brisées*, 127.

6. Fanon pointedly contrasts Sartre's militant model of a black *resistance* to the French language with Leiris's more nuanced theory of a subversion *within* the master discourse by the colonized. See Fanon, *Black Skin, White Masks*, 17–40.

7. See Jean Jamin's notes to Leiris's *Journal*, 858.

8. Leiris, "Phantom Africa," in *Brisées: Broken Branches*, 46; *Brisées*, 55.

9. Leiris, *L'Afrique fantôme*, 264.

10. The publication of Leiris's *Journal* sheds new light on the genesis of the journal that makes up *L'Afrique fantôme*. Shortly before his departure for Africa, Leiris begins to form the idea of what a personal journal might entail, if it truly told all. By scrupulously recounting the day in its infinite details, a picture of life's insignificance would emerge: "It would be clearly established that the most futile things override the serious things [*ont nettement le pas sur les choses graves*]" (Leiris, *Journal*, 147). In these pages from 1929, one sees a literary project taking shape in which writing is conceived as both exhaustive and useless, in which "futility prevails by far over gravity [*la futilité l'emporte de loin sur la gravité*]" (147). Confession, rather than relying on the drama of revelation, would simply be the project of saying *everything*: "A private journal that is truly sincere should bear the trace of no choice as to what is related" (169). Before starting his psychoanalytic cure, then, Leiris already bowed to the first rule of treatment in his writing and anticipates a paradox that will come back to haunt him, notably in *L'Afrique fantôme*. The exhaustive project of writing threatens to exhaust the writer and consume his life: "Under the pretext of writing to exalt your life, you forget to live, because you are writing" (169).

11. Leiris, *Brisées: Broken Branches*, 46; *Brisées*, 54. This formula from the *prière d'insérer* repeats the formula with which the journal of 1929 breaks off, just before the African voyage: "Cette fuite qui consiste à lutter contre l'obsession du temps en lui opposant celle de l'espace" (Leiris, *Journal*, 210).

12. Leiris, *Scratches*, 220; *Biffures*, 258. Interestingly, Lydia Davis's clarifying "and" seems to betray the "cadence" of the dance step that Leiris marks not with a conjunction but with a more elliptical comma. If the fox-trot is, as Leiris says, "an illustration—even a portrait—of my own desire" it would be because of its *paralyzing* cadence, which, for all its moving qualities, leads Leiris to figure crucial spatial and temporal distinctions in terms of "a thin ribbon" and a "threshold" evoked by "the bounds [*les limites*] of those two words." Indeed, "traduire en parade judicieusement réglée" is one of the most succinct formulations of Leiris's autobiography, not only in its evocation of the *rule*, of "showing off," and the work of translation (*traduire*), but in the semantic complexity of the *parade*: deriving from the Latin *parare*, for "warding off," whence the meanings of parrying, ostentation and display, *parade* also carries a sense deriving from the Spanish *parar*, "to stop, stay, rest, end, be at a non-plus, pause" (OED).

13. Leiris, *Scratches*, 210; *Biffures*, 246.

14. Leiris, *L'Afrique fantôme*, 11.

15. "[J]'ai bien l'impression qu'on tourne dans un cercle vicieux: on pille des Nègres, sous prétexte d'apprendre aux gens à les connaître et les aimer, c'est-à-dire, en fin de compte, à former d'autres ethnographes qui iront eux aussi les 'aimer' et les piller" (Leiris, *L'Afrique fantôme*, 1996, 204).

16. "Ils reviendront, ces Dieux que tu pleures toujours! / Le temps va ramener l'ordre des anciens jours" (Nerval, *Selected Writings*, 367).

17. See Rosaldo, *Culture and Truth*, 68–87.

18. There is plenty of evidence to suggest as much. The presence of the mission in many areas could not fail to provoke fear of forced conscription, forced labor, confiscation of goods, and so forth, abuses that could be expected from business representatives and colonial authorities: "En général, dès que nous approchons des villages, les enfants se sauvent. Certains même hurlent de peur, quand nous entrons dans les cases" (Leiris, *L'Afrique fantôme*, 61).

19. See Clifford, *The Predicament of Culture*, 117–51.

20. Michel Leiris, "From the Impossible Bataille to the Impossible *Documents*, in *Brisées: Broken Branches*, 237–47; "De Bataille l'impossible à l'impossible *Documents*" in *Brisées*, 256–266.

21. For the exchange between Leiris and Bataille on this subject, see the texts edited and annoted by Hollier and Jamin in "Aux fins du Collège de Sociologie," 61–77.

22. Lucey, *Gide's Bent*, 51.

23. See Krauss, *The Originality of the Avant-Garde*, 43–85.

24. See Said, *Orientalism*.

25. In this, I am extending on a debate whose bibliography is quite extensive. Countering Said's critique of Orientalism as a discursive field broadly representing Western political and economic interests, Homi Bhabha argues that colonial discourse is fundamentally heterogeneous. Within Bhabha's framework, colonial discourse is maintained in discursive acts whose disavowals, displacements, and rhetorical sleights perform the deconstruction of their own claims. See Bhabha, *The Location of Culture*. For a discussion of the limitations of an ideological definition of exoticism, see, for example, Lowe, *Critical Terrains*, 1–29; and Clifford, *The Predicament of Culture*, 255–76. It should be pointed out that critiques such as Lowe's tend toward the contentious in ascribing to Said a monolithic portrait of colonial discourse; subsequent to *Orientalism*, Said's own work moved into a more nuanced view of the discourse of empire, both by highlighting the resistance of the colonized and by exploring the ambiguities and duplicities of the imperial vision. See Said, *Culture and Imperialism*.

26. Clifford, *The Predicament of Culture*, 127.

27. Cited in Rabinow, *French Modern*, 354.
28. *Documents*' "Dictionary" and Bataille's entry on the "Formless" in particular continue to influence debates in art history, as seen in the recent exhibit at the Centre Georges Pompidou and the accompanying catalogue. See Bois and Krauss, *Informe*.
29. Leiris, *Brisées: Broken Branches*, 18; *Brisées*, 25.
30. Derrida, "White Mythology," in *Margins of Philosophy*.
31. For a discussion of metaphor and travel as circuit of profit and return, see also Van Den Abbeele, *Travel as Metaphor*.
32. See Price and Jamin, "Entretien avec Michel Leiris," 39–40.
33. Clifford, *The Predicament of Culture*, 146.
34. Foucault, *The Order of Things*, xv, xvi.
35. Leiris, *Brisées: Broken Branches*, 19; *Brisées*, 26.
36. Leiris, *Langage tangage*, 41.
37. Leiris, *Brisées: Broken Branches*, 3; *Brisées*, 11.
38. Genette, *Mimologics*, 293.
39. Leiris, *Brisées: Broken Branches*, 3; *Brisées*, 11.
40. Leiris, "Apartheid," 71.
41. Leiris, *Scratches*, 5; *Biffures*, 12.
42. Genette, *Mimologics*, 279.
43. Leiris, *Scratches*, 14; *Biffures*, 20.
44. Fineman, "The Structure of Allegorical Desire," 44, 45.
45. See Hollier, "Le Déséquilibriste," 189–99.
46. Leiris, *Biffures*, 258; *Scratches*, 220.
47. "La signification essentielle que j'attache à mon activité poétique est celle d'un *refus*.... *L'Afrique fantôme* est née de mon refus d'écrire un livre ressortissant au genre 'littérature de voyage'" (Leiris, *Journal*, 335).
48. For an account of the Mission Dakar-Djibouti in relation to colonial politics in Ethiopia, see Caltagirone, "Le Séjour en Ethiopie," 3–11.
49. See Kaufmann, "Michel Leiris," 145–62.
50. Leiris, *L'Afrique fantôme*, 268; cited in Kaufmann, "Michel Leiris," 153.
51. Kaufmann, "Michel Leiris," 154.
52. See Leiris, *Instructions sommaires*.
53. In a letter to his wife, Leiris underscores the disparity between objects in the field (inseparable from the drama of the *find*, to say nothing of theft) and the artifacts destined for the museum: "[Q]uand tu les verras ils seront à Paris, dans une caisse ou une vitrine de musée. Ils auront perdu toute leur fraîcheur et seront tombés au rang d'abjects objets de collection" (Leiris, *L'Afrique fantôme*, 1996, 257).

54. Lacan, *The Four Fundamental Concepts of Psycho-Analysis*, 179; *Le Séminaire, livre XI*, 163. Christopher Lane cites this line in an essay on Gide's African travels, without, however, developing the specific implications of Lacan's formulation ("'Savage Ecstasy,'" 286).

55. Žižek, *Looking Awry*, 5.

56. Lacan, *Ecrits*, 803.

57. Lacan, *The Four Fundamentals*, 181; *Le Séminaire, livre XI*, 165.

58. See, for instance Laplanche, *Le Fourvoiement biologisant*. For a fuller account of Laplanche in relation to Leiris's self-analysis, see my chapter 1.

59. Leiris, *Scratches*, 218; *Biffures*, 255.

60. "La recherche même prend le pas sur l'objet de la recherche" (Leiris, *L'Homme sans honneur*, 50).

61. Leiris, *Frêle bruit*, 224.

62. Lacan, *The Seminar of Jacques Lacan, Book VII*, 54.

63. Bataille, "The Sorcerer's Apprentice," 13.

64. For an account of these thefts, see also Larson, "Ethnography, Thievery, and Cultural Identity," 229–42.

65. Leiris, *L'Afrique fantôme*, 104.

66. Once again, Leiris's wife is the favored ear for his guilty confession: "[D]es aventures comme celles des enlèvements du *kono*, tout compte fait, me laissent sans remords, puisqu'il n'y a pas d'autre moyen d'avoir de tels objets et que le sacrilège lui-même est un élément assez grandiose" (Leiris, *L'Afrique fantôme*, 1996, 204).

67. James Clifford provides an analysis of this pervasive mode of inquest in the fieldwork of Marcel Griaule (see *The Predicament of Culture*, 55–91).

68. Although Leiris is quite forthright in his portrayal of the mission's ethnographic thefts, the entries in which he relates these thefts are among the most heavily edited portions of *L'Afrique fantôme* and the manuscript notebooks on which the book is based. This work of revision contrasts with the bulk of the manuscript and with Leiris's repeatedly stated intention to preserve its character as a journal composed "de 'premier jet'" and published "pratiquement sans retouches" (notebook 4:91), a characterization maintained by his editor, who calls *L'Afrique fantôme* "la transcription littérale du manuscrit" (Jamin, "Présentation de L'Afrique Fantôme," 81). Ruth Larson has noted some of the variants between the two texts, specifically as relates to the thefts (see Larson, "Ethnography, Thievery, and Cultural Identity," 241). In Leiris's manuscript notebooks, the account of the first *kono* theft on September 6, 1931, includes this withering judgment: "Drôle d'opération qui participe du simple bluff, du chantage, de l'abus de pouvoir, de

l'escroquerie et de la pure et simple profanation!" (notebook 1), a line reduced in *L'Afrique* to the more lapidary "Affreux chantage!" (104). Moreover, in the crucial following passage where Leiris speaks of the "vapeur du sacrilège" taking over the ethnographers, the locals are described as "horrifiés" in *L'Afrique*, replacing the more damning "terrifiés" in the manuscript. Similarly, the word "vol" in the manuscript is replaced by "coup" in the entry of September 7, and "voler" by "s'en emparer" in the entry of November 18. "Belle moëlle, dont s'engraisse un musée!" Leiris says on November 16, a bitterly ironic line that is crossed out in the manuscript and does not appear in *L'Afrique*. These alterations reflect a pattern of retractions whose aim is to attenuate Leiris's critical observations, often relating to sexual improprieties—not only his own, but those of his colleagues and the colonial officials encountered en route. Interestingly, several observations of queer sexuality are substantially reworked as well, as if Leiris feared self-incrimination for perhaps taking too much interest in such matters (e.g., notebook 1, May 28; notebook 2, November 10; notebook 3, January 31). Among Leiris's revisions, perhaps most telling, however, is his somewhat devious justification of the ethnographers' thefts and extortions, which does not appear in the manuscript and seems to have been added after the fact: "Aux officiels, toutefois, qui estimeraient que décidément nous en prenons trop à notre aise dans nos transactions avec les nègres, il serait aisé de répondre que tant que l'Afrique sera soumise à un régime aussi inique que celui de l'impôt, des prestations et du service militaire sans contrepartie, ce ne sera pas à eux de faire la petite bouche à propos d'objets enlevés" (*L'Afrique fantôme*, 113). This invocation of judging officials, in an interpolation that defies Leiris's own "principle" of composition (notebook 4:91), is particularly suggestive; the guilt disavowed here bears at once on his ethnographic abuse and his practice of composition. Subsequently, in *La Règle du jeu*, self-portraiture and self-justification will go by way of a more reflexive writing practice, no longer conceived as the straightforward task of speaking the whole truth, but instead a more ethical, if tormented, process of explicit additions, elaborations, and retractions, as conveyed by the title of the initial volume, *Biffures*.

69. Leiris, "The Sacred in Everyday Life," 24.

70. Leiris, *Scratches*, 66; *Biffures*, 80.

71. Leiris, *Manhood*, 120; *L'Age d'homme*, 176.

72. Leiris, *Scratches*, 213; *Biffures*, 249.

73. On the motif of "under erasure," see Spivak, "Translator's Preface," xiv, and my introduction.

74. See Richman, "Leiris's *L'Age d'homme*," 91–110.

75. Freud, *Totem and Taboo*, 73.

76. Laplanche and Pontalis, *The Language of Psycho-Analysis*, 5. To say that Leiris was "acting out" is not to overlook that he undertook his trip at the recommendation of his doctor. Acting out is a common symptom, precisely, within the context of analysis.

77. Leiris is well attuned to the factor of acting out in drunken states, which he tellingly compares to the state of possession: "Caractère théâtral de l'ivresse. Comment on joue à être saoûl. Grandiloquence. Adoption d'attitudes conventionelles. Gesticulation. Récitation de vérités premières. Ton volontiers prophétique. De même qu'un possédé à l'instant où il est mû par l'esprit possesseur, il semble qu'on soit revêtu d'une personnalité d'apparat, dont on a le sentiment qu'elle est plus ressemblante que la vraie" (*L'Homme sans honneur*, 42).

78. Leiris, *Journal*, 41.

79. Clifford, *The Predicament of Culture*, 169.

80. Leiris, *L'Afrique fantôme*, 1996, 581.

81. Leiris, "La Croyance aux génies *zar*," 945.

82. Leiris, *Manhood*, 142; *L'Age d'homme*, 202.

83. Leiris, *L'Homme sans honneur*, 20.

84. Leiris, *La Possession*, 950. This formulation is cited from Leiris's first text on the *zar* cult, which, without fully elaborating the problematic of simulation and theatricality, nevertheless anticipates the developments of the later text. See Leiris, "La Croyance aux génies *zâr*," 942.

85. Leiris, *La Possession*, 952.

86. See Douglas, *Natural Symbols*.

87. Glissant, *Caribbean Discourse*, 26.

88. Mercier, "Présentation de La Possession," 908.

89. Lotringer, "Phantoms of the Opera," 70.

90. Leiris, *La Possession*, 998.

91. Mannoni, *Clefs pour l'Imaginaire*, 11.

92. The lack of a singular fetish-object in Leiris is a recurring topic in *Rules of the Game* and could be considered a significant driving factor of his restless, questing prose. Significantly, this quest culminates in *Frêle bruit* with an elaborate meditation on the mystical grail. That Leiris's exploration of *le merveilleux* calls upon the Arthurian cycle is highly suggestive in the light of the structure of divided belief we are tracing here, given the hybrid nature of the texts as pagan legends overlaid with Christian motifs. Might the grail, then, represent for Leiris an object of belief before mystification?

93. Mannoni, *Clefs pour l'Imaginaire*, 29.

94. Leiris, *Scratches*, 235; *Biffures*, 275.

95. Leiris, *La Possession*, 998.

96. Leiris, *L'Homme sans honneur*, 122–25.

97. Leiris, *Scratches*, 247. The original reads: "Toute ligne qu'une plume a tracée, aussi châtiée qu'elle soit, doit être plus ou moins passible d'une chiromancie et, dans chaque mouvement de chaque main défricheuse de papier, il est probable qu'on peut lire ce qu'est, en son entier, celui qui laisse ainsi mirer son destin à la surface, tranquille ou agitée, d'un geste" (Leiris, *Biffures*, 289).

98. Stoekl, *Politics, Writing, Mutilation*, 53–54.

99. Leiris, *L'Afrique fantôme*, 590.

100. Leiris, *L'Afrique fantôme*, 583.

101. Leiris, *La Possession*, 1045.

102. Butler, *Bodies That Matter*, 15.

103. A fuller account of Leiris's writings on music and theater is beyond the scope of this essay. See especially "Songs" in *Scratches*, 7–17; *Operratiques*.

104. Leiris, *La Possession*, 1061.

105. See Foucault, *The Order of Things*, 373–87.

106. On the sexual politics of fieldwork, see Kulick and Willson, *Taboo*, in which "taboo" reflects not the ordering principle of anthropology or psychoanalysis, but rather the inevitable contamination of fieldwork by the desire of the researcher.

107. Leiris, *Scraps*, 162 (translation modified).

108. Leiris, *Fibrilles*, 86.

109. Leiris, *Scraps*, 172.

110. Leiris, *Fibrilles*, 58.

111. I draw here on Judith Butler's "The Lesbian Phallus and the Morphological Imaginary." Butler's main argument in this essay is with Lacan, who is at pains to define the phallus not as a material organ but as the key signifier of the Symbolic order. And yet, as Butler shows, this abstraction of the phallus enables an even more imperious masculine privilege, but only through a process of rhetorical displacements and disavowals that Butler's reading of Lacan brings to light. Butler argues that Lacan's very negation of a bodily privilege for the phallus is symptomatic of a series of rhetorical displacements that performatively install the phallus in and through those very displacements: "Although Lacan explicitly denounces the possibility that the phallus is a body part or an imaginary effect, that repudiation will be read as constitutive of the very symbolic status he confers on the phallus" (*Bodies That Matter*, 73).

112. Deleuze, "Coldness and Cruelty," 34. Deleuze's reading of Sacher-Masoch challenges the normative account of masochism as pathological submission to castration and the superego, and holds that the pleasures of the masochist are

a defiant resistance to the the Oedipal father. Laplanche's work lends support to Deleuze's challenge to the normative psychoanalytic reading of masochism as perversion; for Laplanche, the subject who aims to recover the origins of his self-constitution is bound to uncover a traumatic and persecutory other at the heart of his primal fantasies.

113. Leiris, *Fibrilles*, 55.

114. Leiris, *Frêle bruit*, 392.

115. A brief look at this crucial passage should not overlook the fact that Leiris does not figure his situation as prompting a *choice* or *option* but rather a "recourse" or "*ressource*," in which the "re-" seems to indicate not a plural but a duplicity within the singular "option." Glossed as such, "ma seule ressource" is itself contradictory and indeed aporetic. Here, at the conclusion of *Rules of the Game*, the elusive rule is figured, then, as the enactment of an *undecidable* choice. Along these lines, we might cast Leiris's trouble with the law and with his *rule* as an "ordeal of the undecidable," as Derrida puts it ("Force of Law," 253). Legal scholar Drucilla Cornell makes clear that such an ordeal does not entail an abandonment of responsibility; rather, undecidability imposes "infinite responsibility" and an intervention of radical ethics into the field of law (*The Philosophy of the Limit*, 169).

116. Mbembe, *On the Postcolony*, 13.

117. See Silverman, *Male Subjectivity at the Margins*, 15–51.

5. Atopia

1. Barthes, "Inaugural Lecture," 458; *Leçon*, 801.

2. See Foucault, "The Discourse on Language"; *L'Ordre du discours*.

3. Barthes, *Roland Barthes by Roland Barthes*, 71.

4. Barthes, *Roland Barthes by Roland Barthes*, 49; *Roland Barthes par Roland Barthes*, 132.

5. Barthes, *A Lover's Discourse*, 34; *Fragments d'un discours amoureux*, 493.

6. Barthes, "Entretien," 774.

7. Barthes, *A Lover's Discourse*, 35; *Fragments d'un discours amoureux*, 494.

8. Barthes, *Roland Barthes by Roland Barthes*, 104; *Roland Barthes par Roland Barthes*, 174.

9. Barthes, *A Lover's Discourse*, 20; *Fragments d'un discours amoureux*, 476.

10. See Culler, *Roland Barthes*, 9–23; Comment, *Roland Barthes*, 13; Bensmaïa, *The Barthes Effect*, 90.

11. Culler, *Roland Barthes*, 12.

12. Doubrovsky, "Une Ecriture tragique," 339.

13. Barthes, *Roland Barthes by Roland Barthes*, 165; *Roland Barthes par Roland Barthes*, 221.

14. Barthes, "Preface to Renaud Camus's *Tricks*," 291; "Préface à *Tricks* de Renaud Camus," 1017.

15. Butler, *Excitable Speech*, 125.

16. As Barthes says, "language—the performance of a language system—is neither reactionary nor progressive; it is quite simply fascist; for fascism does not prevent speech, it compels speech [*le fascisme, ce n'est pas d'empêcher de dire, c'est d'obliger à dire*]" (Barthes, "Inaugural Lecture," 461; *Leçon*, 803).

17. Comment, *Roland Barthes*, 39.

18. Paulhan, *Chroniques de Jean Guérin*, 81.

19. Brown, *Roland Barthes*, 32.

20. See Syrotinski, *Defying Gravity*, 22–23.

21. Barthes, "Literature and Signification," 266.

22. Barthes, "Réponses," 1321.

23. Barthes, "Literature and Signification," 278.

24. Barthes, *Roland Barthes by Roland Barthes*, 84.

25. Barthes, *Mythologies*, Eng., 123; *Mythologies*, Fr., 693.

26. In granting to the colonized the role previously claimed by the proletariat, Barthes suggests that a historical exigency has been passed from the one to the other. In so doing, however, he overlooks Marx's observation that colonization *preceded* industrial exploitation, a point underscored by Lévi-Strauss: "colonization historically and logically precedes capitalism, and the capitalist regime consists in treating Western people as Western people had previously treated native populations. For Marx, the relationship between capitalist and proletarian is thus only another particular case of the relationship between colonizer and colonized" (Lévi-Strauss, "Cultural Discontinuity," 315). We might call Lévi-Strauss's correction here as an instance of the classical chiastic turn of *proteron hysteron* (i.e., the latter first). Accordingly, the colonized reclaims his primary position in the Marxist dialectic, though that primary position is displaced, as always in Lévi-Strauss, by the more primary claim of the primitive aboriginal, and thus ultimately back to the narrative of fatal contact. For his part, Leiris, always more willing than Lévi-Strauss to subject his politics to reflexive critique, and in this sense more of an ethicist than a moralist, gives this dialectical overturning a supplementary twist by noting that his own surrealist anticolonialism derived from a certain bad faith. "Basically," Leiris says, "we were concerned with the condition of the colonized well before we concerned ourselves with the condition of the proletariat. It is extremely likely—and this betrays the posture of the aesthete—that exoticism played a part here. We were much more likely to claim solidarity with 'exotic' oppressed people than with oppressed people closer to home" (Leiris,

"Entretien," 30). In Leiris, dialectical history thus takes shape less as a series of progressive overturnings or rightings of wrongs than as a repeated tangle with problematic inversions; tellingly, in a self-critique that can no doubt be extended to Lévi-Strauss as well, Leiris casts the ethnographer's preference for primitive societies as a kind of "inverted racism [*racisme retourné*]" (37), an argument vigorously advanced in his essay "The Ethnographer Faced with Colonialism."

27. Barthes, *The Eiffel Tower*, 53; *Mythologies*, Fr., 615.

28. Barthes, *Mythologies*, Eng., 76; *Mythologies*, Fr., 638.

29. Barthes, *The Eiffel Tower*, 37–38; *Mythologies*, Fr., 602.

30. See Adorno, *The Stars Down to Earth*.

31. *Mythologies*, Fr., 666.

32. Barthes, *The Eiffel Tower*, 94; *Mythologies*, Fr., 641.

33. Ross, *Fast Cars, Clean Bodies*, 3.

34. Cited in Ross, *Fast Cars, Clean Bodies*, 72.

35. Barthes, *Mythologies*, Eng., 71; *Mythologies*, Fr., 619.

36. This ethical dimension of Barthes's *Mythologies* invites comparison with Levinas, whose *Totalité et infini* opens by evoking the metaphysical "alibi," the illusions of travel, and the ethical approach to the other, beyond appropriation and identity. See Levinas, *Totalité et infini*, 3.

37. See Althusser, "Ideology and Ideological State Apparatuses."

38. Barthes, *Roland Barthes by Roland Barthes*, 6; *Roland Barthes par Roland Barthes*, 88.

39. Brown, *Roland Barthes*, 41–42.

40. Brown, *Roland Barthes*, 29.

41. Barthes, *The Eiffel Tower*, 31; *Mythologies*, Fr., 599.

42. The second to last stanza of Rimbaud's poem reads: "Si je désire une eau d'Europe, c'est la flache / Noire et froide où vers le crépuscule embaumé / Un enfant accroupi plein de tristesses, lâche / Un bateau frêle comme un papillon de mai" (Rimbaud, "Le Bateau ivre," 103).

43. Barthes, *Roland Barthes by Roland Barthes*, 60; *Roland Barthes par Roland Barthes*, 140.

44. Garcin, *Nouvelles Mythologies*, 116–17.

45. See Rancière, *Le Spectateur emancipé*, 118–24.

46. Barthes, *Mythologies*, Eng., 12; *Mythologies*, Fr., 566.

47. Barthes, *S/Z*, Eng., 45; *S/Z*, Fr., 584–85.

48. Barthes, "Texte à deux (parties)," 765.

49. Barthes, *Roland Barthes by Roland Barthes*, 51; *Roland Barthes par Roland Barthes*, 134.

50. Barthes, *The Pleasure of the Text*, 22; *Le Plaisir du texte*, 1505.

51. Culler, *Roland Barthes*, 56.

52. Barthes, *Roland Barthes by Roland Barthes*, 22; *Roland Barthes par Roland Barthes*, 106.

53. See Lee, *Jacques Lacan*, 28.

54. Barthes, *A Lover's Discourse*, 60; *Fragments d'un discours amoureux*, 516.

55. Barthes, *The Pleasure of the Text*, 18–19; *Le Plaisir du texte*, 1503.

56. Lacan, *The Four Fundamental Concepts of Psycho-Analysis*, 62–63; *Le Séminaire, livre XI*, 61.

57. Lacan, *Ecrits*, 803.

58. Barthes, "Texte à deux (parties)," 765.

59. Barthes, *Roland Barthes by Roland Barthes*, 161.

60. See Zižek, *The Sublime Object of Ideology*, 158. I am indebted here to Zižek's formulations, but opposed to the main thrust of his polemic, which pits post-structuralists as a whole against Lacan on the question of metalanguage. My brief account of Barthes's intervention in Lacanian theory shows the extent to which the two are in agreement.

61. Barthes, *Writing Degree Zero*, 11; *Le Degré zéro de l'écriture*, 146.

62. See Sartre, *Qu'est-ce que la littérature?*

63. Barthes, *Writing Degree Zero*, 4 (translation modified); *Le Degré zéro de l'écriture*, 140.

64. Barthes, "The Last Word on Robbe-Grillet?" 199; "Le Point sur Robbe-Grillet?" 1318.

65. Barthes, "The Reality Effect," 143; "L'Effet de réel," 480.

66. Barthes, "Inaugural Lecture," 465; *Leçon*, 806.

67. Barthes, *Empire of Signs*, 3.

68. Barthes, *Empire of Signs*, 9; *L'Empire des signes*, 750.

69. See Barthes, "Writing the Event," 149–54; "L'Ecriture de l'événement," 496–500.

70. Barthes, *Empire of Signs*, 82; *L'Empire des signes*, 802.

71. Jean-Michel Rabaté, in a fine account of Barthes's evolution from the structuralist paradigm, argues that it is not May '68 that constitutes the turning point for Barthes, but rather May '66, the occasion of his first trip to Japan. Interestingly, as Rabaté notes, Barthes's first mention of Derrida occurs in the course of a 1967 essay on Tokyo, "Sémiologie et urbanisme." See Rabaté, introduction, 4; Barthes, "Sémiologie et urbanisme," 439–46.

72. Barthes, *s/z*, Eng., 105.

73. Barthes, *Roland Barthes by Roland Barthes*, 50; *Roland Barthes par Roland Barthes*, 132.

74. See Barthes, "Fromentin," 1399.

75. Barthes, *The Pleasure of the Text*, 10; *Le Plaisir du texte*, 1499.

76. Within contemporary literature, the travel narrative as "discontinuous" text is epitomized by Michel Butor's travelogue *Mobile*, a text of scattered notations that, Barthes notes, are not so much *developed* as *distributed* across the text. Barthes sees Butor's challenge to narrative as inscribing a fertile *discontinuity* within the conventions of the narrative voyage. See Barthes, "Literature and Discontinuity," 171–83; "Littérature et discontinu," 1299–308.

77. Barthes, "Pierre Loti," Eng., 119; "Pierre Loti," Fr., 1409.

78. Barthes, *The Pleasure of the Text*, 30; *Le Plaisir du texte*, 1509.

79. "Children will never be rocked enough," Gide says. "I even think it would be a good plan to calm them and send them to sleep by means of a special pitching-and-tossing apparatus [*d'appareils profondément bousculatoires*]. As for me, I was brought up according to rational methods and by my mother's orders never slept in beds that were not fixed; thanks to which, I am particularly liable to seasickness [*au mal de mer*]" (Gide, *Travels in the Congo*, 3; *Voyage au Congo*, 683).

80. Lucey, *Gide's Bent*, 175.

81. See de Troyes, *Le Roman de Perceval*. Charles Méla provides an illuminating Lacanian reading of *Perceval* as "a story set adrift" ("Perceval," 254) and "haunted by the Father's vacant place" (259). The crucial scene in *Perceval* is of course his witness to the procession of the grail, when he is "fascinated" by a vision that will continue to "petrify" him in his failed quest (275).

82. See Grosrichard, *Structure du sérail*; Rodinson, *La Fascination de l'Islam*.

83. Kandiyoti, "Roland Barthes Abroad," 228.

84. See Barthes, *Incidents*; "Incidents" and "Soirées de Paris."

85. Chambers, *Loiterature*, 250–69.

86. Barthes, "Well, and China?" 116; "Alors, la Chine?" 32.

87. De Certeau, *Heterologies*, 68.

88. Kristeva, *About Chinese Women*, 12; *Des Chinoises*, 14.

89. Barthes, *Roland Barthes by Roland Barthes*, 48; *Roland Barthes par Roland Barthes*, 131.

90. See Barthes, *Carnets du voyage en Chine*.

91. Hayot, *Chinese Dreams*, 149. Hayot provides a detailed and insightful account of the context of Tel quel's Chinese trip and its aftermath.

92. Lowe, *Critical Terrains*, 159.

93. Young, *White Mythologies*, 5.

94. Lowe, *Critical Terrains*, 163.

95. See Sandoval, *Methodology of the Oppressed*.

96. "Often he felt stupid [*bête*]: this was because he had only an *ethical* intelligence [*une intelligence morale*]" (Barthes, *Roland Barthes by Roland Barthes*, 110; *Roland Barthes par Roland Barthes*, 179).

97. See Derrida, "The Deaths of Roland Barthes," 34–67.

98. The recent publication of Barthes's *Journal de deuil* sheds new light on the mourning that orients his reflections in his final book, *Camera Lucida*. Throughout the journal Barthes voices his discouragement at traveling after the death of his mother in 1977. Interestingly, the breakdown of travel evokes an ethics of paralysis, if only in the mode of inarticulate suffering: "Journey from Paris to Tunis. Series of airplane breakdowns. Endless stops [*séjours interminables*] in airports among crowds of Tunisians heading home for the Aïd Kebir. Why does the disaster of this day of accidents go so well with mourning?" (Barthes, *Journal de deuil*, 68).

99. Butler, *Giving an Account of Oneself*, 83.

6. The Wake of Ulysses

1. Bauman, *Globalization*, 113.

2. Derrida, *Margins of Philosophy*, 13.

3. Put another way, the counterpath exposes, within the path of one traveler, the *irony* of travel's general economy. As Polly Pattullo says, "there is a certain irony in the fact that tourists began to arrive in the Caribbean in greater numbers just as the poor of the Caribbean began their own more onerous journey in the opposite direction to work" (*Last Resorts*, 6).

4. See Chakrabarty, *Provincializing Europe*.

5. "Heureux qui, comme Ulysse, a fait un beau voyage, / Ou comme cestuy là qui conquit la toison, / Et puis est retourné, plein d'usage et raison, / Vivre entre ses parents le reste de son aage!" (*Les Regrets*, in Du Bellay, *The Regrets*, 82–83).

6. As Richard Helgerson puts it, "Is the Du Bellay of sonnet 31 longing for his native French *pays*? Or is he rather intent, as he was in the *Defense*, on devising a newly Romanized *patrie*? The poem may say the first, but all its canny art points toward the second" (introduction, 15). Recent critical theory allows us to recognize in this ambiguity a predicament characteristic of postcolonial national identity; nationhood and nativism are often claimed, paradoxically, by means of a belated return home from the metropole. While the influence of the colonizer readily lends itself to challenge and opposition, such critique often inadvertently reinscribes the "home" in mythic terms as autonomous and essential, if only through discursive disavowals and metaphysical claims to nativism. Much postcolonial theory thus calls on deconstruction's insights into retroactive and "prosthetic" origins as a means to undo the tenacious hold of power in myths and figures of

autonomy and national self-identity. David Lloyd's *Anomalous States* remains one of the most articulate expositions of this problematic.

7. See Van den Abbeele, *Travel as Metaphor*.

8. See Derrida, in *Margins of Philosophy*, 209. The play on "usage" and "usure" with which Derrida opens "White Mythology" is present in Du Bellay's poem as well, where the word *usage* suggests, as in Derrida, both gain and loss, the profit of travels and the vanity of knowledge. The poet speaks of the "usage et raison" gained in travel, but longs for a return home that remains to come, and perhaps never will. In this way, the poem of travel and *mal de pays* is also a meditation on time's passage and mortality. The "usage" gained in travel foreshadows this regretful insight in the poem, evoking not only the know-how or social graces learned abroad (as in *l'usage du monde*) but a more deleterious "usage" as *wearing away*. Travel's profits are thus linked to loss in the word *usage*, which subtly rhymes with the key word *voyage* outside of the poem's metrical scheme. If life-as-journey is *usagé*, a tired, hackneyed, and well-worn metaphor, Du Bellay's choice of the word *usage* would seem to implicitly acknowledge this itself, and the poem thereby undercuts its own claims. Suspended by the alternatives of profit and loss, and stuck between the faded appeal of travel and an impossible return home, the poem, however, resolves this tension in a metaphysical turn. The final word in the last line suggests a redemptive destination: the angelic resonance of the name "Angevine" converts the pain of exile into the hope of a journey into the afterlife.

9. Horkheimer and Adorno, *Dialectic of Enlightenment*, 34.

10. See Blanchot, "The Sirens' Song," 59–65.

11. Foucault, *The Order of Things*, 46.

12. Beckett, "The Way," 173.

13. Eyal Amiran makes this a similar point, arguing that "The Way" conveys a journey that, while *unique*, cannot presume *originality* (*Wandering and Home*, 210).

14. As instance of this *retrait*, Derrida quotes Aristotle's citation from *The Odyssey*, which, tellingly enough, delivers metaphorical *transport* in an image of stasis: "'Here stands my ship . . . ,' for to be anchored is one among many ways of being stopped" (Derrida, *Psyche*, 51).

15. Beckett's "∞" is not, in fact, the symmetrical symbol of infinity (as I have rendered it here), but rather an asymmetrical figure eight on its side.

16. Beckett describes Molloy as "free, on the black boat of Ulysses, to crawl toward the East, along the deck. That is a great measure of freedom, for him who has not the pioneering spirit. And from the poop, poring upon the wave, a sadly rejoicing slave, I follow with my eyes the proud and futile wake" (*Molloy*, 51.

17. Ortega y Gasset, *The Dehumanization of Art*, 65.

18. See Duffy, *The Subaltern Ulysses*; Cheng, *Joyce, Race and Empire*; Attridge and Howes, *Semicolonial Joyce*. *Semicolonial Joyce* contains an essay that addresses the theme of what Joyce himself called "Irish paralysis" (Gibbons, "'Have you no homes to go to?'" 153). See also Deane's essay, "Dead Ends." Deane provides a fine reading of the chiasmus that closes "The Dead," in which, as Deane says, "conflict is annulled and the distinction between deathly paralysis and total liberation is . . . cancelled" (36).

19. Maranhão, introduction, xvii.

20. Robeson, *Here I Stand*, 67.

21. A critic such as C. L. R. James would thus take the dialectic at its word, arguing that the true stakes of French revolution were not staged in Paris but in the slave revolution in the colony of San Domingo. See James, *The Black Jacobins*.

22. See Fanon, *Black Skin, White Masks*, 109–40.

23. This predicament would not, of course, prevent Fanon from taking political action and making decisive journeys. Fanon would renounce his French citizenship and enlist in the FLN to contribute to the cause of Algerian liberation. And yet, Marxist and Hegelian models of revolt and revolution were not fully realized in Algeria, not only because the Soviet Union failed to acknowledge and support its colonial liberation movement, but because the struggle did not follow the historical script of contestation, revolt, and freedom. Fanon's writings on Algeria capture the complexity of this postcolonial moment, whose progressive Marxist aspirations are challenged by the fits and starts of nationalist consciousness, ethnic and racial identification, and religion. See Fanon, *The Wretched of the Earth*.

24. Said, *Culture and Imperialism*, xvi.

25. Freud, "The 'Uncanny,'" 217.

26. Selvon, *The Lonely Londoners*, 129.

27. Cited in Gibbons, "'Have you no homes to go to?'", 152.

28. Hertz, *The End of the Line*, 217.

29. It might be objected, of course, that moments of reflection always involve a certain pause and immobilization. But Hertz insists that such moments are, as he puts it, properly *paralyzing*. What Hertz calls "the 'paralyzing' powers of art" (*The End of the Line*, xx) expose one to "moments of shared 'unconsciousness,' when important transmissions are taking place" (xvii). Such moments are moments of uncanny and enigmatic transmissions; they are also moments of a postcolonial uncanny. We might cite, in this regard, the crucial scene in Joyce's "The Dead," where Gabriel, that lonely Dubliner, is rapt in attention at the sight of his wife listening to an old Irish air: "Gabriel was surprised at her stillness

and strained his ear to listen also." Gretta's stillness mirrors that of Gabriel, who "stood still in the gloom of the hall, trying to catch the air that the voice was singing and gazing up at his wife." This moment is, of course, one of failed reflection on Gabriel's part, as he is exposed to an uncanny ghost that, by the end of the story, forces a confrontation with a native identification he has foreclosed in his identification with colonial Irish culture. Hertz has shown how scenes of doubling and reflection tend to resolve their equivocations in a mechanism of scapegoating whereby self-possession and identity are reasserted at the cost of the other. Similarly, Joyce's story shows how Gabriel's misogyny and rejection of Irish identity serve as scapegoating means to his illusory identity, destroyed by the end of the story in the uncanny return of all Gabriel had rejected in his colonized culture. See Joyce, "The Dead," 227.

30. This is not to claim that Selvon's narrative, in claiming to represent his fellow immigrants, offers merely a realist and mimetic portrait. Indeed, his characters often seem to defy categories and explanations. As Moses says, "You work things out in your own mind to a kind of pattern, in a sort of sequence, and one day bam! something happen to throw everything out of gear, what you expect to happen never happen, what you don't expect to happen always happen, and you have to start thinking all over again" (*The Lonely Londoners*, 56).

31. Boudjedra, *Topographie*.
32. Heath, *The Nouveau Roman*, 151.
33. Robbe-Grillet, *Snapshots*, 49; *Instantanés*, 78.
34. Boudjedra, *Lettres algériennes*, 11.
35. Graebner, *History's Place*, 294.
36. Boudjedra, *Fascination*, 239.
37. Apter, *Continental Drift*, 195.
38. See Culbert, "On the Trace of the Other."
39. Sebbar, *Métro*, 96.
40. The image of a "Marianne voilée" first appeared in the extreme right-wing magazine *Minute* on July 16, 1983, and later on the cover of *Figaro Magazine* on October 26, 1985, accompanied by the title "Serons-nous encore français dans 30 ans?" Such right-wing discourse implies the incompatibility of republican values with a perceived threat from the French Muslim population. While trying to stake out a more tolerant position, defenders of *laïcité* on the left have also invoked the right's provocative figure; Laurent Fabius, for instance, has echoed ethnophobic fears in stating that "Marianne ne peut pas être voilée" (Speech to Socialist Party Congress, Dijon, May 17, 2003), a position he reiterated in the context of the anti-burka debates of 2009, not without inadvertently hardening his own formula: "Marianne ne doit pas être voilée" (RMC [Radio Monte-Carlo], June 24, 2009).

41. See Bottici, *A Philosophy of Political Myth*, 252.

42. The year 1973 saw the highest incidence up to that date of racist attacks in France against Algerians. The media fanned the flames of this violence, with justifications that included the oil crisis and the Arab-Israeli war of October. In response to the violence, on September 20 the Algerian government suspended all immigration to France. (Arriving as he did on September 26, Boudjedra's immigrant seems to have slipped through, however). An important consequence of the violence was the French government decision in 1974 to halt the recruitment of Algerian laborers, key contributors up to then to French postwar economic growth. This decision coincides with the end of the *trente glorieuses* of French prosperity. See Ben Jelloun, *Hospitalité française*, 112–13.

43. In the years following its initial publication in 1984, the topic of hospitality gained new currency with the intervention of Derrida's deconstructive ethics of hospitality. The reissue of *Hospitalité française* thus includes a long introduction drawing on Derrida and Levinas, among others, to frame an ethics of hospitality for contemporary immigration debates.

44. Begag, *Ethnicity and Equality*, 41.

45. See Maspero, *Roissy Express*.

46. Silverstein, *Algeria in France*, 113.

47. The riots of 2005 confirmed this diagnosis for Silverstein. In a commentary written during the riots, he speaks of "an enduring logic of colonial rule" in the spatial segregation of the *banlieues* and their management by the state and the forces of order. See Silverstein and Tetrault, "Urban Violence in France."

48. Likewise, the 2004 law against the Muslim headscarf repeated the forcible unveiling of Algerian women during the height of the war. Fanon's insights into the tactical and shifting symbolic nature of the veil remain pertinent fifty years later, and serve as a corrective to the panicked view of its purportedly backward, religious, and fundamentalist significance. See Fanon, "Algeria Unveiled," 35–68.

49. Silverstein, *Algeria in France*, 115.

50. De Certeau, *The Practice of Everyday Life*, xix.

51. Benjamin, *The Arcades Project*, 518; cited in Apter, *Continental Drift*, 194.

52. See Tiedmann, "Dialectics at a Standstill," 929–45.

53. A manifesto for popular and ordinary practices of freedom and mobility, de Certeau's seminal text gained a new and uncanny resonance after the events of 9/11. Beginning on top of the World Trade Center, the text leads the reader on an "Icarian fall" from the heights: "Must one finally fall back into the dark space where crowds move back and forth, crowds that, though visible from on high, are themselves unable to see down below?" (*Practice of Everyday Life*, 92).

54. De Certeau's "Walking in the City" is clearly indebted to the Situationist theory of urban drift, or *dérive*. An early contribution to the theory of drift and psychogeography is Abdelhafid Khatib's "Essai de description psychogéographique des Halles," published in the *Internationale Situationniste* in 1958. The editors of the journal point out that Khatib's essay remains incomplete, as he was arrested in the course of his urban research due to curfews against North Africans. This interference of the police in Khatib's experiment in urban mobility is deeply ironic, though it only confirms the purpose of Khatib's and the editors' work in charting spaces of freedom in the city. Guy Debord's famous "Theory of the *dérive*" immediately follows Khatib's essay. See Khatib, "Essai de description psychogéographique des Halles," 13–18. Debord's essay, "Theory of the *dérive*," may be found in *Situationist International Anthology*, 50–54.

55. Augé, *Non-Places*, 79.

56. See Ben Jelloun, *La Plus haute des solitudes*.

57. On October 17, 1961, as many as two hundred Algerian immigrants were murdered by the police in Paris. These murders followed a peaceful demonstration against the war and against a curfew specifically targeting the Algerian population.

58. Haneke, *Caché*.

59. See Einaudi, *La Bataille de Paris*; Einaudi and Kagan, *17 Octobre 1961*; Sebbar, *La Seine était rouge*. Einaudi and Kagan's book contains graphic photos of this event whose history has long been suppressed.

60. The son's body is denied repatriation in Algeria, due to his father's collaboration with the French during the war. When Meriem herself finally returns to Algeria, she goes straight to the graves of her parents, and decides to live out her days in the cemetery. See Charef, *Le Harki de Meriem*.

61. Derrida, *Aporias*, 61.

62. Derrida, *The Work of Mourning*, 45.

63. This "return of the dead" is literally invoked in the French word for ghost, *revenant*.

64. Derrida, *Of Hospitality*, 91.

65. Ben Jelloun, *Hospitalité française*, 109–115.

66. Butler, *Precarious Life*, 22.

67. Djebar says, "No; I say no to all ceremonies: those of farewell, those of piety, those of chagrin which seek their own comforts, those of consolation" (*Algerian White*, 53 [translation modified]).

68. Djebar, *Fantasia*, 115–16.

69. Butler, *Precarious Life*, 23.

70. Michael O'Riley provides an extensive treatment of the question of haunting in the work of Assia Djebar. See O'Riley, *Postcolonial Haunting and Victimization*.

71. Derrida, *Paper Machine*, 66.

72. Derrida, *Of Hospitality*, 79–81.

73. Derrida, *Paper Machine*, 67.

74. Spivak, *In Other Worlds*, 112. Spivak adopts the expression from Marcuse. See Marcuse, "Repressive Tolerance."

75. See Hargreaves, "Translator's Introduction."

76. Wallerstein, "Integration to What?" 113.

77. See Amin, *The Liberal Virus*, 40. While Amin's book helpfully dispels the myth of inclusiveness underlying the liberal premise of social and economic integration, his argument finesses the paradox that he himself invokes, namely that of an integration that excludes, whose haunted topography we have been pursuing here.

78. See Hardt and Negri, *Multitude;* Balibar, *We, the People of Europe?*

79. Curiously, Begag sees even racially based humor as an exercise in tolerance and civil exchange. "Rire de l'autre, c'est déjà l'accepter en son sein, lui donner une place, l'accueillir, comme on accueille en soi sa propre part d'étrangeté" (Begag, *L'intégration*, 63). This language of welcome and hospitality does not seem to worry about the asymmetries of power that structure the language of racial humor. In this light it is worth pointing out that the riots of 2005 were immediately preceded by the outbreak of the Danish cartoon scandal, in which defamatory pictures of the prophet Mohammed were published in a Danish newspaper, to the dismay of Muslims worldwide. Without claiming a direct causal relationship between the two events, the least that can be said is that the French suburban rioters were responding to a broad social and cultural exclusion, reinforced by an increasingly repressive security state, which allied their griefs with a larger European Muslim community and a besieged Arab and Muslim world.

80. See Lévi-Strauss, "Race and History," 341. It is worth pointing out that Lévi-Strauss's broad and synoptic study on race, commissioned for publication by UNESCO, as was Leiris's "Race and Civilization," contrasts significantly with the latter, in which racial politics are addressed in the light of decolonization movements, minority identity, and activist art and cultural production. Nonetheless, we might invoke Lévi-Strauss's text to counter Begag's judgment of the immobile "rusters," whose tactics, in any case, are mobile, and whose resistance should no doubt be seen as something other than a failure to "get moving." As Lévi-Strauss says, "Each time we tend to classify a human culture as inert or static, we must

ask ourselves if this apparent lack of mobility does not result from our ignorance of its true interests, conscious or unconscious; and if, possessing criteria different from our own, this culture is not—as far as we are concerned—victim of the same illusion."

81. A brief look at the language of political denigration illuminates the merging consensus of right and left in the recent discourse and practice of French interior security. In 1998 socialist interior minister Jean-Pierre Chevènement invoked the term *sauvageons* to refer to young delinquents (Chevènement, "Sauvageon versus racaille"). Though Chevènement has insisted that the term, meaning "wild stock," simply derives from horticulture, the connotations of "sauvage" also carry an unmistakable legacy of colonial and early ethnological discourse. In a televised appearance on October 25, 2005, two days before the outbreak of the suburban riots, Sarkozy used the term *racaille* to refer to suburban delinquents ("scum" or "rabble," though the French word is significantly more offensive), and he later insisted on the term, despite the public uproar it provoked. "Ce sont des voyous, des racailles, je persiste et je signe," Sarkozy said at the height of the riots, and his lexical intransigence went so far as to appeal to tautology: "On l'appelle un voyou parce que c'est un voyou" (Sarkozy, interview). Derrida's own lexical inquiry into the notion of the savage and the *voyou*, or "rogue," underscores the uncanny pertinence of Sarkozy's sovereign tautology; for Derrida, reading political theory in the wake of 9/11, the idea of the "rogue" combines two opposed yet interlinked concepts of being "above the laws" and "without laws" (*The Beast and the Sovereign*, 18): "Sovereign and beast seem to have in common their being-outside-the-law.... Sharing this common being-outside-the-law, beast, criminal, and sovereign have a troubling resemblance: they call on each other and recall each other, from one to the other; there is between sovereign, criminal and beast a sort of obscure and fascinating complicity, or even a worrying mutual attraction, a worrying familiarity, an *unheimlich*, uncanny reciprocal haunting" (17). *The Beast and the Sovereign*, Derrida's final seminar, reprises a motif we have traced here in all of his work, that of the *pas* (step/not), cast throughout the seminar in terms of the insistent and obsessive trace of the savage wolf in political discourse. This *pas de loup* suggestively conveys as well the longstanding and elusive target of deconstruction: "Loup.... Malfaçon dans un ouvrage de construction" (*Petit Robert*).

82. The CPE, or Contrat Première Embauche (First Employment Contract), makes up article 8 of the *loi sur l'égalité des chances* developed in response to the fall 2005 riots. The CPE provided incentives for employers to hire youths under twenty-six-years old; its most controversial feature is that it would have imposed an initial trial period of two years during which the employer could fire his

young employee without need for justification. Michel Kokoreff sees the CPE as amounting to nothing less than "an institutionalization of *précarité*" (Kokoreff, *Sociologie des émeutes*, 103).

83. See Kokoreff, *Sociologie des émeutes*, 10.

84. Kokoreff, *Sociologie des émeutes*, 312. Alain Finkielkraut echoes this attitude of Sarkozy by eliminating all sociological explanations to posit instead an "ethnic" threat against the French nation. Asked to answer whether the riots reflect a "failure of integration," Finkielkraut stated, "Il n'y a pas de lien de cause à effet entre l'aggravation des inégalités, la tristesse des banlieues, le chômage, la pauvreté, la précarité, et des actes pareils. Nul déterminisme économique ne peut rendre raison de ces saccages et de cette volonté de tuer.... Ce ne sont pas des émeutes sociales, ce ne sont pas des émeutes de la faim, ce ne sont pas des émeutes économiques, ce sont des émeutes ethniques dirigées contre la France" (interview).

85. Kokoreff, *Sociologie des émeutes*, 119.

86. Asad, *Genealogies of Religion*, 272.

87. Asad, "Trying to Understand French Secularism," 508.

88. Girard, *Violence and the Sacred*, 85.

89. Balibar, *We, the People of Europe?* 40.

90. Bhabha, "Novel Metropolis," 18.

91. Butler, *Bodies that Matter*, 45.

92. Derrida, *Specters of Marx*, 39.

Bibliography

Adorno, Theodor W. *The Stars Down to Earth and Other Essays on the Irrational in Culture*. Edited by Stephen Crook. London: Routledge, 1994.

Al-Kassim, Dina. *On Pain of Speech: Fantasies of the First Order and the Literary Rant*. Berkeley: University of California Press, 2010.

Alloula, Malek. *The Colonial Harem*. Translated by Myrna Godzich and Wlad Godzich. Minneapolis: University of Minnesota Press, 1986.

Althusser, Louis. "Ideology and Ideological State Apparatuses." In *Lenin and Philosophy*. New York: Monthly Review Press, 1971.

Amin, Samir. *The Liberal Virus: Permanent War and the Americanization of the World*. Translated by James Membrez. New York: Monthly Review Press, 2004.

Amiran, Eyal. *Wandering and Home: Beckett's Metaphysical Narrative*. University Park: Pennsylvania State Press, 1993.

Apter, Emily. *Continental Drift: From National Characters to Virtual Subjects*. Chicago: University of Chicago Press, 1999.

Asad, Talal, ed. *Anthropology and the Colonial Encounter*. Atlantic Highlands NJ: Humanities Press, 1973.

———. *Genealogies of Religion: Discipline and Reasons of Power in Christianity and Islam*. Baltimore: Johns Hopkins University Press, 1993.

———. "Trying to Understand French Secularism." In *Political Theologies*. Edited by Hent de Vries, 494–526. New York: Fordham University Press, 2006.

Attridge, Derek, and Marjorie Howes, eds. *Semicolonial Joyce*. Cambridge: Cambridge University Press, 2000.

Augé, Marc. *L'Impossible voyage*. Paris: Payot, 1997.

———. *Non-Places: Introduction to an Anthropology of Supermodernity*. Translated by John Howe. London: Verso, 1995.

Badré, Frédéric. *Paulhan le juste*. Paris: Grasset, 1996.

Balibar, Etienne. *We, the People of Europe? Reflections on Transnational Citizenship*. Translated by James Swenson. Princeton: Princeton University Press, 2004.

Barthèlemy, Guy. *Fromentin et l'écriture du désert*. Paris: L'Harmattan, 1997.

Barthes, Roland. *Carnets du voyage en Chine*. Paris: Christian Bourgois, 2009.

———. *Critical Essays*. Translated by Richard Howard. Evanston: Northwestern University Press, 1972. Translated from *Essais critiques*, in *Oeuvres complètes*, vol. 1, 1165–1377.

———. "The Death of the Author." In *Image, Music, Text*, 142–48. Translated by Stephen Heath. New York: Hill and Wang, 1977. Translated from "La Mort de l'auteur," in *Oeuvres complètes*, vol. 2, 491–95.

———. *The Eiffel Tower and Other Mythologies*. Translated by Richard Howard. Berkeley: University of California Press, 1997. Translated from "La Tour Eiffel," in *Oeuvres complètes*, vol. 1, 1379–1400.

———. *Empire of Signs*. Translated by Richard Howard. New York: Hill and Wang, 1982. Translated from *L'Empire des signes*, in *Oeuvres complètes*, vol. 2, 743–831.

———. "Entretien." In *Oeuvres complètes*, vol. 3, 774–79.

———. "Fromentin: *Dominique*." In *New Critical Essays*, 91–104. Translated by Richard Howard. New York: Hill and Wang, 1980. Translated from "Fromentin: 'Dominique,'" *Nouveaux essais critiques*, in *Oeuvres complètes*, vol. 2, 1392–1400.

———. "Inaugural Lecture." Translated by Richard Howard. In *A Barthes Reader*. Edited by Susan Sontag, 457–78. New York: Hill and Wang, 1982. Translated from *Leçon*, in *Oeuvres complètes*, vol. 3, 799–814.

———. *Incidents*. Translated by Richard Howard. Berkeley: University of California Press, 1992. Translated from "Incidents," in *Oeuvres complètes*, vol. 3, 1255–72; and "Soirées de Paris," in *Oeuvres complètes*, vol. 3, 1273–86.

———. *Journal de deuil*. Paris: Seuil/Imec, 2009.

———. "The Last Word on Robbe-Grillet?" In *Critical Essays*, 197–204. Translated from "Le Point sur Robbe-Grillet?" in *Essais critiques*, in *Oeuvres complètes*, vol. 1, 1317–22.

———. "Literature and Signification." In *Critical Essays*, 261–79.

———. "Literature and Discontinuity." In *Critical Essays*, 171–83. Translated from "Littérature et discontinu," in *Essais critiques*, in *Oeuvres complètes*, vol. 1, 1299–1308.

———. *A Lover's Discourse: Fragments*. Translated by Richard Howard. New York: Hill and Wang, 1978. Translated from *Fragments d'un discours amoureux*, in *Oeuvres complètes*, vol. 3, 457–687.

———. *Mythologies*. Translated by Annette Lavers. New York: Hill and Wang, 1972. Translated from *Mythologies*, in *Oeuvres complètes*, vol. 1, 561–722.

———. *Oeuvres complètes*. 3 vols. Paris: Seuil, 1992–95.
———. "Pierre Loti: *Aziyadé*." In *New Critical Essays*. Translated by Richard Howard. New York: Hill and Wang, 1980. Translated from "Pierre Loti: 'Aziyadé,'" in *Nouveaux essais critiques*, in *Oeuvres complètes*, vol. 2, 1401–11.
———. *The Pleasure of the Text*. Translated by Richard Miller. New York: Hill and Wang, 1975. Translated from *Le Plaisir du texte*, in *Oeuvres complètes*, vol. 2, 1493–1592.
———. "Préface." *Essais critiques*. In *Oeuvres complètes*. Vol. 1, 1169–76.
———. "Preface to Renaud Camus's *Tricks*." In *The Rustle of Language*, 291–95. Translated by Richard Howard. New York: Hill and Wang, 1986. Translated from "Préface à *Tricks* de Renaud Camus," in *Oeuvres complètes*, vol. 3, 1017–20.
———. "The Reality Effect." In *The Rustle of Language*, 141–48. Translated by Richard Howard. New York: Hill and Wang, 1986. Translated from "L'Effet de réel," in *Oeuvres complètes*, vol. 2, 479–84.
———. "Réquichot et son corps." In *Oeuvres complètes*. Vol. 2, 1623–42.
———. Réponses." In *Oeuvres complètes*. Vol. 2, 1307–24.
———. *Roland Barthes by Roland Barthes*. Translated by Richard Howard. New York: Hill and Wang, 1977. Translated from *Roland Barthes par Roland Barthes*, in *Oeuvres complètes*, vol. 3, 79–250.
———. *The Rustle of Language*. Translated by Richard Howard. New York: Hill and Wang, 1986.
———. "Sémantique de l'objet." In *Oeuvres complètes*. Vol. 2, 65–73.
———. "Sémiologie et urbanisme." In *Oeuvres complètes*. Vol. 2, 439–46.
———. *S/Z*. Translated by Richard Miller. New York: Hill and Wang, 1974. Translated from *S/Z*, in *Oeuvres complètes*, vol. 2, 555–741.
———. "Texte à deux (parties)." In *Oeuvres complètes*. Vol. 3, 761–67.
———. "L'Utopie." In *Oeuvres complètes*. Vol. 3, 44.
———. "Well, and China?" Translated by Lee Hildreth. *Discourse* 8 (Fall/Winter 1986–87): 116–20. Translated from "Alors, la Chine?" in *Oeuvres complètes*, vol. 3, 32–35.
———. *Writing Degree Zero*. Translated by Annette Lavers and Colin Smith. New York: Hill and Wang, 1968. Translated from *Le Degré zéro de l'écriture*, in *Oeuvres complètes*, vol. 1, 137–87.
———. "Writing the Event." In *The Rustle of Language*, 149–54. Translated from "L'Ecriture de l'événement," in *Oeuvres complètes*, vol. 2, 496–500.
Bataille, Georges. "The Sorcerer's Apprentice." Translated by Betsy Wing. In *The College of Sociology 1937–39*. Edited by Denis Hollier, 12–23. Minnesota: University of Minnesota Press, 1988.

Baudelaire, Charles. *The Flowers of Evil*. Translated by James McGowan. Oxford: Oxford University Press, 1993.

———. *Oeuvres complètes*. Paris: Gallimard, 1961.

———. *Oeuvres complètes*. Paris: Seuil, 1968.

———. *The Painter of Modern Life and Other Essays*. Translated by Jonathan Mayne. New York: Da Capo, 1986.

Bauman, Zygmunt. *Globalization: The Human Consequences*. New York: Columbia University Press, 1998.

Beckett, Samuel. "First Love." In *The Complete Short Prose, 1929–1989*. Edited by S. E. Gontarski, 25–45. New York: Grove Press, 1995.

———. *Molloy*. In *Three Novels*, 1–170. Translated by Patrick Bowles and Samuel Beckett. New York: Grove Press, 1965.

———. *Premier amour*. Paris: Editions de Minuit, 1970.

———. "The Way." In *No Symbols Where None Intended: A Catalogue of Books, Manuscripts, and Other Material Relating to Samuel Beckett in the Collections of the Humanities Research Center*. Edited by Carlton Lake, 173. Austin: Humanities Research Center, University of Texas, 1984.

Begag, Azouz. *Ethnicity and Equality: France in the Balance*. Translated by Alec G. Hargreaves. Lincoln: University of Nebraska Press, 2007.

———. *L'Intégration*. Paris: Le Cavalier Bleu, 2003.

Behdad, Ali. *Belated Travelers: Orientalism in the Age of Colonial Dissolution*. Durham: Duke University Press, 1994.

Belaval, Yvon. Présentation to Jean Paulhan, *Traité du ravissement*, 11–18. Paris: Périple, 1983.

Ben Jelloun, Tahar. *Hospitalité française: Racisme et immigration maghrébine*. Paris: Seuil, 1997.

———. *La Plus haute des solitudes: Misère affective et sexuelle d'émigrés nord-africains*. Paris: Seuil, 1977.

Benjamin, Walter. *The Arcades Project*. Translated by Howard Eiland and Kevin McLaughlin. Cambridge MA: Harvard University Press, 1999.

———. *Illuminations*. Translated by Harry Zohn. New York: Schocken, 1969.

Bennington, Geoffrey. "X." In *Interrupting Derrida*, 76–92. London: Routledge, 2000.

Bensmaïa, Réda. *The Barthes Effect: The Essay as Reflective Text*. Translated by Pat Fedkiew. Minneapolis: University of Minnesota Press, 1987.

Bermann, Sandra. Introduction to *Nation, Language, and the Ethics of Translation*. Edited by Sandra Bermann and Michael Wood, 1–10. Princeton: Princeton University Press, 2005.

Bermann, Sandra, and Michael Wood, eds. *Nation, Language, and the Ethics of Translation*. Princeton: Princeton University Press, 2005.

Bersani, Leo, and Ulysse Dutoit. *Arts of Impoverishment: Beckett, Rothko, Resnais*. Cambridge MA: Harvard University Press, 1993.

Bhabha, Homi. *The Location of Culture*. London: Routledge, 1994.

———. "Novel Metropolis." *New Statesman and Society*. February 16, 1990, 16–18.

Blanchot, Maurice. *L'Amitié*. Paris: Gallimard, 1971.

———. "The Ease of Dying." In Jean Paulhan, *Progress in Love on the Slow Side*, 122–40. Translated by Christine Moneera Laennec and Michael Syrotinski. Lincoln: University of Nebraska Press, 1994.

———. *Faux pas*. Paris: Gallimard, 1943.

———. "How Is Literature Possible?" In *The Blanchot Reader*. Translated by Michael Syrotinski. Edited by Michael Holland, 49–60. Oxford: Blackwell, 1995.

———. *The Instant of My Death*. Translated by Elizabeth Rottenberg. Stanford: Stanford University Press, 2000.

———. "The Most Profound Question." In *The Infinite Conversation*, 11–24. Translated by Susan Hanson. Minneapolis: University of Minnesota Press, 1993.

———. "The Paradox of Aytré." In *The Work of Fire*, 61–73. Translated by Charlotte Mandell. Stanford: Stanford University Press, 1995.

———. *Le Pas au-delà*. Paris: Gallimard, 1973.

———. "The Sirens' Song." In *The Sirens' Song*. Translated by Sacha Rabinovitch. Edited by Gabriel Josopovici, 59–65. Bloomington: Indiana University Press, 1982.

———. *The Space of Literature*. Translated by Ann Smock. Lincoln: University of Nebraska Press, 1982. Translated from *L'Espace littéraire* (Paris: Gallimard, 1955).

———. *The Step Not Beyond*. Translated by Lycette Nelson. Albany: State University of New York Press, 1992.

———. "Le Terrorisme, méthode de salut publique." *Combat*, July 7, 1936, 106.

———. *The Work of Fire*. Translated by Charlotte Mandell. Stanford: Stanford University Press, 1995. Translated from *La Part du feu* (Paris: Gallimard, 1949).

———. *The Writing of the Disaster*. Translated by Ann Smock. Lincoln: University of Nebraska Press, 1986.

Blix, Göran. *Paris to Pompeii: French Romanticism and the Cultural Politics of Archaeology*. Philadelphia: University of Pennsylvania Press, 2009.

Bloom, Peter J. "Trans-Saharan Automotive Cinema." In *Virtual Voyages: Cin-*

ema and Travel. Edited by Jeffrey Ruoff, 139–56. Durham: Duke University Press, 2006.

Bois, Yve-Alain, and Rosalind Krauss. *Informe: Mode d'emploi*. Paris: Centre Georges Pompidou, 1996.

Bonnefoy, Yves. *L'Arrière-pays*. Paris: Gallimard, 2003.

Boothby, Richard. *Death and Desire: Psychoanalytic Theory in Lacan's Return to Freud*. New York: Routledge, 1991.

Borer, Alain. "Note de l'éditeur." In *Pour une littérature voyageuse*. Edited by Alain Borer, 7–15. Brussels: Editions Complexe, 1992.

Bottici, Chiara. *A Philosophy of Political Myth*. Cambridge: Cambridge University Press, 2007.

Boudjedra, Rachid. *Fascination*. Paris: Grasset, 2000.

——. *Lettres algériennes*. Paris: Grasset, 1995.

——. *Timimoun*. Paris: Denoël, 1994.

——. *Topographie idéale pour une agression caractérisée*. Paris: Denoël, 1975.

Brantlinger, Patrick. *Dark Vanishings: Discourse on the Extinction of Primitive Races, 1800–1930*. Ithaca: Cornell University Press, 2003.

Breton, André. "A Great Black Poet." In Aimé Césaire, *Notebook of a Return to the Native Land*. Translated by Clayton Eshleman and Annette Smith. Middletown CT: Wesleyan University Press, 2001.

Brooks, Peter. *Reading for the Plot*. Cambridge MA: Harvard University Press, 1984.

Brown, Andrew. *Roland Barthes: The Figures of Writing*. Oxford: Oxford University Press, 1992.

Butler, Judith. *Bodies That Matter: On the Discursive Limits of "Sex."* New York: Routledge, 1993.

——. *Excitable Speech: A Politics of the Performative*. New York: Routledge, 1997.

——. *Giving an Account of Oneself*. New York: Fordham University Press, 2005.

——. *Precarious Life: The Powers of Mourning and Violence*. London: Verso, 2004.

——. *The Psychic Life of Power*. Stanford: Stanford University Press, 1997.

——. *Subjects of Desire: Hegelian Reflections in Twentieth-Century France*. New York: Columbia University Press, 1987.

Caillié, René. *Journal de Voyage à Temboctou et à Jenné dans l'Afrique Centrale*. 1830; Paris: Le Club des Editeurs, 1961.

———. *Travels through Central Africa to Timbuktoo*. 2 vols. London: Frank Cass and Co., 1968.

———. *Voyage à Tombouctou*. 1830; Paris: La Découverte, 2007.

Caltagirone, Benedetto. "Le Séjour en Ethiopie de la mission Dakar-Djibouti." *Gradhiva* 5 (1988): 3–11.

Cardonne, Elisabeth. Introduction to Eugène Fromentin, *Une Année dans le Sahel*, 9–31. Paris: Flammarion, 1991.

Caruth, Cathy. "Trauma and Experience: Introduction." In *Trauma: Explorations in Memory*. Edited by Cathy Caruth, 3–12. Baltimore: Johns Hopkins University Press, 1995.

———. *Unclaimed Experience: Trauma, Narrative, and History*. Baltimore: Johns Hopkins University Press, 1996.

Césaire, Aimé. *Notebook of a Return to the Native Land*. Translated by Clayton Eshleman and Annette Smith. Middletown CT: Wesleyan University Press, 2001.

Chakrabarty, Dipesh. *Provincializing Europe: Postcolonial Thought and Historical Difference*. Princeton: Princeton University Press, 2000.

Chambers, Ross. *Gérard de Nerval et la poétique du voyage*. Paris: José Corti, 1969.

———. *Loiterature*. Lincoln: University of Nebraska Press, 1999.

Charef, Mehdi. *Le Harki de Meriem*. Paris: Mercure de France, 1989.

Chemama, Roland. "L'Expérience du proverbe et le discours psychanalytique." *Ornicar?* 17–18 (1979): 43–55.

Cheng, Vincent. *Joyce, Race and Empire*. Cambridge: Cambridge University Press, 1995.

Chevènement, Jean-Pierre. "Sauvageon versus racaille." March 30, 2007. http://www.chevenement.fr/Sauvageon-versus-racaille_a277.html (accessed January 20, 2010).

Christin, Anne-Marie. *Fromentin conteur d'espace: Essai sur l'oeuvre algérienne*. Paris: Le Sycomore, 1982.

Clancy-Smith, Julia. *Rebel and Saint: Muslim Notables, Populist Protest, Colonial Encounters (Algeria and Tunisia, 1800–1904)*. Berkeley: University of California Press, 1994.

Clastres, Pierre. *Archeology of Violence*. Translated by Jeanine Herman. New York: Semiotext(e), 1994. Translated from *Recherches d'anthropologie politique* (Paris: Seuil, 1980).

———. *Society against the State: Essays in Political Anthropology*. Translated by Robert Hurley and Abe Stein. New York: Zone Books, 1989.

Clifford, James. *On the Edges of Anthropology (Interviews)*. Chicago: Prickly Paradigm Press, 2003.

———. "Partial Truths." *Writing Culture: The Poetics and Politics of Ethnography*. Edited by James Clifford and George E. Marcus, 1–26. Berkeley: University of California Press, 1986.

———. *The Predicament of Culture: Twentieth-Century Ethnography, Literature, and Art*. Cambridge MA: Harvard University Press, 1988.

———. *Routes: Travel and Translation in the Late Twentieth Century*. Cambridge MA: Harvard University Press, 1997.

Clifford, James, and George E. Marcus, eds. *Writing Culture: The Poetics and Politics of Ethnography*. Berkeley: University of California Press, 1986.

Coetzee, J. M. *Waiting for the Barbarians*. London: Penguin, 1980.

———. *White Writing*. New Haven: Yale University Press, 1988.

Comment, Bernard. *Roland Barthes: Vers le neutre*. Paris: Christian Bourgois, 1991.

Compagnon, Antoine. "Who is the Real One?" In *Writing the Image after Roland Barthes*. Edited by Jean-Michel Rabaté, 196–200. Philadelphia: University of Pennsylvania Press, 1997.

Conrad, Joseph. *Heart of Darkness*. In *Heart of Darkness and The Secret Sharer*, 63–164. New York: New American Library, 1997.

Copjec, Joan. *Read My Desire*. Cambridge MA: MIT Press, 1994.

Cornell, Drucilla. *The Philosophy of the Limit*. London: Routledge, 1992.

Culbert, John. "On the Trace of the Other: Memory, Melancholia and Repression in Rachid Boudjedra's *Timimoun*." *L'Esprit créateur* 43, no. 1 (2003): 69–80.

Culler, Jonathan. *Roland Barthes*. New York: Oxford University Press, 1983.

———. "The Semiotics of Tourism." In *Framing the Sign: Criticism and Its Institutions*, 152–67. Norman: University of Oklahoma Press, 1988.

Daudet, Alphonse. *Tartarin de Tarascon*. Paris: Livre de Poche, 1982.

Daumas, Eugène. *Le Grand désert, ou Itinéraire d'une caravane du Sahara au pays des nègres*. Paris: Napoléon Chaix, 1848.

Deane, Seamus. "Dead Ends: Joyce's Finest Moments." In *Semicolonial Joyce*. Edited by Derek Attridge and Marjorie Howes, 21–36. Cambridge: Cambridge University Press, 2000.

Debord, Guy. "Theory of the *dérive*." *Situationist International Anthology*. Edited and translated by Ken Knabb, 50–54. Berkeley CA: Bureau of Public Secrets, 1981.

de Certeau, Michel. *Heterologies: Discourse on the Other*. Translated by Brian Massumi. Minneapolis: University of Minnesota Press, 1986.

———. *The Practice of Everyday Life*. Translated by Steven Rendall. Berkeley: University of California Press, 1984.

de Lauretis, Teresa. "Desire in Narrative." In *Alice Doesn't: Feminism, Semiotics, Cinema*, 103–57. Bloomington: Indiana University Press, 1984.

Deleuze, Gilles. "Coldness and Cruelty." In *Masochism*, 7–138. Translated by Jean McNeil. New York: Zone, 1989.

Deleuze, Gilles, and Claire Parnet. *Dialogues*. Translated by Hugh Tomlinson and Barbara Habberjam. New York: Columbia University Press, 1987.

de Man, Paul. *Blindness and Insight*. Minneapolis: The University of Minnesota Press, 1983.

Derrida, Jacques. *Aporias*. Translated by Thomas Dutoit. Stanford: Stanford University Press, 1993.

———. *Archive Fever: A Freudian Impression*. Translated by Eric Prenowitz. Chicago: University of Chicago Press, 1996.

———. *The Beast and the Sovereign*. Vol. 1. Translated by Geoffrey Bennington. Chicago: University of Chicago Press, 2009.

———. "The Deaths of Roland Barthes" In *The Work of Mourning*. Edited by Pascale-Anne Brault and Michael Naas, 34–67. Chicago: University of Chicago Press, 2001. Translated from "Les Morts de Roland Barthes," *Poétique* 47 (September 1981): 269–92.

———. "Faith and Knowledge." In *Religion*. Edited by Jacques Derrida and Gianni Vattimo, 1–78. Stanford: Stanford University Press, 1998.

———. "Force of Law: The 'Mystical Foundation of Authority.'" Translated by Mary Quaintance. In *Acts of Religion*. Edited by Gil Anidjar, 230–98. New York and London: Routledge, 2002.

———. "The Law of Genre." Translated by Avital Ronell. *Critical Inquiry* 7, no. 1 (1980): 55–81.

———. *Learning to Live Finally: An Interview with Jean Birnbaum*. Translated by Pascale-Anne Brault and Michael Naas. Hoboken NJ: Melville House Publishing, 2007.

———. *Margins of Philosophy*. Translated by Alan Bass. Chicago: University of Chicago Press, 1982.

———. *Mémoires: For Paul de Man*. Translated by Cecile Lindsay, Jonathan Culler, and Eduardo Cadava. New York: Columbia University Press, 1986.

———. *Of Grammatology*. Translated by Gayatri Chakravorty Spivak. Baltimore: Johns Hopkins University Press, 1976. Translated from *De la grammatologie* (Paris: Minuit, 1967).

———. *Of Hospitality / Anne Dufourmantelle Invites Jacques Derrida to Respond.* Translated by Rachel Bowlby. Stanford: Stanford University Press, 2000.

———. *Paper Machine.* Translated by Rachel Bowlby. Stanford: Stanford University Press, 2005.

———. *Parages.* Paris: Galilée, 1986.

———. *Positions.* Chicago: University of Chicago Press, 1981.

———. *The Post Card: From Socrates to Freud and Beyond.* Translated by Alan Bass. Chicago: University of Chicago Press, 1987.

———. *Psyche: Inventions of the Other.* Vol. 1. Edited by Peggy Kamuf and Elizabeth Rottenberg. Stanford: Stanford University Press, 2007.

———. *Resistances of Psychoanalysis.* Translated by Peggy Kamuf, Pascale-Anne Brault, and Michael Naas. Stanford: Stanford University Press.

———. *Specters of Marx: The State of the Debt, the Work of Mourning, and the New International.* Translated by Peggy Kamuf. New York: Routledge, 1994.

———. *The Truth in Painting.* Translated by Geoff Bennington and Ian McLeod. Chicago: University of Chicago Press, 1987. Translated from *La Vérité en peinture* (Paris: Flammarion, 1978).

———. *Without Alibi.* Translated by Peggy Kamuf. Stanford: Stanford University Press, 2002.

———. *The Work of Mourning.* Edited by Pascale-Anne Brault and Michael Naas. Chicago: University of Chicago Press, 2001.

———. *Writing and Difference.* Translated by Alan Bass. Chicago: University of Chicago Press, 1978.

de Troyes, Chrétien. *Le Roman de Perceval, ou le conte du Graal.* Edited by William Roach. Geneva: Droz, 1959.

Djebar, Assia. *Algerian White.* Translated by David Kelley and Marjolijn de Jager. New York: Seven Stories Press, 2000.

———. *Fantasia: An Algerian Cavalcade.* Translated by Dorothy S. Blair. Portsmouth NH: Heinemann, 1993.

———. *Women of Algiers in Their Apartment.* Translated by Marjolijin de Jager. Charlottesville: University Press of Virginia, 1999.

Doane, Mary Anne. *Femmes Fatales: Feminism, Film Theory, Psychoanalysis.* New York: Routledge, 1991.

Dobie, Madeleine. *Foreign Bodies: Gender, Language, and Culture in French Orientalism.* Stanford: Stanford University Press, 2004.

Donadey, Anne. *Recasting Postcolonialism: Women Writing between Worlds.* Hanover NH: Heinemann, 2001.

Doubrovsky, Serge. "Une Ecriture tragique." *Poétique* 47 (1981): 329–54.

Douglas, Mary. *Natural Symbols: Explorations in Cosmology.* New York: Random House, 1973.

Du Bellay, Joachim. *The Regrets; With the Antiquities of Rome, Three Latin Elegies and The Defense and Illustration of the French Language.* Translated and edited by Richard Helgerson. Philadelphia: University of Pennsylvania Press, 2006.

Duffy, Enda. *The Speed Notebook: Velocity, Pleasure, Modernism.* Durham: Duke University Press, 2009.

———. *The Subaltern Ulysses.* Minneapolis: University of Minnesota Press, 1994.

Du Mesnil, Armand. "Zorr." In Eugène Fromentin, *Oeuvres complètes*, 1229–48. Paris: Gallimard, 1984.

Durou, Jean-Marc. *L'Exploration du Sahara.* Paris: Actes Sud, 1993.

Echenoz, Jean. *Courir.* Paris: Editions de Minuit, 2008.

Edwards, Brent. *The Practice of Diaspora: Literature, Translation and the Rise of Black Internationalism.* Cambridge MA: Harvard University Press, 2003.

Einaudi, Jean-Luc. *La Bataille de Paris.* Paris: Seuil, 1991.

Einaudi, Jean-Luc, and Elie Kagan. *17 Octobre 1961.* Paris: Actes Sud, 2001.

Fabian, Johannes. *Anthropology with an Attitude: Critical Essays.* Stanford: Stanford University Press, 2001.

———. *Out of Our Minds: Reason and Madness in the Exploration of Central Africa.* Berkeley: University of California Press, 2000.

———. *Time and the Other: How Anthropology Makes Its Object.* New York: Columbia University Press, 1983.

Fanon, Frantz. "Algeria Unveiled." In *A Dying Colonialism*, 35–68. New York: Grove Press, 1965.

———. *Black Skin, White Masks.* Translated by Charles Lam Markmann. New York: Grove Press, 1967.

———. *The Wretched of the Earth.* Translated by Constance Farrington. New York: Grove Press, 1963.

Fineman, Joel. "The Structure of Allegorical Desire." In *Allegory and Representation.* Edited by Stephen Greenblatt, 26–60. Baltimore: Johns Hopkins University Press, 1981.

Finkielkraut, Alain. Interview. *Qui Vive.* Radio de la Communauté Juive, November 6, 2005.

Flaubert, Gustave. *Sentimental Education.* Translated by Robert Baldick. Edited by Geoffrey Wall. London: Penguin, 2004.

Fletcher, John. "Introduction: Psychoanalysis and the Question of the Other." In Jean Laplanche, *Essays on Otherness*, 1–51. London: Routledge, 1999.

Forsdick, Charles. *Travel in Twentieth-Century French and Francophone Cultures.* Oxford: Oxford University Press, 2005.

Foucault, Michel. "The Discourse on Language." *The Archaeology of Knowledge and The Discourse on Language,* 215–37. Translated by A. M. Sheridan Smith. New York: Pantheon, 1982. Translated from *L'Ordre du discours* (Paris: Gallimard, 1971).

———. *The Order of Things: An Archaeology of the Human Sciences.* New York: Vintage, 1994. Translated from *Les Mots et les choses* (Paris: Gallimard, 1966).

———. "A Preface to Transgression." In *Language, Counter-memory, Practice.* Edited by Donald F. Bouchard, 29–52. Ithaca: Cornell University Press, 1977.

———. "Questions on Geography." In *Power/Knowledge.* Translated and edited by Colin Gordon, 63–77. New York: Pantheon, 1980.

Freud, Sigmund. *Beyond the Pleasure Principle.* Translated by James Strachey. New York: Norton, 1961.

———. *Civilization and Its Discontents.* Translated by James Strachey. New York: W. W. Norton, 1961.

———. "Delusions and Dreams in Jensen's *Gradiva.*" *Writings on Art and Literature.* Edited and translated by James Strachey, 3–86. Stanford: Stanford University Press, 1997.

———. "Fixation to Traumas—The Unconscious." In *Introductory Lectures on Psychoanalysis,* 273–85. Translated by James Strachey. New York : Norton, 1966.

———. *Moses and Monotheism.* Translated by Katherine Jones. New York: Vintage, 1939.

———. "Notes upon a Case of Obsessional Neurosis." In *Three Case Histories.* Translated by James Strachey. Edited by Philip Rieff, 1–82. New York: Collier, 1993.

———. *Sexuality and the Psychology of Love.* New York: Macmillan, 1963.

———. "Some Points in a Comparative Study of Organic Hysterical Paralyses" (1893). In *Early Psychoanalytic Writings.* Translated by M. Meyer. Edited by Philip Rieff, 51–65. New York: Macmillan, 1963.

———. *Studies in Parapsychology.* Edited by Philip Rieff. New York: Collier Books, 1963.

———. *Totem and Taboo: Some Points of Agreement between the Mental Lives of Savages and Neurotics.* Translated by James Strachey. New York: Norton, 1950.

———. "The 'Uncanny.'" *Writings on Art and Literature.* Translated and edited by James Strachey, 193–233. Stanford: Stanford University Press, 1997.

Fromentin, Eugène. *Between Sea and Sahara: An Orientalist Adventure.* Translated by Blake Robinson. London: Tauris Parke, 2004. Translated from *Une Année dans le Sahel*, in *Oeuvres complètes*, 185–365.

———. *Correspondance d'Eugène Fromentin*. Vol. 1. Edited by Barbara Wright. Paris: CNRS-Editions, 1995.

———. *Dominique*. Translated by Edward Marsh. London: Soho Book Company, 1986. Translated from version published in *Oeuvres complètes*, 367–564.

———. *Un Eté dans le Sahara*. In *Oeuvres complètes*, 1–183.

———. "La Fin du ramadan." In *Oeuvres complètes*, 866–67.

———. *Lettres de jeunesse*. Geneva: Slatkine, 1973.

———. "Notes et variantes." In *Oeuvres complètes*.

———. *Oeuvres complètes*. Paris: Edited by Guy Sagnes. Gallimard, 1984.

Garcin, Jérôme, ed. *Nouvelles Mythologies*. Paris: Seuil, 2007.

Gasché, Rodolphe. "The Felicities of Paradox." In *Maurice Blanchot: The Demand of Writing*. Edited by Carolyn Bailey Gill, 34–69. London: Routledge, 1996.

———. "Reading Chiasms." In *Of Minimal Things: Studies on the Notion of Relation*, 263–84. Stanford: Stanford University Press, 1999.

Gautier, Théophile. "Arria Marcella." In *The Quartette*, 315–367. Translated by F. C. de Sumichrast. Boston: C. T. Brainard Publishing, 1901. Translated from "Arria Marcella," in *Récits fantastiques*, 235–72 (Paris: Flammarion, 1981).

———. *Emaux et camées*. Edited by Guy Sagnes. Paris: Gallimard, 1981.

———. *Mademoiselle de Maupin*. Paris: Flammarion, 1966.

———. *Le Roman de la momie*. Paris: René Hilsum, 1933.

Genet, Jean. *The Thief's Journal*. Translated by Bernard Frechtman. New York: Grove Press, 1964.

Genette, Gérard. *Mimologics*. Translated by Thaïs E. Morgan. Lincoln: University of Nebraska Press, 1994.

Gibbons, Luke. "'Have you no homes to go to?': Joyce and the Politics of Paralysis." In *Semicolonial Joyce*. Edited by Derek Attridge and Marjorie Howes, 150–71. Cambridge: Cambridge University Press, 2000.

Gide, André. *Amyntas*. 1906; New York: Ecco Press, 1988.

———. *L'Immoraliste*. Paris: Mercure de France, 1902.

———. *Si le grain ne meurt*. In *Journal 1939–1949 / Souvenirs*, 347–615. Paris: Gallimard, 1954.

———. *Travels in the Congo*. Translated by Dorothy Bussy. New York: Knopf, 1929. Translated from *Voyage au Congo* (Paris: Gallimard, 1954).

Gilroy, Paul. *The Black Atlantic: Modernity and Double Consciousness*. Cambridge MA: Harvard University Press, 1993.

Girard, René. *Violence and the Sacred*. Translated by Patrick Gregory. Baltimore: Johns Hopkins University Press, 1977.

Glissant, Edouard. *Caribbean Discourse: Selected Essays*. Translated by J. Michael Dash. Charlottesville: University Press of Virginia, 1989.

Goethe, Johann Wolfgang von. *Wilhelm Meister's Years of Apprenticeship*. Vol. 1. Translated by H. M. Waidson. London: John Calder, 1977.

Graebner, Seth. *History's Place: Nostalgia and the City in French Algerian Literature*. Lanham MD: Lexington Books, 2007.

Gregg, John. *Maurice Blanchot and the Literature of Transgression*. Princeton: Princeton University Press, 1994.

Grosrichard, Alain. *Structure du sérail: La Fiction du despotisme asiatique dans l'Occident classique*. Paris: Seuil, 1979.

Haneke, Michael, dir. *Caché*. Film. Paris: Les Films du Losange, 2005.

Hardt, Michael, and Antonio Negri. *Multitude: War and Democracy in the Age of Empire*. New York: Penguin, 2004.

Hargreaves, Alec. "Translator's Introduction." In Azouz Begag, *Ethnicity and Equality*, vii–xxii. Lincoln: University of Nebraska Press, 2007.

Hayot, Eric. *Chinese Dreams: Pound, Brecht, Tel quel*. Ann Arbor: University of Michigan Press, 2004.

Heath, Stephen. *The Nouveau Roman: A Study in the Practice of Writing*. London: Elek, 1972.

———. *Vertige du déplacement: Lecture de Barthes*. Paris: Fayard, 1974.

Helgerson, Richard. Introduction to Joachim du Bellay, *The Regrets; With the Antiquities of Rome, Three Latin Elegies and The Defense and Illustration of the French Language*. Translated and edited by Richard Helgerson, 1–36. Philadelphia: University of Pennsylvania Press, 2006.

Hertz, Neil. *The End of the Line: Essays on Psychoanalysis and the Sublime*. New York: Columbia University Press, 1985.

———. Foreword to Sigmund Freud, *Writings on Art and Literature*, ix–xx. Stanford: Stanford University Press, 1997.

Hill, Leslie. *Beckett's Fiction: In Different Words*. Cambridge: Cambridge University Press, 1990.

———. *Blanchot: Extreme Contemporary*. London: Routledge, 1997.

Hollier, Denis. "Le Déséquilibriste." *Critique* 418 (1982): 189–99.

———, ed., *The College of Sociology, 1937–39*, Translated by Betsy Wing. Minneapolis: University of Minnesota Press, 1988.

Hollier, Denis, and Jean Jamin. "Aux fins du Collège de Sociologie." *Gradhiva* 13 (1993): 61–77.

Horkheimer, Max, and Theodor W. Adorno. *Dialectic of Enlightenment*. Translated by John Cumming. New York: Continuum, 1972.

James, C. L. R. *The Black Jacobins: Toussaint l'Ouverture and the San Domingo Revolution*. New York: Vintage, 1989.

Jamin, Jean. "Les Chemins de la Gradiva." *Gradhiva* 2 (1987): 1–6.

———. "Présentation de L'Afrique Fantôme." In Michel Leiris, *Miroir de l'Afrique*. Edited by Jean Jamin, 78–79. Paris: Gallimard, 1996.

Jay, Martin. *Downcast Eyes: The Denigration of Vision in Twentieth-Century French Thought*. Berkeley: University of California Press, 1993.

Jensen, Wilhelm. *Gradiva*. Translated by Helen M. Downey. Los Angeles: Sun and Moon Press, 1993.

Joyce, James. "The Dead." *The Portable James Joyce*. Edited by Harry Levin, 190–242. New York: Penguin, 1976.

Kandiyoti, Dalia. "Roland Barthes Abroad." In *Writing the Image after Roland Barthes*. Edited by Jean-Michel Rabaté, 228–42. Philadelphia: University of Pennsylvania Press, 1997.

Kant, Immanuel. *Critique of Judgment*. Translated by Werner S. Pluhar. Indianapolis: Hackett, 1987.

Katz, Daniel. *Saying I No More: Subjectivity and Consciousness in the Prose of Samuel Beckett*. Evanston: Northwestern University Press, 1999.

Kaufmann, Vincent. "Michel Leiris: 'On ne part pas.'" *Revue des Sciences Humaines* 214 (1989): 145–62.

Khatib, Abdelhafid. "Essai de description psychogéographique des Halles." *Internationale Situationniste* no. 2 (December 1958): 13–18.

Killick, Andrew P. "The Penetrating Intellect." In *Taboo: Sex, Identity and Erotic Subjectivity in Anthropological Fieldwork*. Edited by Don Kulick and Margaret Willson, 76–106. London: Routledge, 1995.

Kincaid, Jamaica. *A Small Place*. London: Virago, 1988.

———. "In History." *Calalloo* 20, no. 1 (1997): 1–7.

Knowles, Owen. Introduction to Joseph Conrad, *Almayer's Folly: A Story of an Eastern River*. Edited by Owen Knowles, xvii–xliii. London: J. M. Dent, 1995.

Kokoreff, Michel. *Sociologie des émeutes*. Paris: Payot, 2008.

Kofman, Sarah. *Freud and Fiction*. Translated by Sarah Wykes. Boston: Northeastern University Press, 1991.

Krakauer, Jon. *Into Thin Air: A Personal Account of the Mount Everest Disaster*. New York: Anchor Books, 1998.

Krauss, Rosalind. *The Originality of the Avant-Garde and Other Modernist Myths*. Cambridge MA: MIT Press.

Kristeva, Julia. *About Chinese Women*. Translated by Anita Barrows. New York: Marion Boyars, 1986. Translated from *Des Chinoises* (Paris: Editions des Femmes, 1974).

Kulick, Don, and Margaret Willson, eds. *Taboo: Sex, Identity and Erotic Subjectivity in Anthropological Fieldwork*. London: Routledge, 1995.

Lacan, Jacques. *Ecrits*. Paris: Seuil, 1966.

———. *Ecrits II*. Paris: Seuil, 1971.

———. *Ecrits: A Selection*. Translated by Alan Sheridan. New York: Norton, 1977.

———. *Le séminaire, livre xx: Encore*. Paris: Seuil, 1975.

———. *The Four Fundamental Concepts of Psycho-Analysis*. Translated by Alan Sheridan. New York: Norton, 1978. Translated from *Le Séminaire, livre XI: Les Quatre concepts fondamentaux de la psychanalyse* (Paris: Seuil, 1973).

———. *On Feminine Sexuality, the Limits of Love and Knowledge: The Seminar of Jacques Lacan, Book xx, Encore*. Edited by Jacques-Alain Miller. Translated by Bruce Fink. New York: Norton, 1999.

———. *The Seminar of Jacques Lacan, Book VII. The Ethics of Psychoanalysis*. Edited by Jacques-Alain Miller. Translated by Dennis Porter. New York: Norton, 1992.

Lafouge, Jean-Pierre. *Etude sur l'orientalisme d'Eugène Fromentin dans ses "récits algériens."* New York: Peter Lang, 1988.

Lambry, Léon. *Dans les sables rouges*. Collection Printemps no. 58. Paris: Dalzan, 1933.

Lane, Christopher. "'Savage Ecstasy': Colonialism and the Death Drive." In *The Psychoanalysis of Race*. Edited by Christopher Lane, 282–304. New York: Columbia University Press, 1998.

Laplanche, Jean. *Essays on Otherness*. Edited by John Fletcher. London: Routledge, 1999.

———. *Le Fourvoiement biologisant de la sexualité chez Freud*. Paris: Les Empêcheurs de Penser en Rond, 1993.

———. *Life and Death in Psychoanalysis*. Translated by Jeffrey Mehlman. Baltimore: Johns Hopkins University Press, 1976.

Laplanche, Jean, and Jean-Bertrand Pontalis. "Fantasy and the Origins of Sexuality." In *Formations of Fantasy*. Edited by Victor Burgin, James Donald and Cora Kaplan, 5–34. London: Methuen, 1986.

———. *The Language of Psychoanalysis*. Translated by Donald Nicholson-Smith. New York: Norton, 1973.

Larson, Ruth. "Ethnography, Thievery, and Cultural Identity: A Rereading of

Michel Leiris' *L'Afrique fantôme*." *Publications of the Modern Language Association* 112 (March 1997): 229–42.

Le Bris, Michel. "Fragments du royaume." In *Pour une littérature voyageuse*. Edited by Alain Borer, 138–39. Brussels: Editions Complexe, 1992.

Le Bris, Michel, and Jean Rouaud, eds. *Pour une littérature-monde*. Paris: Gallimard, 2007.

Le Bris, Michel, et al. "Pour une littérature-monde en français." *Le Monde des livres*, March 16, 2007, 2.

Lee, Jonathan Scott. *Jacques Lacan*. Amherst: University of Massachusetts Press, 1991.

Leiris, Michel. *L'Afrique fantôme*. Paris: Gallimard, 1981.

———. *L'Afrique fantôme*. In *Miroir de L'Afrique*. Edited by Jean Jamin, 87–869. Paris: Gallimard, 1996.

———. "Apartheid." Translated by Peggy Kamuf. In *For Nelson Mandela*. Edited by Jacques Derrida and Mustapha Tlili, 71. New York: Seaver Books, 1987.

———. *Brisées: Broken Branches*. Translated by Lydia Davis. San Francisco: North Point Press, 1989. Translated from *Brisées* (Paris: Mercure de France, 1966).

———. "La Croyance aux génies *zâr* en Ethiopie du Nord." In *Miroir de l'Afrique*. Edited by Jean Jamin, 923–45. Paris: Gallimard, 1996.

———. *Fibrilles*. Paris: Gallimard, 1966.

———. *Frêle bruit*. Paris: Gallimard, 1976.

———. *L'Homme sans honneur: Notes pour le sacré dans la vie quotidienne*. Edited by Jean Jamin. Paris: Jean-Michel Place, 1994.

———. *Instructions sommaires pour les collecteurs d'objets ethnographiques*. Paris: Musée d'Ethnographie et Mission Dakar-Djibouti, 1931.

———. *Journal*. Edited by Jean Jamin. Paris: Gallimard, 1992.

———. *Langage tangage ou ce que les mots me disent*. Paris: Gallimard, 1985.

———. *Manhood: A Journey from Childhood into the Fierce Order of Virility*. Translated by Richard Howard. San Francisco: North Point Press, 1984. Translated from *L'Age d'homme* (Paris: Gallimard, 1939).

———. Notebooks. Manuscript. Lake Collection, Humanities Research Center, University of Texas.

———. *Nuits sans nuit et quelques jours sans jour*. Paris: Gallimard, 1961.

———. *Operratiques*. Paris: P. O. L., 1992.

———. *La Possession et ses aspects théâtraux chez les Ethiopiens de Gondar*. In *Miroir de L'Afrique*. Edited by Jean Jamin, 949–1061. Paris: Gallimard, 1996.

———. "Race et Civilisation." In *Cinq études d'ethnologie*, 9–80. Paris: Denoël, 1969.

———. "The Sacred in Everyday Life." Translated by Betsy Wing. In *The College of Sociology*. Edited by Denis Hollier, 98–102. Minnesota: University of Minnesota Press, 1988.

———. *Scraps*. Translated by Lydia Davis. Baltimore: Johns Hopkins University Press, 1997. Translated from *Fourbis* (Paris: Gallimard, 1955).

———. *Scratches*. Translated by Lydia Davis. New York: Paragon House, 1991. Translated from *Biffures* (Paris: Gallimard, 1948).

Levinas, Emmanuel. "Philosophy and the Idea of Infinity." In *Collected Philosophical Papers*, 47–60. Translated by Alphonso Lingis. The Hague: Martinus Nijhoff, 1977.

———. *Totalité et infini: Essai sur l'extériorité*. The Hague: Martinus Nijhoff, 1961.

Lévi-Strauss, Claude. "Cultural Discontinuity and Economic and Social Development." In *Structural Anthropology*. Vol. 2, 312–22. Translated by Monique Layton. Chicago: University of Chicago Press, 1983.

———. "Jean-Jacques Rousseau, Founder of the Sciences of Man." In *Structural Anthropology*. Vol. 2, 33–43. Translated by Monique Layton. Chicago: University of Chicago Press, 1983.

———. "Race and History." In *Structural Anthropology*. Vol. 2, 323–62. Translated by Monique Layton. Chicago: University of Chicago Press, 1976.

———. *The Savage Mind*. Chicago: University of Chicago Press, 1966. Translated from *La Pensée sauvage* (Paris: Plon, 1962).

———. *Tristes Tropiques*. Translated by John and Doreen Weightman. London: Penguin, 1992. Translated from *Tristes tropiques* (Paris: Plon, 1955).

Lévy-Bruhl, Lucien. *Les Fonctions mentales dans les sociétés inférieures*. Paris: Alcan, 1910.

———. *La Mentalité primitive*. Paris: Alcan, 1923.

Lloyd, David. *Anomalous States: Irish Writing and the Post-Colonial Moment*. Durham: Duke University Press, 1993.

Lorcin, Patricia M. E. *Imperial Identities: Stereotyping, Prejudice and Race in Colonial Algeria*. London: I. B. Tauris, 1995.

Lotman, Jurij. "The Origin of Plot in the Light of Typology." *Poetics Today* 1, no. 1–2 (1979): 161–84.

Lotringer, Sylvère. "Phantoms of the Opera." *Diacritics* 23, no. 4 (1993): 62–71.

Loutfi, Martine Astier. *Littérature et Colonialisme: L'Expansion coloniale vue dans la littérature romanesque française 1871–1914*. Paris: Mouton, 1971.

Lowe, Lisa. *Critical Terrains*. Ithaca: Cornell University Press, 1991.

Lucey, Michael. *Gide's Bent*. New York: Oxford University Press, 1995.

Lyotard, Jean-François. *The Differend: Phrases in Dispute*. Translated by Georges Van Den Abbeele. Minneapolis: University of Minnesota Press, 1988.

———. *Lessons on the Analytic of the Sublime*. Translated by Elizabeth Rottenberg. Stanford: Stanford University Press, 1994.

———. *The Postmodern Condition: A Report on Knowledge*. Translated by Geoff Bennington and Brian Massumi. Minneapolis: University of Minnesota Press, 1984.

MacCannell, Dean. *The Tourist: A New Theory of the Leisure Class*. New York: Schocken, 1976.

Malabou, Catherine, and Jacques Derrida. *Counterpath: Traveling with Jacques Derrida*. Translated by David Wills. Stanford: Stanford University Press, 2004.

Malinowski, Bronislaw. *Argonauts of the Western Pacific*. Prospect Heights IL: Waveland Press, 1984.

Mannoni, Octave. *Clefs pour l'Imaginaire ou l'Autre Scène*. Paris: Seuil, 1969.

———. *Prospero and Caliban: The Psychology of Colonization*. Translated by Pamela Powesland. Ann Arbor: University of Michigan Press, 1991.

Maranhão, Tullio. Introduction to *Translation and Ethnography: The Anthropological Challenge of Intercultural Understanding*. Edited by Tullio Maranhão and Bernhard Streck, xi–xxvi. Tucson: University of Arizona Press, 2003.

Maranhão, Tullio, and Bernhard Streck, eds. *Translation and Ethnography: The Anthropological Challenge of Intercultural Understanding*. Tucson: University of Arizona Press, 2003.

Marcuse, Herbert. "Repressive Tolerance." In Robert Paul Wolff, Barrington Moore, and Herbert Marcuse, *Critique of Pure Tolerance*, 81–117. Boston: Beacon Press, 1965.

Maspero, François. *Roissy Express: A Journey through the Paris Suburbs*. Translated by Paul Jones. New York: Verso, 1994.

Massonet, Stéphane. "Quelques lettres à propos du relativisme culturel." *Gradhiva* 19 (1996): 97–114.

Maupassant, Guy de. *Au soleil*. Paris: Conard, 1924.

———. *Bel-Ami*. Translated by Margaret Maulden. Oxford: Oxford University Press, 2001.

———. *Selected Short Stories*. Translated by Roger Colet. London: Penguin, 1971.

Mbembe, Achille. *On the Postcolony*. Berkeley: University of California Press, 2001.

Mehlman, Jeffrey. *Genealogies of the Text: Literature, Psychoanalysis, and Politics in Modern France*. Cambridge: Cambridge University Press, 1995.

———. *Legacies: Of Anti-Semitism in France*. Minneapolis: University of Minnesota Press, 1983.

Méla, Charles. "Perceval." In *Literature and Psychoanalysis: The Question of Reading Otherwise*. Edited by Shoshana Felman, 253–79. Baltimore: Johns Hopkins University Press, 1982.

Mellah, Fawzi. *Clandestin en Méditerranée*. Paris: Le Cherche Midi, 2000.

Memmi, Albert. *The Colonizer and the Colonized*. Translated by Howard Greenfeld. Boston: Beacon Press, 1967.

Mercier, Jacques. "Présentation de La Possession et ses aspects théâtraux chez les Ethiopiens de Gondar." In Michel Leiris, *Miroir de l'Afrique*, 891–911. Paris: Gallimard: 1996.

Mérimée, Prosper. "La Vénus d'Ille." In *Romans et nouvelles*. Edited by Henri Martineau. Paris: Gallimard, 1951.

Miller, Christopher. *The French Atlantic Triangle: Literature and Culture of the Slave Trade*. Durham: Duke University Press, 2008.

———. *Theories of Africans: Francophone Literature and Anthropology in Africa*. Chicago: University of Chicago Press, 1990.

Miller, D. A. *Bringing Out Roland Barthes*. Berkeley: University of California Press, 1992.

Milne, Anna-Louise. *The Extreme In-Between: Jean Paulhan's Place in the Twentieth Century*. Oxford: Legenda, 2006.

Milner, Jean-Claude. "La Technique littéraire des paradoxes de Zénon." In *Détections fictives*, 45–71. Paris: Seuil, 1985.

Morand, Paul. *Eloge du repos: Apprendre à se reposer*. Paris: Arléa, 1996.

Nancy, Jean-Luc. "The Sublime Offering." In *Of the Sublime: Presence in Question*. Edited and translated by Jeffrey S. Librett, 25–54. Albany: State University of New York Press, 1993.

Nerlich, Michael. *Ideology of Adventure: Studies in Modern Consciousness, 1100–1750*. Translated by Ruth Crowley. Minneapolis: University of Minnesota Press, 1987.

Nerval, Gérard de. "Isis." In *Oeuvres*. Vol. 1, 317–28. Edited by Albert Béguin and Jean Richer. Paris: Gallimard (Bibliothèque de la Pléiade), 1952.

———. *Selected Writings*. Translated by Richard Seiburth. London: Penguin, 1999.

———. *Voyage en Orient*. In *Oeuvres*. Vol. 2, 171–840. Edited by Jean Guillaume and Claude Pichois. Paris: Gallimard (Bibliothèque de la Pléiade), 1984.

Newman, Michael. "The Trace of Trauma." In *Maurice Blanchot: The Demand of Writing*. Edited by Carolyn Bailey Gill, 153–73. London: Routledge, 1996.

Nizan, Paul. *Aden, Arabie*. Paris: François Maspero, 1960.

North, Michael. *The Final Sculpture: Public Monuments and Modern Poets*. Ithaca: Cornell University Press, 1985.

O'Riley, Michael. *Postcolonial Haunting and Victimization: Assia Djebar's New Novels*. New York: Peter Lang, 2007.

Ortega y Gasset, José. *The Dehumanization of Art and Other Essays on Art, Culture, and Literature*. Translated by Helene Weyl, Paul Snodgress, Joseph Frank, and Willard R. Trask. Princeton: Princeton University Press, 1968.

Ortner, Sherry B. *Life and Death on Mt. Everest: Sherpas and Himalayan Mountaineering*. Princeton: Princeton University Press, 1999.

Pattullo, Polly. *Last Resorts: The Cost of Tourism in the Caribbean*. London: Cassell, 1996.

Paulhan, Jean. "Anarchie." In *Oeuvres complètes*. Vol. 4, 452–56.

———. *Aytré qui perd l'habitude*. Le Revest-les-Eaux: Spectres Familiers, 1988.

———. "Aytré qui perd l'habitude." In *Oeuvres complètes*. Vol. 1, 237–60.

———. *Chroniques de Jean Guérin*. Paris: Editions des Cendres, 1991.

———. "Cours de malgache." In *Cahiers Jean Paulhan*. Vol. 2, 175–90. Paris: Gallimard, 1982.

———. "La Demoiselle aux miroirs." In *Oeuvres complètes*. Vol. 2, 169–83.

———. "Entretien avec Robert Mallet." In *Oeuvres complètes*. Vol. 1, 299–311.

———. "L'Expérience du proverbe." In *Oeuvres complètes*. Vol. 2, 97–124.

———. *The Flowers of Tarbes, or Terror in Literature*. Translated by Michael Syrotinski. Urbana: University of Illinois Press, 2006. Translated from *Les Fleurs de Tarbes ou la Terreur dans les Lettres* (Paris: Gallimard, 1990).

———. *Le Fruit dans la forêt*. Paris: Seghers, 1990.

———. "Le Guerrier appliqué." In *Oeuvres complètes*. Vol. 1, 163–215.

———. *Les Hain-teny merina*. Paris: Geuthner, 1913.

———. *Les Hain-tenys*. Paris: Gallimard, 1939.

———. "Les Hain-tenys, poésie de dispute." 1939. In *Oeuvres complètes*. Vol. 2, 67–96.

———. "Happiness in Slavery." In Pauline Réage, *Story of O*, xxi–xxxvi. Translated by Sabine d'Estrée. New York: Grove Press, 1965.

———. *L'Innocence utile*. Paris: L'Echoppe, 1994.

———. "Jules Vallès." In *Oeuvres complètes*. Vol. 4, 57–63.

———. "Le Marquis de Sade et sa complice." In *Oeuvres complètes*. Vol. 4, 9–36.

———. "La Mentalité primitive et l'illusion des explorateurs." In *Oeuvres complètes*. Vol. 2, 141–53.

———. *Oeuvres complètes*. Vol. 1. Paris: Cercle du Livre Précieux, 1966.

———. *Oeuvres complètes*. Vol. 1, *Récits*. Edited by Bernard Baillaud. Paris: Gallimard, 2006.

———. *Oeuvres complètes*. Vol. 2. Paris: Cercle du Livre Précieux, 1966.

———. *Oeuvres complètes*. Vol. 4. Paris: Cercle du Livre Précieux, 1969.

———. *Oeuvres complètes*. Vol. 5. Paris: Cercle du Livre Précieux, 1970.

———. *Of Chaff and Wheat: Writers, War and Treason*. Translated by Richard Rand. Urbana: University of Illinois Press, 2004. Translated from "De la paille et du grain," in *Oeuvres complètes*, vol. 5, 313–406.

———. *On Poetry and Politics*. Translated by Jennifer Bajorek, Charlotte Mandell, and Eric Trudel. Edited by Jennifer Bajorek and Eric Trudel. Urbana: University of Illinois Press, 2008.

———. *Progress in Love on the Slow Side*. Translated by Christine Moneera Laennec and Michael Syrotinski. Lincoln: University of Nebraska Press, 1994.

———. "La Rhétorique renaît de ses cendres." In *Oeuvres complètes*. Vol. 2, 155–67.

———. "Sacred Language." Translated by Betsy Wing. *The College of Sociology 1937–39*. Edited by Denis Hollier, 304–21. Minneapolis: University of Minnesota Press, 1988.

———. "Sémantique du proverbe." In *Cahiers Jean Paulhan*. Vol. 2, 266–311. Paris: Gallimard, 1982.

———. *La Vie est pleine de choses redoutables*. Edited by Claire Paulhan. Paris: Seghers, 1989.

Porch, Douglas. *The Conquest of the Sahara*. London: Jonathan Cape, 1984.

Pratt, Mary Louise. *Imperial Eyes: Travel Writing and Transculturation*. London: Routledge, 1992.

Price, Sally, and Jean Jamin. "Entretien avec Michel Leiris." *Gradhiva* 4 (1988): 29–56.

Rabaté, Jean-Michel. Introduction to *Writing the Image after Roland Barthes*. Edited by Jean-Michel Rabaté, 1–16. Philadelphia: University of Pennsylvania Press, 1997.

Rabinow, Paul. *French Modern: Norms and Forms of the Social Environment*. Cambridge MA: MIT Press, 1989.

Rancière, Jacques. *Le Spectateur emancipé*. Paris: La Fabrique d'Editions, 2008.

Réage, Pauline. *Story of O*. Translated by Sabine d'Estrée. New York: Grove Press, 1965.

Richard, Jean-Pierre. *Littérature et sensation*. Paris: Seuil, 1954.

Richman, Michèle. "Leiris's *L'âge d'homme*: Politics and the Sacred in Everyday Ethnography." *Yale French Studies* 81 (1992): 91–110.
Rimbaud, Arthur. "Le Bateau ivre." In *Oeuvres complètes*, 100–103. Paris: Gallimard, 1954.
Robbe-Grillet, Alain. *C'est Gradiva qui vous appelle*. Paris: Minuit, 2002.
———. *Snapshots*. Translated by Bruce Morrissette. New York: Grove Press, 1968. Translated from *Instantanés* (Paris: Minuit, 1962).
———. *Topology of a Phantom City*. Translated by J. A. Underwood. New York: Grove Press, 1977.
———, dir. *Gradiva*. Film. Paris: Acajou Films, 2006.
Robeson, Paul. *Here I Stand*. Boston: Beacon Press, 1958.
Rodinson, Maxime. *La Fascination de l'Islam*. Paris: François Maspero, 1980.
Rosaldo, Renato. *Culture and Truth: The Remaking of Social Analysis*. Boston: Beacon Press, 1989.
Rosello, Mireille. *Postcolonial Hospitality: The Immigrant as Guest*. Stanford: Stanford University Press, 2001.
Ross, Kristin. *Fast Cars, Clean Bodies: Decolonization and the Reordering of French Culture*. Cambridge MA: MIT Press, 1995.
Royle, Nicholas. *The Uncanny*. London: Routledge, 2003.
Rousseau, Jean-Jacques. *Reveries of the Solitary Walker*. Translated by Peter France. London: Penguin, 1979. Translated from *Les Rêveries du promeneur solitaire*, edited by Erik Leborgne (Paris: Flammarion, 1997).
Sagnes, Guy. "Les Voyages de Fromentin en Algérie." In Eugène Fromentin, *Oeuvres complètes*, 1251–59. Paris: Gallimard, 1984.
Said, Edward. *Culture and Imperialism*. New York: Vintage, 1994.
———. *Orientalism*. New York: Random House, 1978.
Saint-Exupéry, Antoine de. *Terre des hommes*. Paris: Gallimard, 1939.
Sandoval, Chela. *Methodology of the Oppressed*. Minneapolis: University of Minnesota Press, 2000.
Sarkozy, Nicolas. Interview. *A vous de juger*. France 2, November 10, 2005.
Sarraute, Nathalie. *Oeuvres complètes*. Paris: Gallimard, 1996.
Sartre, Jean-Paul. *Qu'est-ce que la littérature?* Paris: Gallimard, 1948.
Savin, Tristan. "La Saga Le Clézio." *Lire*, November 2008, 34–37.
Sebbar, Leïla. *Métro: Instantanés*. Monaco: Editions du Rocher, 2007.
———. *La Seine était rouge. Paris, octobre 1961*. Paris: Thierry Magnier, 1999.
Segonds, Jean-Philippe. "Le Retour de Jean Guérin." In Jean Paulhan, *Chroniques de Jean Guérin*. Edited by Jean-Philippe Segonds, 9–20. Paris: Editions des Cendres, 1991.

Selvon, Sam. *The Lonely Londoners*. Harlow, UK: Longman, 1985.

Sieburth, Richard. "Introductory Note to 'Angélique' and 'Sylvie,'." In Gérard de Nerval, *Selected Writings*, 61–65. London: Penguin, 1999.

———. "Leiris/Nerval: A Few File Cards." *October* 112 (2005): 51–62.

Silverman, Kaja. *Male Subjectivity at the Margins*. London: Routledge, 1992.

Silverstein, Paul A. *Algeria in France: Transpolitics, Race, and Nation*. Bloomington: Indiana University Press, 2004.

Silverstein, Paul, and Chantal Tetrault. "Urban Violence in France." Middle East Report Online. November 2005. http://www.merip.org/mero/interventions/silverstein_tetreault_interv.htm (accessed December 15, 2009).

Simon, Claude. *The Flanders Road*. Translated by Richard Howard. New York: George Braziller, 1961.

Skeat, Walter W. *A Concise Etymological Dictionary of the English Language*. New York: Putnam, 1980.

Smock, Ann. "More on 'Writing and Deference.'" *Representations*, no. 18 (Spring 1987): 158–64.

———. *What Is There to Say?* Lincoln: University of Nebraska Press, 2003.

Spivak, Gayatri Chakravorty. *A Critique of Postcolonial Reason: Toward a History of the Vanishing Present*. Cambridge MA: Harvard University Press, 1999.

———. *In Other Worlds: Essays in Cultural Politics*. New York: Routledge, 1988.

———. "Translating into English." In *Nation, Language, and the Ethics of Translation*. Edited by Sandra Bermann and Michael Wood, 93–110. Princeton: Princeton University Press, 2005.

———. "Translator's Preface." In Jacques Derrida, *Of Grammatology*. Translated by Gayatri Chakravorty Spivak, ix–xc. Baltimore: Johns Hopkins University Press, 1974.

Stoekl, Allan. *Politics, Writing, Mutilation*. Minneapolis: University of Minnesota Press, 1985.

Syrotinski, Michael. *Defying Gravity: Jean Paulhan's Interventions in Twentieth-Century French Intellectual History*. Albany: State University of New York Press, 1998.

———. Introduction to Jean Paulhan, *Progress in Love on the Slow Side*, vii–xxii. Translated by Christine Moneera Laennec and Michael Syrotinski. Lincoln: University of Nebraska Press, 1994.

———, ed. "The Power of Rhetoric, the Rhetoric of Power: Jean Paulhan's Fiction, Criticism, and Editorial Activity." Special issue, *Yale French Studies* 106 (2004).

Terdiman, Richard. *Discourse/Counter-Discourse: The Theory and Practice of Sym-*

bolic Resistance in Nineteenth-Century France. Ithaca: Cornell University Press, 1985.

Thompson, James, and Barbara Wright. *La Vie et l'oeuvre d'Eugène Fromentin*. Paris: ACR, 1987.

Tiedmann, Rolf. "Dialectics at a Standstill." In Walter Benjamin, *The Arcades Project*. Translated by Howard Eiland and Kevin McLaughlin, 929–45. Cambridge MA: Harvard University Press, 1999.

Todorov, Tzvetan. *On Human Diversity: Nationalism, Racism, and Exoticism in French Thought*. Translated by Catherine Porter. Cambridge MA: Harvard University Press, 1993.

Ungar, Steven. *Scandal and Aftereffect: Blanchot and France since 1930*. Minneapolis: University of Minnesota Press, 1995.

Van Den Abbeele, Georges. *Travel as Metaphor: from Montaigne to Rousseau*. Minneapolis: University of Minnesota Press, 1992.

Virilio, Paul. *Open Sky*. Translated by Julie Rose. London: Verso, 1997.

Waberi, Abdourahman A. *Aux Etats-Unis d'Afrique*. Paris: Jean-Claude Lattès, 2006.

Wallerstein, Immanuel. "Integration to What? Marginalization from What?" In *The End of the World as We Know It: Social Science for the Twenty-First Century*, 104–17. Minneapolis: University of Minnesota Press, 1999.

Wieners, Brad. "The 25 (Essential) Books for the Well-Rounded Explorer." *Outside*, January 2003, http://outside.away.com/outside/features/200301/200301_adventure_canon_1.html (accessed February 7, 2010).

Wright, Barbara. *Eugène Fromentin: A Life in Art and Letters*. Bern: Peter Lang, 2000.

Yeshua, Silvio. "Jean Paulhan et les hain-teny: De l'étude savante au récit initiatique." In *Cahiers Jean Paulhan*. Vol. 2, 338–56. Paris: Gallimard, 1982.

Young, Robert. *White Mythologies: Writing History and the West*. London: Routledge, 1990.

Žižek, Slavoj. *Looking Awry*. Cambridge MA: MIT Press, 1991.

———. *The Sublime Object of Ideology*. London: Verso, 1989.

Zweig, Paul. *The Adventurer*. Princeton: Princeton University Press, 1974.

Index

About Chinese Women (Des Chinoises) (Kristeva), 307
Abyssinia, Leiris in, 226
"acting out," 244, 390n76
Adorno, Theodor W., 273, 320
adventure literature, 30–32, 35, 364n64
The Adventurer (Zweig), 35–36
L'Afrique fantôme (Leiris), 60–61, 201–9, 214, 224–34, 237–40, 247–48
"Aggressivity in Psychoanalysis" ("L'Agressivité en psychanalyse") (Lacan), 38
Algeria, 353. *See also* Algerian War; anti-Arab violence; French Algeria
Algerian War, 54, 343–45
alibi, 268, 274–75
Al-Kassim, Dina, 92, 363n57
allegory, 66, 222–24
Alloula, Malek, 41
Almayer's Folly (Conrad), 364n61
Althusser, Louis, 275
American literature, and travel, 97–98
Amin, Samir, 349, 403n77
"The Analytic of the Sublime" (Kant), 137
"Antéros" (Nerval), 88
anthropology, 3–6, 8, 13, 19, 59–62, 247, 318, 357n4. *See also* ethnography
anti-Arab violence, 329–30, 339–40, 342, 401n42, 401nn47–48, 402n57, 402nn59–60
aporia, 10–12, 17, 20–21, 107, 138, 144, 242; Derrida on, 64, 368n22
Apter, Emily, 142, 337

archaeology, 78, 83–84
Archeology of Violence (Recherches d'anthropologie politique) (Clastres), 357n3, 357–58n5
arche-violence model, 27, 363n52
archive fever, 80, 90, 91, 141, 148, 369n46
Archive Fever (Mal d'archive) (Derrida), 79–80
Argonauts of the Western Pacific (Malinowski), 357n3
Aristotle, 42
"Arria Marcella" (Gautier), 80–87, 369–70n57
L'Arrière-pays (Bonnefoy), 371n67
arrivant, 48, 106–7, 144, 148, 335–36
art, 72–73, 123, 135
"l'Art" (Gautier), 82, 369n49
Asad, Talal, 318, 352–53
atopie, 46, 260, 262, 308
Augé, Marc, 151, 342
Aurélia (Nerval), 93
Aurora (Leiris), 93
Aury, Dominique, 196–97
Au soleil (Maupassant), 151–52
authenticity, search for, 40, 365–66n78
autobiography: and anthropology, 61–62; elements of in writing, 220–22, 231–36, 238, 240–45, 247–51
Aux Etats-Unis d'Afrique (Waberi), 375n54
"Aytré Who Gets Out of the Habit" ("Aytré qui perd l'habitude") (Paulhan), 158–61, 165–66, 173, 175, 188, 194, 196, 379n5, 379n10

Aziyadé (Loti), 119, 301–2, 304

Badré, Frédéric, 188, 192–93
Balibar, Étienne, 353–54
The Ballad of Reading Gaol (Wilde), 236
Bandung Conference, 53–54
Barthèlemy, Guy, 133–34, 137
Barthes, Roland, 14, 46, 138, 257–312; on atopia, 260, 262; on *Aziyadé*, 119; on *bêtise*, 283–84; *Camera Lucida*, 282, 310, 312, 397n98; and China, 305–8; and classification, 260–62, 264, 290; on colonialism, 268–69, 305, 393–94n26; critique of *The Lost Continent*, 54; "Death of the Author," 110–11, 113, 117–18, 261; on *dérive*, 266, 278, 280, 293, 306–7; Derrida on, 310; and desire, 260–62, 264, 289, 293–94, 303–4; on *Dominique*, 118–19, 121; *The Eiffel Tower*, 280; *Empire of Signs*, 288, 297–98; and the ethical, 310–11, 397n96; and Flaubert, 282–84, 294; on Freud, 287; on *Gradiva*, 77; on haiku, 298–300; and identity, 289; and the Imaginary, 290; "Inaugural Lecture," 257–62, 267, 272, 280, 297; *Incidents*, 304–5; and irony, 283; and Japan, 297–300, 395n71; "The Jet-man," 269; and Lacanian theory, 395n60; and language, 263–64, 266–67, 294, 298–99, 301–2, 393n16; on literary style, 295–96; on love, 284–85, 286–91; and the Nouveau Roman, 330–31; on the occult, 271–73; and Orientalism, 300, 303–4; and the other, 260–61, 267, 306–7; on paralysis, 259–60; and Paulhan, 193, 266; *The Pleasure of the Text*, 280, 285, 292, 300; on popular culture, 267–73, 284; on power, 258–59; and *punctum*, 68–69; "The Reality Effect," 297; and sexuality, 46, 264–66; and structuralism, 263; on the Text, 260; on tourism, 268–69, 303; on utopia, 258–59; "Well, and China?" 305–8. See also *Mythologies*; *S/Z*; *Writing Degree Zero*

Bataille, Georges, 16, 37, 45, 209–10, 214, 232–33, 387n28; and Leiris, 237, 240; and Paulhan, 188
Baudelaire, Charles, 7, 39, 78–79
Bauman, Zygmunt, 315–16
Beckett, Samuel, 3, 11–15, 17, 46, 50, 321–22, 370n61, 377n93
Begag, Azouz, 339, 347–51, 351–52, 403n79
Behdad, Ali, 91, 146–47
Bel-Ami (Maupassant), 99–100, 151–52, 372n4
Belaval, Yvon, 173
Benjamin, Walter, 170, 341
Ben Jelloun, Tahar, 339, 342, 345, 347
Bensmaïa, Réda, 262
Bermann, Sandra, 14
Bersani, Leo, 12
bêtise (stupidity), 283–84, 285, 296, 310
Between Sea and Sahara (*Une Année dans le Sahel*) (Fromentin), 100–102, 107, 112–15, 129, 140–41, 373n5, 373n17, 373n28
Beyond the Pleasure Principle (Freud), 42, 44–47, 74, 137, 287–88, 292–93
Bhabha, Homi, 130, 354, 386n25
The Black Jacobins (James), 22
Black Skin, White Masks (Peau noire, masques blancs) (Fanon), 56, 365n74
Blanchot, Maurice, 45, 157–58, 160–73, 177, 379n10, 380n33; on Paulhan, 182, 188–89, 383n88
Bonnefoy, Yves, 90, 371n67
Boothby, Richard, 376n83
borders, 64. See also boundaries
Bottici, Chiara, 338
Boudjedra, Rachid, 48, 329–39, 354–55
boundaries, 103, 107, 131–32, 135, 137–39, 142–44
Bouvard et Pécuchet (Flaubert), 282–83
Brantlinger, Patrick, 357n3
breasts, as symbol/metaphor, 71–72, 81–87
Breton, André, 58–59
Le Bris, Michel, 358n12
Brooks, Peter, 45–46
Brown, Andrew, 278–79
Butler, Judith, 14, 246, 264, 311, 354,

360n31; on Hegel, 56, 181, 367n8; on mourning, 345–46; on power, 190–92

Caché (film), 342, 344
Caillié, René, 124, 375n53
Caillois, Roger, 194–95
Camera Lucida (La Chambre claire) (Barthes), 282, 310, 312, 397n98
Camus, Albert, 273
Camus, Renaud, 264
The Canterbury Tales (Chaucer), 65
capitalism, 31–32
Carnets du voyage en Chine (Barthes), 308
Caruth, Cathy, 28, 171–72
castration, 89, 113, 184, 222–23, 243, 372n4; and Leiris, 70–71, 73, 224, 231, 246, 249, 251
Césaire, Aimé, 54–56, 58–59, 250, 323, 354–55
Of Chaff and Wheat (De la paille et du grain) (Paulhan), 187–90, 193–94
Chakrabarty, Dipesh, 318
Chambers, Ross, 15–17, 21, 87, 305, 375n44
La Chanson de Roland, 32
Charef, Mehdi, 342, 402n60
Chemama, Roland, 179–80
chiasmus, 12, 18, 165, 189–92, 197, 259, 272, 360–61n39, 361–62n46, 377n89
"A Child Is Being Beaten" (Freud), 197
China, 305–9
Christin, Anne-Marie, 141
"Civilization" ("Civilisation") (Leiris), 217
Civilization and Its Discontents (Freud), 78, 85–86
classification, 260–62, 264–66, 290
Clastres, Pierre, 3–5, 7, 357n3, 357–58n5
Le Clézio, J. M. G., 7
Clifford, James, 21–22, 49, 59–61, 203, 210–13, 216, 239, 318
Coetzee, J. M., 140, 147, 377n89
Collège de France, 257
Collège de Sociologie, 157, 210, 235
colonialism, 3–4, 92–93, 117–18, 130, 148, 393–94n26; advocacy of, 372n75; and anthropology, 357n4; and Barthes, 268–69, 305, 393–94n26; and ethnography, 203–4, 213–14; and exoticism, 211; and French language, 203, 384n6; and identity, 324–25; "imperialist nostalgia," 20, 41, 208; and Leiris, 227–28, 250; opposition to, 53–54, 325, 399n23; politics of, 111–12, 126, 151, 173; and psychology, 39, 110–11, 365n74; and the sublime, 140; and travel, 121–26; and travel writing, 97–115, 121, 372n4
Comment, Bernard, 262, 265
communism, 204
Conrad, Joseph, 7–8, 30–31, 109, 329; writing style of, 364n61
Copjec, Joan, 42–44
Corneille, Pierre, 34
corrida (bullfight), 36–37, 240, 251
Courir (Echenoz), 7
CPE law (*Contrat Première Embauche*, First Employment Contract), 351–52, 404–5n82
Critical Terrains (Lowe), 309–11
Critique of Judgment (Kant), 137
Critique of Postcolonial Reason (Spivak), 26–27
"La Croyance aux génies *zar*" (Leiris), 240
Culler, Jonathan, 40, 262, 265, 288
Culture and Imperialism (Said), 102, 326

Dakar-Djibouti Mission, 201–2, 205–9, 212, 226–30; subjects hiding from ethnographers, 209, 386n18; and theft of sacred objects, 233–34, 388–89n68, 388n66
Dans le labyrinthe (Robbe-Grillet), 331
Daudet, Alphonse, 98
Daumas, Eugène, 115–16, 142
"The Dead" (Joyce), 399n29
death, 45, 63–66, 129, 136, 167–68, 196, 384n104; in "Aytré qui perd l'habitude," 161–62
death drive theory, 34, 38, 43–45, 119, 121, 149; Laplanche on, 86
"The Death of the Author" ("La Mort de l'auteur") (Barthes), 110–11, 113, 117–18, 261

de Certeau, Michel, 8, 306–7, 340–42, 401n53, 402n54
de Certeau, Michel, 8, 306–7, 340–42, 401n53, 402n54
deconstruction, 11, 172, 317, 321, 344, 397–98n6
The Dehumanization of Art (Ortega y Gasset), 30–31
Delacroix, Eugène, 102, 112–13, 114, 134, 154
Deleuze, Gilles, 77, 97–99, 251, 391–92n112
"Delfica" (Nerval), 88–89, 208, 370n62
"Delusions and Dreams in Jensen's *Gradiva*" (Freud), 75–77, 79
de Man, Paul, 79, 163, 167
dérive (drift), 46–48, 119, 121, 266, 278, 280, 293, 300, 304, 402n54
Derrida, Jacques, 17–18, 44–45, 64, 67–69, 343–47, 358–59n18; on aporia, 368n22; and archive fever, 79–80, 141; on the *arrivant*, 106, 144; on Barthes, 310; on Blanchot, 165; career as footnote, 363n51; on Kant, 138; *Margins of Philosophy*, 398n8; on memory of the present, 148–49; on metaphor, 215–16, 398n14; on nostalgia, 316–22; on *paralyse*, 10–11; on Rousseau, 20; on the sublime, 149; on translation, 363–64n59; *Writing and Difference*, 378n97
desire, 136–37, 260–62, 264, 289, 293–94, 303–4; and the other, 86–87, 123
Dialectic of Enlightenment (Horkheimer and Adorno), 320
Dickens, Charles, 326
"Dictionary" (column in *Documents*), 214, 387n28
Dictionnaire des idées reçues (Flaubert), 218, 283
digression, 15–16
"The Discourse on Language" (*L'Ordre du discours*) (Foucault), 11, 258
Djebar, Assia, 105–6, 148, 154, 345, 402n67, 403n70
Doane, Mary Ann, 89
Dobie, Madeleine, 372n75

Documents (magazine), 209–10, 211–17
Dominique (Fromentin), 102, 107, 118–19, 121–23, 141–42, 377n93
Don Quixote (Cervantes), 321
Doubrovsky, Serge, 262–63
Douglas, Mary, 242
Downcast Eyes (Jay), 48–49
"The Drunken Boat" ("Le Bateau ivre") (Rimbaud), 269, 280, 394n42
Du Bellay, Joachim, 319, 398n8
Du Bois, W. E. B., 323
Duffy, Enda, 360n34
Du Mesnil, Armand, 108, 112, 114

"The Ease of Dying" ("La Facilité de mourir") (Blanchot), 163, 167–68, 383n88
Echenoz, Jean, 7
Einstein, Carl, 210
Le Cid (Corneille), 34
Eloge du repos (Morand), 365n69
Emawayish, Leiris's infatuation with, 239, 242, 246
Empire of Signs (*L'Empire des signes*) (Barthes), 288, 297–98
"Entretien avec Robert Mallet" (Paulhan), 180–81, 382n73
entropology, 3–4, 357n3
"The Escalator" ("L'Escalier mécanique") (Robbe-Grillet), 331–32
"Essai de description psychogéographique des Halles" (Khatib), 402n54
Essays on Otherness (Laplanche), 83–84
Un Eté dans le Sahara (Fromentin), 100–104, 107–13, 115, 120–35, 139, 142–48, 150, 373n17, 373n26
the ethical, Barthes on, 310–11, 397n96
Ethnicity and Equality (Begag), 347–51, 403n79
"The Ethnographer Faced with Colonialism" ("L'Ethnographe devant le colonialisme") (Leiris), 203–4, 213
ethnography: and aporia, 242; Clifford on, 210, 212, 216; and colonialism, 203–4, 213; effect of on indigenous cultures,

3–4, 207–8, 386n15, 391n106; and Leiris, 201–7, 212–13, 228–29, 238–40; and the other, 204; and power relations, 203; professionalization of, 212–13; and surrealism, 209–10; and travel, 5–6. *See also* anthropology; Lévi-Strauss
Etonnants Voyageurs festival, 7, 358n12
exoticism, 211–14, 226–27, 268–69. *See also* orientalism
"The Experience of the Proverb" ("L'Expérience du proverbe") (Paulhan), 177, 179

Fabian, Johannes, 5–6, 8–9, 13, 61, 62, 145–46, 318
Fanon, Franz, 56, 59, 310, 354–55, 365n74, 367n3; and colonial resistance, 325, 399n23
Fantasia (Djebar), 105–6
Fascination (Boudjedra), 336–37
femme fatale, 370n64
fetishism, 243–44
"La Fin du Ramadan" (Fromentin), 146
Fineman, Joel, 65–66, 87, 224
fixation, 80–81, 169, 380n41
The Flanders Road (La Route des Flandres) (Simon), 32–35, 331
Flaubert, Gustave, 7, 48, 98, 218, 282–84, 294, 327–28
The Flowers of Tarbes (Les Fleurs de Tarbes) (Paulhan), 164–66, 170–71, 175, 181, 187, 266–67
footnotes: as alternative history, 24–26; Derrida's career as, 363n51
Forsdick, Charles, 8
fort-da game, 47, 119, 292–93
Foucault, Michel, 11, 16, 56, 122, 191, 247, 258, 321
French Algeria, 98–111, 121–22, 125–26, 151. *See also* Algeria; Algerian War
French language, and colonialism, 203, 384n6
Freud, Sigmund, 30, 38, 73, 75–79, 85–86, 89, 136–38, 197; *Beyond the Pleasure Principle*, 42, 44–47, 74, 287–88, 292–93; and boundaries, 376n83; death drive theory, 34; *Totem and Taboo*, 233, 238, 247; traumatic neurosis theory, 169–72
Freud and Fiction (Kofman), 77
Fromentin, Eugène, 100–102, 104–8, 115–25, 130–36, 140–55; as *arrivant*, 106, 144; and castration, 113; and orientalism, 108–10, 374n33; and painting, 127–29, 133–34, 140; power of memory, 147–48, 378n103; Richard on, 120–23, 139–40, 377n93; travels of, 126–27. *See also Un Eté dans le Sahara; Between Sea and Sahara; Dominique*
"Fromentin: *Dominique*" (Barthes), 149
the frontier, 97–98, 104, 107, 122, 131–32
"Frontier Thesis," 97
The Future of an Illusion (Freud), 89

Gallimard, Michel, 273
Gautier, Théophile, 80–87, 90–92, 92, 369n46, 369n49
gender roles, 46–47, 71, 184–85, 366n87
Genet, Jean, 56
Genette, Gérard, 218–19, 221
geste (the gesture), 244–46
Gide, André, 125–26, 211, 302
Girard, René, 353
Giving an Account of Oneself (Butler), 311
Glissant, Edouard, 28
Glossary: My Glosses' Ossuary (Glossaire: J'y serre mes gloses) (Leiris), 217–19
Goethe, Johann Wolfgang von, 85, 88, 370n61
Gradiva (Jensen), 75–79, 87
Gradhiva (journal), 93–94
Graebner, Seth, 335
Of Grammatology (De la grammatologie) (Derrida), 18–20, 67
Le Grand désert (Daumas), 115, 142
Great Expectations (Dickens), 326
Griaule, Marcel, 202
"Le Guerrier appliqué" (Paulhan), 166, 170
guilt, Paulhan on, 175, 381n55

haiku, 298–300

hain-teny (traditional Malagasy poetry), 158, 173, 176–77, 184–85, 193, 381n51
Les Hain-teny merina (Paulhan), 177
Les Hain-tenys (Paulhan, 1939), 177, 180
Haneke, Michael, 342
"Happiness in Slavery" ("Le Bonheur dans l'esclavage") (Paulhan), 197
Le Harki de Meriem (Charef), 342, 402n60
Hayot, Eric, 309
Heart of Darkness (Conrad), 7, 109, 329
Heath, Stephen, 262, 331
Hegel, Georg Wilhelm Friedrich, 56, 167–68, 180–81, 320, 367n8
Heidegger, Martin, 163, 167, 359n21
Hertz, Neil, 71–73, 73, 138–39, 327–28, 376–77n87
Hill, Leslie, 12, 14, 380n33
Hoffmann, E. T. A., 77
Hollier, Denis, 157, 225
home, return to, 319–20, 397–98n6
homosexuality, 263–66. *See also* queer narrative; queer transports; queer travel
the horizon, 122–23, 128–31, 133–35, 140–43, 145
Horkheimer, Max, 320
"The Horla" ("Le Horla") (Maupassant), 152
Hospitalité française (Ben Jelloun), 339
hospitality, 339, 343–44, 346–47, 355, 401n43
"How Is Literature Possible?" ("Comment la littérature est-elle possible?") (Blanchot), 164, 171
Hugo, Victor, 92, 372n72

identity, 289; and colonialism, 324–25; and homosexuality, 266; and the other, 264, 274, 394n36
Ideology of Adventure (Nerlich), 31–32, 320
the Imaginary, 37–39, 42, 47, 137, 288–90, 304, 309
imaginary travel, 39–41, 47
immigrant narrative, 47–48, 57–58, 317–18, 323, 325–26, 328–35, 339–50, 353–55, 397n3
imperialism. *See* colonialism

"imperialist nostalgia," 20, 41, 208, 357n3
"Inaugural Lecture" (*Leçon*) (Barthes), 257–62, 267, 272, 280, 297
Incidents (Barthes), 304–5
"In History" (Kincaid), 22–29
The Instant of My Death (L'Instant de ma mort) (Blanchot), 168
Institut d'Ethnologie, 213
"In the Corridors of the Metro" ("Dans les couloirs du métropolitain") (Robbe-Grillet), 331–32
irony, 283
Isis (goddess), 92
"Isis" (Nerval), 89, 90–91
Islamophobia, 338, 352. *See also* anti-Arab violence

Jakobson, Roman, 179, 183, 223–24
James, C. L. R., 22
Japan, 297–300, 395n71
Jay, Martin, 48–49
Jensen, Wilhelm, 75–77, 87, 90
"The Jet-man" ("L'Homme-Jet") (Barthes), 269
Joyce, James, 322–23, 399n29

Kant, Immanuel, 26, 135–38, 149
Kaufman, Vincent, 228
Khatib, Abdelhafid, 402n54
Kincaid, Jamaica, 22–29, 354–55
Klein, Melanie, 71
Kofmann, Sarah, 77
Kojève, Alexandre, 167
Kokoreff, Michel, 351–52, 405n84
Krakauer, Jon, 364n64
Krauss, Rosalind, 211
Kristeva, Julia, 305–7, 309, 376–77n87

Lacan, Jacques, 39–40, 47, 183–84, 195; 223; on aim *vs.* goal, 229–30; Derrida on, 44–45; and *fort-da* game, 292–93; and the Imaginary, 37–38, 288–90; on Paulhan, 179; on "The Purloined Letter," 162; on satisfaction, 232–33; and the sublime, 136–37; on trauma, 170, 293; on Zeno's paradox, 43

Lafouge, Jean-Pierre, 116–17
Lamartine, Alphonse de, 120
The Land of Thirst (painting), 128
Lane, Christopher, 388n54
language: and abstract thought in traditional societies, 177–78, 381–82n65; and anthropology, 13; and Barthes, 263–64, 266–67, 294, 298–99, 301–2, 307–8, 393n16; foreign influences on, 190; and Leiris, 217–24, 251; and Paulhan, 174–76, 179–82; and power, 258. *See also* French language
Laplanche, Jean, 30, 69, 81–84, 111, 169; on "going astray," 230; on origins, 72; on primal seduction, 86; on sexuality, 69, 71–72; on translation, 363–64n59
Lefebvre, Henri, 272
Leiris, Michel, 36–39, 46, 59–66, 70–75, 90–94, 201–10, 217–26, 231–46, 235–47; African journal of, 385n10–11; and castration, 249, 251; Clifford on, 239; critique of colonialism, 227–28, 250; and ethnography, 212–13, 228–29, 238–40; and language, 251; "Metaphor," 214–18, 225; and the paradox of writing, 385n10, 385n12; and politics, 219–20; psychoanalysis of, 390n76; *Scratches (Biffures)*, 220–23, 236; *Souple mantique*, 217–18; and structuralism, 247; and theater/theatricality, 249–50, 390n84. *See also L'Afrique fantôme*; *Manhood (L'Age d'homme)*; *Rules of the Game (La Règle du jeu)*; *Scraps (Fourbis)*
Lettres algériennes (Boudjedra), 333–34
Levinas, Emmanuel, 140
Lévi-Strauss, Claude, 3, 8, 18–19, 357n2; compared to Leiris, 204, 393n26; debate on cultural relativism, 194–95; on ethnographic travel, 5–6, 11; "Race and History," 350, 403–4n80; on Rousseau, 361–62n46. *See also Tristes Tropiques*
Lévy-Bruhl, Lucien, 176–77, 178
limits, 135, 137, 142, 150. *See also* boundaries
literature: adventure, 30–32, 35, 364n64; American, 97–98; French, 29–30, 48–49, 97–98; postcolonial, 323–24, 328, 399–400n29; postmodern, 31, 33–34, 35, 47; Spanish, 31; terror in, 171, 380n48
"Literature and the Right to Death" ("La Littérature et le droit à la mort") (Blanchot), 167
Lloyd, David, 370n61
"loiterature," 15–16, 375n44
Loiterature (Chambers), 15–16
The Lonely Londoners (Selvon), 326–29, 400n30
Looking Awry (Žižek), 230
Lorcin, Patricia, 116
The Lost Continent (film), 54
Loti, Pierre, 114, 119, 301–2, 304
Lotman, Jurij, 366n87
Lotringer, Sylvère, 242
Loutfi, Martine, 122
love, 235–36, 284–85, 286–91
A Lover's Discourse (Fragments d'un discours amoreaux) (Barthes), 46–47, 260, 284, 285–91, 312
Lowe, Lisa, 309–11
Lucey, Michael, 211, 302
Lyotard, Jean-François, 31, 137, 364n62

MacCannell, Dean, 40
MacCarthy, Oscar, 116
Madagascar, 158–59, 173–74; folklore of, 177. *See also hain-teny*
Mademoiselle de Maupin (Gautier), 91–92
Malinowski, Bronislaw, 357n3
Manhood (L'Age d'homme) (Leiris), 36–37, 61, 201, 223, 236–37, 239–40, 246
Mannoni, Dominique-Octave, 39–40, 173, 197, 243–44, 365n74, 381n51
Maranhão, Tullio, 324
Margins of Philosophy (Marges de la philosophie) (Derrida), 67, 398n8
Marianne (symbol of France), 337–38, 400n40
"Le Marquis de Sade et sa complice" (Paulhan), 196–97
Martinique, 53–54, 58–59, 74
Marx, Karl, 15

Marxism, 270, 281; critique of *The Odyssey*, 320–21
masochism, 196, 251, 391–92n112
Maspero, François, 274, 339–40
Maupassant, Guy de, 99–100, 151–54, 372n4, 378n113
Maurras, Charles, 171
Mauss, Marcel, 202, 210
Mbembe, Achille, 252
Mehlman, Jeffrey, 189–91
Mellah, Fawzi, 57–58
Memmi, Albert, 110–11
Mémoires: For Paul de Man (Mémoires: pour Paul de Man) (Derrida), 79
memory: intrusive, 72; power of, 147–48, 378n103; of the present, 148–49
"La Mentalité primitive et l'illusion des explorateurs" (Paulhan), 186–87
Mercier, Jacques, 242
Mérimée, Prosper, 372n72
metaphor, 215–17, 222–26, 319–22, 398n14
"Metaphor" ("Métaphore") (Leiris), 214–16, 218, 225
Methodology of the Oppressed (Sandoval), 310
Métro: Instantanés (Sebbar), 337–38
Michelin Blue Guide, 122, 268, 277, 303
Miller, Christopher, 56, 159
Miller, Jacques-Alain, 281
Milner, Jean-Claude, 43
Mimologics (Mimologiques) (Genette), 218–19
Molloy (Beckett), 3, 322–23, 398n16
Molloy (character in *Molloy*), 3, 7, 11, 357n3

Morand, Paul, 36, 365n69
"Mors" (chapter in *Scraps*), 67–69, 73–74, 235. See also *Scraps (Fourbis)* (Leiris)
Musée de l'Homme, 212–13
myth, 268, 270–72, 274–75, 277–81
Mythologies (Barthes), 46, 48, 117, 266–82, 284–85, 288, 292, 297, 300, 303–4, 307, 310–11, 334
"Myth Today" ("Le Mythe, aujourd'hui") (Barthes), 277, 282

Nachträglichkeit, 81–83
Naipaul, V. S., 323
Nancy, Jean-Luc, 149–50
Napoléon Bonaparte, 92
narrative, 13; and Barthes, 288, 297, 300, 305; in postmodern literature, 31, 33–35, 47, 364n62. See also immigrant narrative; queer narrative
Native Americans, 21–22
native informant, 26
négritude, 54–56, 59
Nerlich, Michael, 31–32, 35, 320
Nerval, Gérard de, 87–91, 92–93, 208, 371n67
Nietzsche, Friedrich, as adventure hero, 35
Nizan, Paul, 98
nostalgia, 316–17, 345; "imperialist nostalgia," 20, 41, 208
Notebook of a Return to the Native Land (Cahier d'un retour au pays natal) (Césaire), 54–56, 323
Notre-Dame de Paris (Hugo), 92
Nouveau Roman, 330–31, 335
Nouvelles Mythologies (Garcin, ed), 281
NRF *(Nouvelle Revue Française)*, 157, 186, 193, 378n3

occult, 152–53, 271–73
"Octavie" (Nerval), 87–89, 369–70n57
The Odyssey (Homer), 320–22, 330, 335
Oedipus, 138, 290, 376–77n87, 391–92n112
"On the Superiority of Anglo-American Literature" (Deleuze and Parnet), 97–99
orientalism, 92, 102–4, 112–15, 123, 146; and Barthes, 300, 303–4; and Fromentin, 108–10, 374n33; and taboos, 154. See also exoticism
Orientalism (Said), 92, 102, 212, 386n25
origins, 65, 70–71, 72, 80, 91
Ortega y Gasset, José, 30–31, 322
the other, 39, 203–4; as the *arrivant*, 106–7; and art, 123; Barthes on, 260–61, 267, 306–7; death as, 45; and desire, 86–87, 123; and Fromentin, 101–2; and hospitality, 343–44; and identity, 264,

274, 394n36; Lacan on, 223; and Leiris, 66, 236; as love object, 286–87; and myth, 270; and *Nachträglichkeit*, 83; and Paulhan, 179, 187; and primal seduction, 72; and resistance to historical appropriation, 27; and symbolism, 223, 230; and time, 145–46; and travel, 107, 117–18; "vengeful Other," 266, 288, 306; woman as, 71
Out of Our Minds (Fabian), 9

On Pain of Speech (Al-Kassim), 363n57
"The Paradox of Aytré" ("Le Paradoxe d'Aytré") (Blanchot), 160–61
paralyse, Derrida on, 10–11, 165, 358–59n18
paralysis/paralyses, 16–17, 21; Barthes on, 259–60; and French literature, 7–8, 29–30; and Freud, 73, 169; in postcolonial context, 318; and travel, 9–10, 317
"Paris Not Flooded" ("Paris n'a pas été inondé") (Barthes), 279
Parnet, Claire, 97–99
pas (step/not), 45, 48, 90, 369n46, 379n30, 404n81
Paulhan, Jean, 40, 157–59, 161–77, 179–84, 193–97, 378nn2–73; and Barthes, 266; Blanchot on, 182, 188–89, 383n88; *Of Chaff and Wheat*, 189–90; on death, 167–68, 196, 384n104; on gender roles, 184; on guilt, 175, 381n55; *Les Haintenys*, 177, 180; journals of, 382n82; and language, 174–76, 179–82; "La Mentalité primitive et l'illusion des explorateurs," 186–87; and postwar politics, 187–90, 193–95, 383n85. *See also* "Aytré qui perd l'habitude"; *The Flowers of Tarbes (Les Fleurs de Tarbes)*; "Progress in Love on the Slow Side"
Paulhan le juste (Badré), 192–93
Perceval (Chrétien de Troyes), 302, 396n81
"Persephone" ("Perséphone") (Leiris), 67–68
phallus, as symbol/metaphor, 251–53, 391n111
pigeonholed (Barthes), 260

pleasure, 280
The Pleasure of the Text (Le Plaisir du texte) (Barthes), 280, 285, 292, 300
La Plus haute des solitudes (Ben Jelloun), 342
Poe, Edgar Allan, 162
politics: of colonialism, 111–12, 126, 151, 173; and Leiris, 206–7, 219–20; and Paulhan, 187–90, 193–94, 383n85; sexual, 60, 391n106
Pompeii, 75–77, 79–81, 84–85, 90
Pontalis, Jean-Bertrand, 111
popular culture, 267–73, 284, 334
possession (to be possessed), 239–41, 246, 249–50, 390n84
La Possession (Leiris), 239–47
postcards, colonial, 41, 113, 365–66n78
postcolonial critique, 26
postmodernism, 31, 33–34, 35, 47, 318
poststructuralism, 247, 300
power, 258–59; of memory, 147–48, 378n103; and racial humor, 403n79
power relations, and ethnography, 203
Pratt, Mary Louise, 122, 148
The Predicament of Culture (Clifford), 59–60
"A Preface to Transgression" ("Préface à la transgression") (Foucault), 16
Premier amour (First Love) (Beckett), 370n61, 377n93
primal seduction, 72, 81, 86
Prime Mover, 42
"Progress in Love on the Slow Side" ("Progrès en amour assez lents") (Paulhan), 166, 168, 180, 185–86, 382n82
Prospero and Caliban (Psychologie de la colonisation) (Mannoni), 39–40, 365n74
Proust, Marcel, 31, 72, 89–90, 287
proverbs, 175–80, 183, 381n56
The Psychic Life of Power (Butler), 181, 190–91
psychoanalysis, 36–37; and imaginary travel, 39–41; and Leiris, 201–2, 238, 240, 390n76
psychology of colonialism, 39, 110, 365n74

punctum, 68–69, 72, 75
"The Purloined Letter" (Poe), 162

queer narrative, 118, 302–3, 337
queer transports, 121
queer travel, 114
Qu'est-ce que la littérature? (Sartre), 295

"Race and History" ("Race et histoire") (Lévi-Strauss), 350, 403–4n80
Racine, Jean, 31
racism. *See* anti-Algerian violence
Raft of the Medusa (painting), 128
Rancière, Jacques, 281–82, 338
rant, theory of, 29, 363n57
Reading for the Plot (Brooks), 45–46
Réage, Pauline (pseud. of Dominique Aury), 196
the Real, 137, 292–94, 297–98, 309
"The Reality Effect" ("L'Effet de réel") (Barthes), 297
récits, 163, 166, 168–70, 172, 177, 379n11, 380n44; definition, 161–62
The Regrets (Les Regrets) (Du Bellay), 319, 398n8
religion, 240
repetition compulsion, 119
repression, 78–79
La Répudiation (Boudjedra), 337
Reveries of the Solitary Walker (Les Rêveries du promeneur solitaire) (Rousseau), 361–62n46
rhetoric, 164
Richard, Jean-Pierre, 120–21, 137, 139–40, 377n93
Richman, Michèle, 237
Rimbaud, Arthur, 208, 269, 280, 394n42
Rivet, Paul, 213
Robbe-Grillet, Alain, 90, 297, 331–32
Robeson, Paul, 325
Roissy Express (Maspero), 339–40
Roland Barthes by Roland Barthes (Roland Barthes par Roland Barthes) (Barthes), 277, 281
role reversals, 196–97

Le Roman de la momie (Gautier), 369n46
Rosaldo, Renato, 20, 103, 208
Rosello, Mireille, 153
Ross, Kristin, 272–74
Rousseau, Jean-Jacques, 20, 361–62n46
Rules of the Game (La Règle du jeu) (Leiris), 53, 61, 72, 218, 222–23, 235, 244, 252
Rushdie, Salman, 352

Sacher-Masoch, Leopold von, 77, 196–97
the sacred, 237–38
Sade, Donatien Alphonse François, Marquis de, 196–97
sadism, 186
Sagan, Françoise, 273
Sagnes, Guy, 112
Le Sahara algérien (Daumas), 115–16
Said, Edward, 92, 102, 109, 212, 326, 386n25
Saint-Exupéry, Antoine de, 126, 375n56
"The Sandman" (Hoffmann), 77
Sandoval, Chela, 310–11
Sarkozy, Nicolas, 350–52, 404n81
Sarraute, Nathalie, 36, 331
Sartre, Jean-Paul, 56, 204, 295
The Satanic Verses (Rushdie), 352
Scraps (Fourbis) (Leiris), 53, 62–65, 248
Scratches (Biffures) (Leiris), 220–23, 236
Sebbar, Leïla, 337–38
Selvon, Sam, 326–29, 354–55, 400n30
"Sémantique du proverbe" (Paulhan), 176
Senghor, Léopold Sédar, 59
Sentimental Education (L'Education sentimentale) (Flaubert), 7, 48, 327–28
"The Severe Recovery" ("La Guérison sévère") (Paulhan), 166, 196
sex, and Leiris, 239–40, 246
sexual conquest, sharing of as homosocial convention, 113, 374n31
sexuality, 69, 71–72, 82–83, 263–66
sexual politics, 60, 391n106
sexual roles. *See* gender roles
Sieburth, Richard, 89, 93
Silverman, Kaja, 252
Simon, Claude, 32–35, 46, 331

"The Sirens' Song" ("Le Chant des Sirènes") (Blanchot), 170, 320, 380n44
A Small Place (Kincaid), 28–29
Smock, Ann, 166–67
Snapshots (Instantanés) (Robbe-Grillet), 331
the sojourn, 301
Sollers, Philippe, 305
Souple mantique (Leiris), 217–18
The Space of Literature (L'Espace littéraire) (Blanchot), 162–63
speech, and writing, 19
The Speed Notebook (Duffy), 360n34
Spivak, Gayatri, 14, 20, 25–28
The Step Not Beyond (Le Pas au-delà) (Blanchot), 167, 379n30
Stoekl, Allan, 245
The Story of O (Histoire d'O) (Aury), 196–97
"The Storyteller" (Benjamin), 170
structuralism, 5–6, 223, 247, 263, 282
style nègre, 211
subjection, 40, 190–91
the sublime, 135–40, 149
The Sublime Object of Ideology (Žižek), 294, 395n60
surrealism, 209–10
Sylvie (Nerval), 89
the Symbolic, 42, 44, 47, 137, 223, 237, 288, 309; and Barthes, 292–93, 298, 301; and Leiris, 251
Syrotinski, Michael, 168–69, 182, 266–67
S/Z (Barthes), 14, 46–48, 263, 283–84, 300, 308, 311

Tartarin de Tarascon (Daudet), 98
teeth, as symbol/metaphor, 87–88, 90
Tel quel group, 282, 305–6, 308–9
Terdiman, Richard, 49
Terre des hommes (Saint-Exupéry), 126, 375n56
the Text, Barthes on, 260
theater/theatricality, and Leiris, 238–42, 244, 245–47, 249–50, 390n84
The Thief's Journal (Journal du voleur) (Genet), 56
Into Thin Air (Krakauer), 364n64

the Thing, Lacan, 231–32
Thompson, James, 128
the threshold, 143–44, 347
Time and the Other (Fabian), 5–6
Timimoun (Boudjedra), 337
"To a Woman Passing By" ("A une passante") (Baudelaire), 79
Topographie idéale pour une agression caractérisée (Boudjedra), 329–30, 332–33, 335–39, 341, 354
Totem and Taboo (Freud), 233, 238, 247
tourism, 4–5, 28–29, 40–41, 103, 151, 315–17, 397n3; and adventure travel, 32; Barthes on, 268–69, 303; economy of, 208; and travel critique, 7. *See also* travel
Toussaint L'Ouverture, François-Dominique, 22, 362–63n48
trace, 89–90, 141, 322, 377n93; and Derrida, 300; and Fromentin, 106; in Leiris, 236–37; in Paulhan, 160
Traité du ravissement (Paulhan), 173
translation, 363–64n59; anthropological, 13–14, 359n28; cultural, 30, 106, 361n42
trauma, 170, 196, 222, 293
traumatic neurosis theory, 169–72
travel, 3–13, 268–70, 397n3; Barthes on, 47; and colonialism, 97–110, 121–26; and death, 136; Derrida on, 321; as displacement, 216; as failed escape, 201, 228–29; and freedom, 325; imaginary, 39–41, 47; Lévi-Strauss on, 53–54; and literature, 48–49, 97–98; and the other, 107, 117–18; and paralysis, 358–59n18; and sacrilege, 145–46. *See also* immigrant narrative
Travel as Metaphor (Van Den Abbeele), 319
Travels in the Congo (Voyage au Congo) (Gide), 302, 396n79
Travels through Central Africa to Timbuktoo (Journal de voyage à Temboctou) (Caillié), 375n53
travel writing: and anthropology, 3; and colonialism, 97–115, 121, 372n4; postcolonial, 21, 317–18
Tricks (R. Camus), 264

Tristes Tropiques (Lévi-Strauss), 3–8, 18–19, 53–54, 58–59, 68, 208, 357n2
Trocadéro museum, 213
The Truth in Painting (La Vérité en peinture) (Derrida), 17–18
Turner, Frederick Jackson, 97

Ulysses (Joyce), 322–24, 326, 329, 336–37
"The Uncanny" (Freud), 77
"under erasure," 91, 237; defined, 359n21
Ungar, Steven, 171
Unhappy Consciousness, Hegel on, 180–81
The Unnamable (Beckett), 12
"Useful Innocence" ("L'Innocence utile") (Paulhan), 174–75, 185
utopia, 258–59, 296

vagabonds, 315–17, 397n3
Van Den Abbeele, Georges, 319
"La Vénus d'Ille" (Mérimée), 372n72
Venus in Furs (Sacher-Masoch), 77
Verne, Jules, 269
Vertige du déplacement (Heath), 262
La Vie errante (Maupassant), 151–52
Virilio, Paul, 14–15
Le Voyageur (Bonnefoy), 371n67

Waberi, Abdourahman, 124–25, 375n54
Waiting for the Barbarians (Coetzee), 147
"Walking in the City" ("Marches dans la ville") (de Certeau), 340–42, 401n53, 402n54
Wallerstein, Immanuel, 349
"The Way" (Beckett), 50, 321–22
"Well, and China?" ("Alors, la Chine?") (Barthes), 305–8
Wilde, Oscar, 235
Wilhelm Meister's Years of Apprenticeship (Goethe), 88, 370n61
Women of Algiers (painting), 102, 112–13, 154
The Work of Fire (La Part du feu) (Blanchot), 165
Worstward Ho (Beckett), 12, 321–22
Wright, Barbara, 128, 373n5
writing, paradox of, 206, 385n10, 385n12
Writing and Difference (L'Ecriture et la différence) (Derrida), 378n97
Writing Degree Zero (Le Degré zéro de l'écriture) (Barthes), 258, 263, 294–96
"Writing the Event" ("L'Ecriture de l'événement") (Barthes), 300

Yanomami, 3
Yeshua, Silvio, 176–77, 184
Young, Robert, 309

Zeno's paradoxes, 41–43, 181, 366n79
Žižek, Slavoj, 41–42, 136–37, 229–30, 294, 395n60
Zweig, Paul, 35–36